KURO ZAKURO

2

Story and Art by
YOSHINORI NATSUME

KURO ZAKURO

CHARACTERS

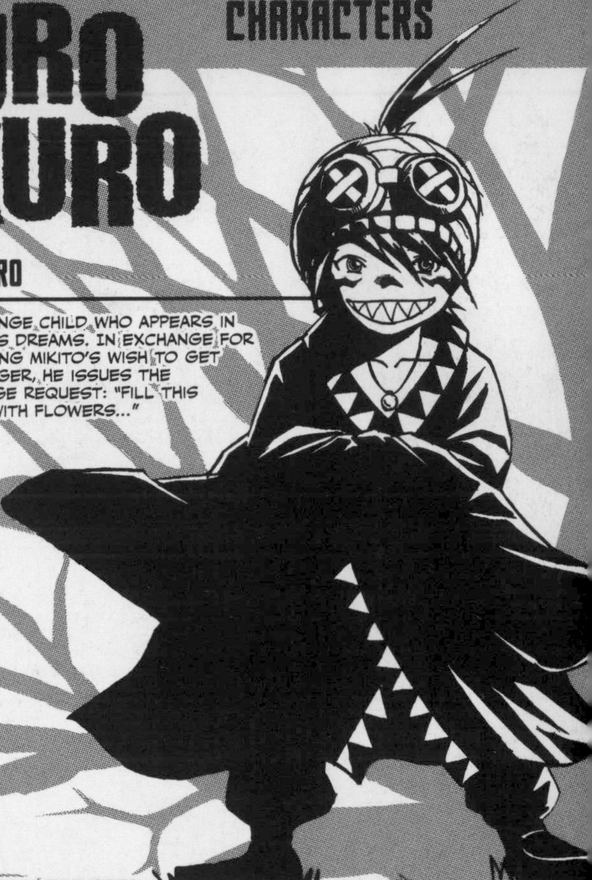

ZAKURO

A STRANGE CHILD WHO APPEARS IN MIKITO'S DREAMS. IN EXCHANGE FOR GRANTING MIKITO'S WISH TO GET STRONGER, HE ISSUES THE STRANGE REQUEST: "FILL THIS TREE WITH FLOWERS..."

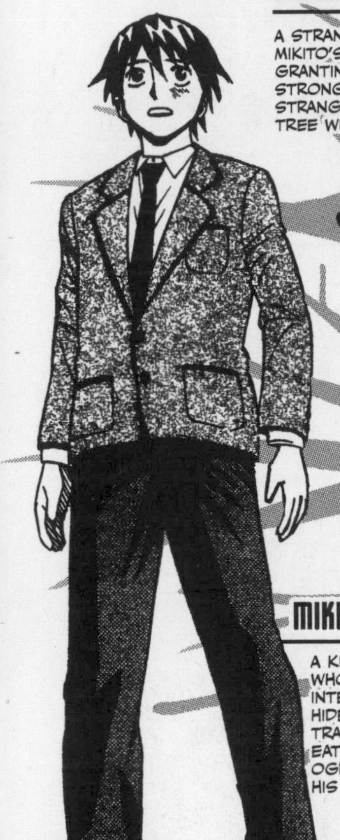

MIKITO SAKURAI

A KINDHEARTED HIGH SCHOOL KID WHO ALWAYS PUTS OTHER PEOPLE'S INTERESTS BEFORE HIS OWN. HE HIDES THE FACT THAT HE'S TRANSFORMING INTO A MAN-EATING OGRE, FIGHTING HIS OGRE INSTINCTS WITH ALL HIS MIGHT...

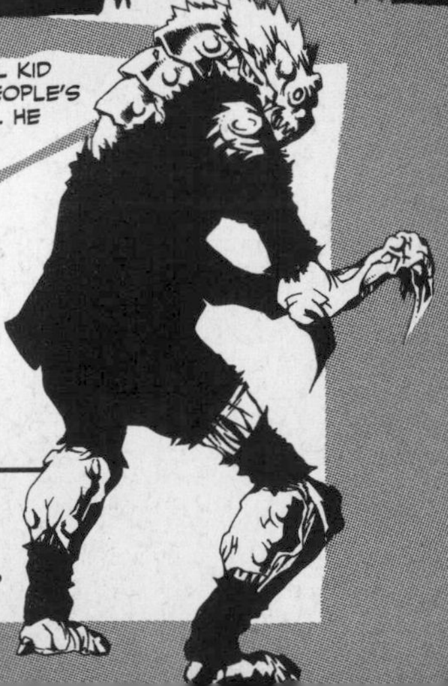

OGRE

THIS IS WHAT BECOMES OF HUMANS WHO SWALLOW AN OGRE SEED. THEIR PHYSICAL ABILITIES AND APPETITE INCREASE, AND THEY DEVELOP VIOLENT IMPULSES.

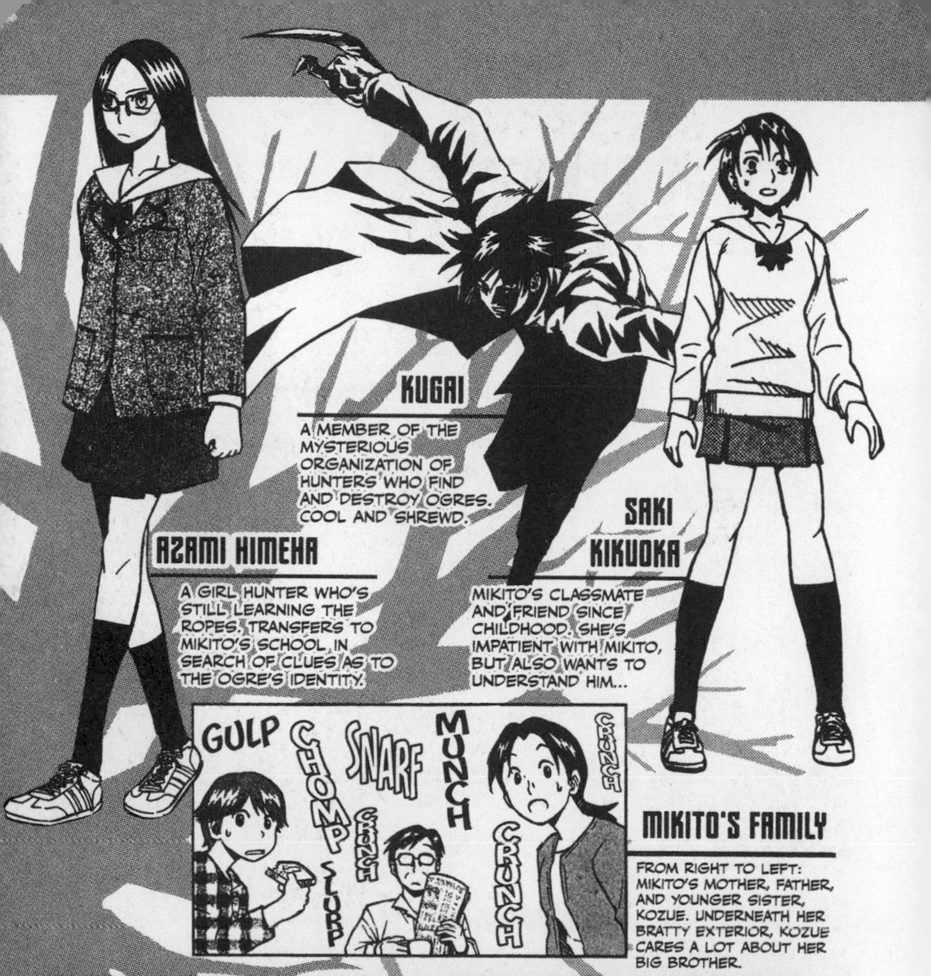
KUGAI
A MEMBER OF THE MYSTERIOUS ORGANIZATION OF HUNTERS WHO FIND AND DESTROY OGRES. COOL AND SHREWD.
SAKI KIKUOKA
MIKITO'S CLASSMATE AND FRIEND SINCE CHILDHOOD. SHE'S IMPATIENT WITH MIKITO, BUT ALSO WANTS TO UNDERSTAND HIM...
AZAMI HIMEHA
A GIRL HUNTER WHO'S STILL LEARNING THE ROPES. TRANSFERS TO MIKITO'S SCHOOL IN SEARCH OF CLUES AS TO THE OGRE'S IDENTITY.
CRUNCH
MUNCH
CRUNCH
SNARF
CRUNCH
CHOMP
SLURP
GULP
MIKITO'S FAMILY
FROM RIGHT TO LEFT: MIKITO'S MOTHER, FATHER, AND YOUNGER SISTER, KOZUE. UNDERNEATH HER BRATTY EXTERIOR, KOZUE CARES A LOT ABOUT HER BIG BROTHER.

The Story Up Until Now

HIGH SCHOOL STUDENT MIKITO SAKURAI'S GENTLENESS AND PASSIVITY HAVE EARNED HIM CONTEMPT FROM HIS CLASSMATES AND HARASSMENT FROM THE SCHOOL'S BULLIES. ONE DAY A STRANGE CHILD CALLED ZAKURO APPEARS IN MIKITO'S DREAMS. THE NEXT DAY MIKITO NOTICES VARIOUS PHYSICAL AND PSYCHOLOGICAL CHANGES INCLUDING ENHANCED PHYSICAL ABILITIES AND VIOLENT IMPULSES. HE EVEN BEGINS TO FEEL URGES TO EAT HIS FAMILY AND CLASSMATES—ALL SIGNS THAT MIKITO IS TRANSFORMING INTO A MAN-EATING MONSTER CALLED AN OGRE.

SOON MIKITO LEARNS OF THE HUNTERS AND THEIR SECRET PLEDGE TO PROTECT HUMANS FROM OGRES. A HUNTER CALLED KUGAI IDENTIFIES MIKITO AS AN OGRE WITH HIS OGRE-DETECTING BELL, BUT MIKITO ESCAPES BY THE SKIN OF HIS TEETH. SOON AFTERWARD ANOTHER HUNTER CALLED AZAMI BECOMES MIKITO'S CLASSMATE! WILL MIKITO BE ABLE TO KEEP HIS IDENTITY A SECRET?

KUROZAKURO Volume 2

Contents

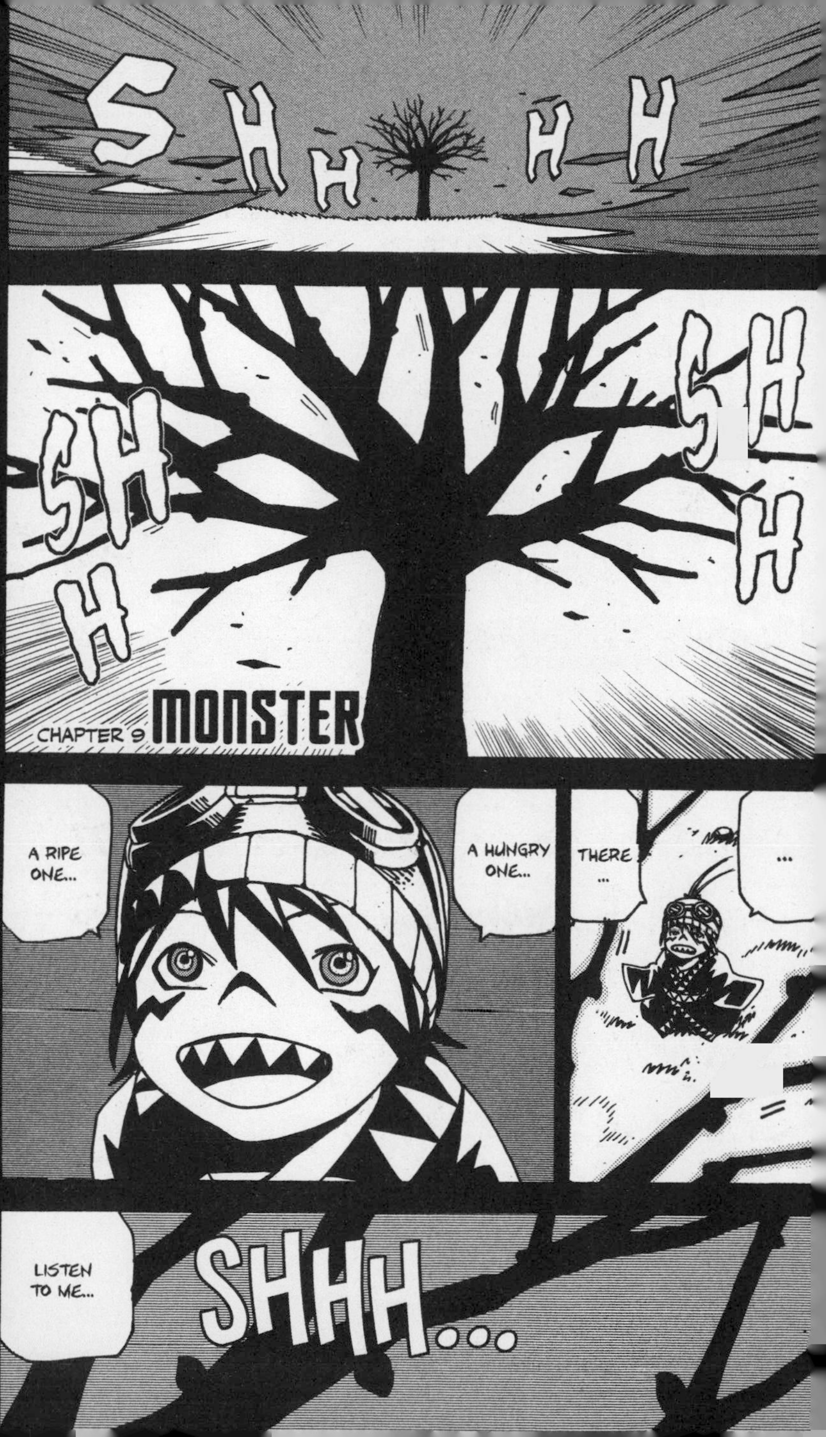
SHHHHH
SHH
SHH
CHAPTER 9 MONSTER
...
THERE ...
A HUNGRY ONE...
A RIPE ONE...
SHHH...
LISTEN TO ME...

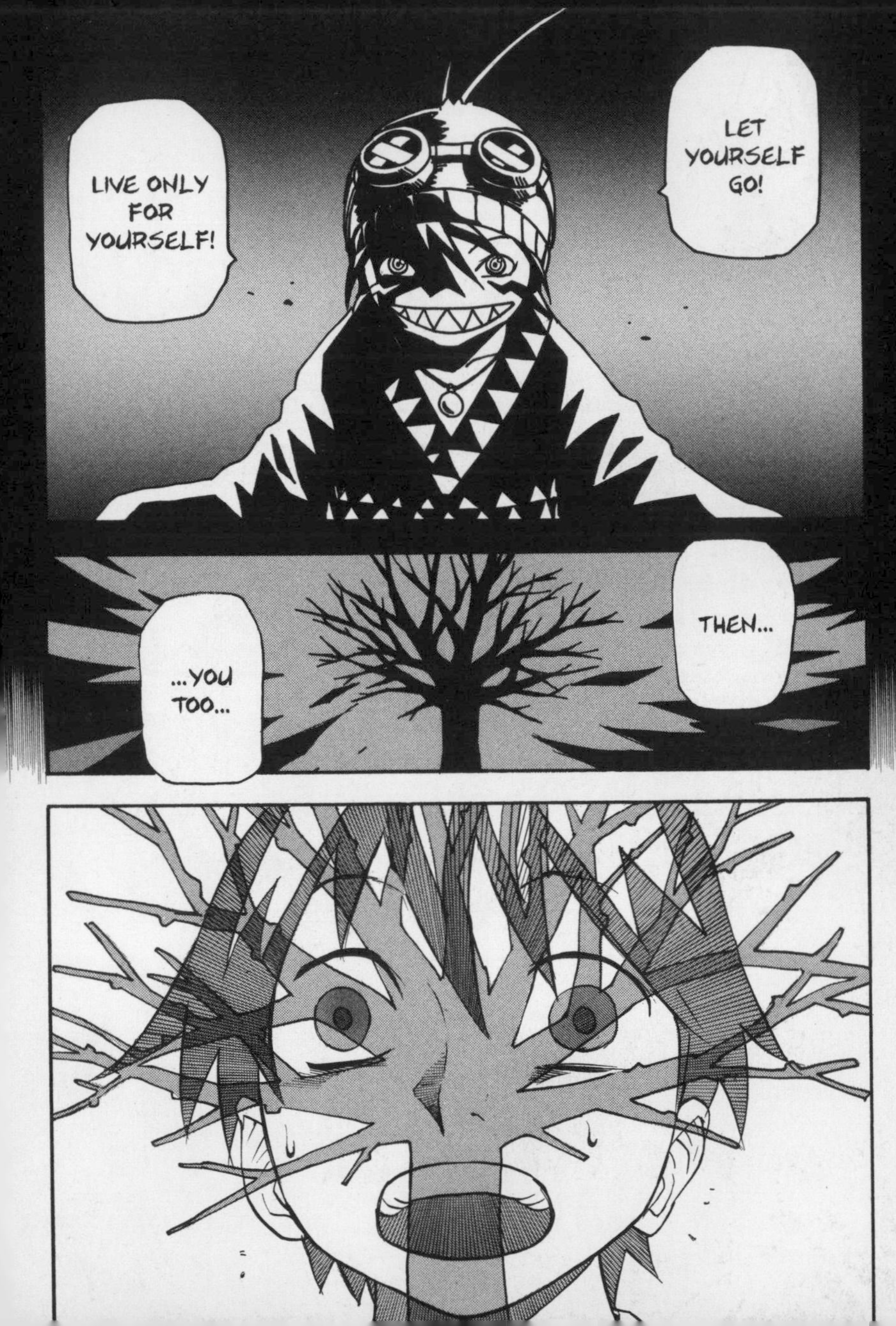
LET YOURSELF GO!
LIVE ONLY FOR YOURSELF!
THEN...
...YOU TOO...

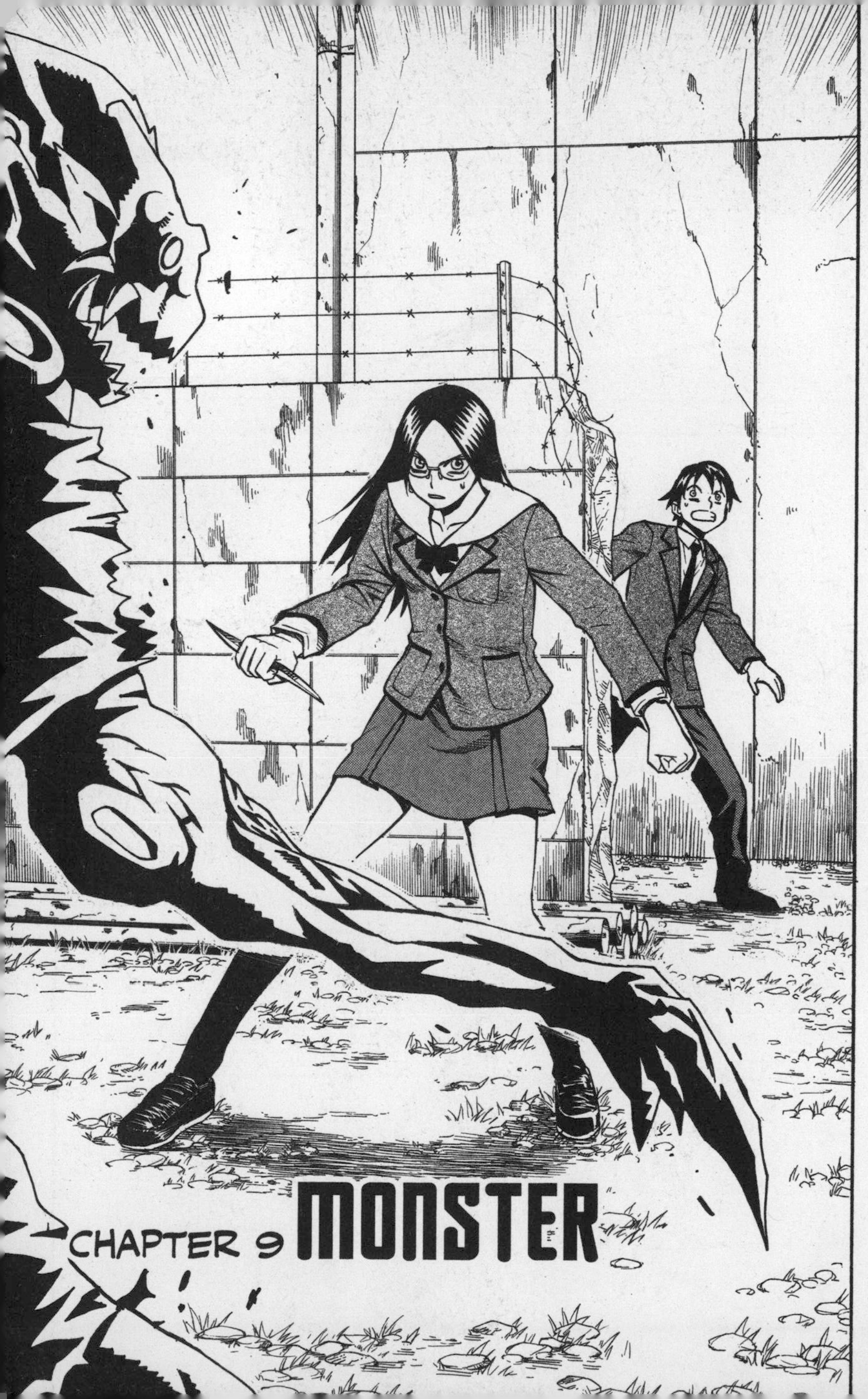
CHAPTER 9 MONSTER

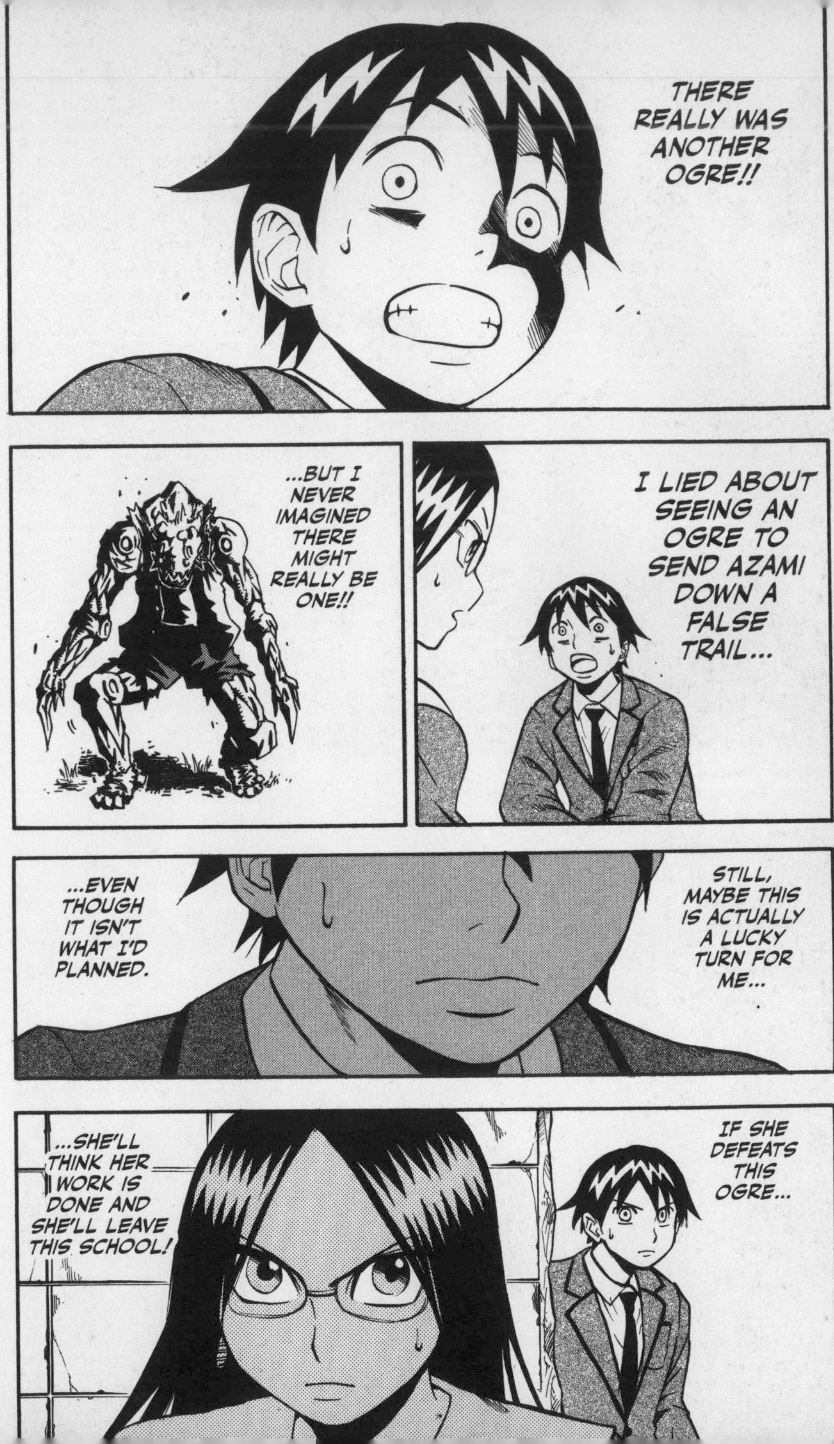
THERE REALLY WAS ANOTHER OGRE!!
I LIED ABOUT SEEING AN OGRE TO SEND AZAMI DOWN A FALSE TRAIL...
...BUT I NEVER IMAGINED THERE MIGHT REALLY BE ONE!!
STILL, MAYBE THIS IS ACTUALLY A LUCKY TURN FOR ME...
...EVEN THOUGH IT ISN'T WHAT I'D PLANNED.
IF SHE DEFEATS THIS OGRE...
...SHE'LL THINK HER WORK IS DONE AND SHE'LL LEAVE THIS SCHOOL!

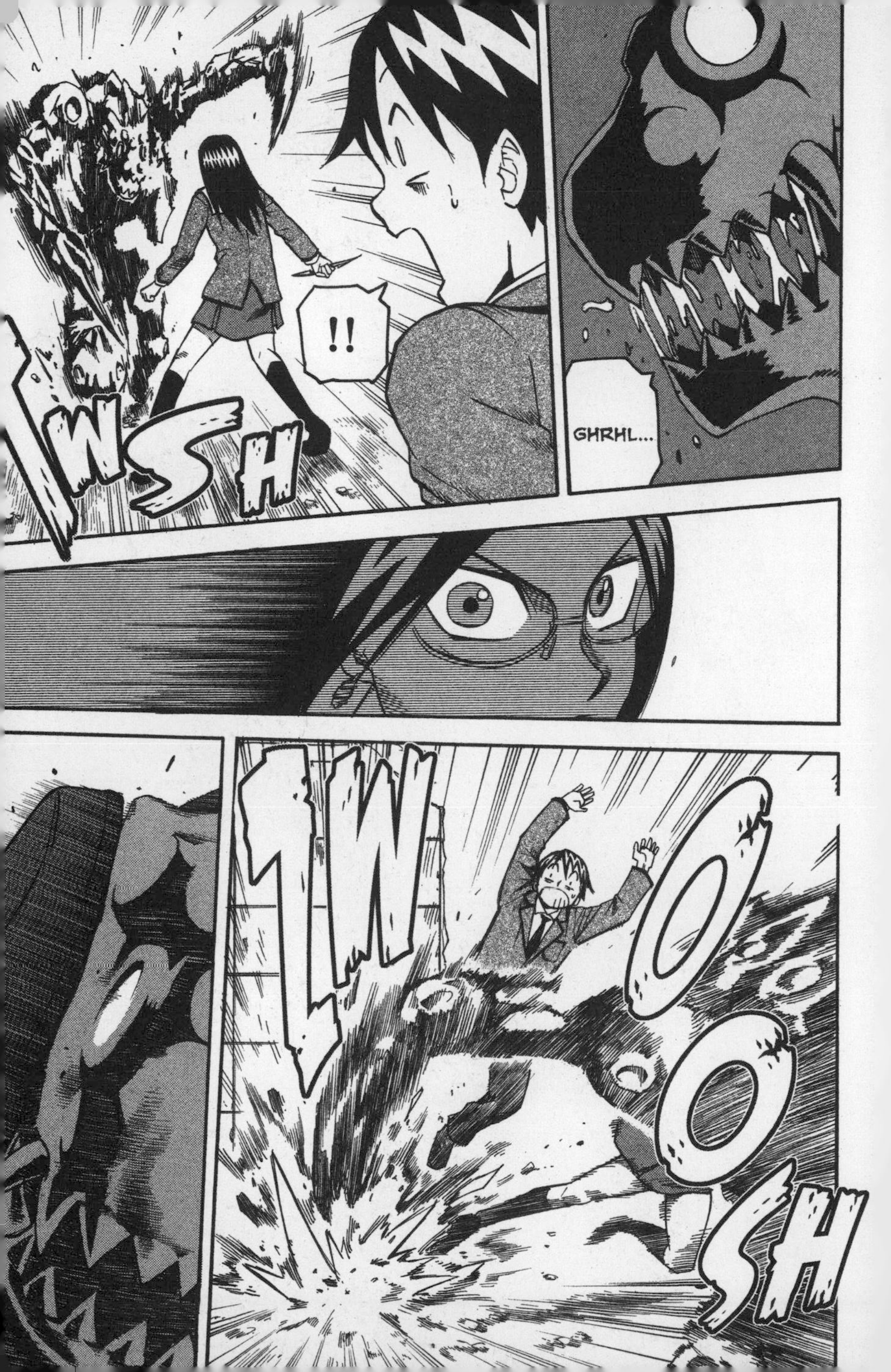
GHRHL...
!!
WSH
WOOSH

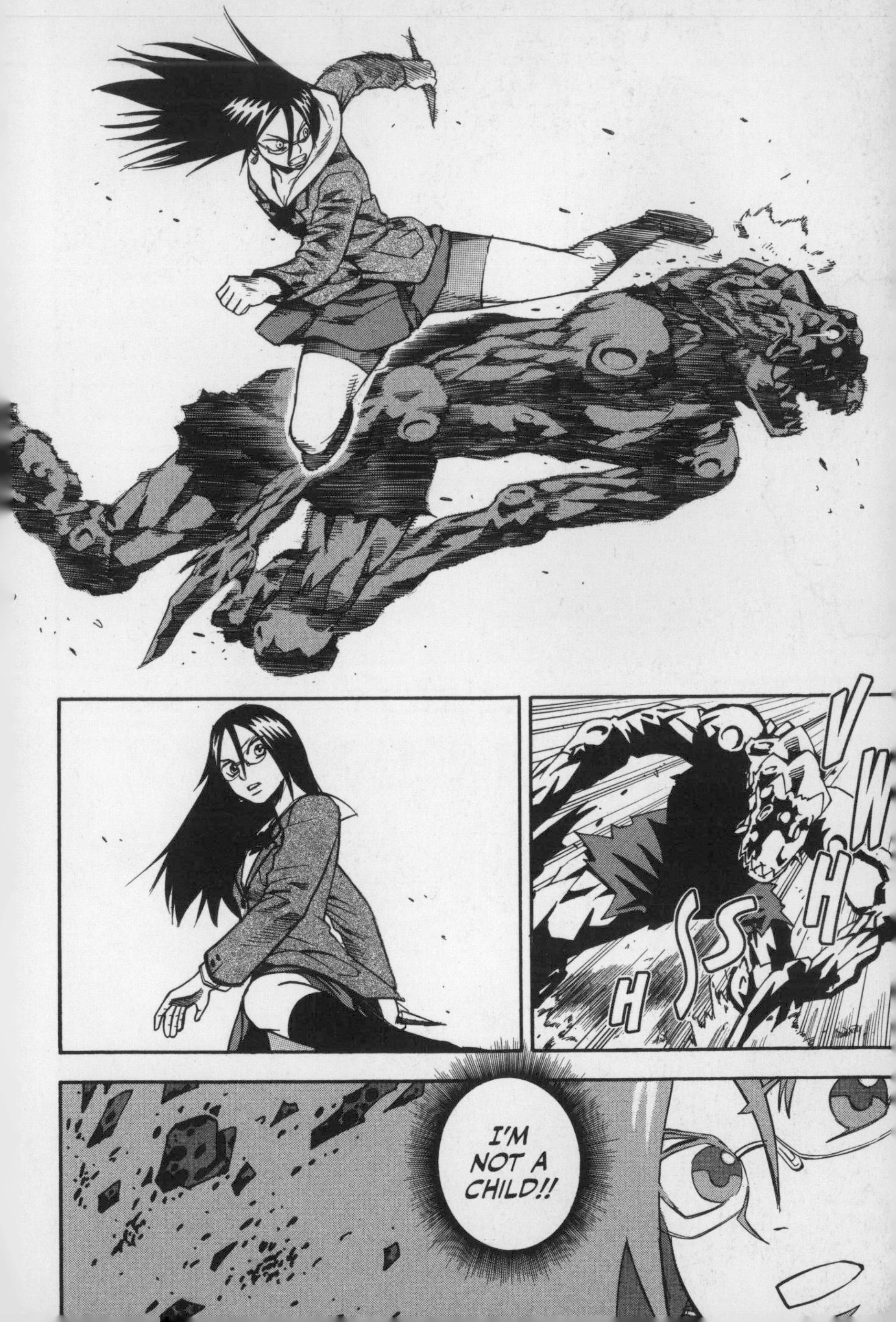
I'M NOT A CHILD!!

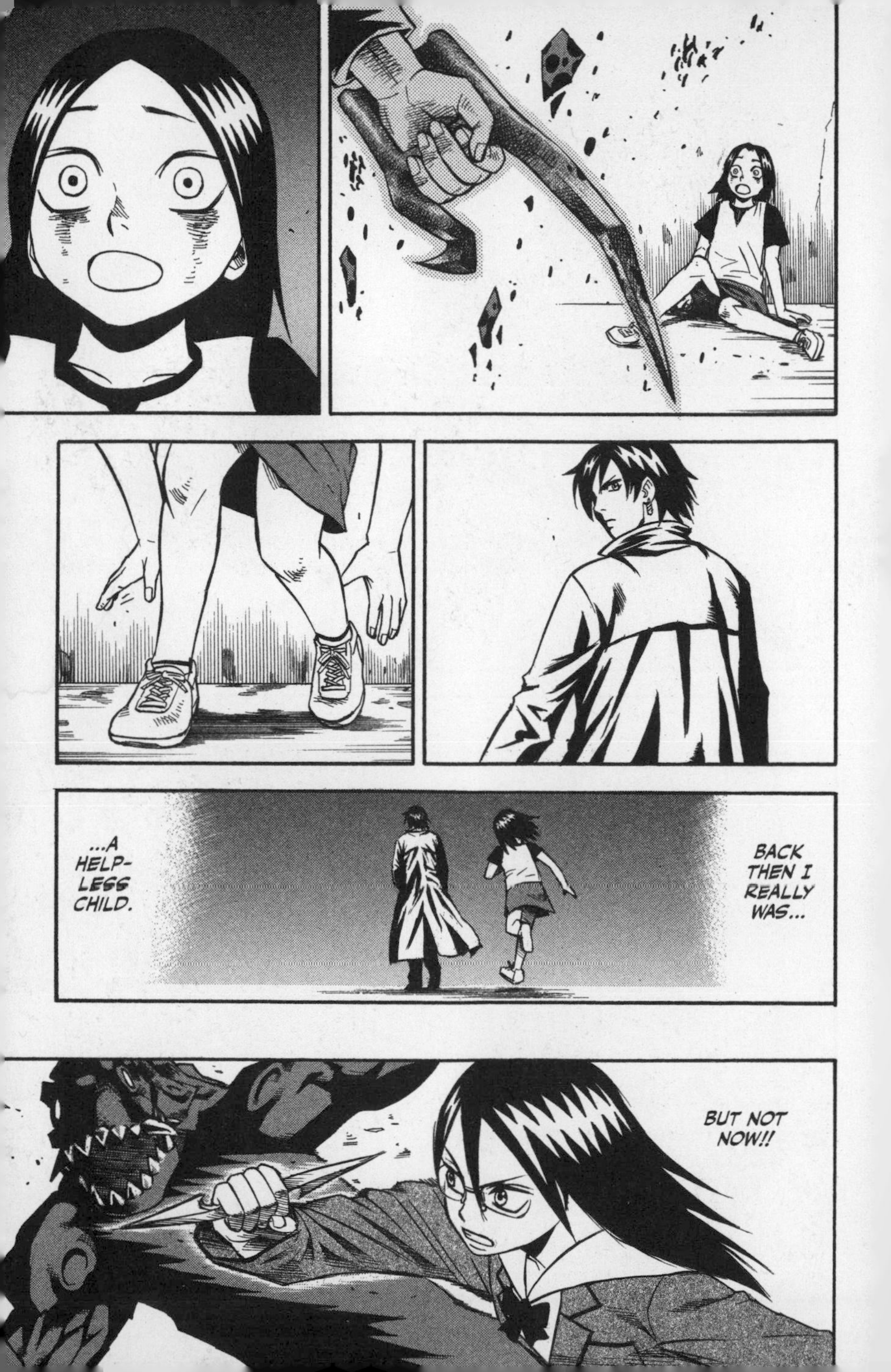
BACK THEN I REALLY WAS...
...A HELP-LESS CHILD.
BUT NOT NOW!!

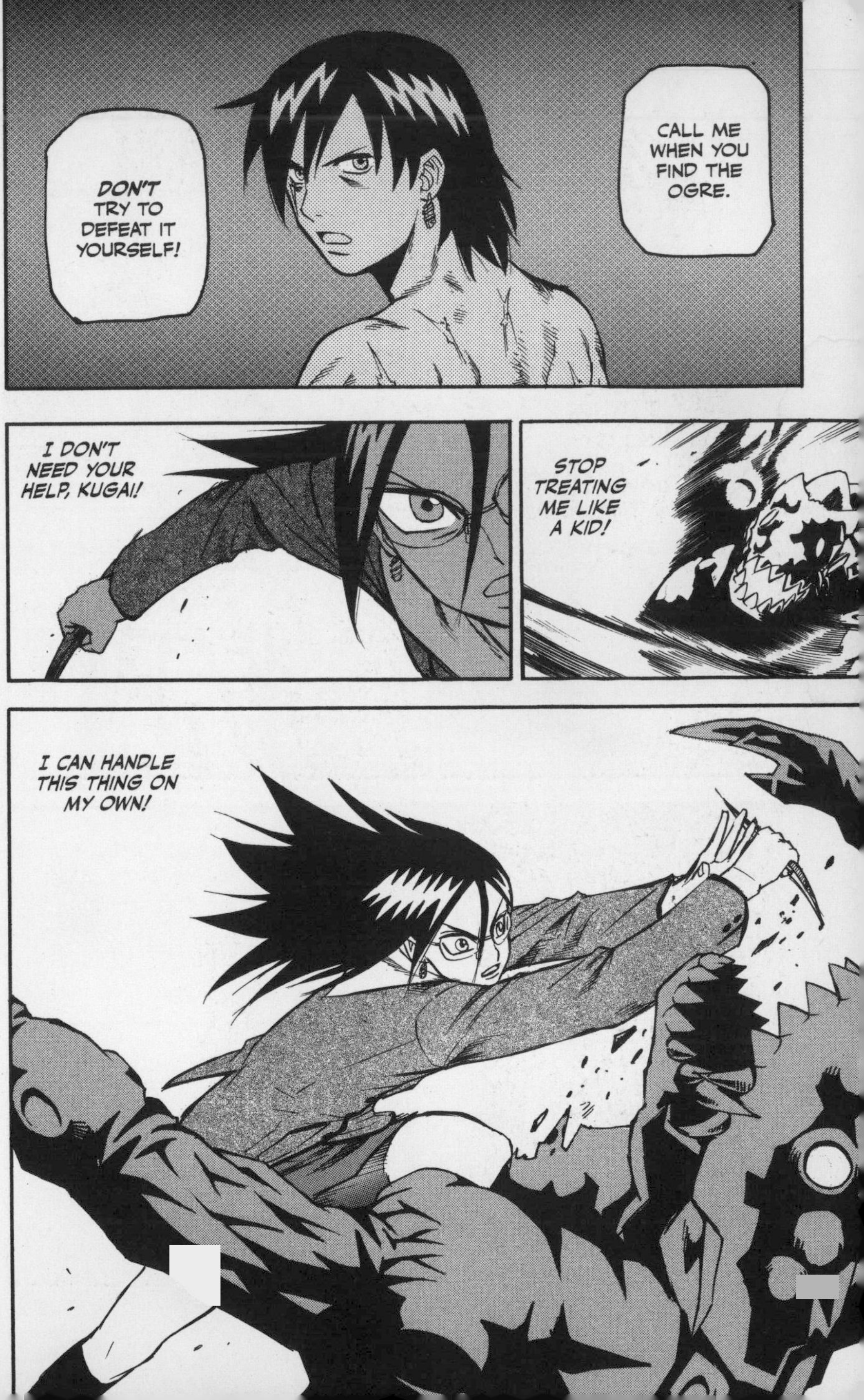
CALL ME WHEN YOU FIND THE OGRE.
DON'T TRY TO DEFEAT IT YOURSELF!
STOP TREATING ME LIKE A KID!
I DON'T NEED YOUR HELP, KUGAI!
I CAN HANDLE THIS THING ON MY OWN!

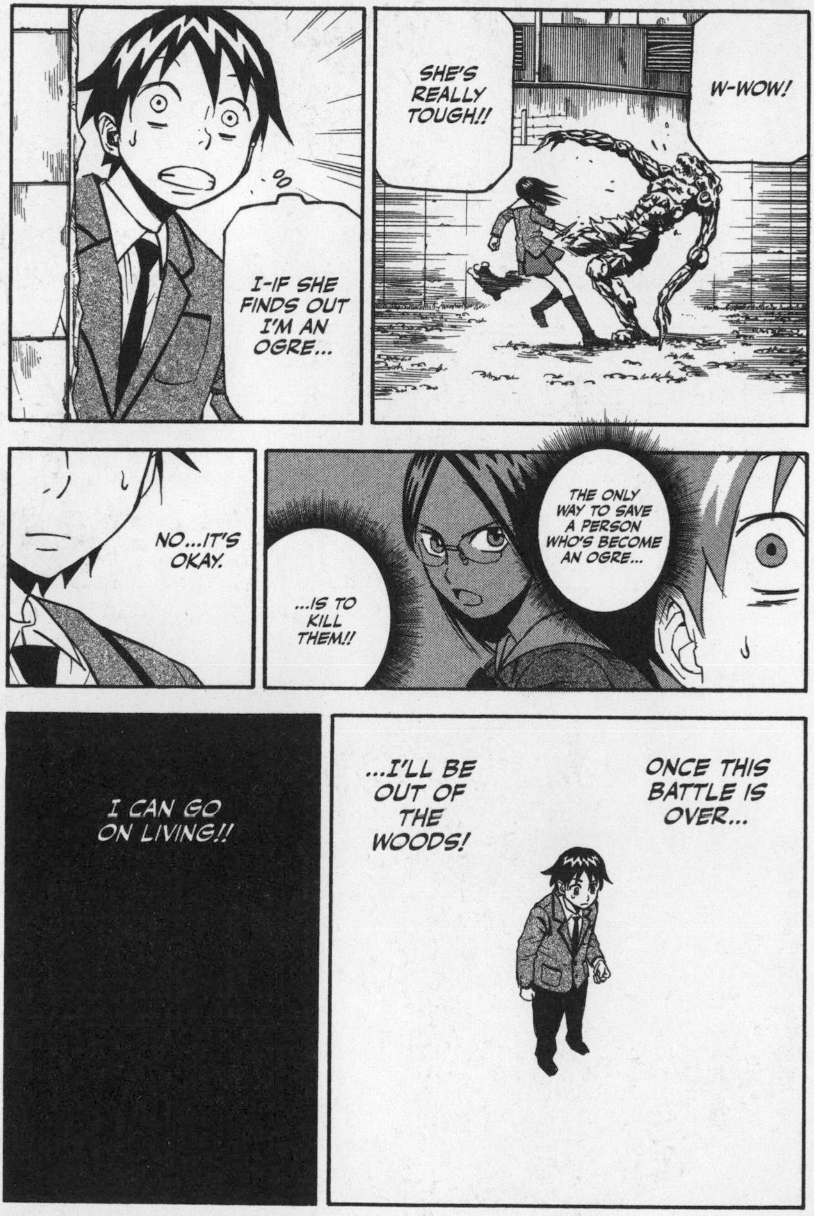
W-WOW!
SHE'S REALLY TOUGH!!
I-IF SHE FINDS OUT I'M AN OGRE...
THE ONLY WAY TO SAVE A PERSON WHO'S BECOME AN OGRE...
...IS TO KILL THEM!!
NO...IT'S OKAY.
ONCE THIS BATTLE IS OVER...
...I'LL BE OUT OF THE WOODS!
I CAN GO ON LIVING!!

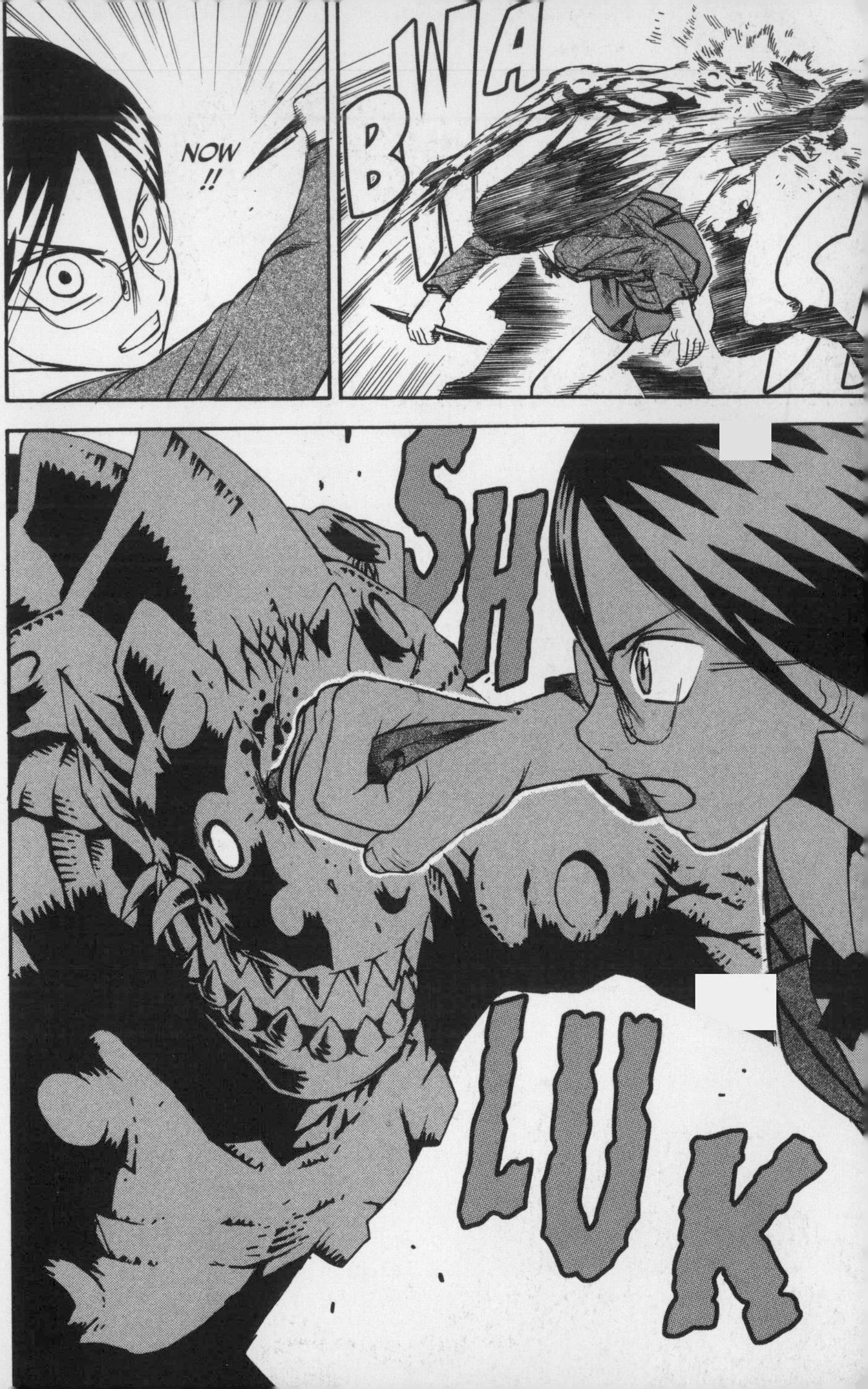
BWA
NOW !!
SH
LUK

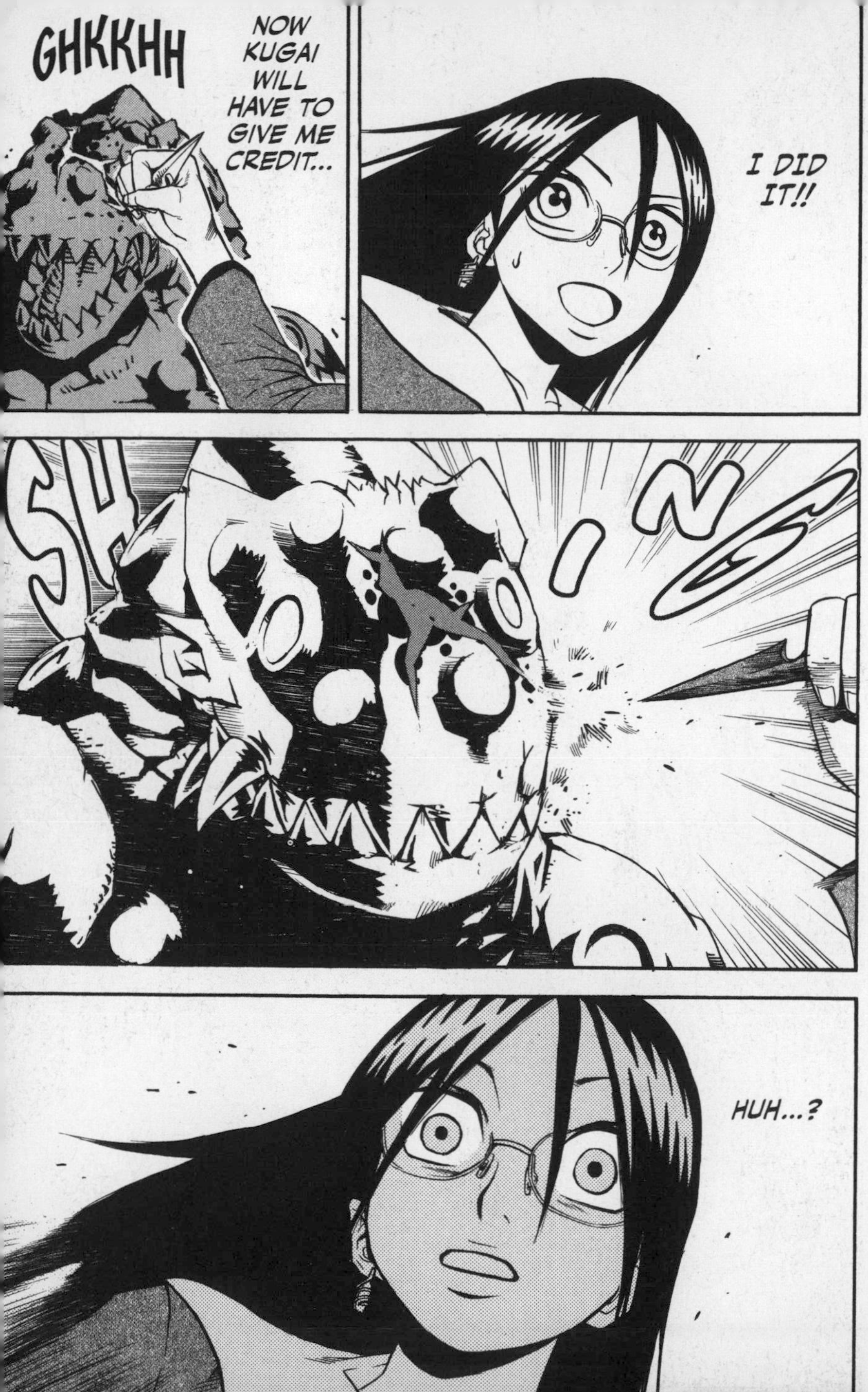
I DID IT!!
NOW KUGAI WILL HAVE TO GIVE ME CREDIT...
GHKKHH
SHING
HUH...?

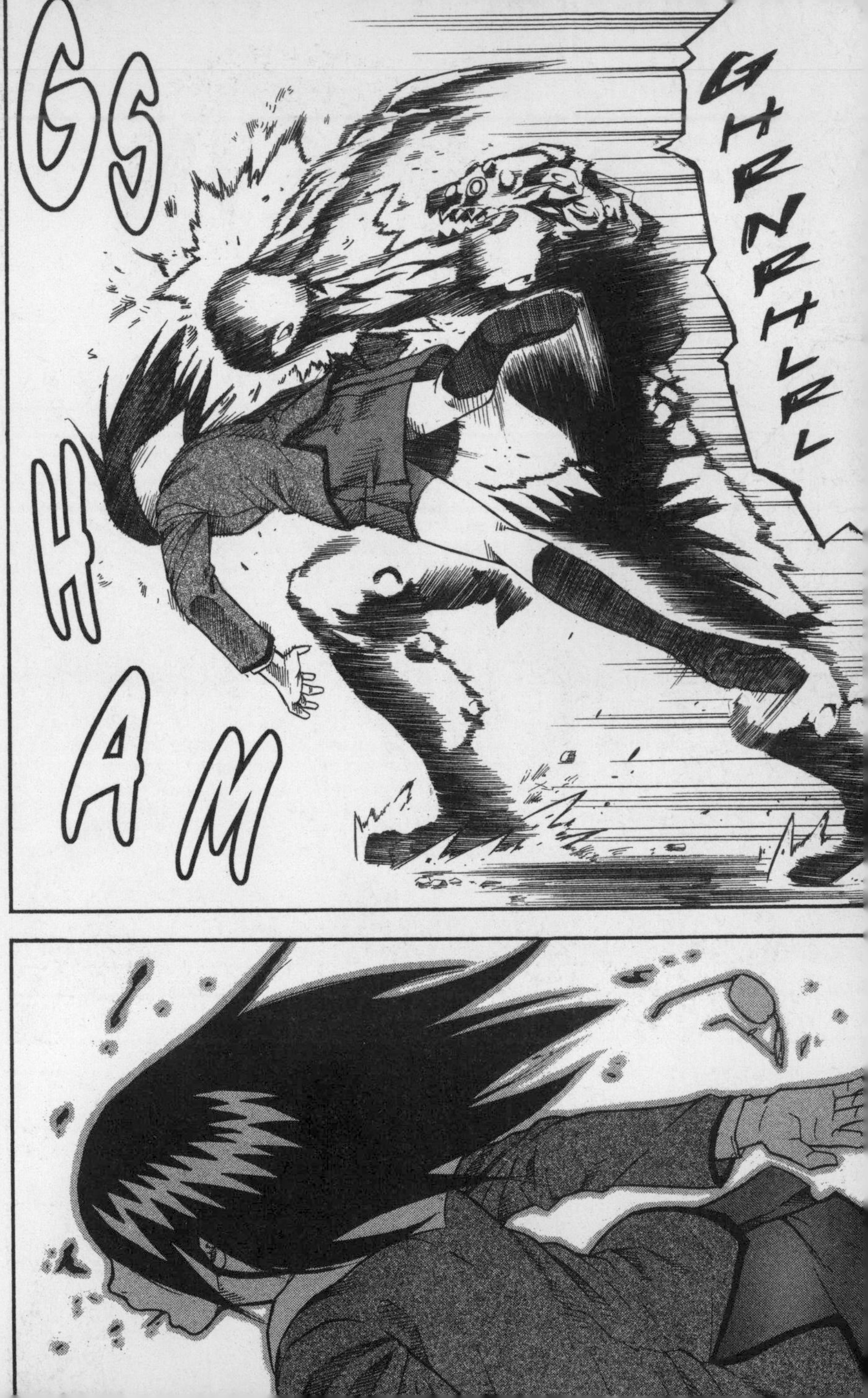
GHRRRHRRR
GSHAM

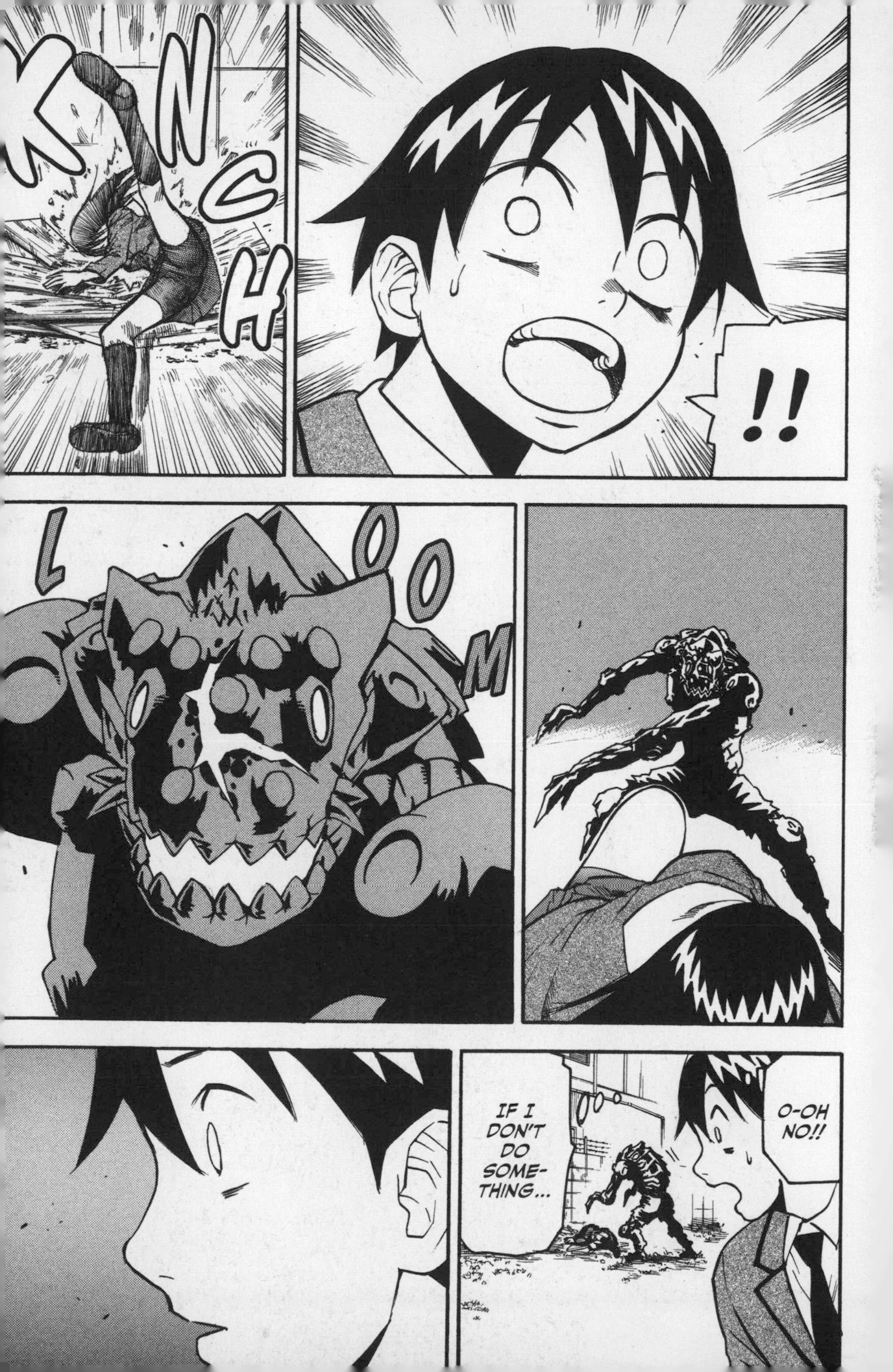
!!
NCH
LOOOM
O-OH NO!!
IF I DON'T DO SOME- THING...

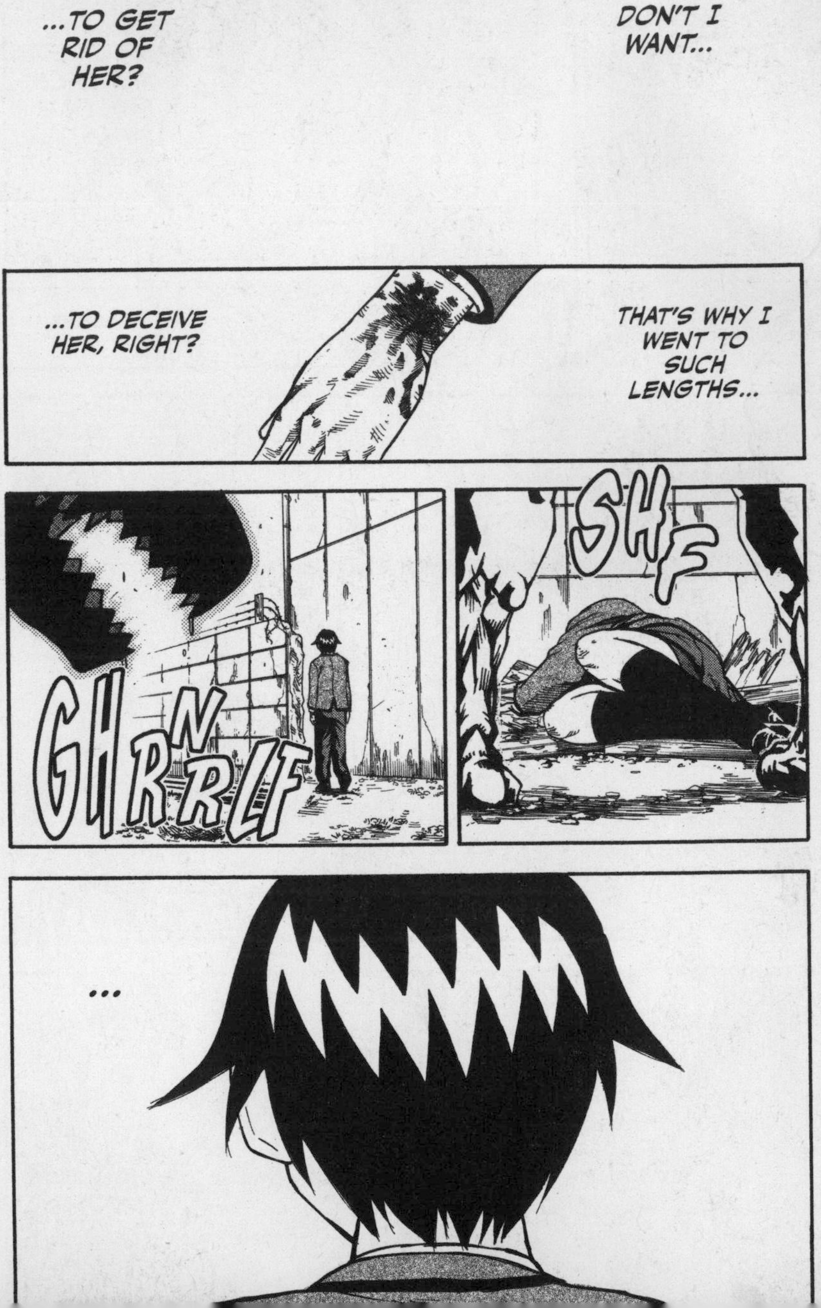
DON'T I WANT...
...TO GET RID OF HER?
THAT'S WHY I WENT TO SUCH LENGTHS...
...TO DECEIVE HER, RIGHT?
SHF
GHRNRLF
...

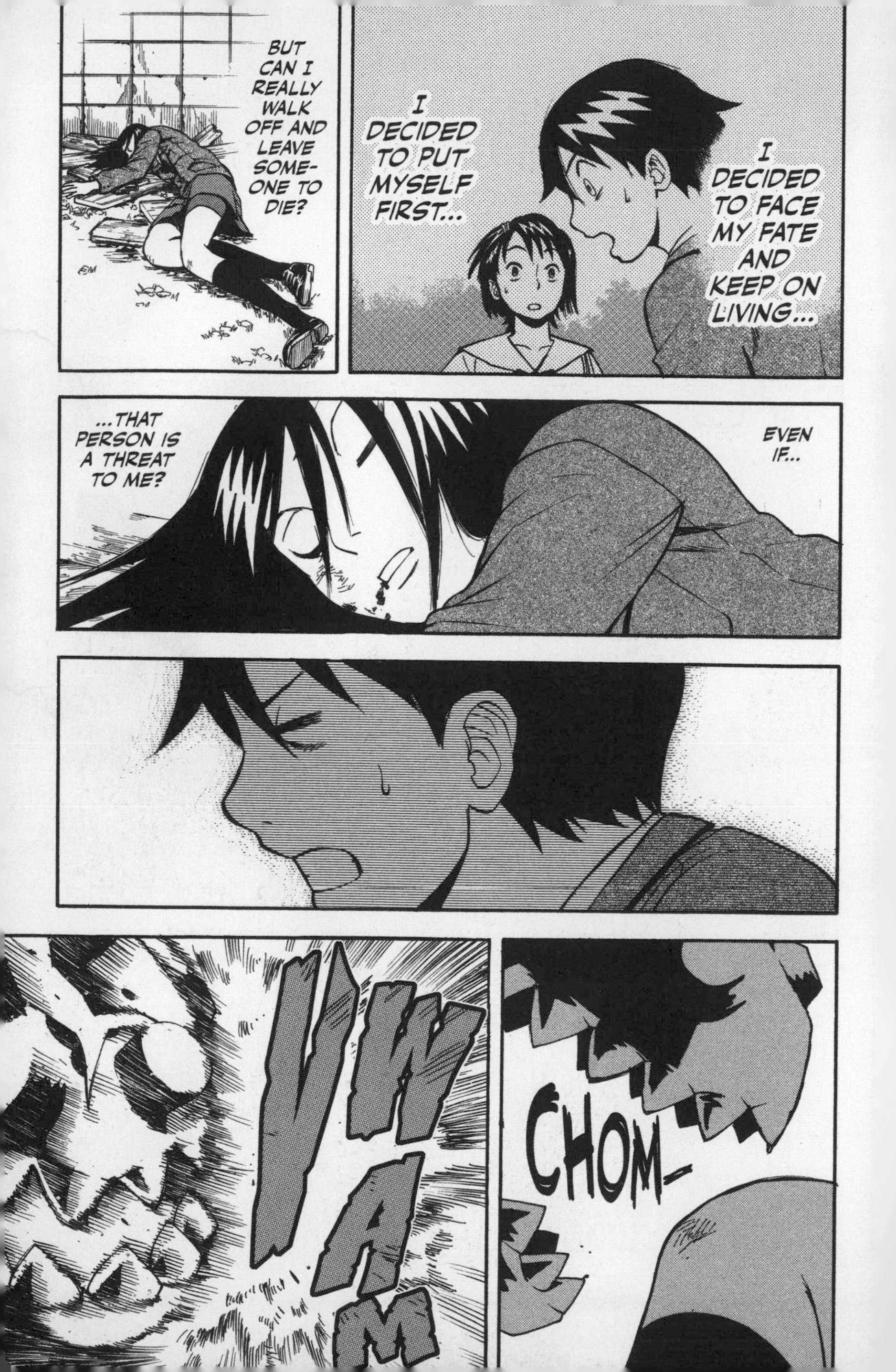
I DECIDED TO FACE MY FATE AND KEEP ON LIVING...
I DECIDED TO PUT MYSELF FIRST...
BUT CAN I REALLY WALK OFF AND LEAVE SOME-ONE TO DIE?
EVEN IF...
...THAT PERSON IS A THREAT TO ME?
CHOM-
WHAM

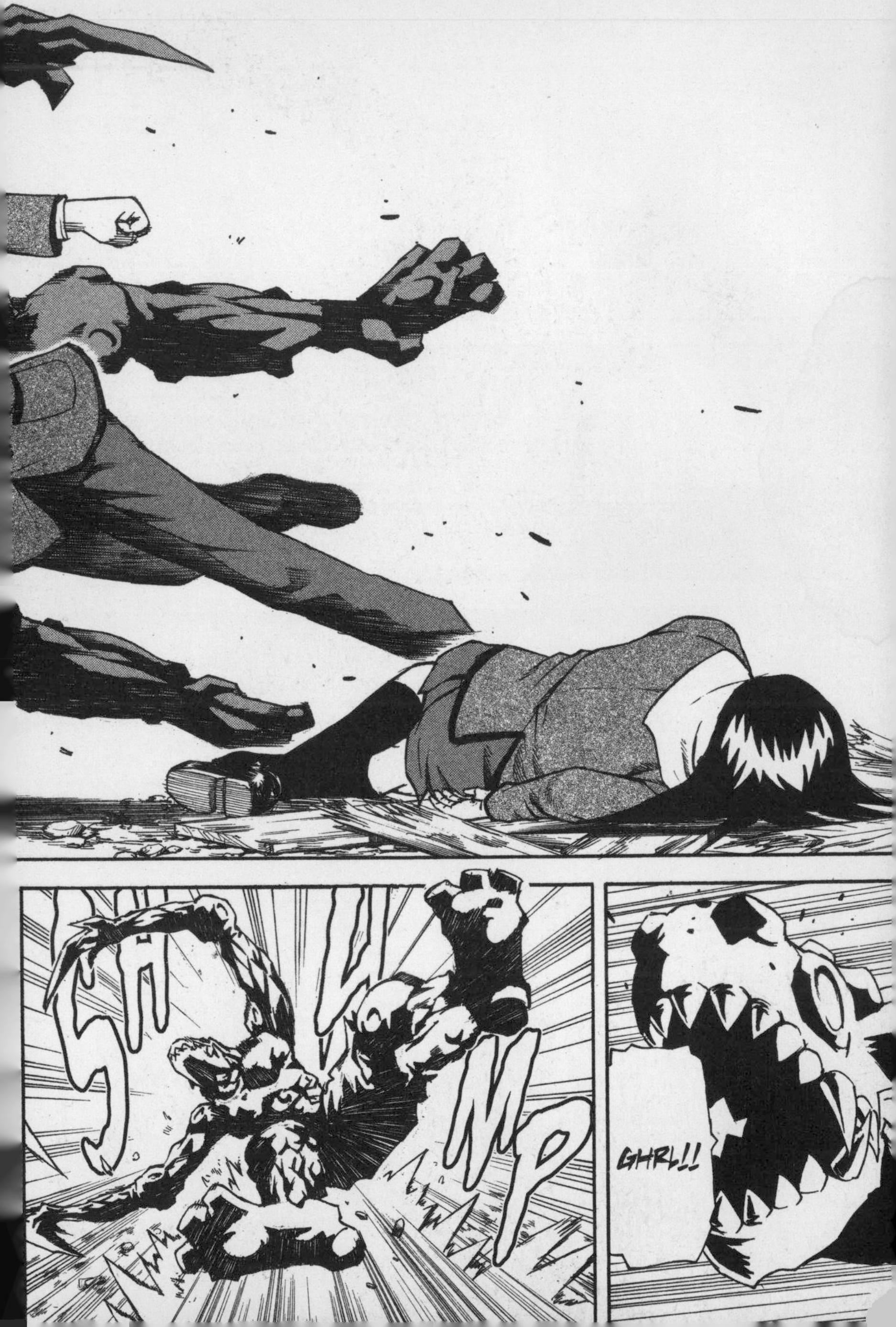
GHRL!!

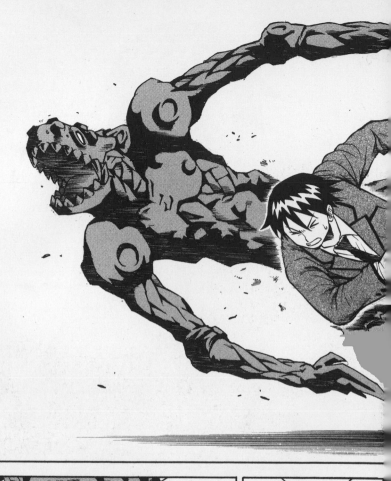

NO. IF I EVER CHANGE THAT MUCH...

...I REALLY WON'T BE HUMAN ANYMORE!!

HAHH

HAHH

S H P

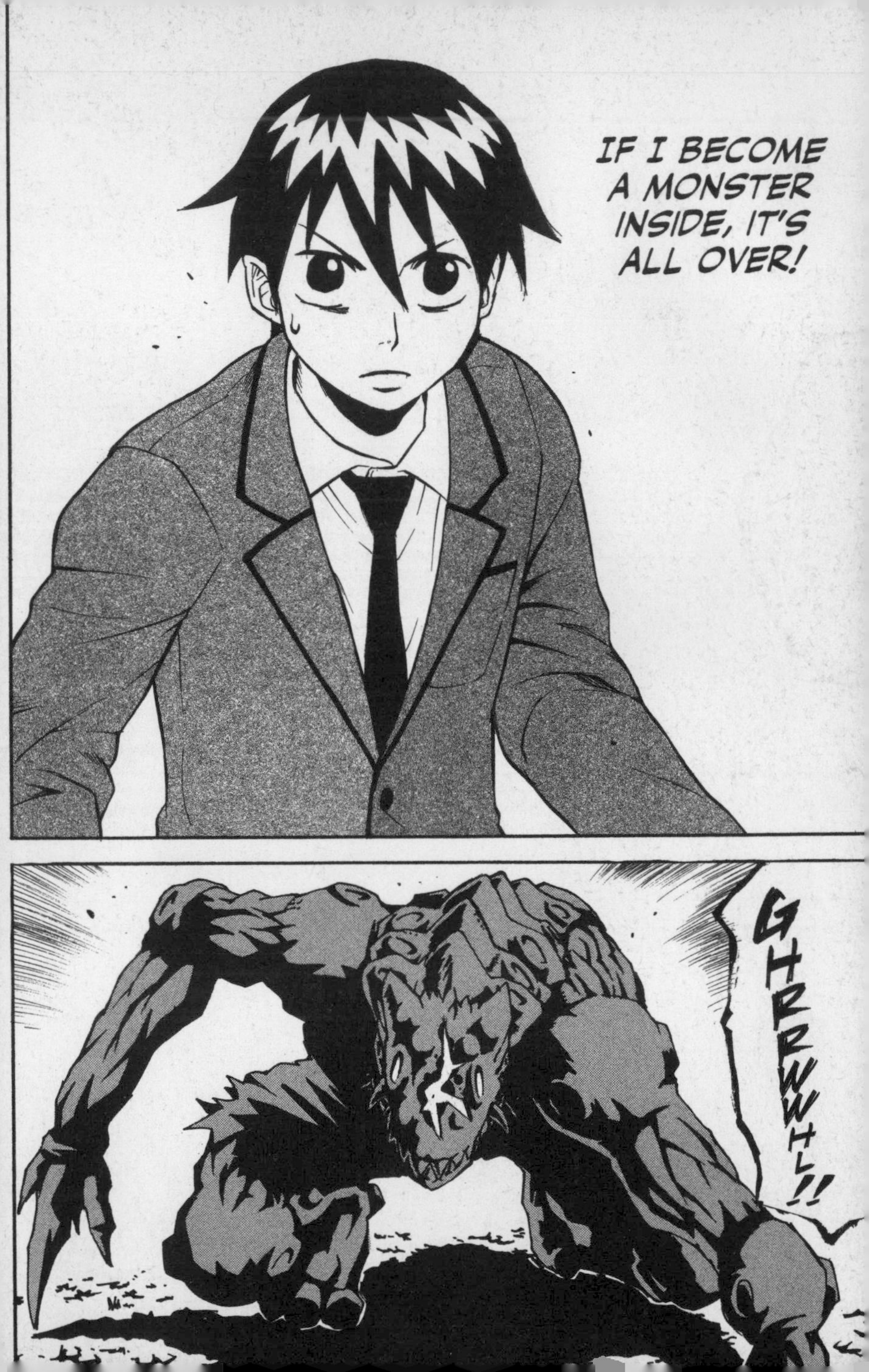
IF I BECOME A MONSTER INSIDE, IT'S ALL OVER!
GHRRWHL!!

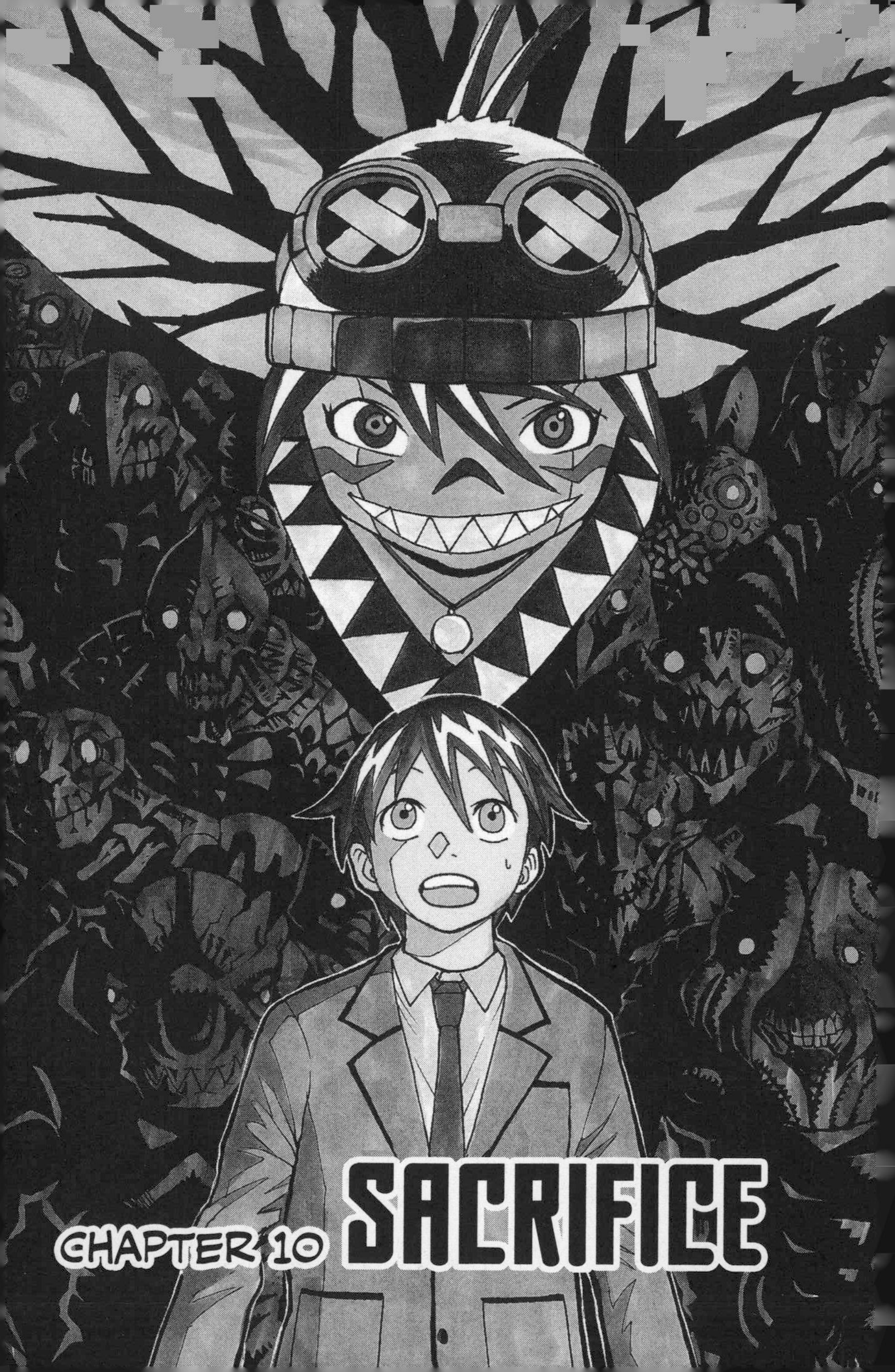
CHAPTER 10
SACRIFICE

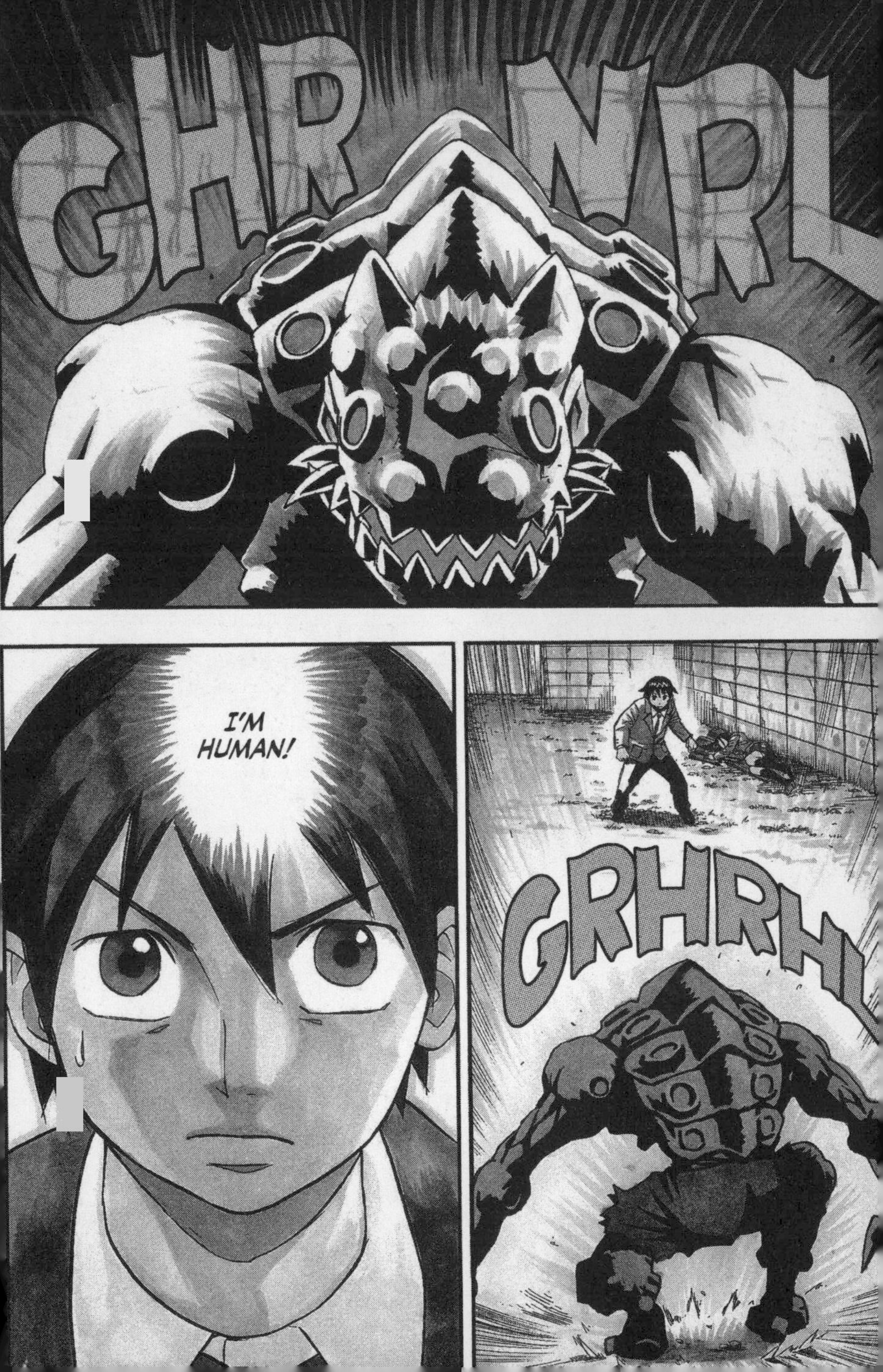
GHRNRL
GRHRH
I'M HUMAN!

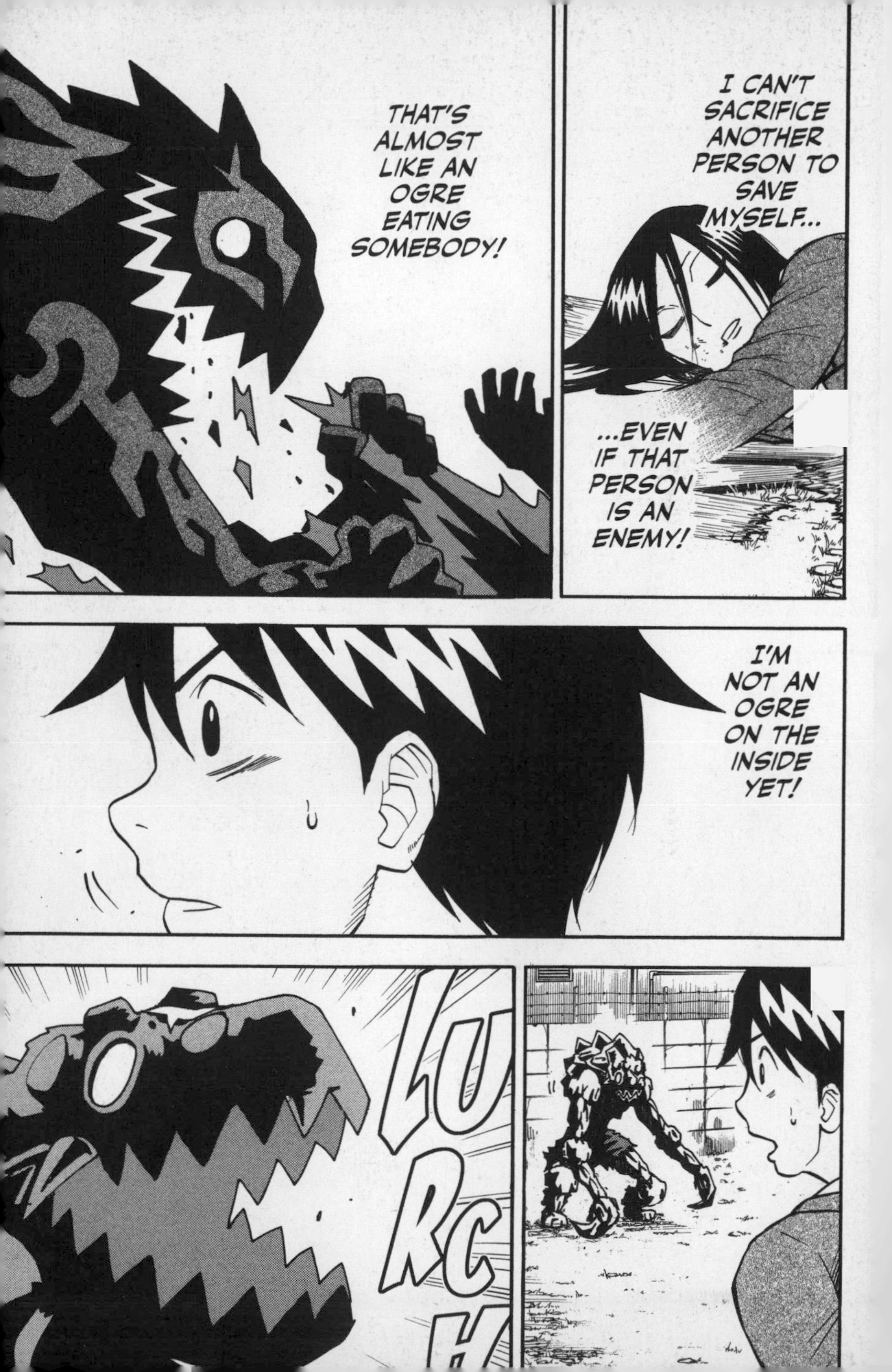
I CAN'T SACRIFICE ANOTHER PERSON TO SAVE MYSELF...
...EVEN IF THAT PERSON IS AN ENEMY!
THAT'S ALMOST LIKE AN OGRE EATING SOMEBODY!
I'M NOT AN OGRE ON THE INSIDE YET!
LURCH

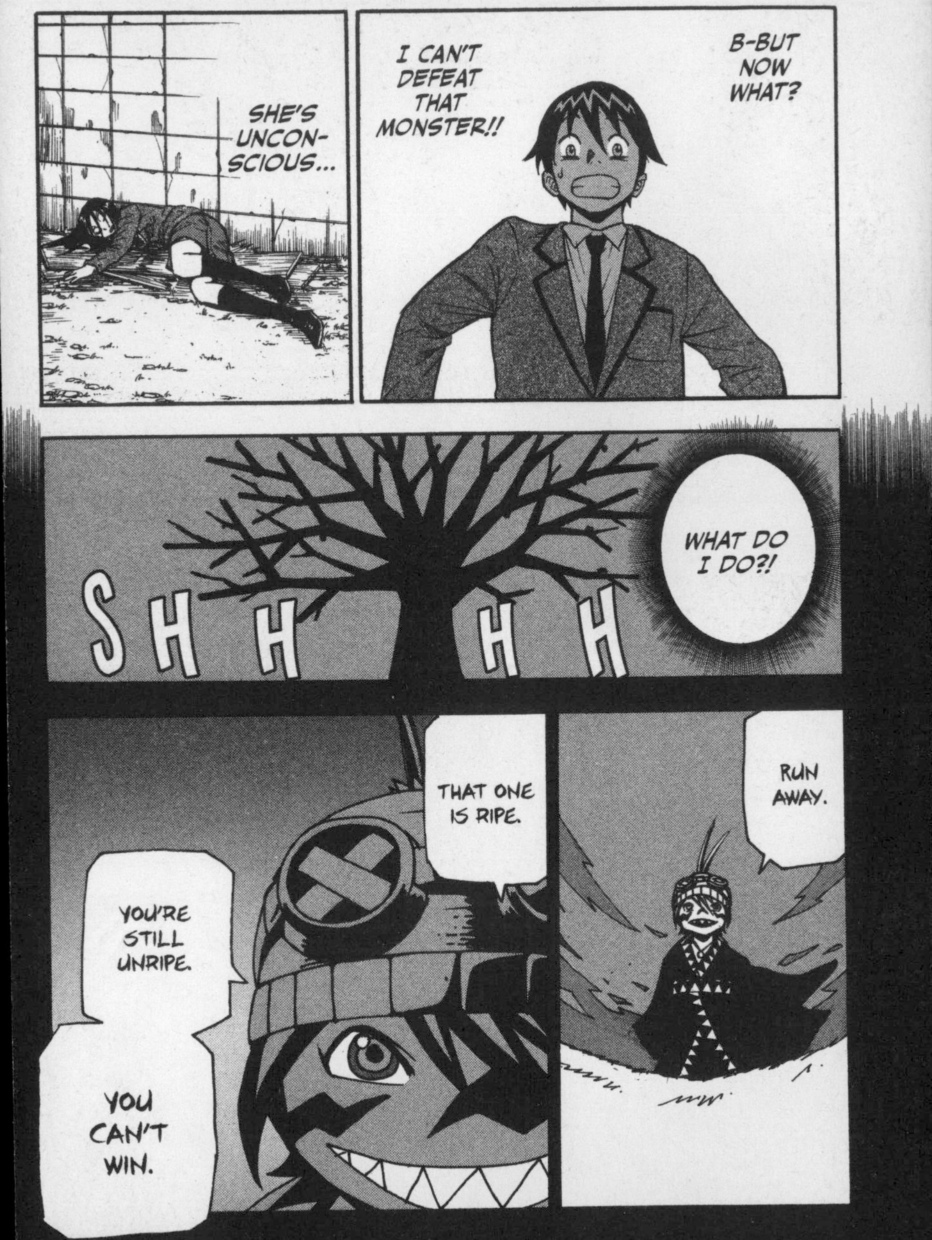
B-BUT NOW WHAT?
I CAN'T DEFEAT THAT MONSTER!!
SHE'S UNCON-SCIOUS...
WHAT DO I DO?!
SHHHH
RUN AWAY.
THAT ONE IS RIPE.
YOU'RE STILL UNRIPE.
YOU CAN'T WIN.

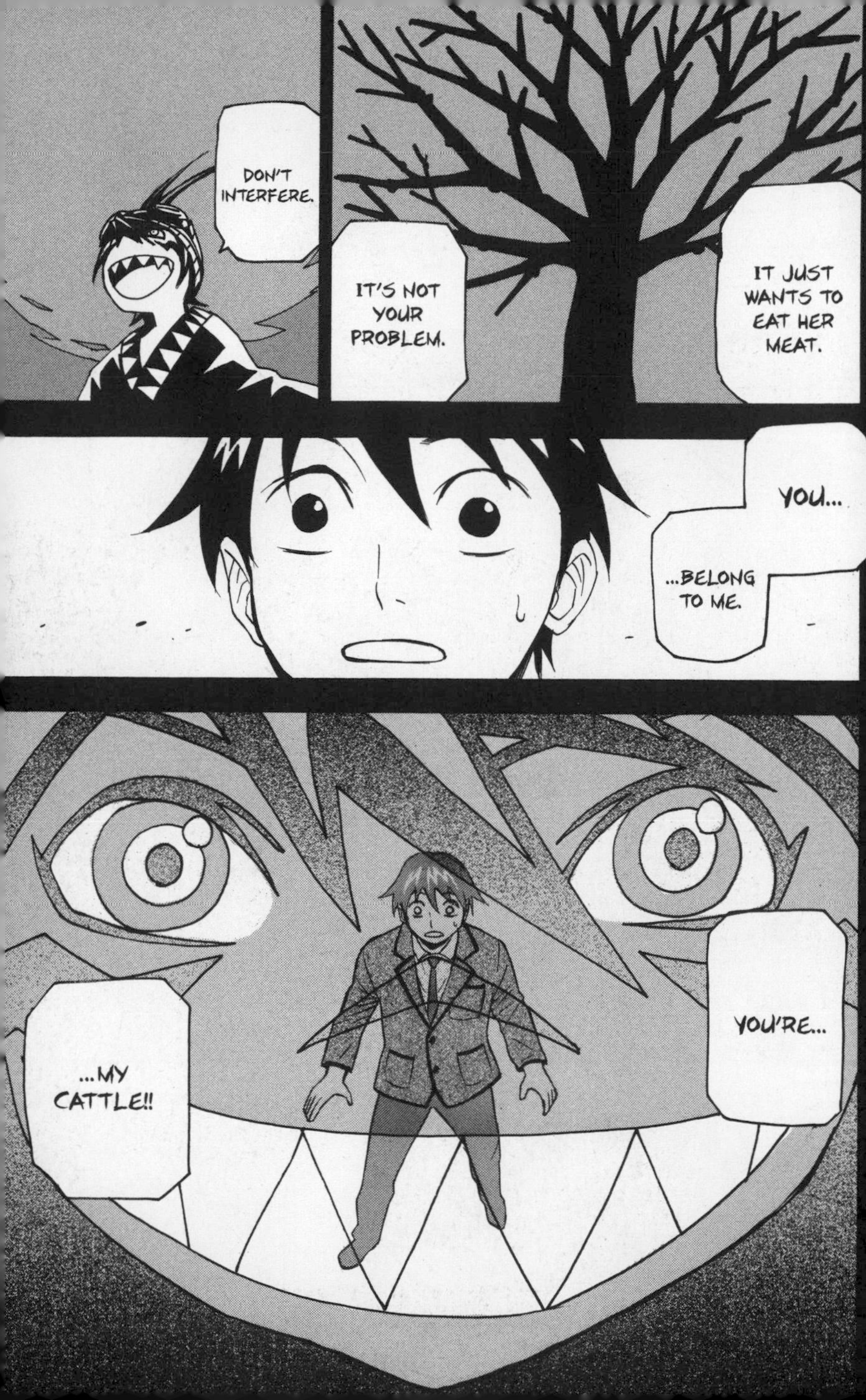
IT JUST WANTS TO EAT HER MEAT.
IT'S NOT YOUR PROBLEM.
DON'T INTERFERE.
YOU...
...BELONG TO ME.
YOU'RE...
...MY CATTLE!!

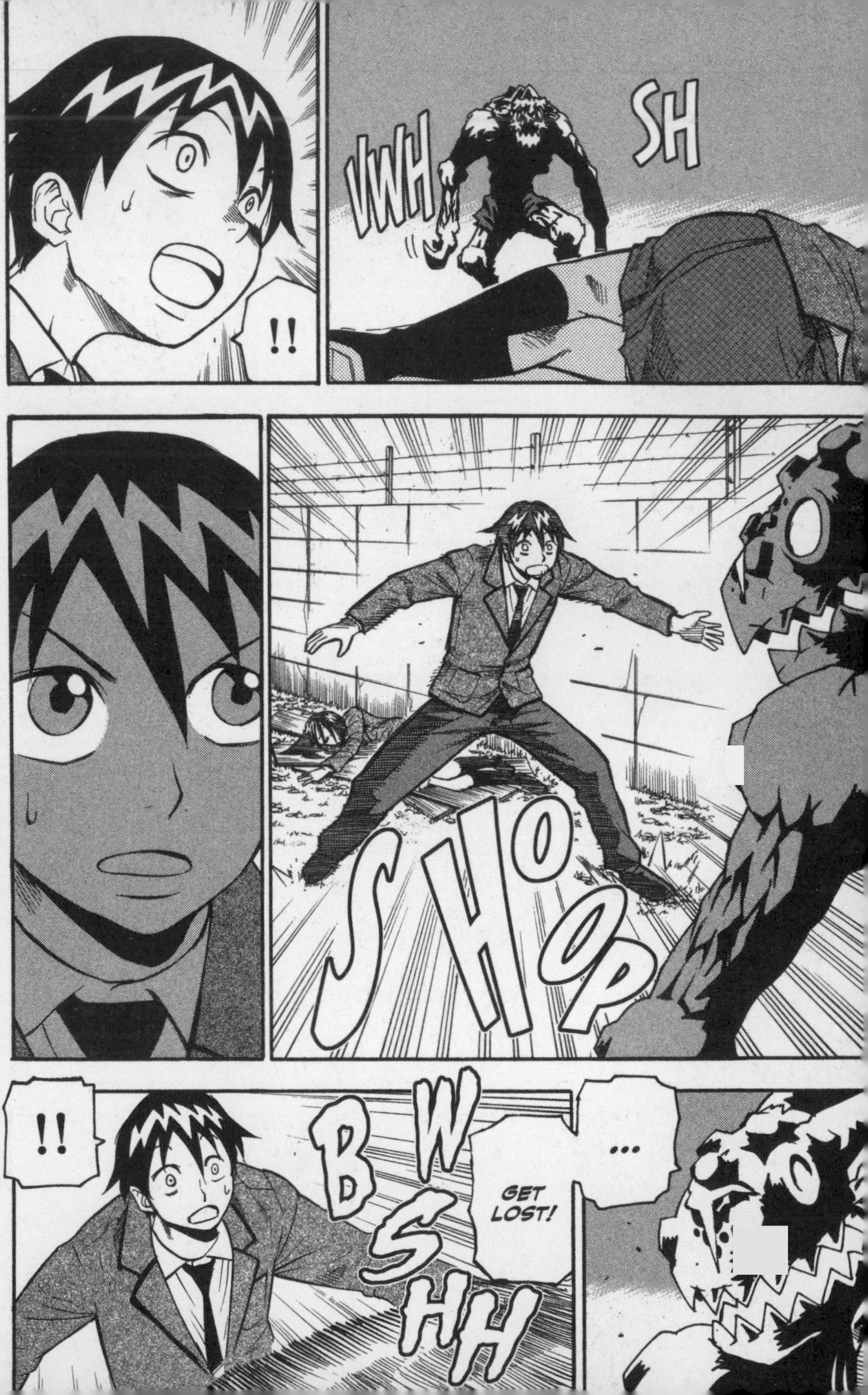
VWH
SH
!!
SHOOP
...
GET LOST!
BWSHH
!!

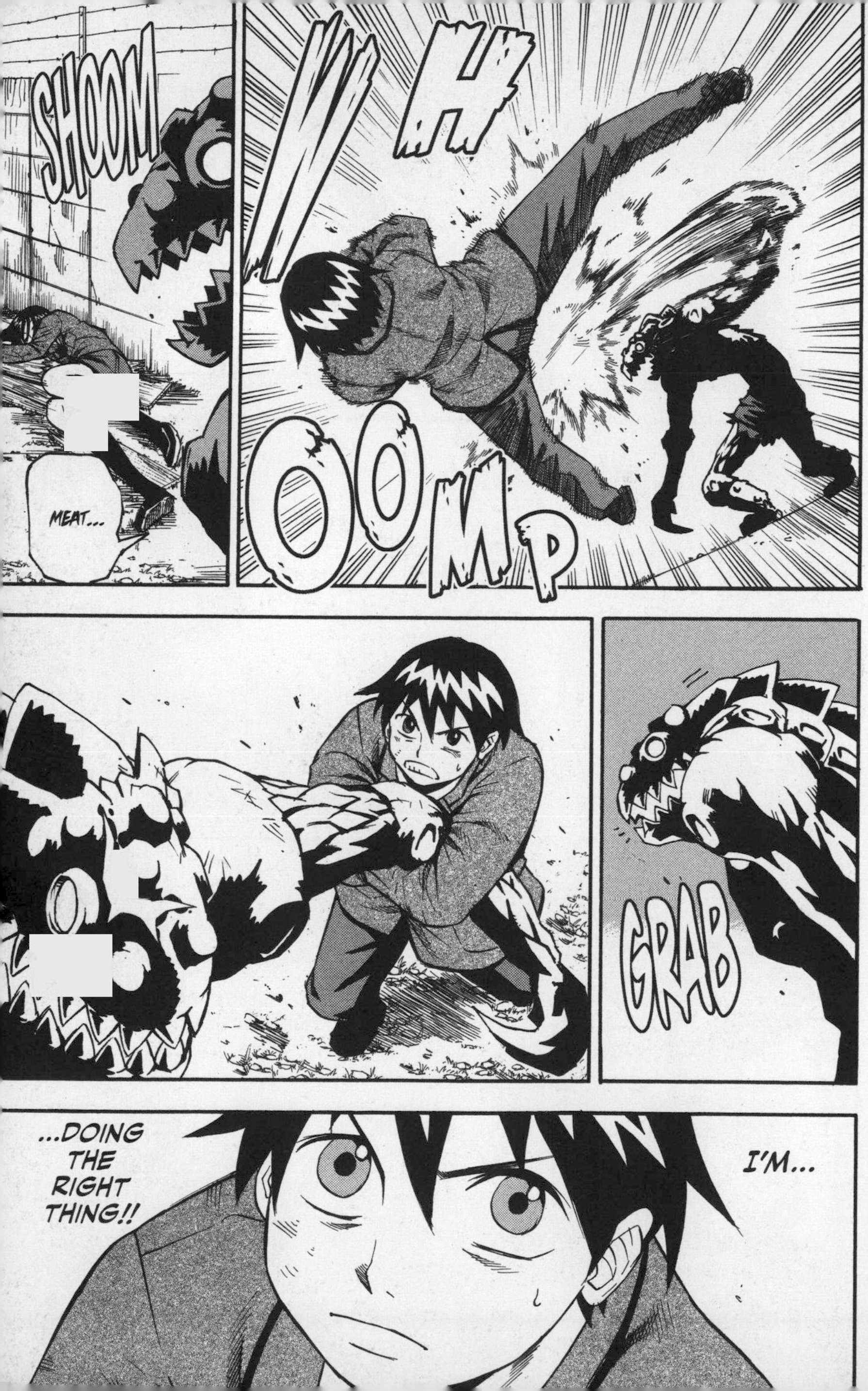
WHOOMP
SHOOM
MEAT...
GRAB
I'M...
...DOING THE RIGHT THING!!

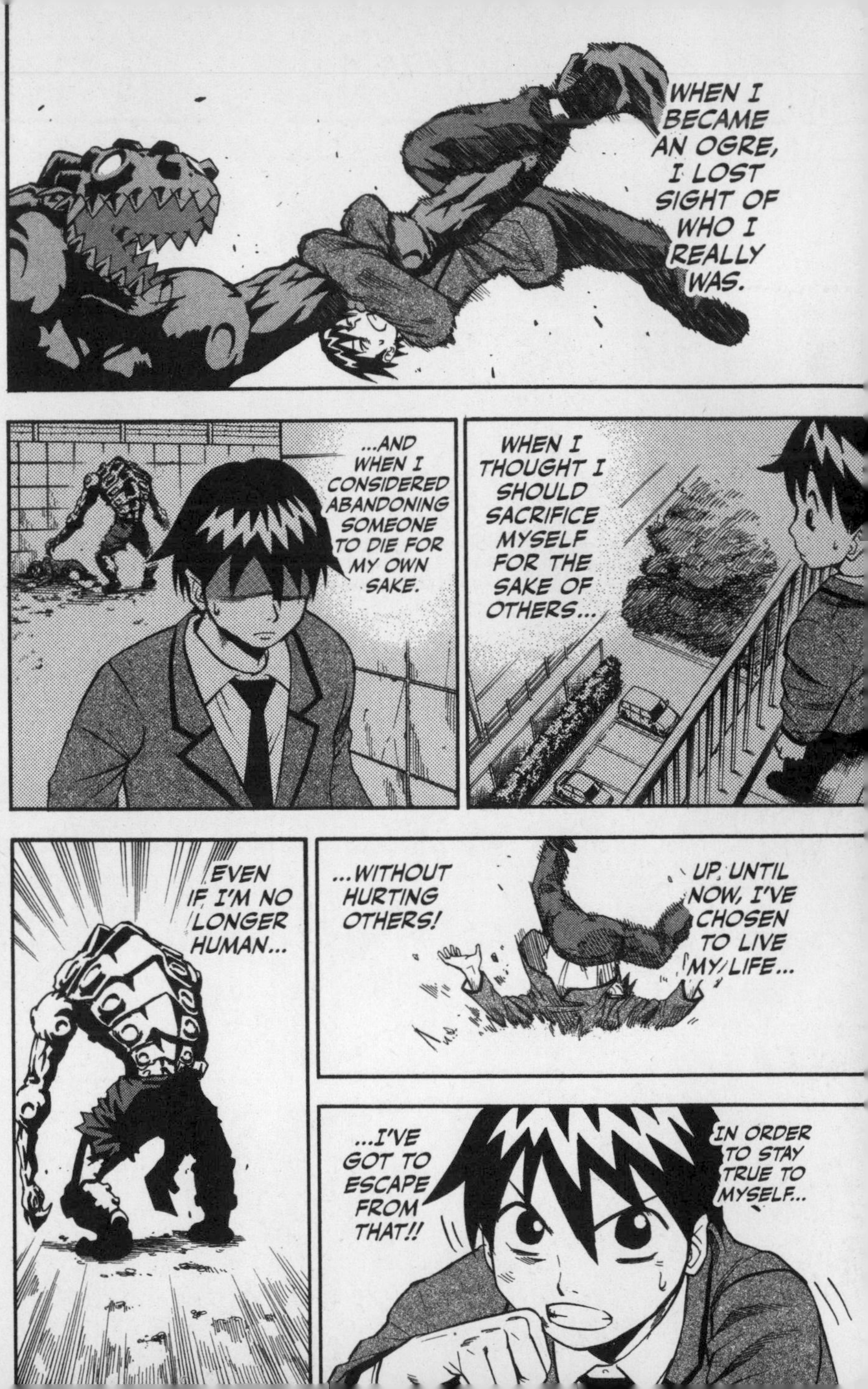
WHEN I BECAME AN OGRE, I LOST SIGHT OF WHO I REALLY WAS.
WHEN I THOUGHT I SHOULD SACRIFICE MYSELF FOR THE SAKE OF OTHERS...
...AND WHEN I CONSIDERED ABANDONING SOMEONE TO DIE FOR MY OWN SAKE.
UP UNTIL NOW, I'VE CHOSEN TO LIVE MY LIFE...
...WITHOUT HURTING OTHERS!
IN ORDER TO STAY TRUE TO MYSELF...
...I'VE GOT TO ESCAPE FROM THAT!!
EVEN IF I'M NO LONGER HUMAN...

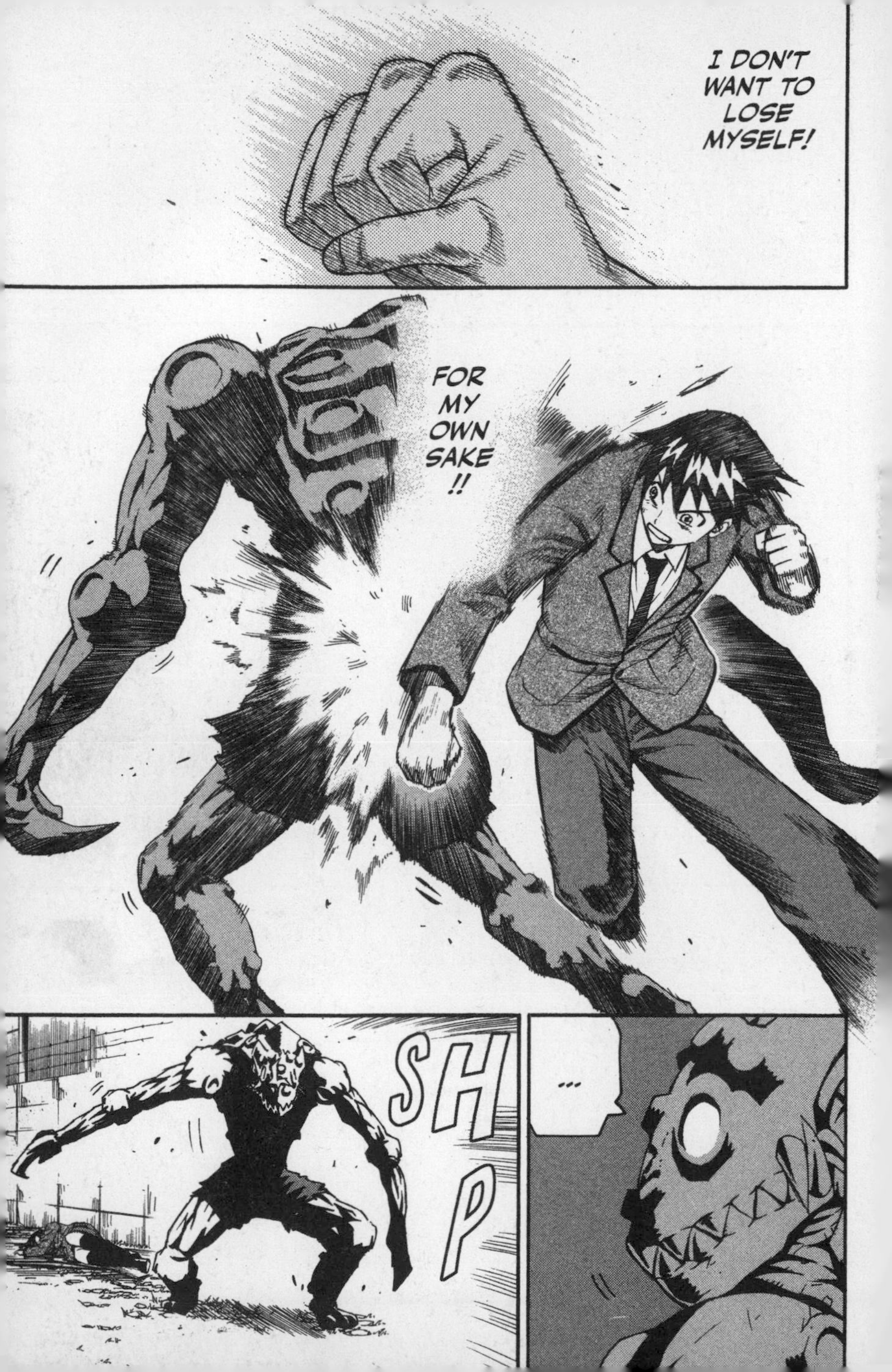
I DON'T WANT TO LOSE MYSELF!
FOR MY OWN SAKE !!
...
SHP

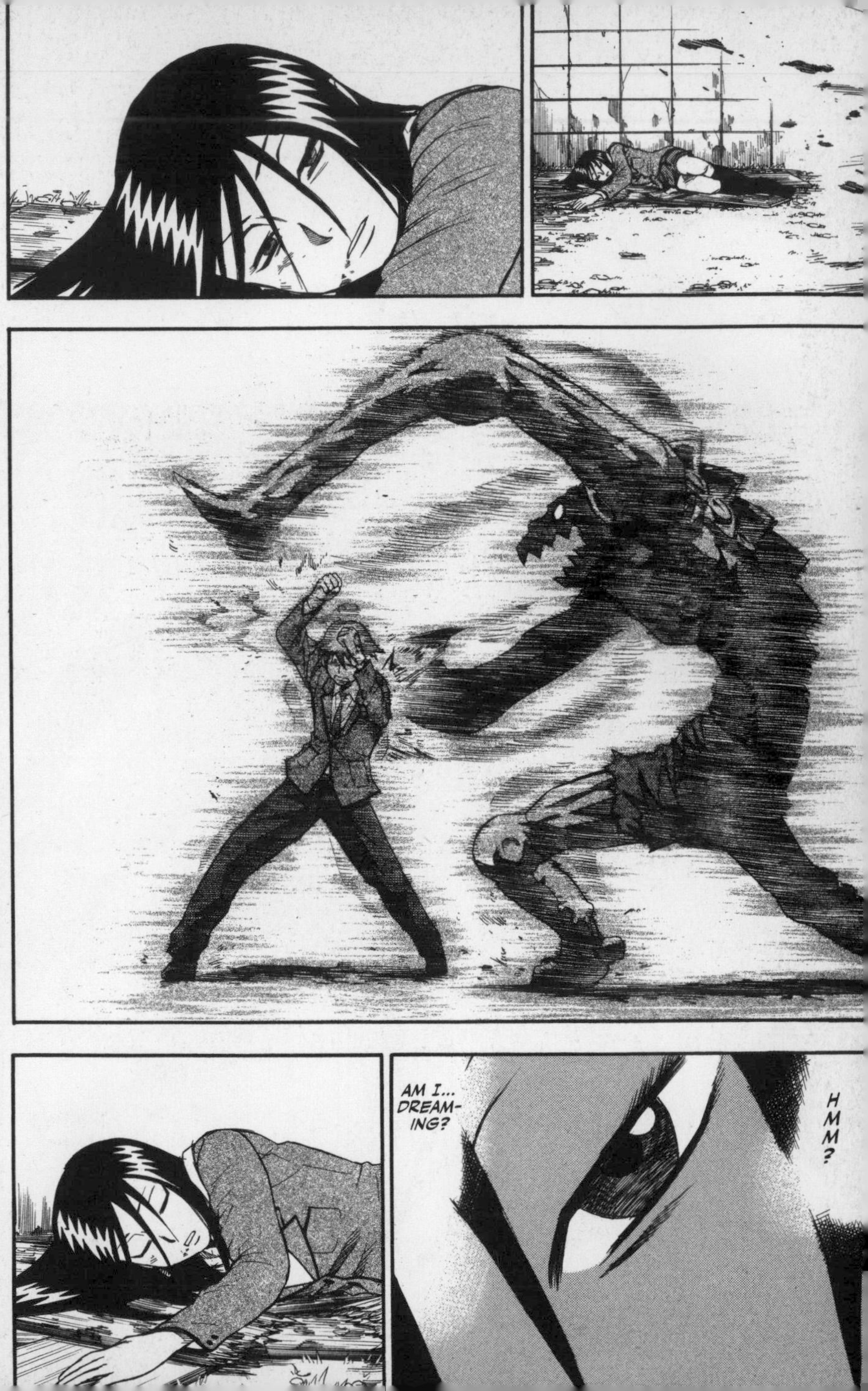
HMM?
AM I... DREAMING?

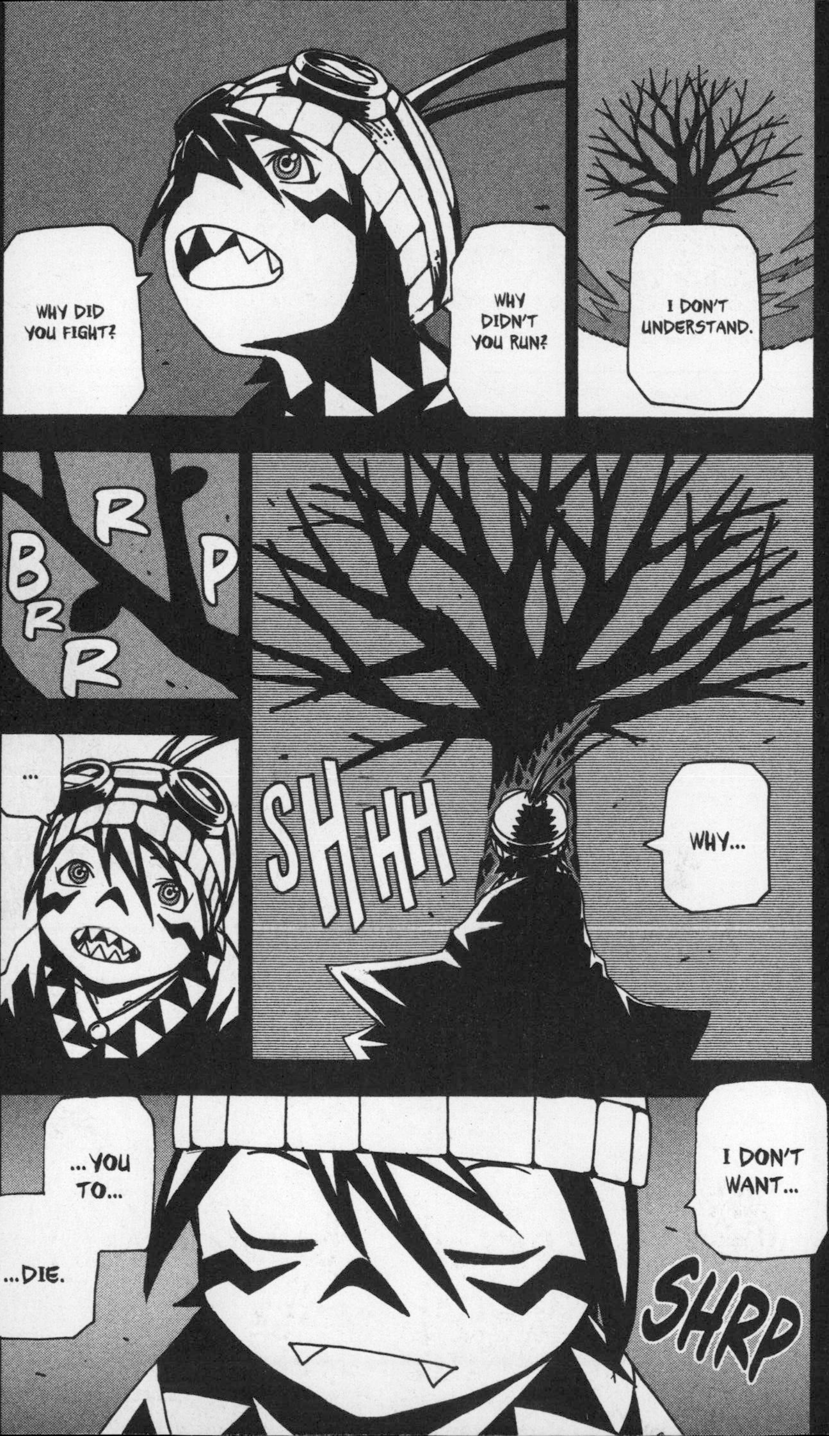
I DON'T UNDERSTAND.
WHY DIDN'T YOU RUN?
WHY DID YOU FIGHT?
WHY...
SHHH
BRRRP
...
I DON'T WANT...
SHRP
...YOU TO...
...DIE.

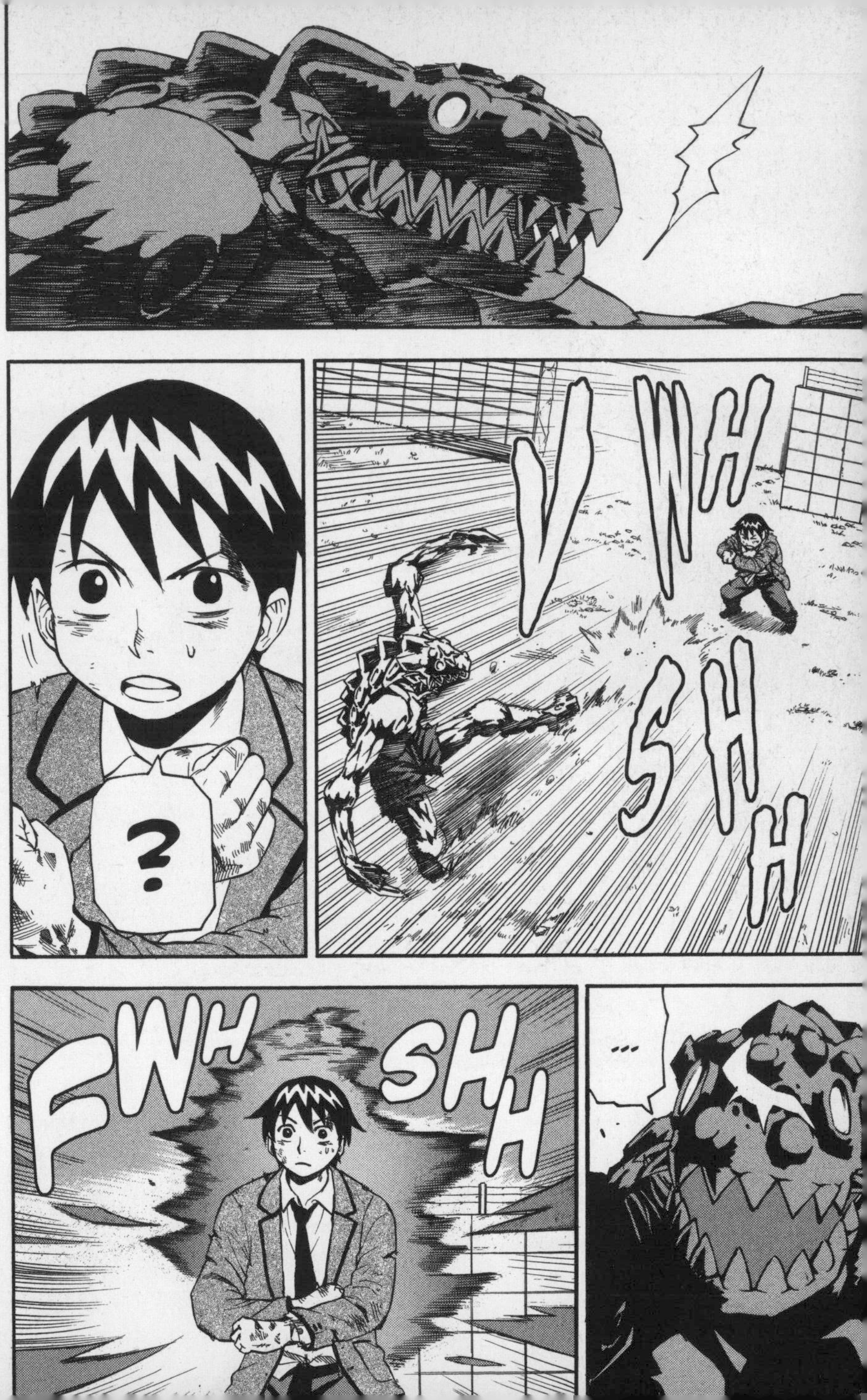
VWHSHH
?
...
FWHSHH

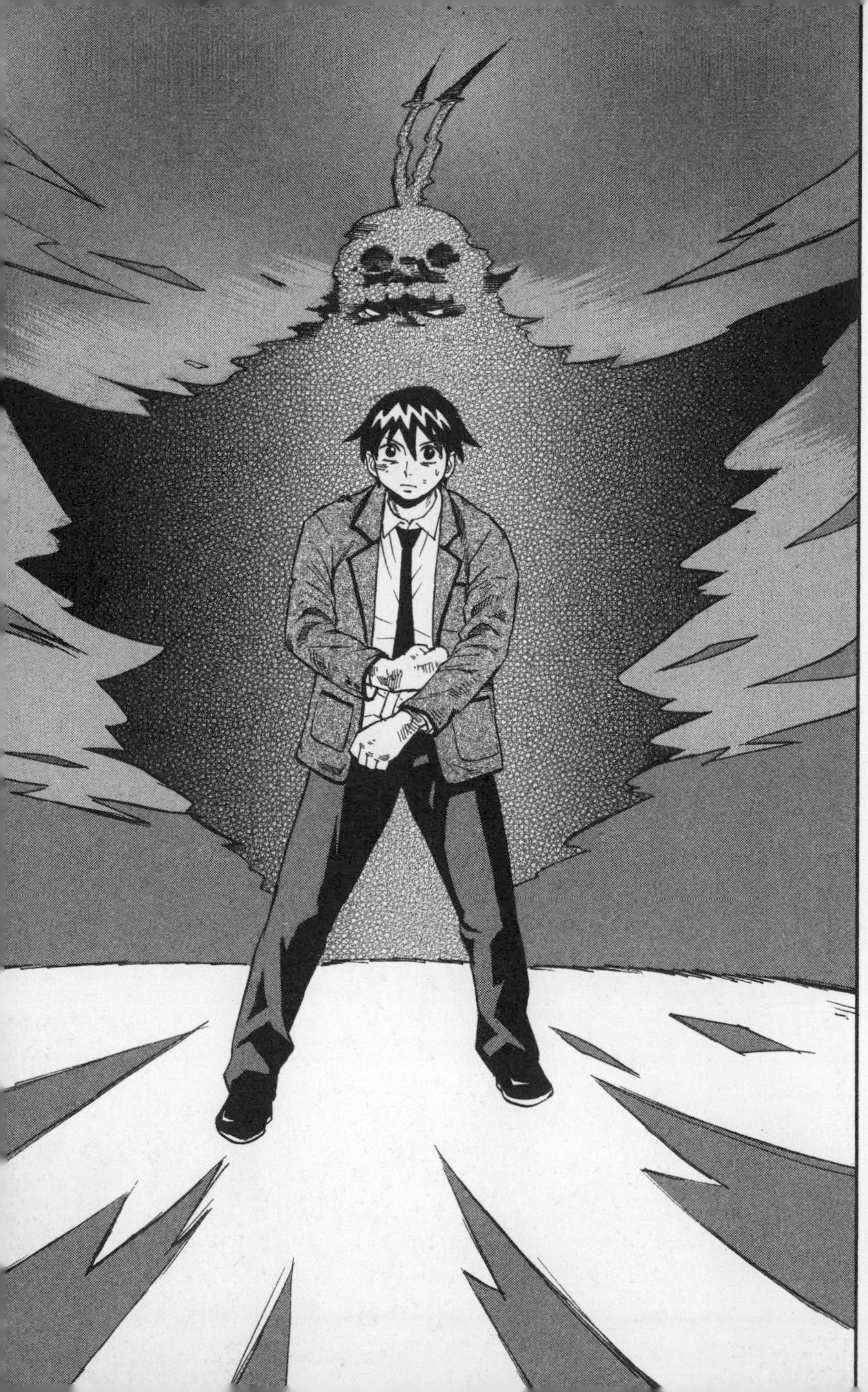

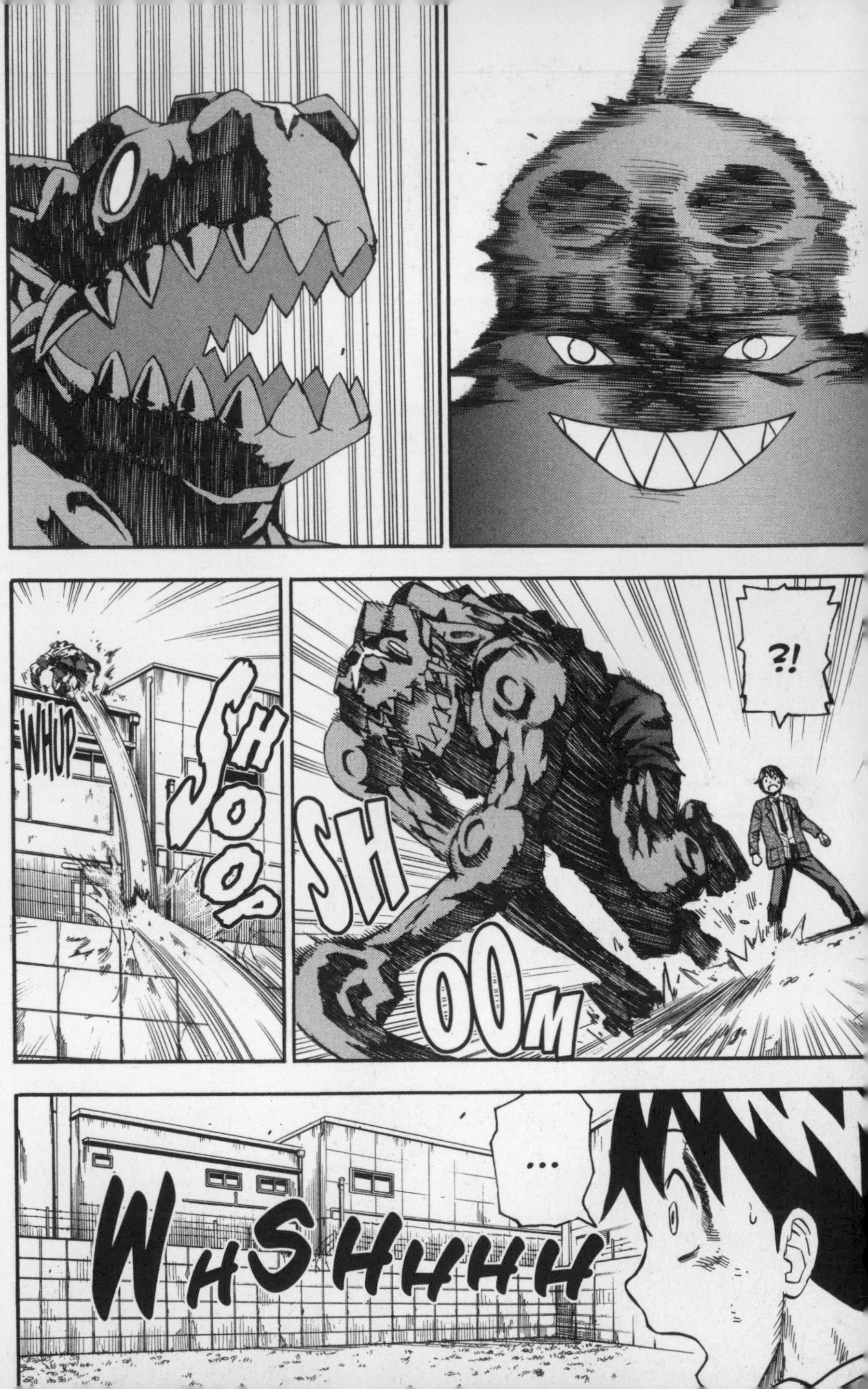

?!
SHOOM
SHOOP
WHUP
...
WHSHHHH

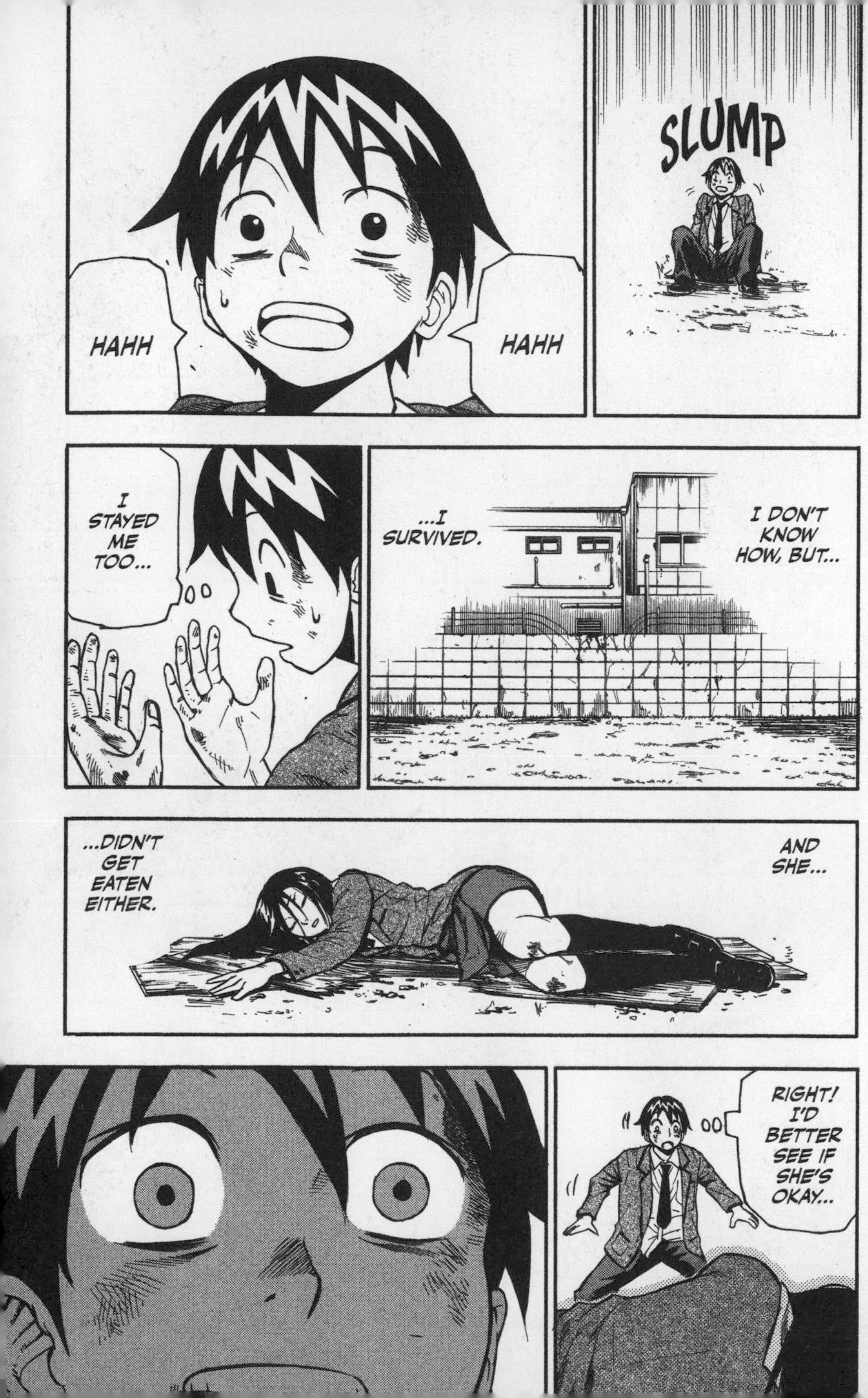
SLUMP
HAHH
HAHH
I DON'T KNOW HOW, BUT...
...I SURVIVED.
I STAYED ME TOO...
AND SHE...
...DIDN'T GET EATEN EITHER.
RIGHT! I'D BETTER SEE IF SHE'S OKAY...

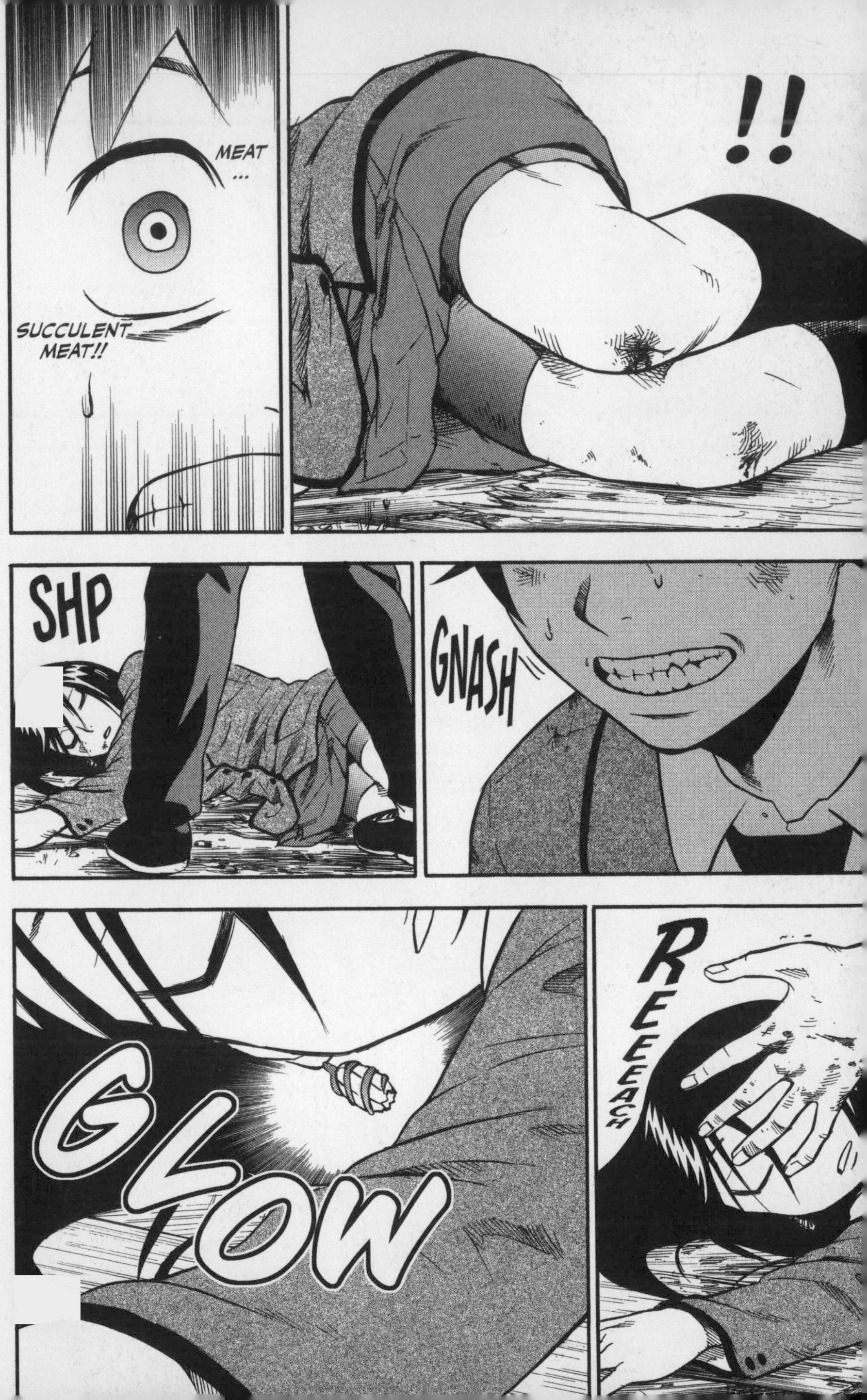
!!
MEAT ...
SUCCULENT MEAT!!
GNASH
SHP
REEEACH
GLOW

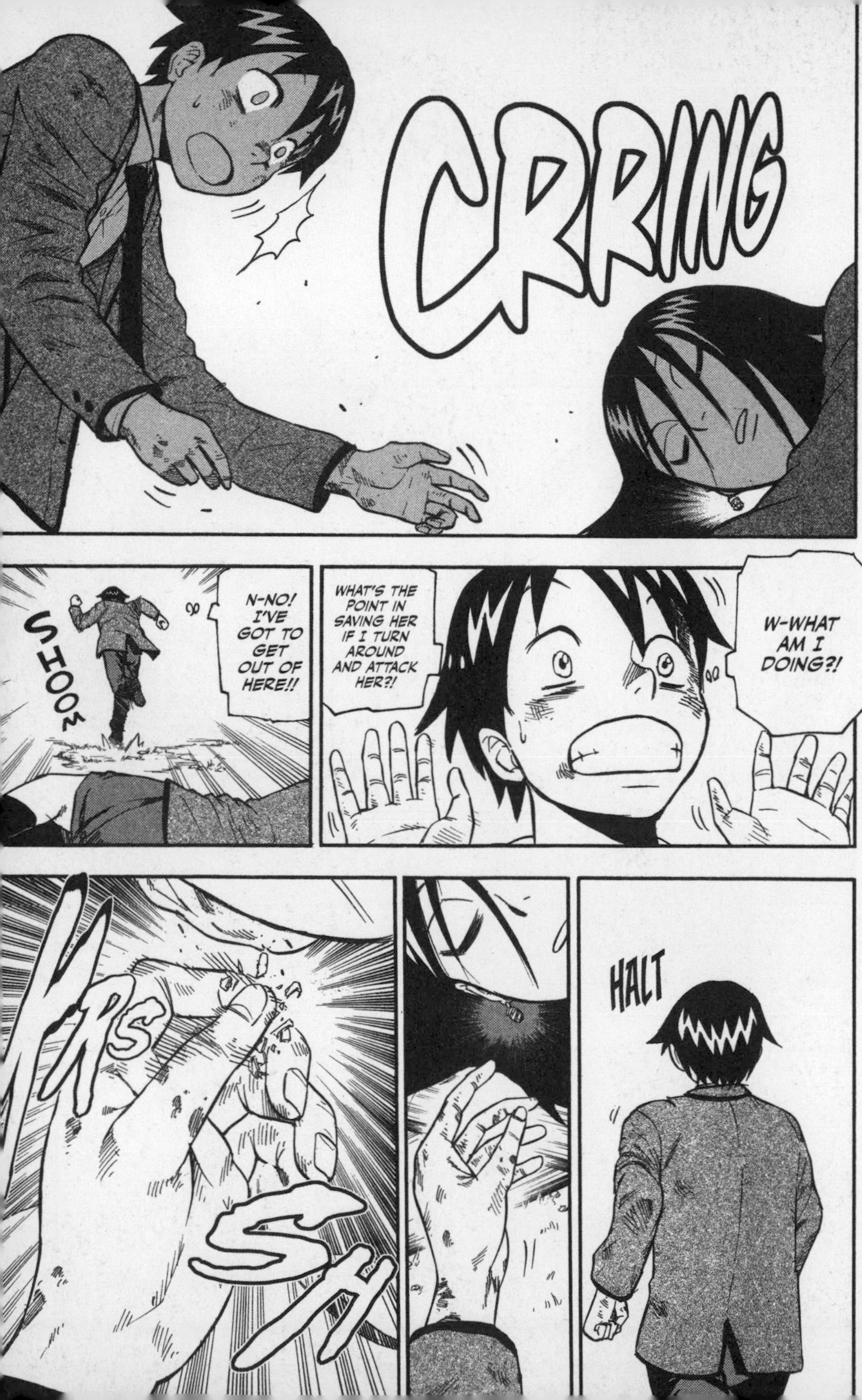
CRRING
W-WHAT AM I DOING?!
WHAT'S THE POINT IN SAVING HER IF I TURN AROUND AND ATTACK HER?!
N-NO! I'VE GOT TO GET OUT OF HERE!!
SHOOM
HALT

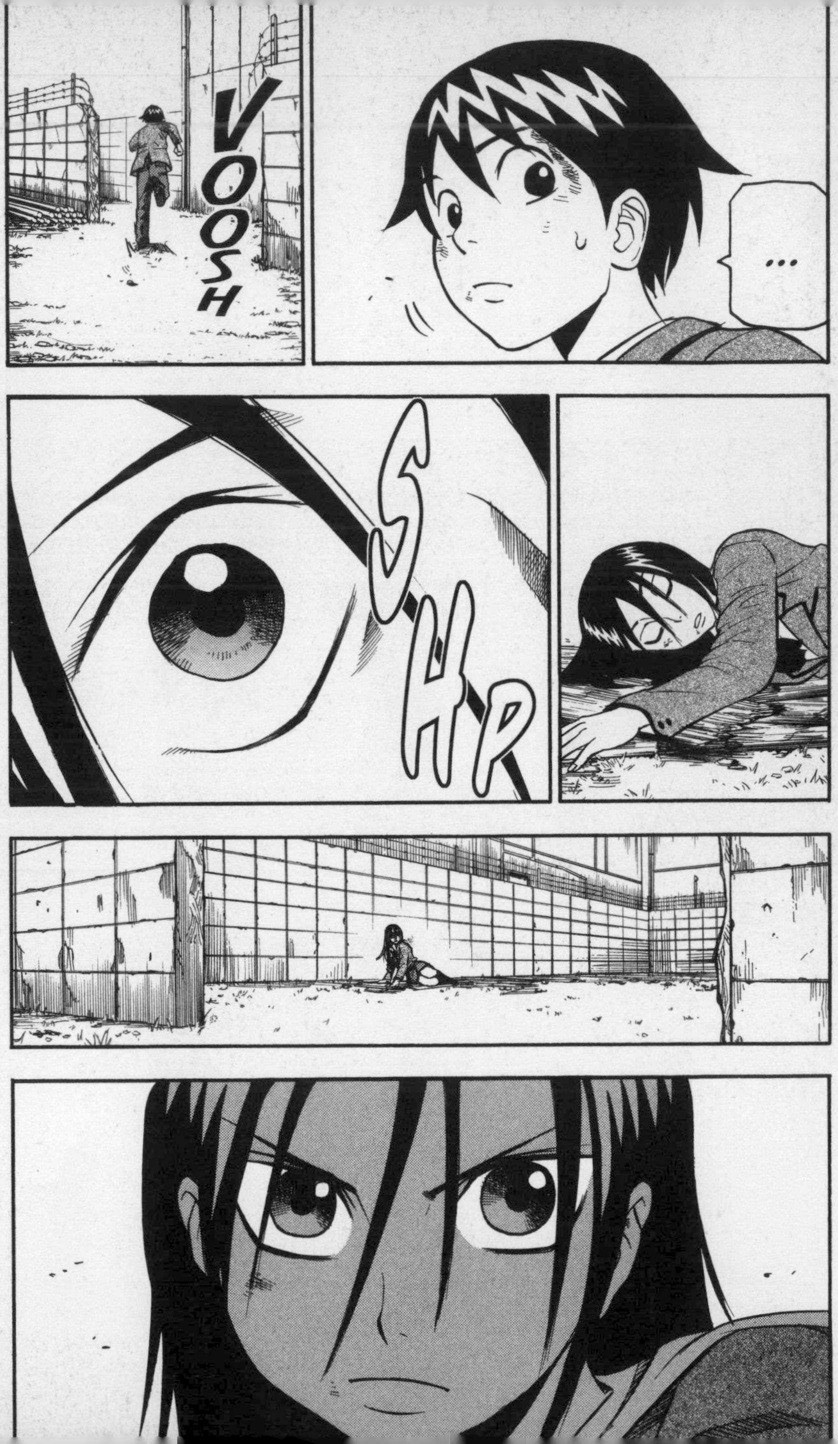
...
VOOSH
SHP

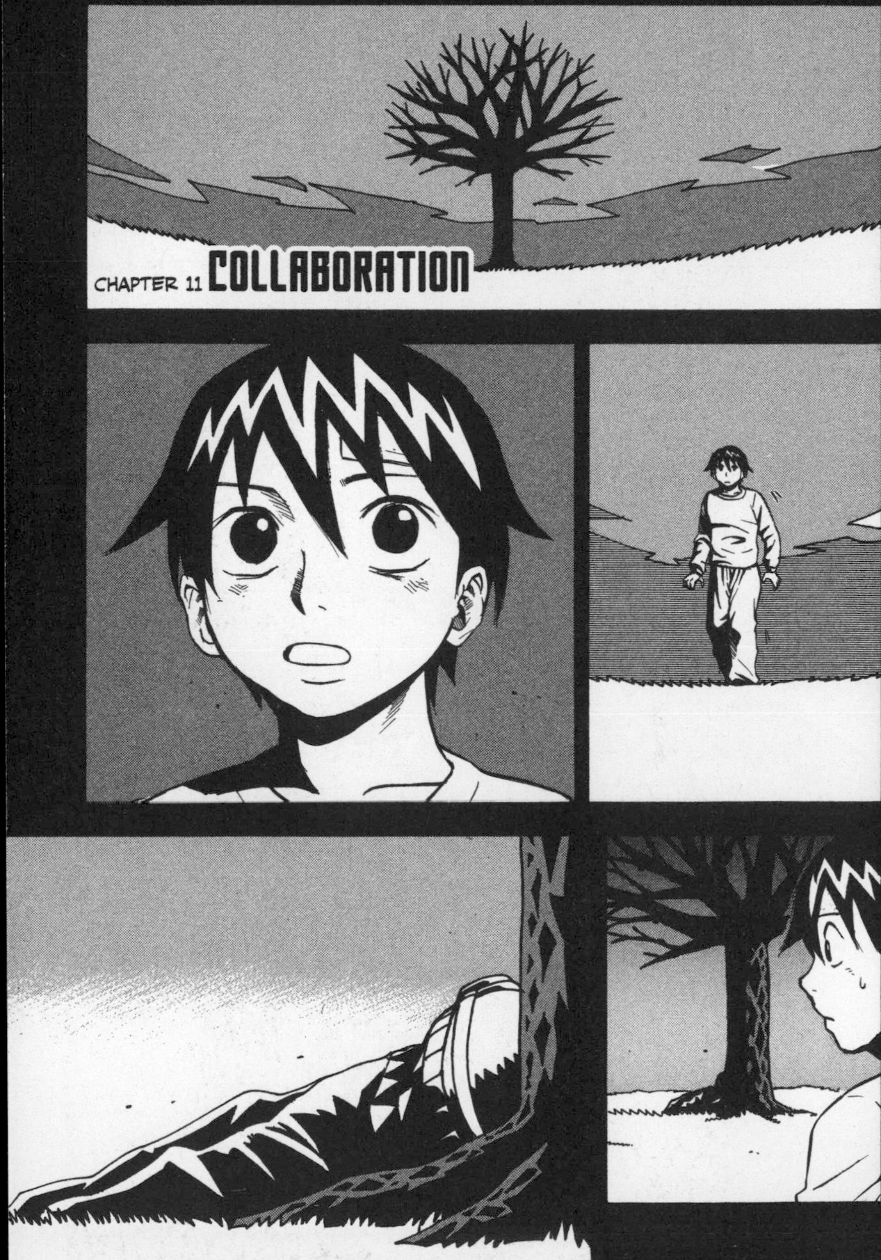
CHAPTER 11 COLLABORATION

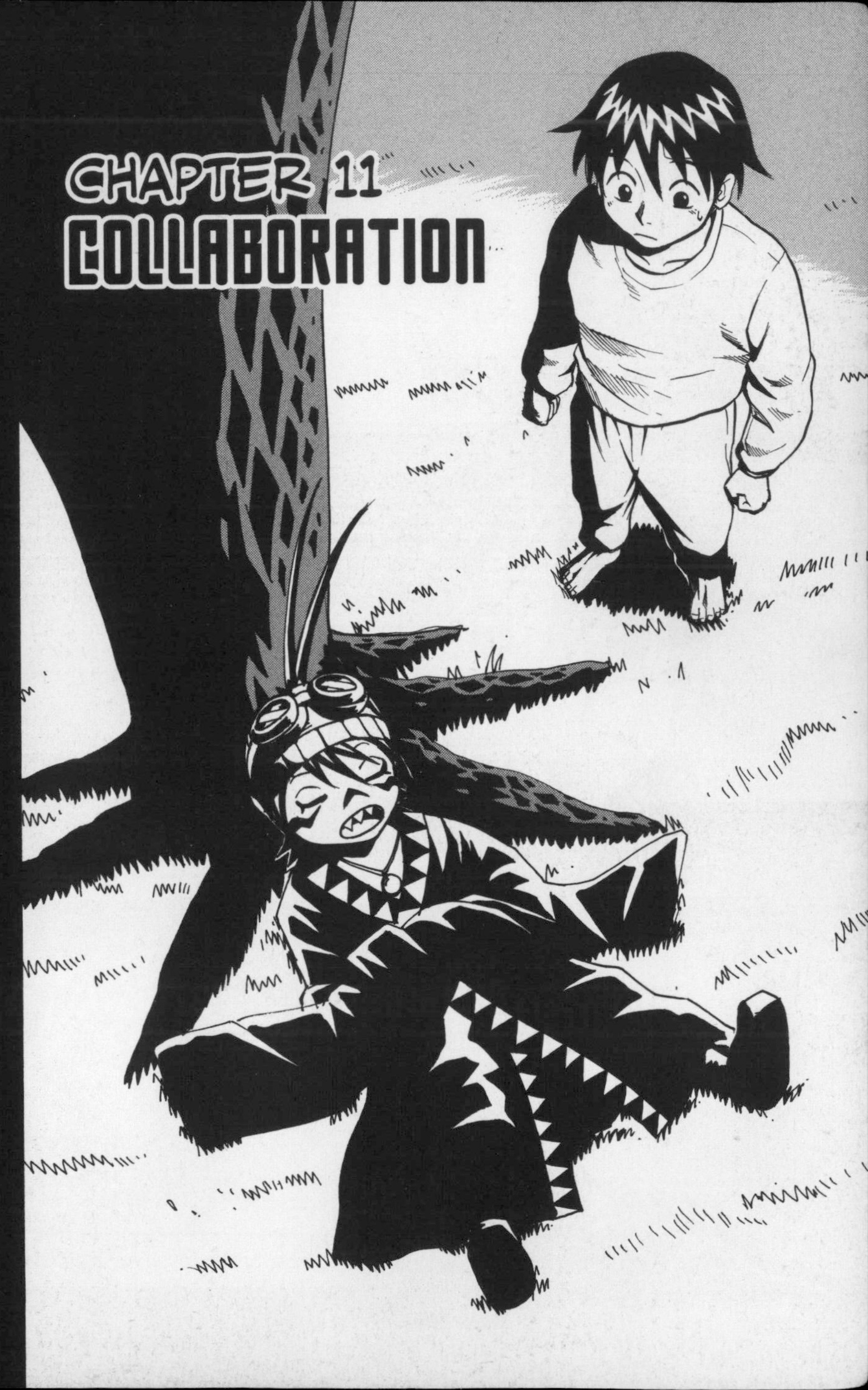
CHAPTER 11
COLLABORATION

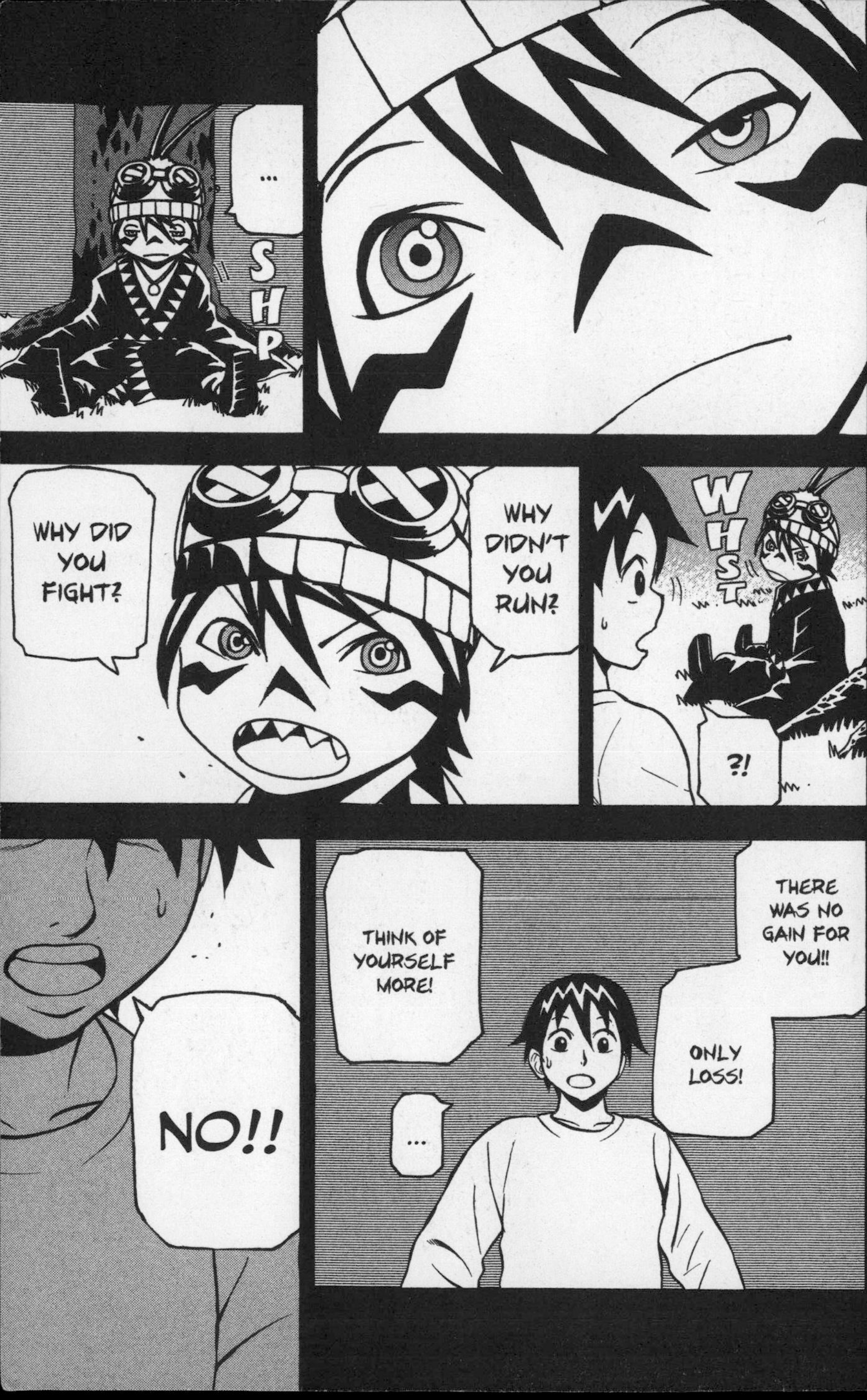
...
SHP
WHST
?!
WHY DIDN'T YOU RUN?
WHY DID YOU FIGHT?
THERE WAS NO GAIN FOR YOU!!
ONLY LOSS!
THINK OF YOURSELF MORE!
...
NO!!

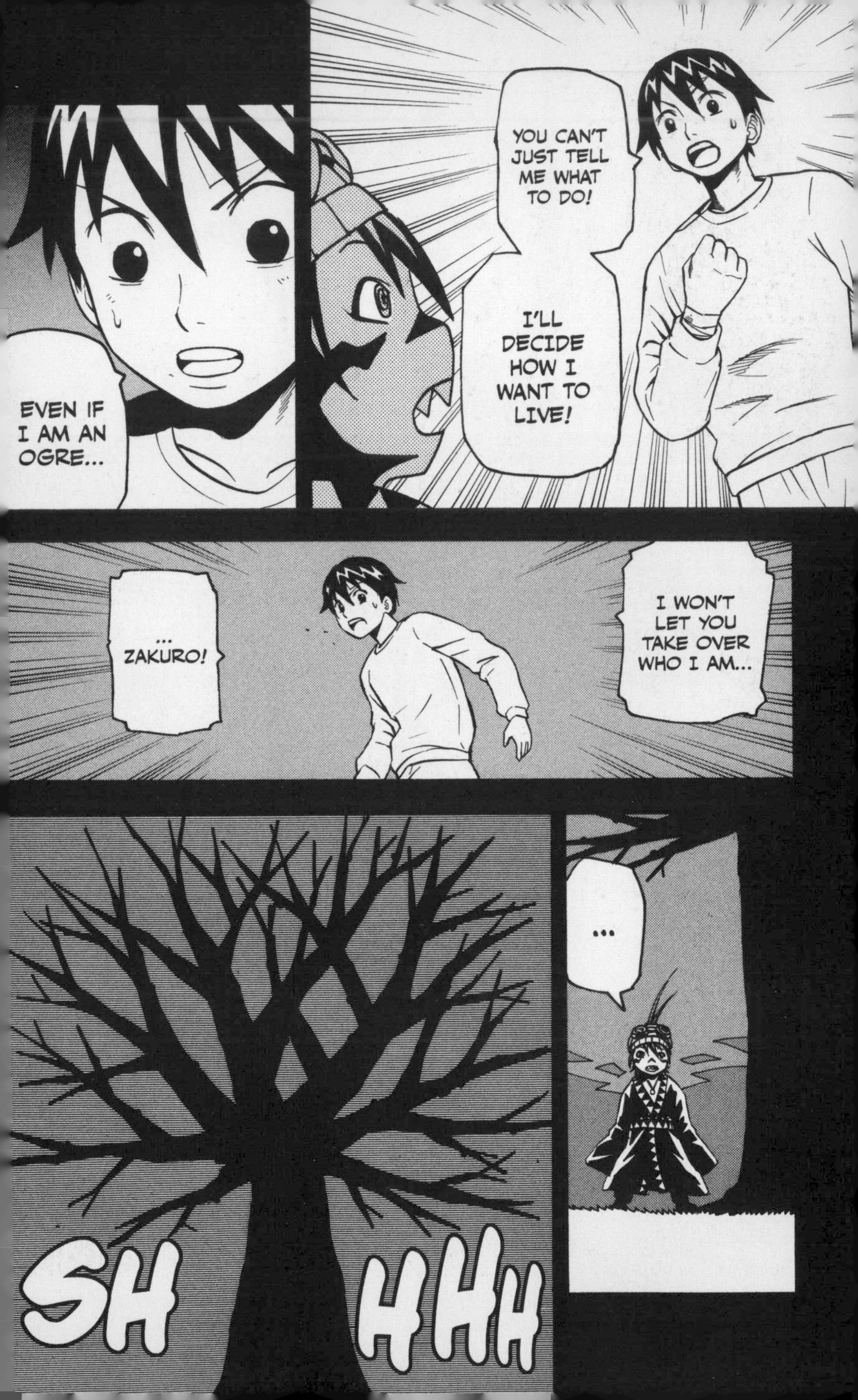
YOU CAN'T JUST TELL ME WHAT TO DO!
I'LL DECIDE HOW I WANT TO LIVE!
EVEN IF I AM AN OGRE...
I WON'T LET YOU TAKE OVER WHO I AM...
... ZAKURO!
...
SHHHH

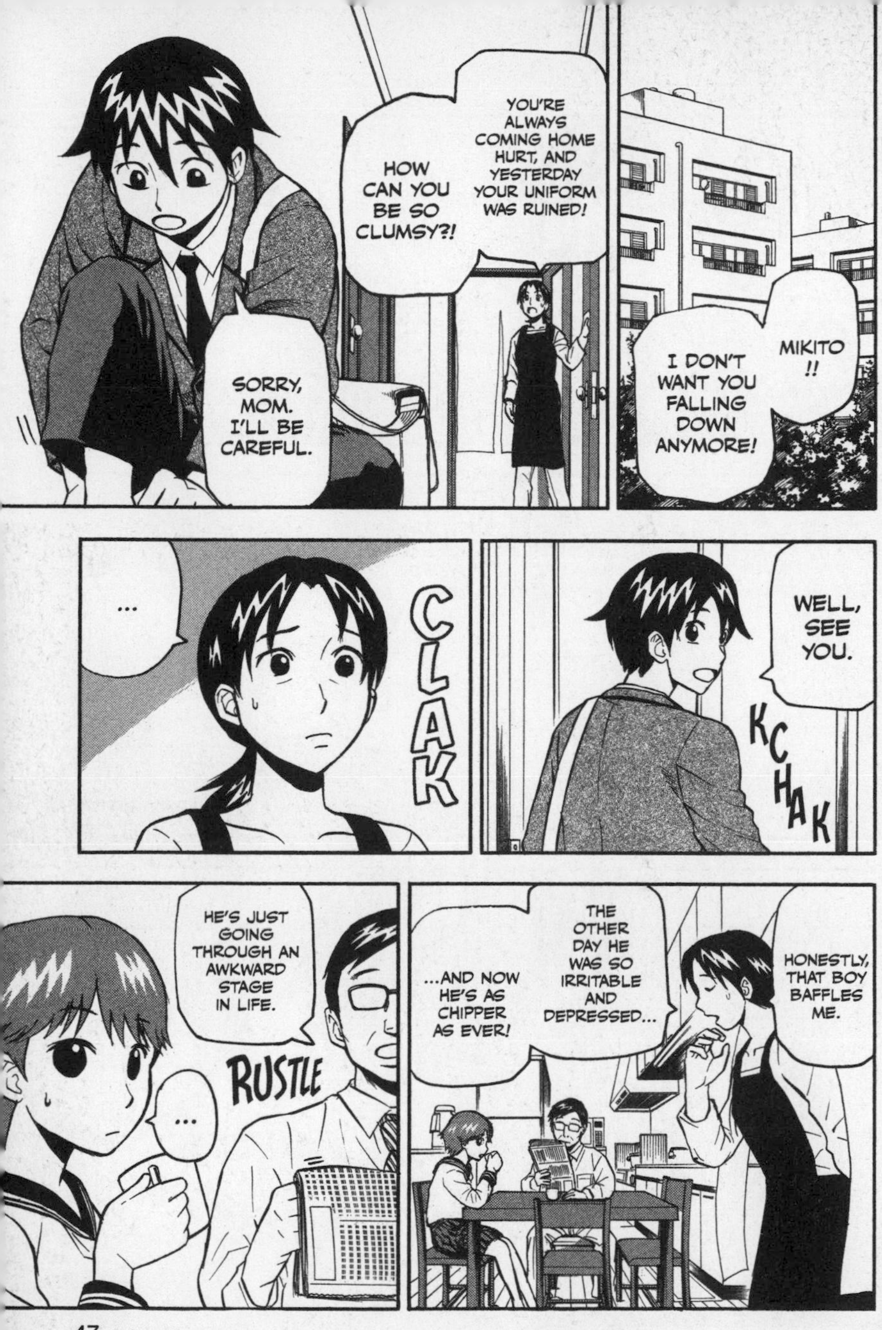
MIKITO !!
I DON'T WANT YOU FALLING DOWN ANYMORE!
YOU'RE ALWAYS COMING HOME HURT, AND YESTERDAY YOUR UNIFORM WAS RUINED!
HOW CAN YOU BE SO CLUMSY?!
SORRY, MOM. I'LL BE CAREFUL.
WELL, SEE YOU.
KCHAK
CLAK
...
HONESTLY, THAT BOY BAFFLES ME.
THE OTHER DAY HE WAS SO IRRITABLE AND DEPRESSED...
...AND NOW HE'S AS CHIPPER AS EVER!
HE'S JUST GOING THROUGH AN AWKWARD STAGE IN LIFE.
RUSTLE
...

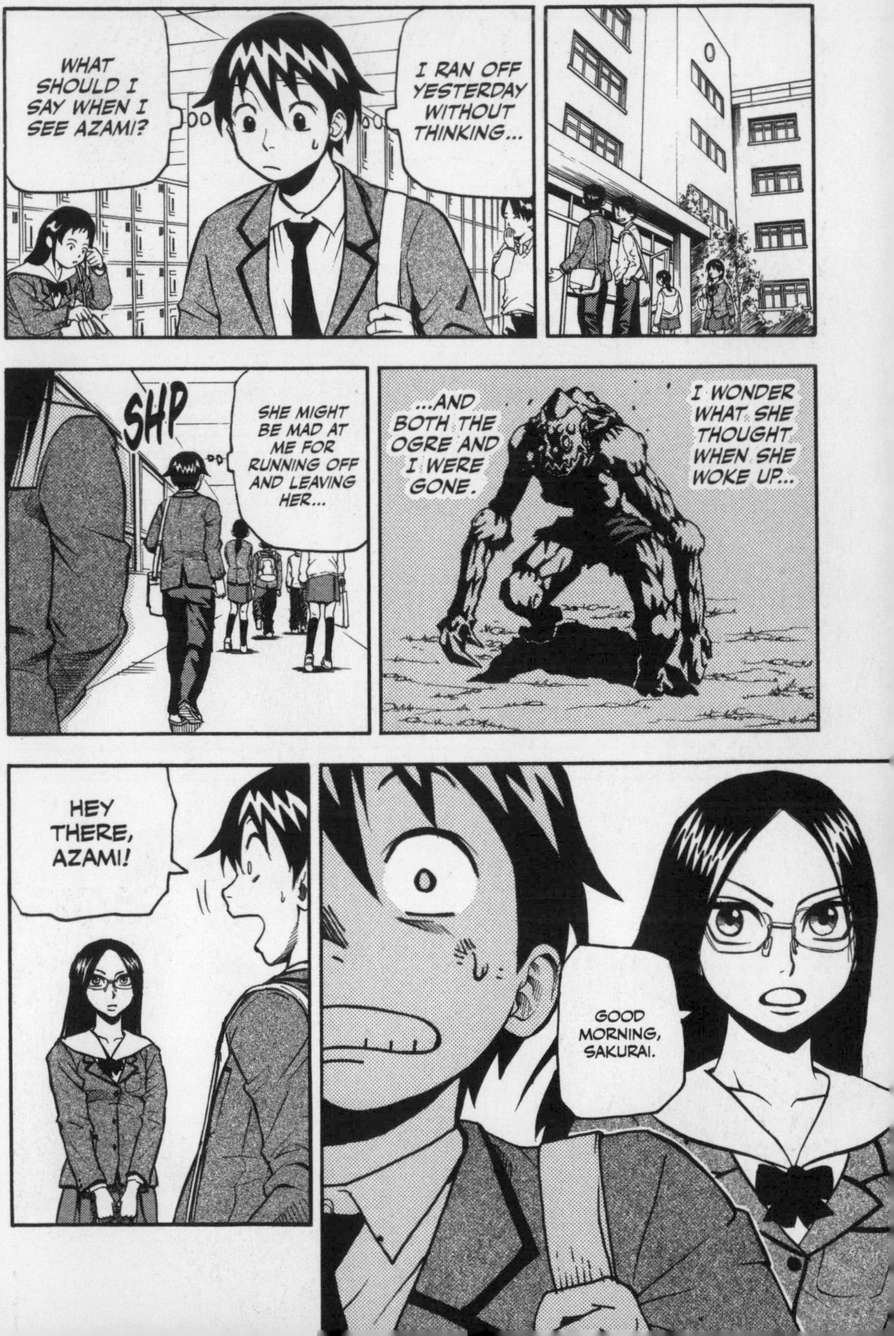
I RAN OFF YESTERDAY WITHOUT THINKING...
WHAT SHOULD I SAY WHEN I SEE AZAMI?
I WONDER WHAT SHE THOUGHT WHEN SHE WOKE UP...
...AND BOTH THE OGRE AND I WERE GONE.
SHP
SHE MIGHT BE MAD AT ME FOR RUNNING OFF AND LEAVING HER...
GOOD MORNING, SAKURAI.
HEY THERE, AZAMI!

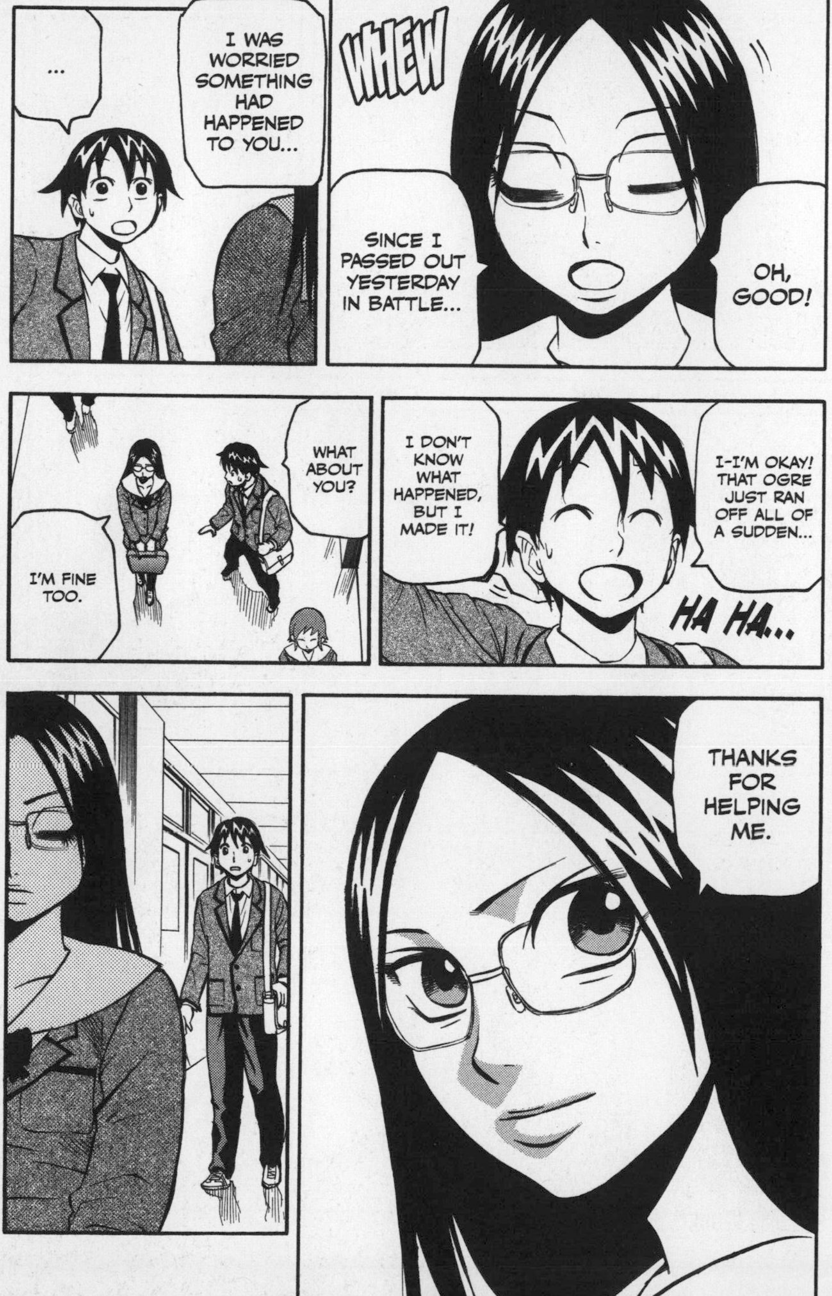
WHEW
OH, GOOD!
SINCE I PASSED OUT YESTERDAY IN BATTLE...
I WAS WORRIED SOMETHING HAD HAPPENED TO YOU...
...
I-I'M OKAY! THAT OGRE JUST RAN OFF ALL OF A SUDDEN...
I DON'T KNOW WHAT HAPPENED, BUT I MADE IT!
HA HA...
WHAT ABOUT YOU?
I'M FINE TOO.
THANKS FOR HELPING ME.

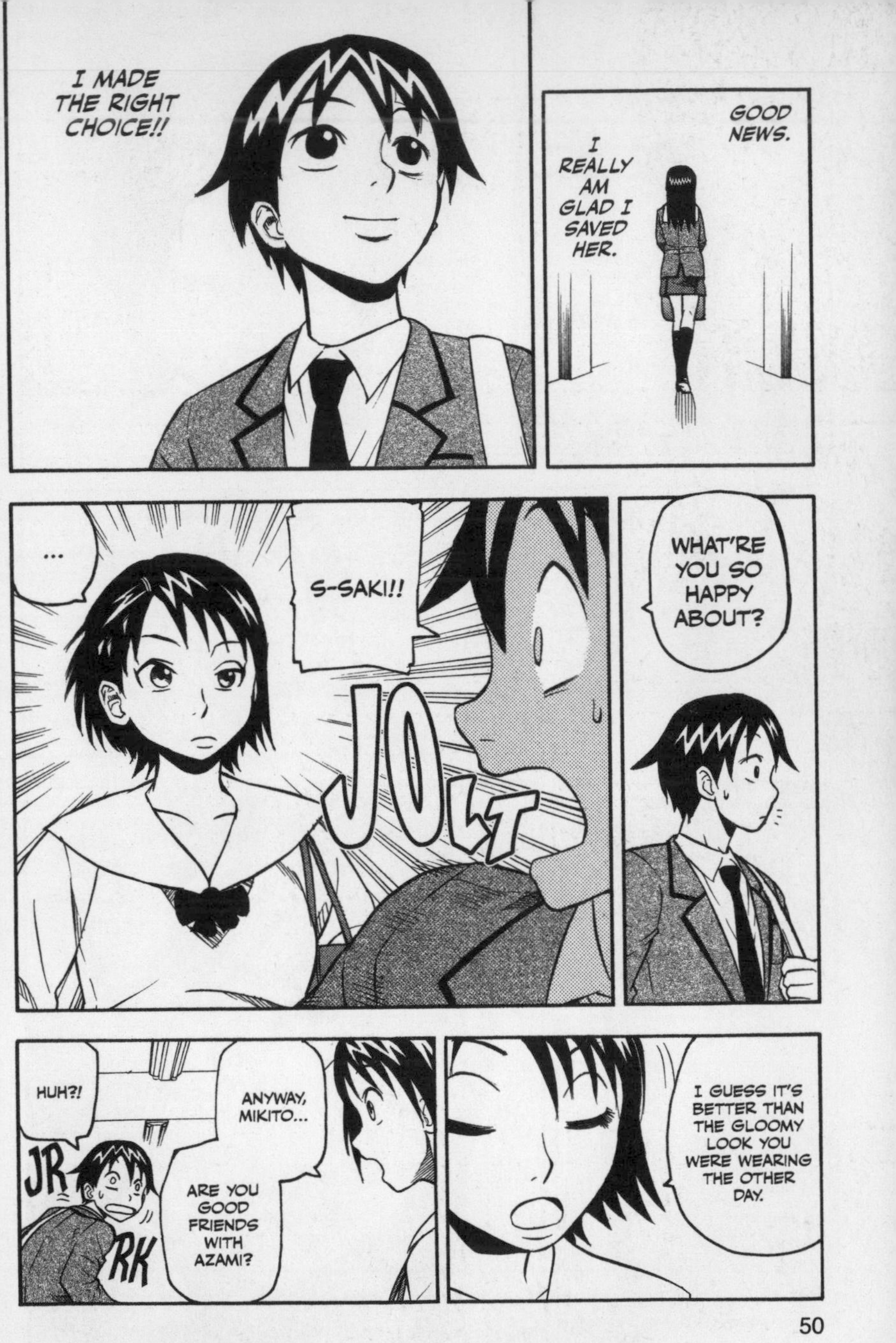
GOOD NEWS.
I REALLY AM GLAD I SAVED HER.
I MADE THE RIGHT CHOICE!!
WHAT'RE YOU SO HAPPY ABOUT?
S-SAKI!!
JOLT
...
I GUESS IT'S BETTER THAN THE GLOOMY LOOK YOU WERE WEARING THE OTHER DAY.
ANYWAY, MIKITO...
ARE YOU GOOD FRIENDS WITH AZAMI?
HUH?!
JRRK

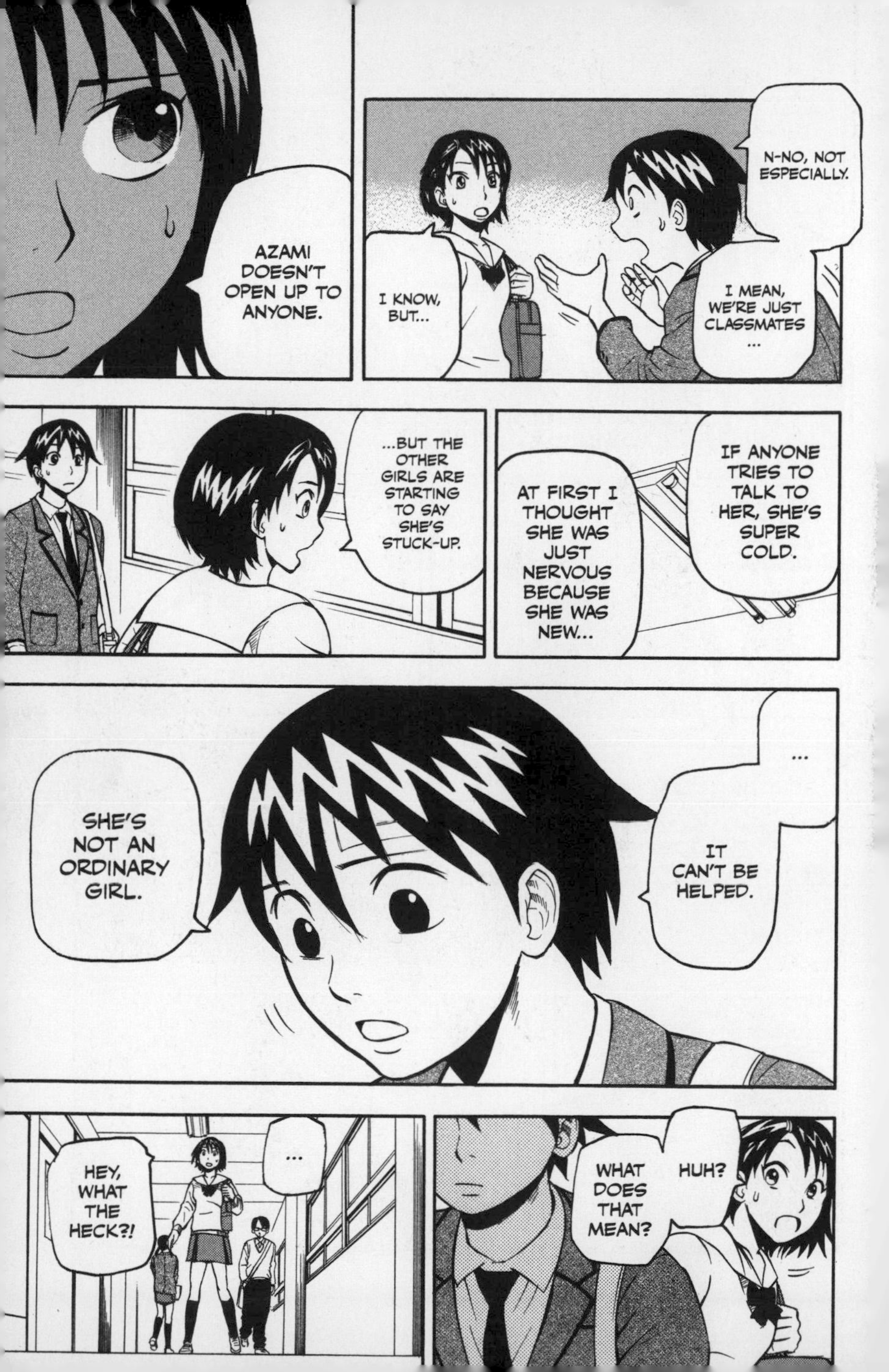
N-NO, NOT ESPECIALLY.
I MEAN, WE'RE JUST CLASSMATES ...
I KNOW, BUT...
AZAMI DOESN'T OPEN UP TO ANYONE.
IF ANYONE TRIES TO TALK TO HER, SHE'S SUPER COLD.
AT FIRST I THOUGHT SHE WAS JUST NERVOUS BECAUSE SHE WAS NEW...
...BUT THE OTHER GIRLS ARE STARTING TO SAY SHE'S STUCK-UP.
...
IT CAN'T BE HELPED.
SHE'S NOT AN ORDINARY GIRL.
HUH?
WHAT DOES THAT MEAN?
...
HEY, WHAT THE HECK?!

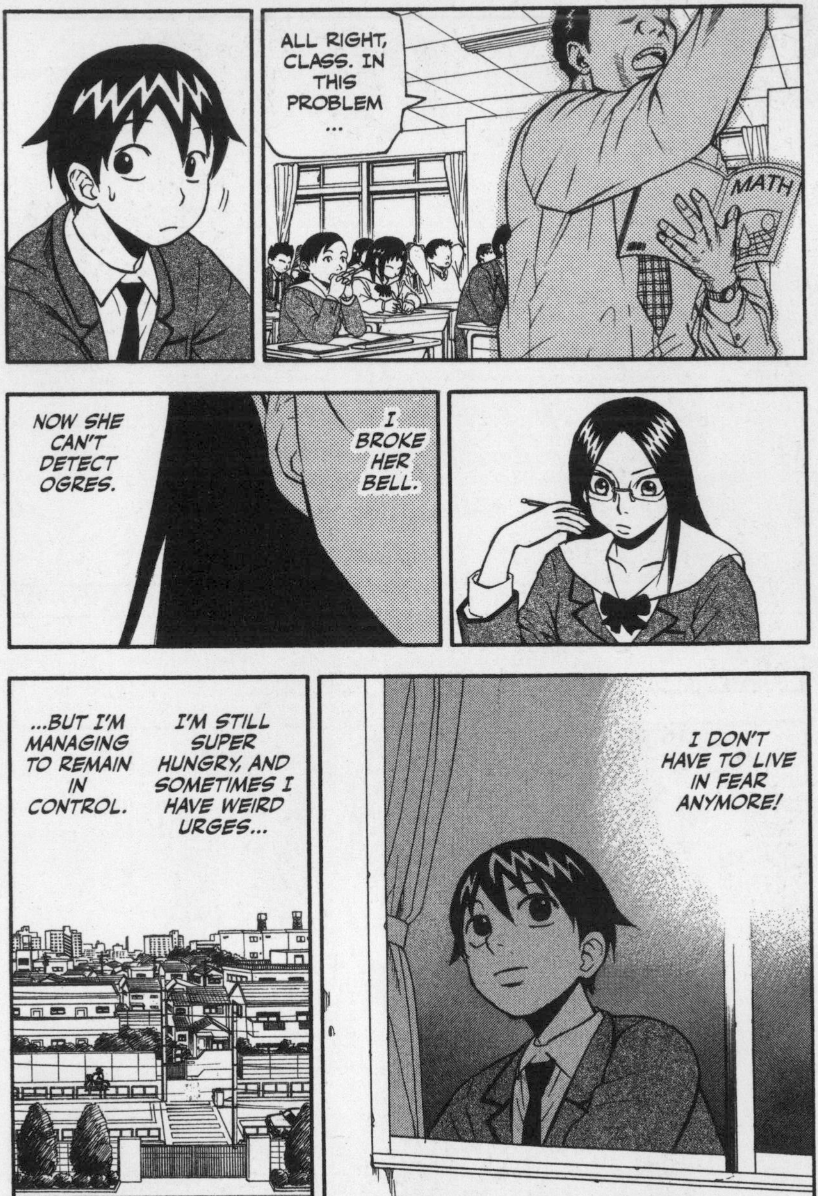
ALL RIGHT, CLASS. IN THIS PROBLEM ...
MATH
I BROKE HER BELL.
NOW SHE CAN'T DETECT OGRES.
I DON'T HAVE TO LIVE IN FEAR ANYMORE!
I'M STILL SUPER HUNGRY, AND SOMETIMES I HAVE WEIRD URGES...
...BUT I'M MANAGING TO REMAIN IN CONTROL.

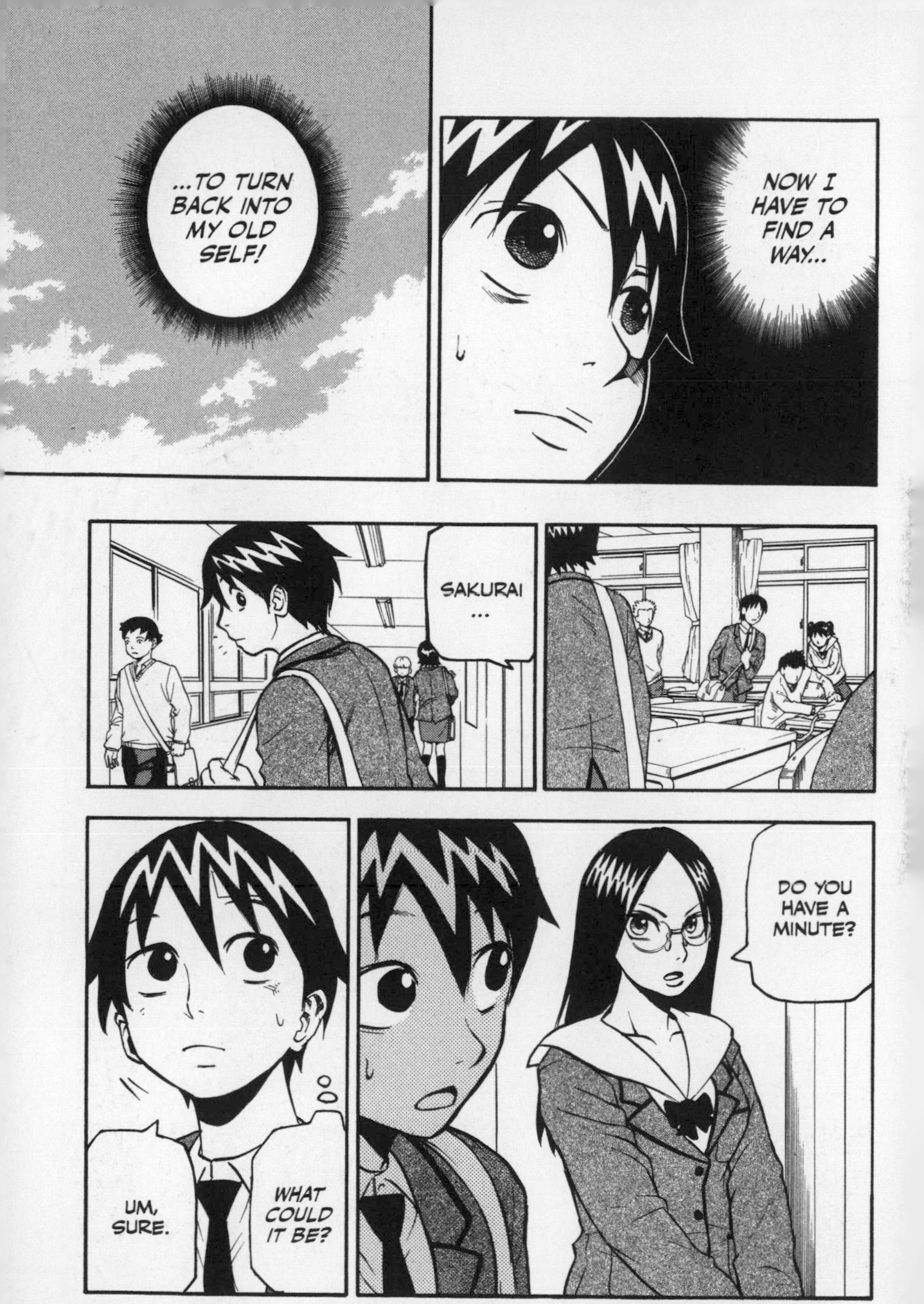
NOW I HAVE TO FIND A WAY...
...TO TURN BACK INTO MY OLD SELF!
SAKURAI ...
DO YOU HAVE A MINUTE?
WHAT COULD IT BE?
UM, SURE.

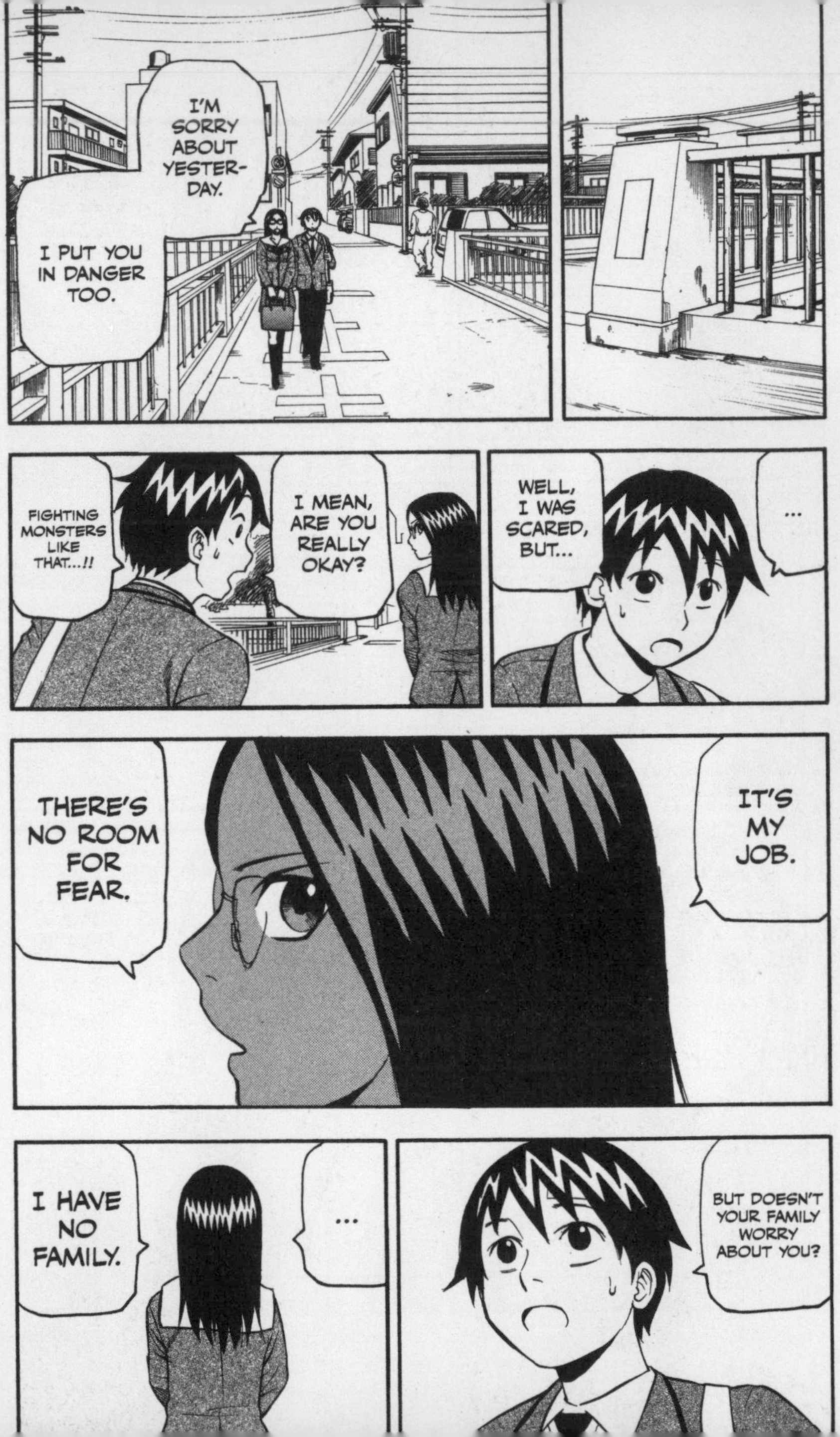
I'M SORRY ABOUT YESTER-DAY.
I PUT YOU IN DANGER TOO.
...
WELL, I WAS SCARED, BUT...
I MEAN, ARE YOU REALLY OKAY?
FIGHTING MONSTERS LIKE THAT...!!
IT'S MY JOB.
THERE'S NO ROOM FOR FEAR.
BUT DOESN'T YOUR FAMILY WORRY ABOUT YOU?
...
I HAVE NO FAMILY.

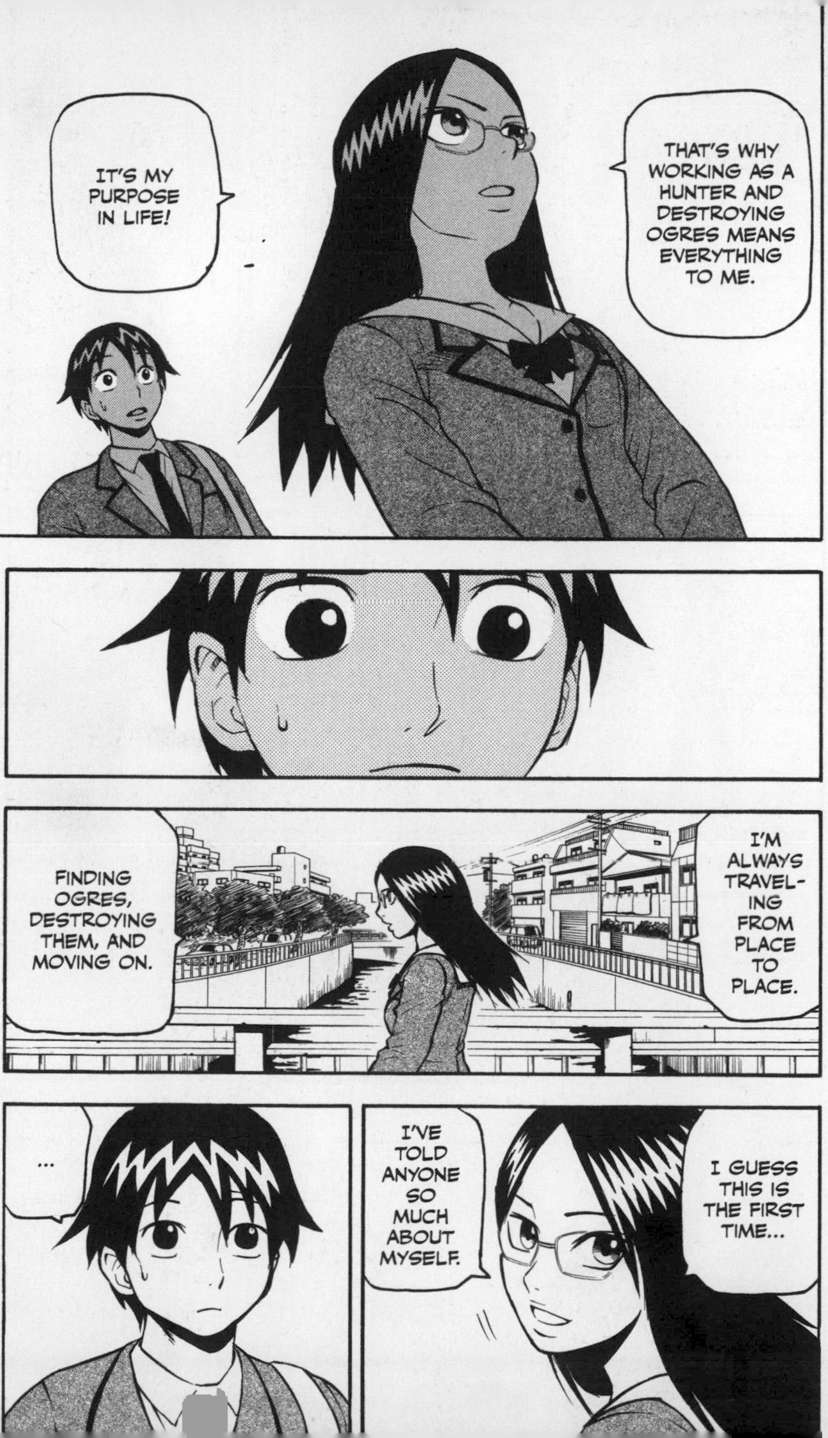
THAT'S WHY WORKING AS A HUNTER AND DESTROYING OGRES MEANS EVERYTHING TO ME.
IT'S MY PURPOSE IN LIFE!
I'M ALWAYS TRAVEL-ING FROM PLACE TO PLACE.
FINDING OGRES, DESTROYING THEM, AND MOVING ON.
I GUESS THIS IS THE FIRST TIME...
I'VE TOLD ANYONE SO MUCH ABOUT MYSELF.
...

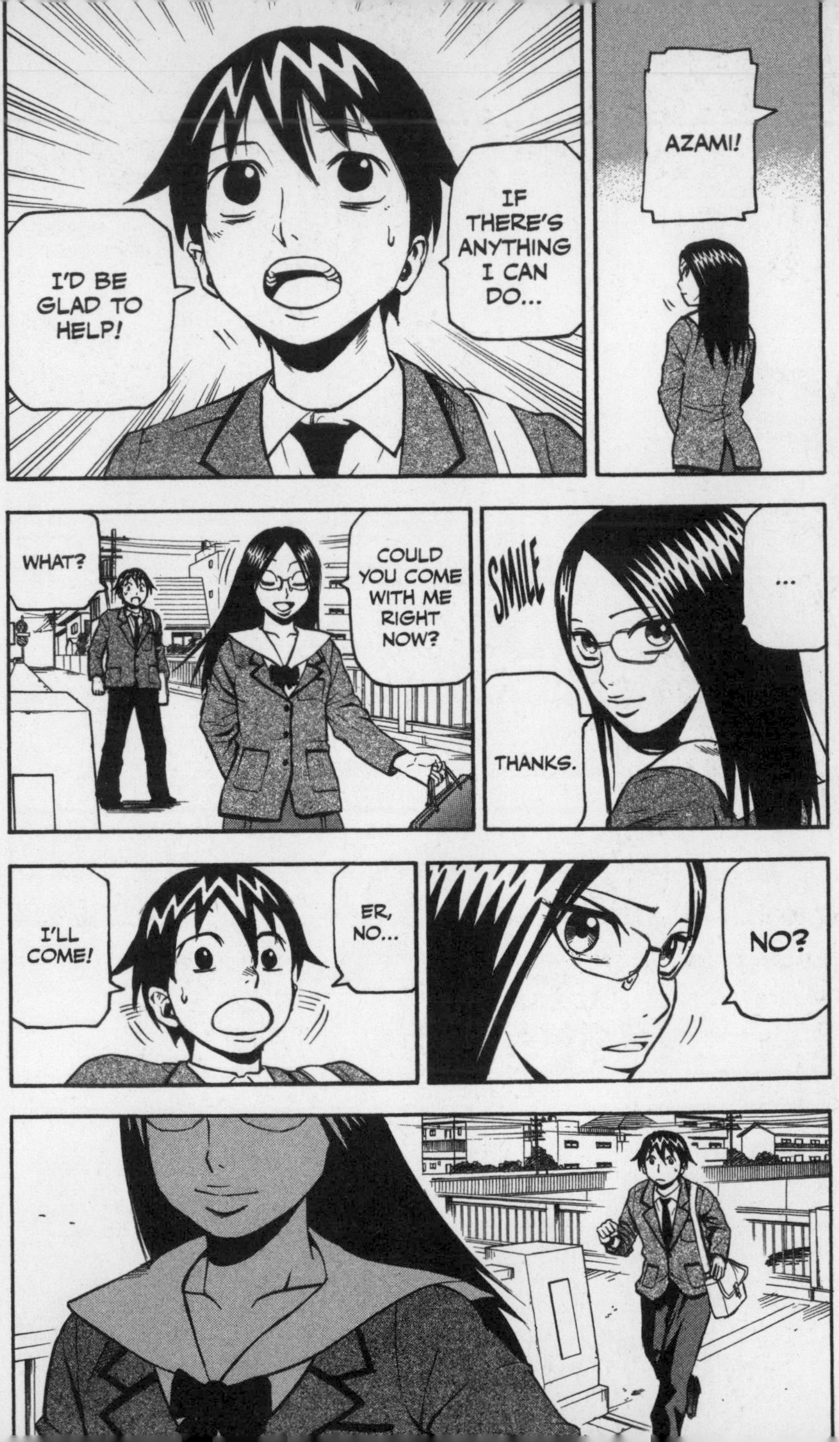
AZAMI!
IF THERE'S ANYTHING I CAN DO...
I'D BE GLAD TO HELP!
...
SMILE
THANKS.
COULD YOU COME WITH ME RIGHT NOW?
WHAT?
NO?
ER, NO...
I'LL COME!

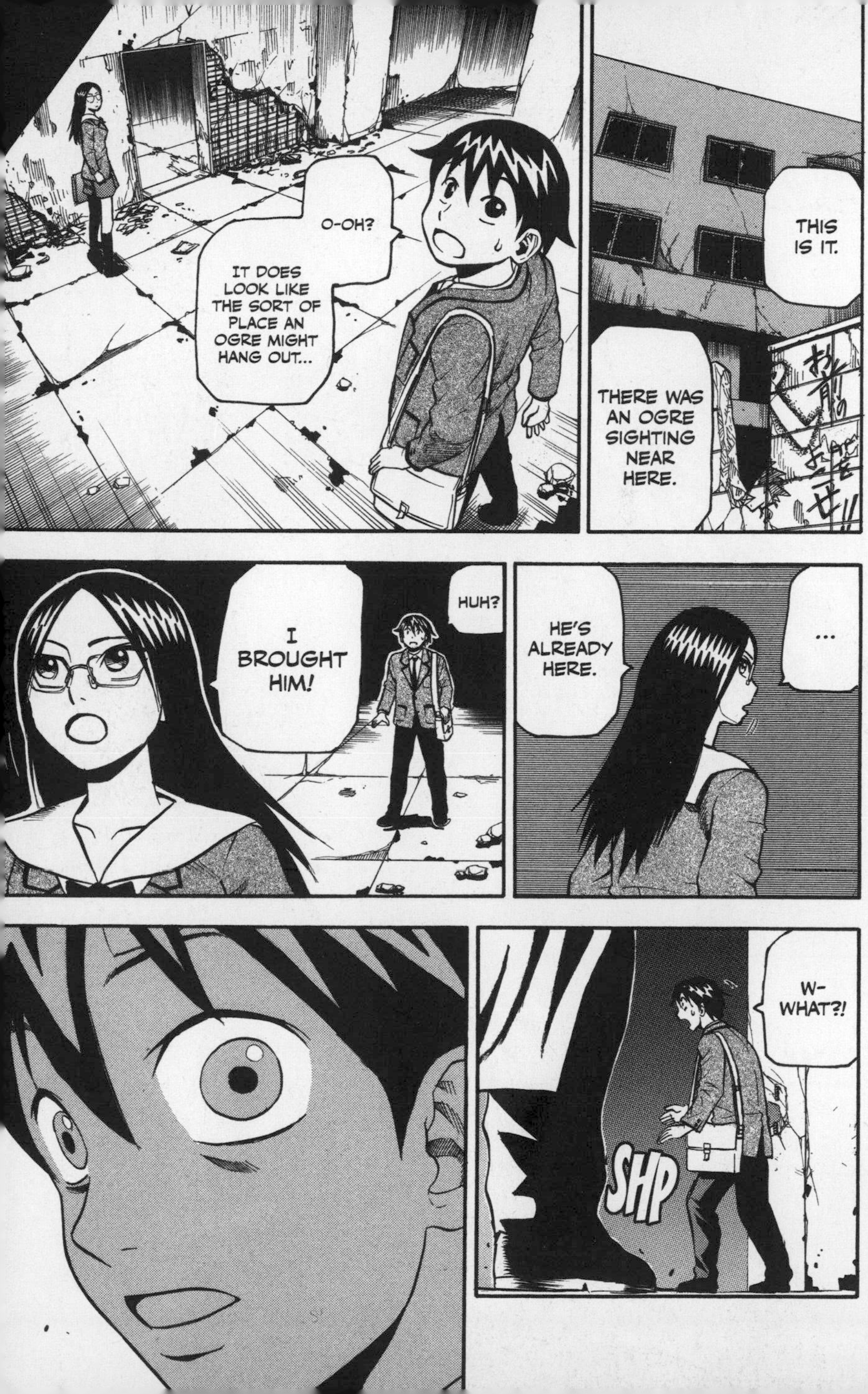
THIS IS IT.
THERE WAS AN OGRE SIGHTING NEAR HERE.
O-OH?
IT DOES LOOK LIKE THE SORT OF PLACE AN OGRE MIGHT HANG OUT...
...
HE'S ALREADY HERE.
HUH?
I BROUGHT HIM!
W-WHAT?!
SHP

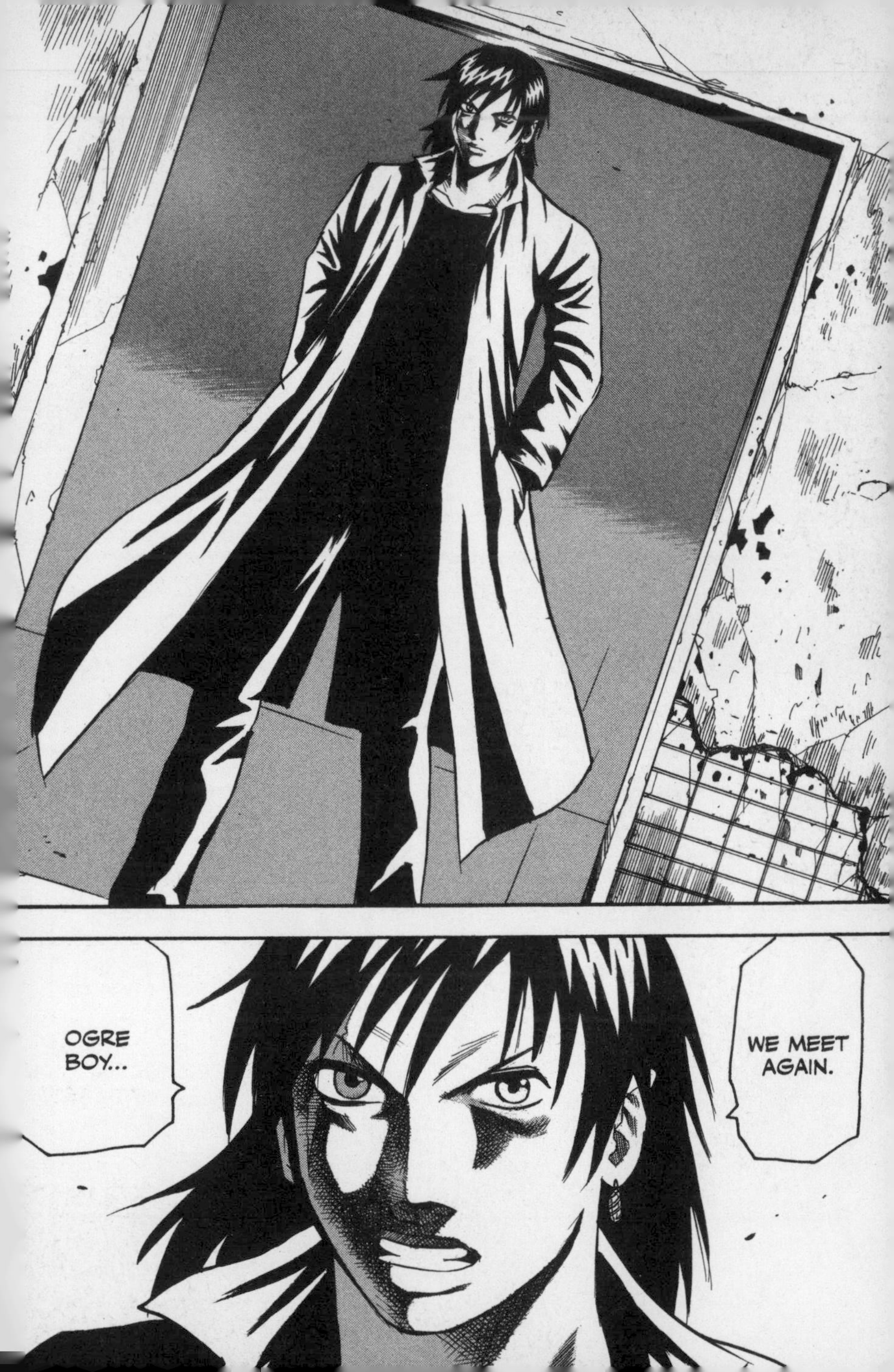
WE MEET AGAIN.
OGRE BOY...

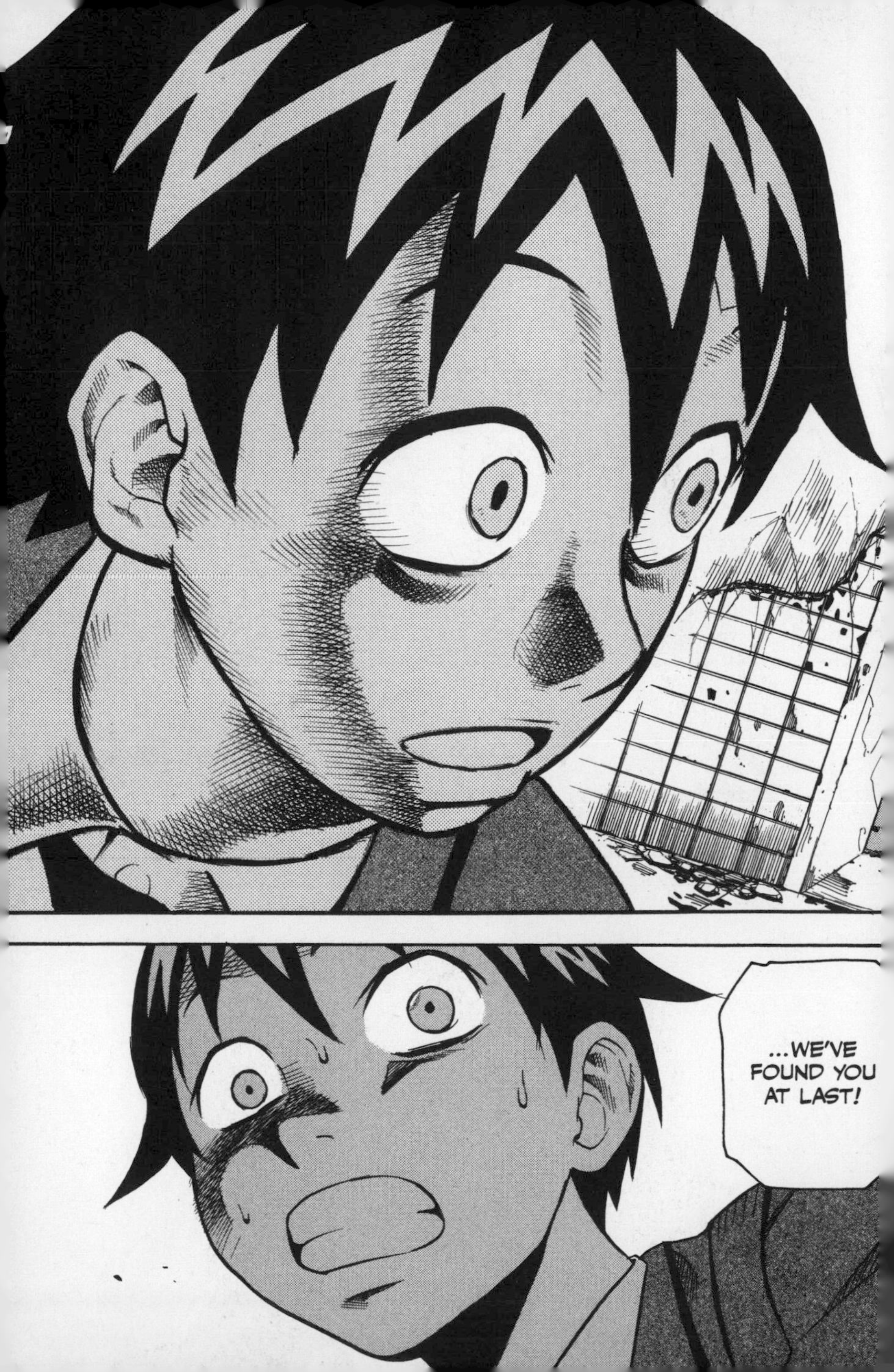
...WE'VE FOUND YOU AT LAST!

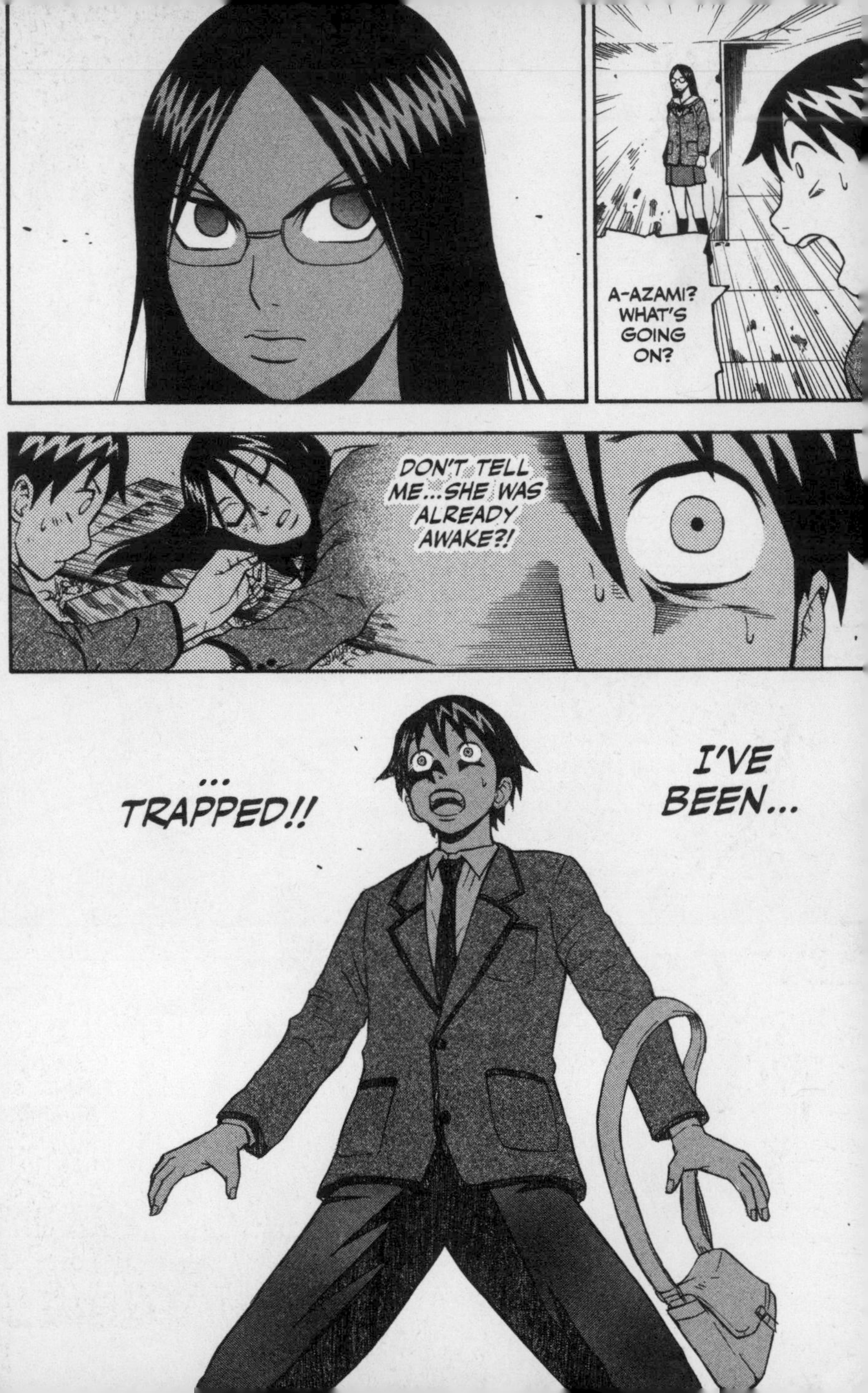
A-AZAMI? WHAT'S GOING ON?
DON'T TELL ME...SHE WAS ALREADY AWAKE?!
I'VE BEEN...
...TRAPPED!!

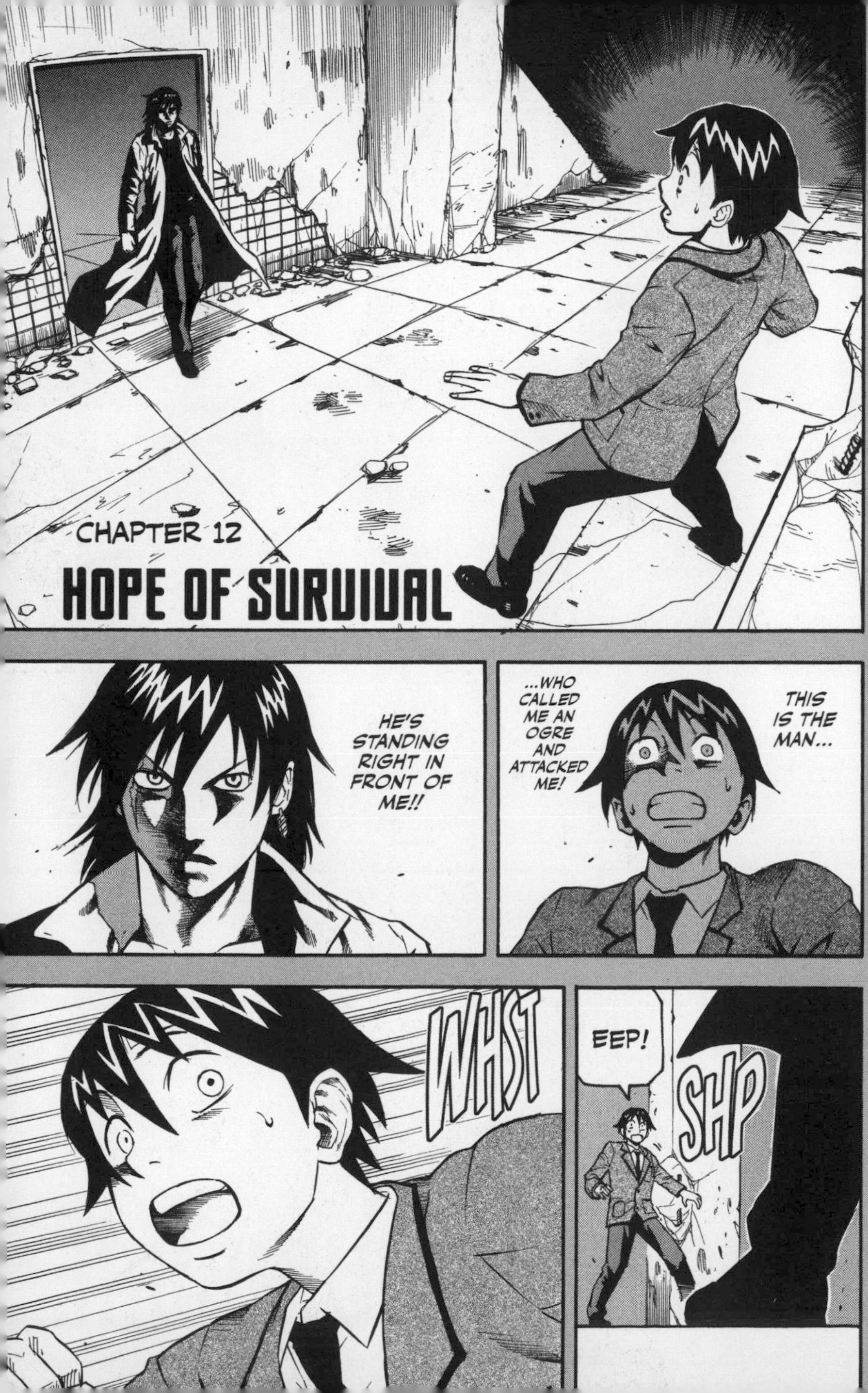
CHAPTER 12
HOPE OF SURVIVAL
THIS IS THE MAN...
...WHO CALLED ME AN OGRE AND ATTACKED ME!
HE'S STANDING RIGHT IN FRONT OF ME!!
EEP!
SHP
WHST

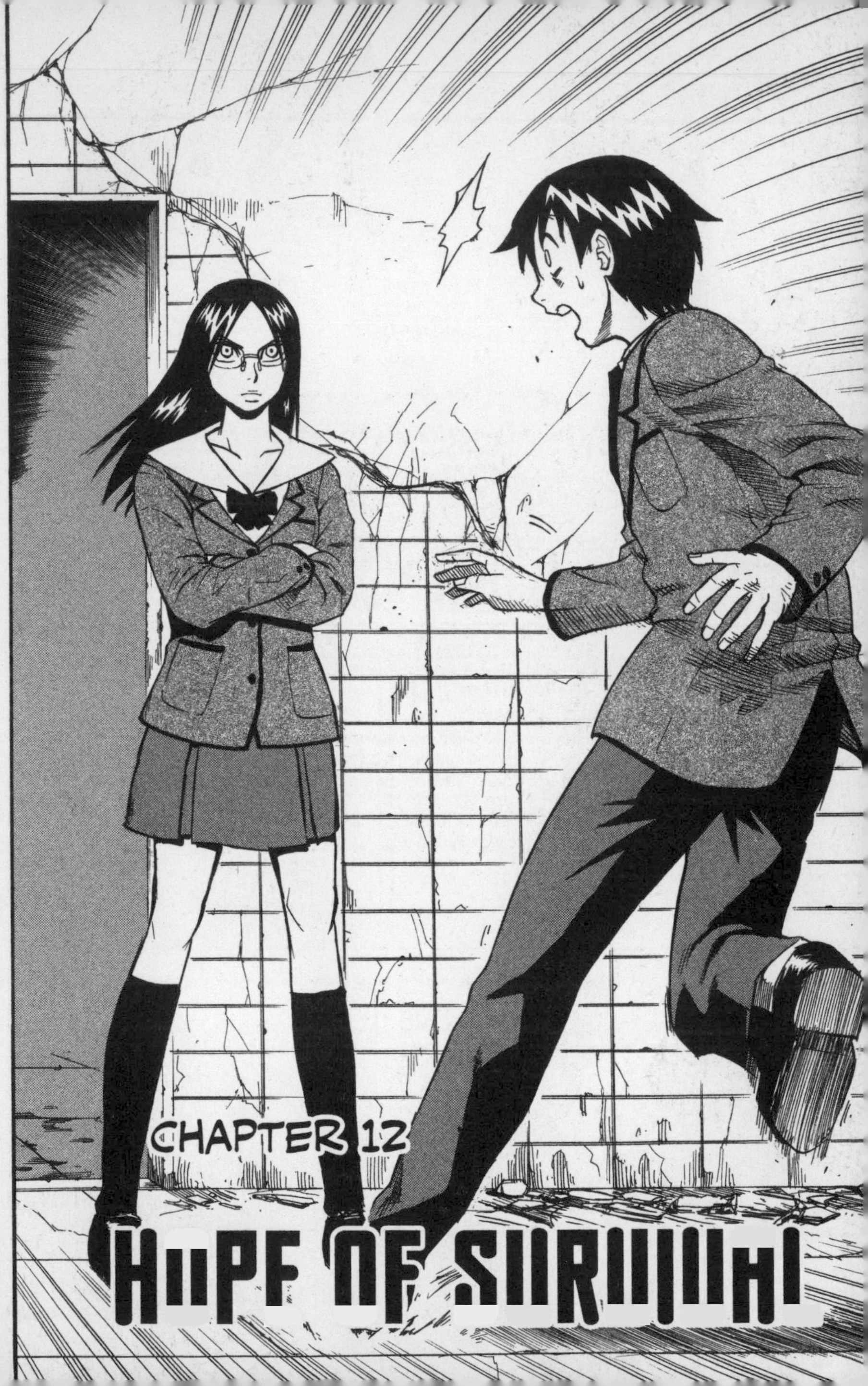
CHAPTER 12
HOPE OF SURVIVAL

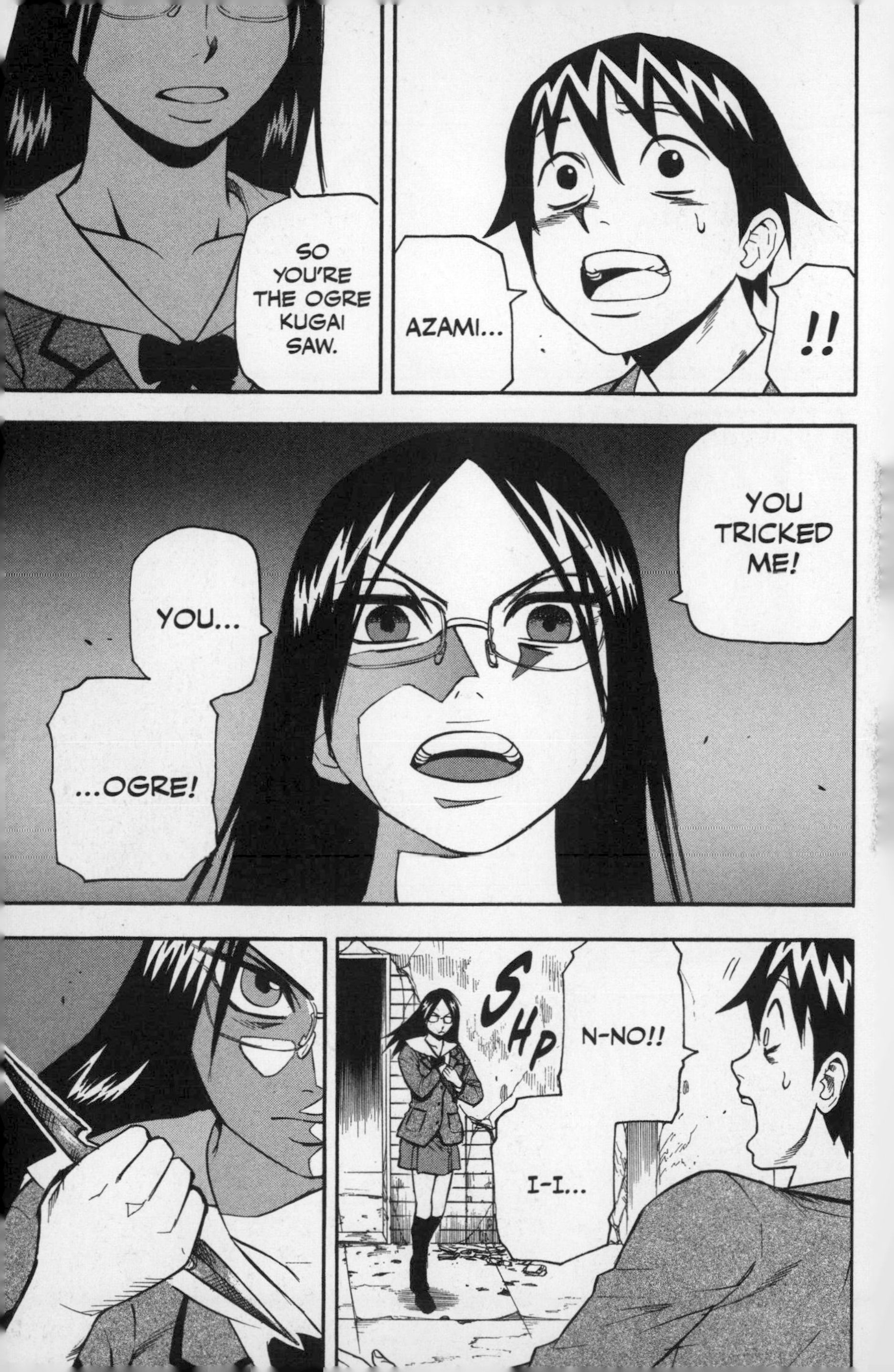
!!
AZAMI...
SO YOU'RE THE OGRE KUGAI SAW.
YOU TRICKED ME!
YOU...
...OGRE!
N-NO!!
SHP
I-I...

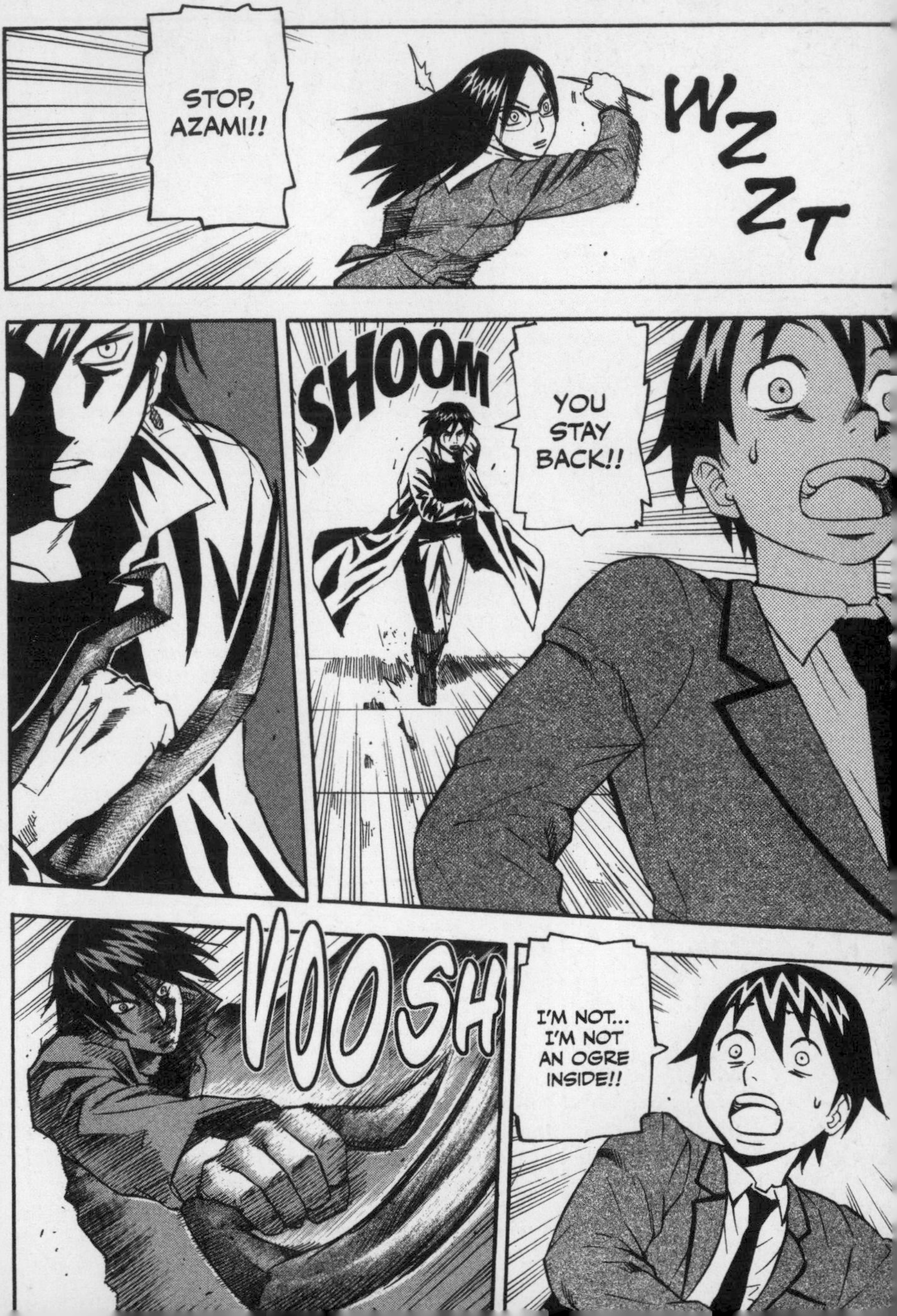
WZZT
STOP, AZAMI!!
YOU STAY BACK!!
SHOOM
I'M NOT... I'M NOT AN OGRE INSIDE!!
VOOSH

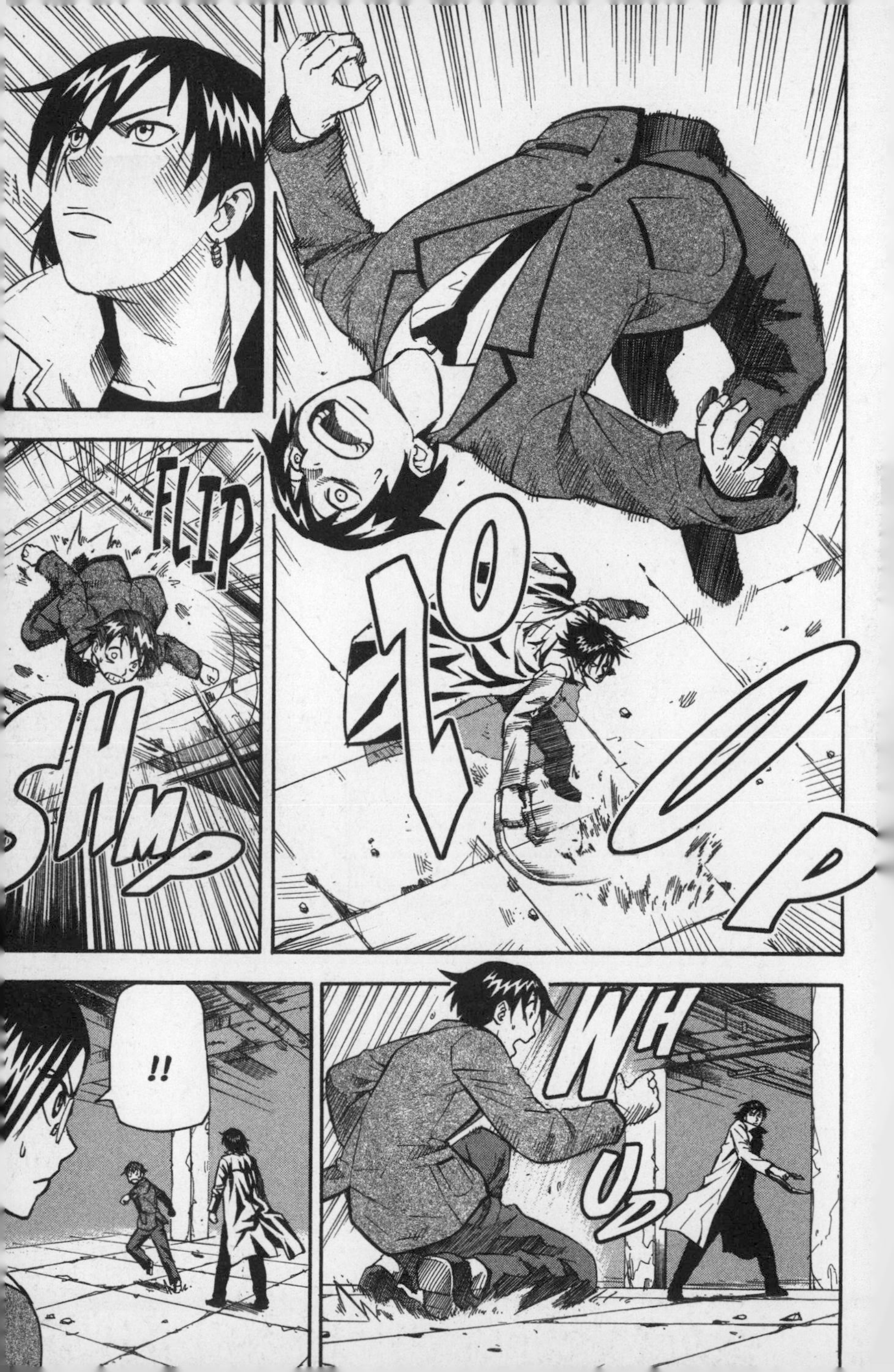
LOOP
FLIP
SHMP
WHUD
!!

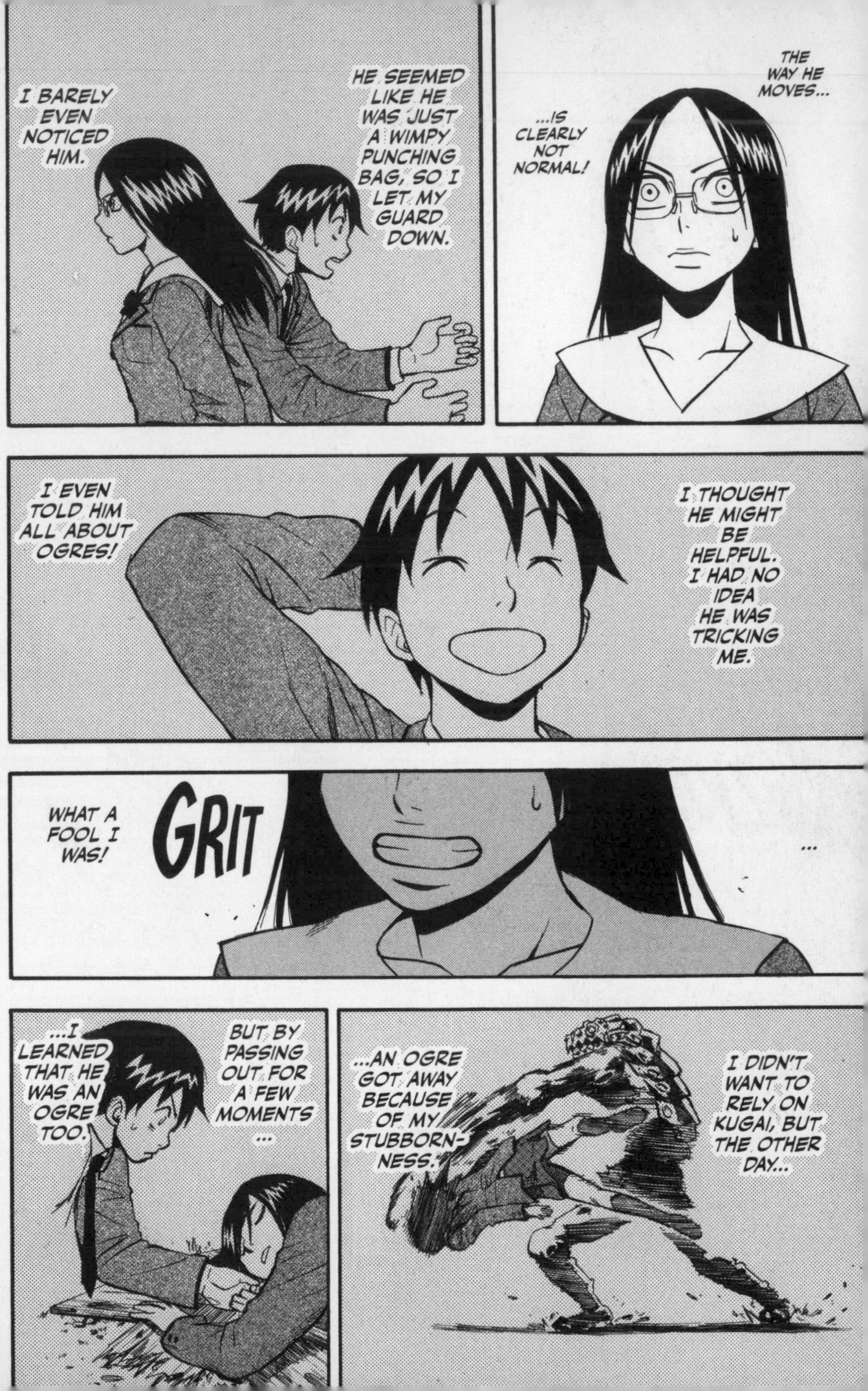
THE WAY HE MOVES...
...IS CLEARLY NOT NORMAL!
HE SEEMED LIKE HE WAS JUST A WIMPY PUNCHING BAG, SO I LET MY GUARD DOWN.
I BARELY EVEN NOTICED HIM.
I THOUGHT HE MIGHT BE HELPFUL. I HAD NO IDEA HE WAS TRICKING ME.
I EVEN TOLD HIM ALL ABOUT OGRES!
...
GRIT
WHAT A FOOL I WAS!
I DIDN'T WANT TO RELY ON KUGAI, BUT THE OTHER DAY...
...AN OGRE GOT AWAY BECAUSE OF MY STUBBORN-NESS.
BUT BY PASSING OUT FOR A FEW MOMENTS ...
...I LEARNED THAT HE WAS AN OGRE TOO.

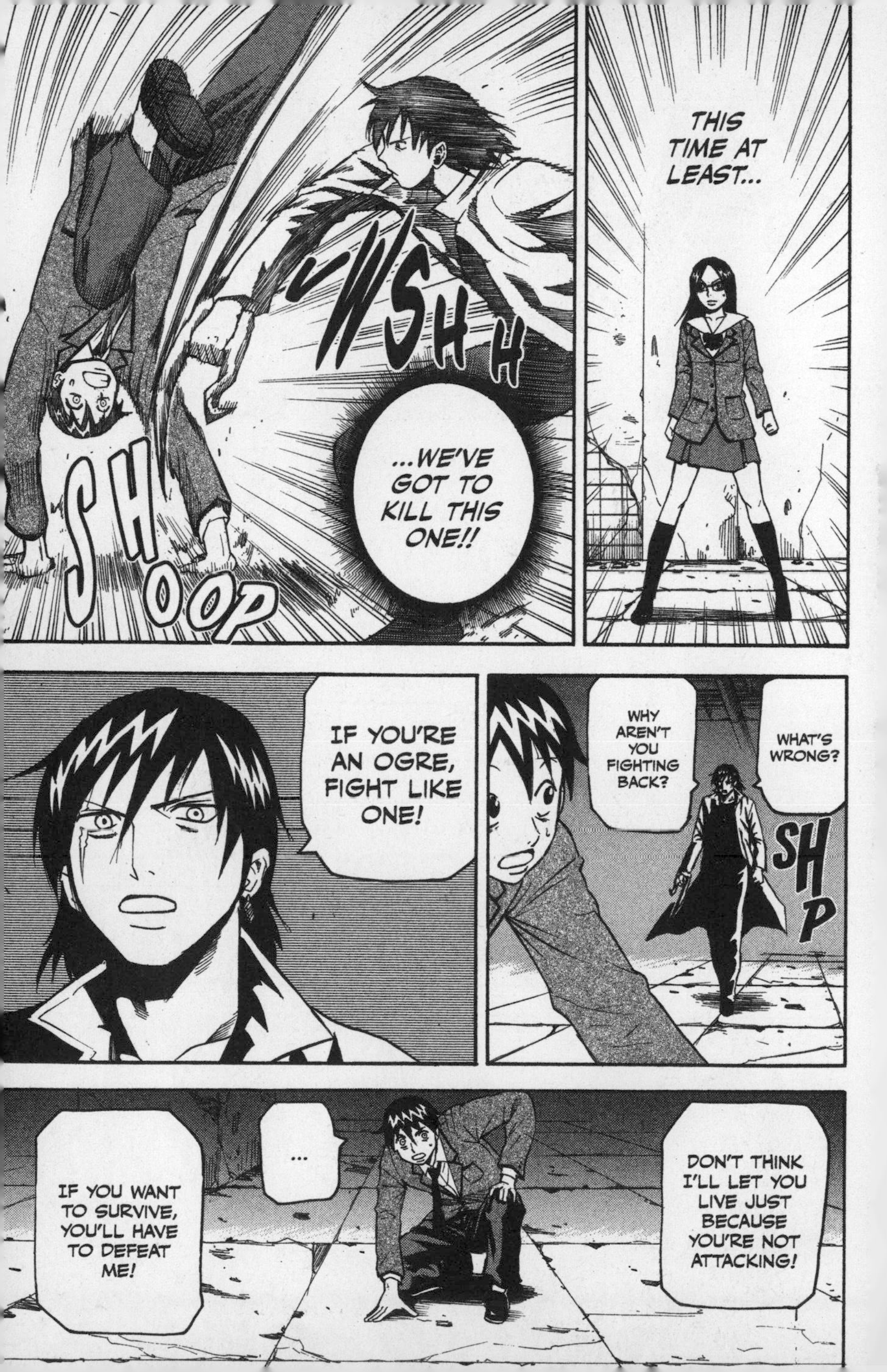
THIS TIME AT LEAST...
WHSHH
...WE'VE GOT TO KILL THIS ONE!!
SHOOP
WHAT'S WRONG?
WHY AREN'T YOU FIGHTING BACK?
SHP
IF YOU'RE AN OGRE, FIGHT LIKE ONE!
DON'T THINK I'LL LET YOU LIVE JUST BECAUSE YOU'RE NOT ATTACKING!
...
IF YOU WANT TO SURVIVE, YOU'LL HAVE TO DEFEAT ME!

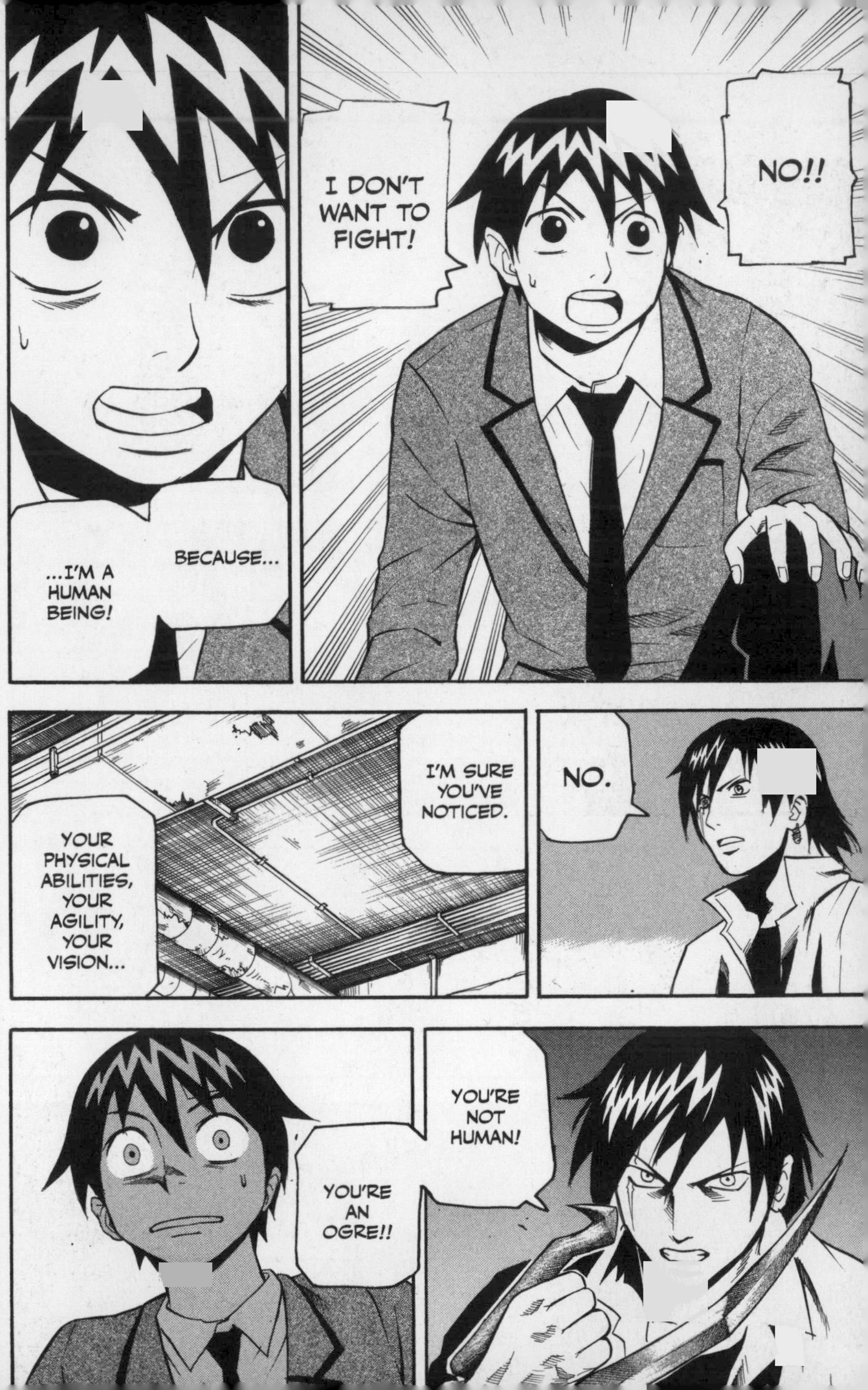
NO!!
I DON'T WANT TO FIGHT!
BECAUSE...
...I'M A HUMAN BEING!
NO.
I'M SURE YOU'VE NOTICED.
YOUR PHYSICAL ABILITIES, YOUR AGILITY, YOUR VISION...
YOU'RE NOT HUMAN!
YOU'RE AN OGRE!!

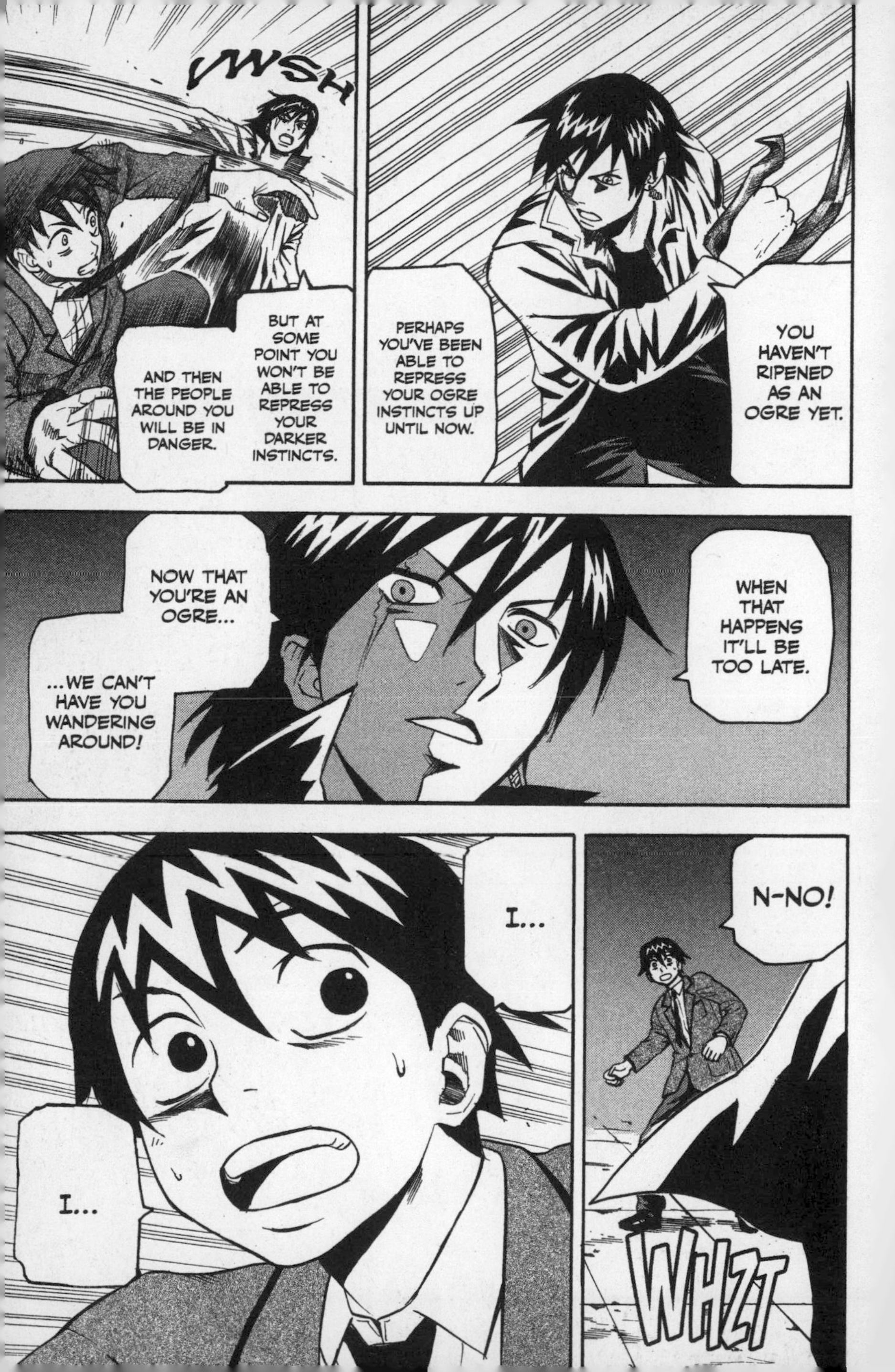
YOU HAVEN'T RIPENED AS AN OGRE YET.
PERHAPS YOU'VE BEEN ABLE TO REPRESS YOUR OGRE INSTINCTS UP UNTIL NOW.
VWSH
BUT AT SOME POINT YOU WON'T BE ABLE TO REPRESS YOUR DARKER INSTINCTS.
AND THEN THE PEOPLE AROUND YOU WILL BE IN DANGER.
WHEN THAT HAPPENS IT'LL BE TOO LATE.
NOW THAT YOU'RE AN OGRE...
...WE CAN'T HAVE YOU WANDERING AROUND!
N-NO!
WHZT
I...
I...

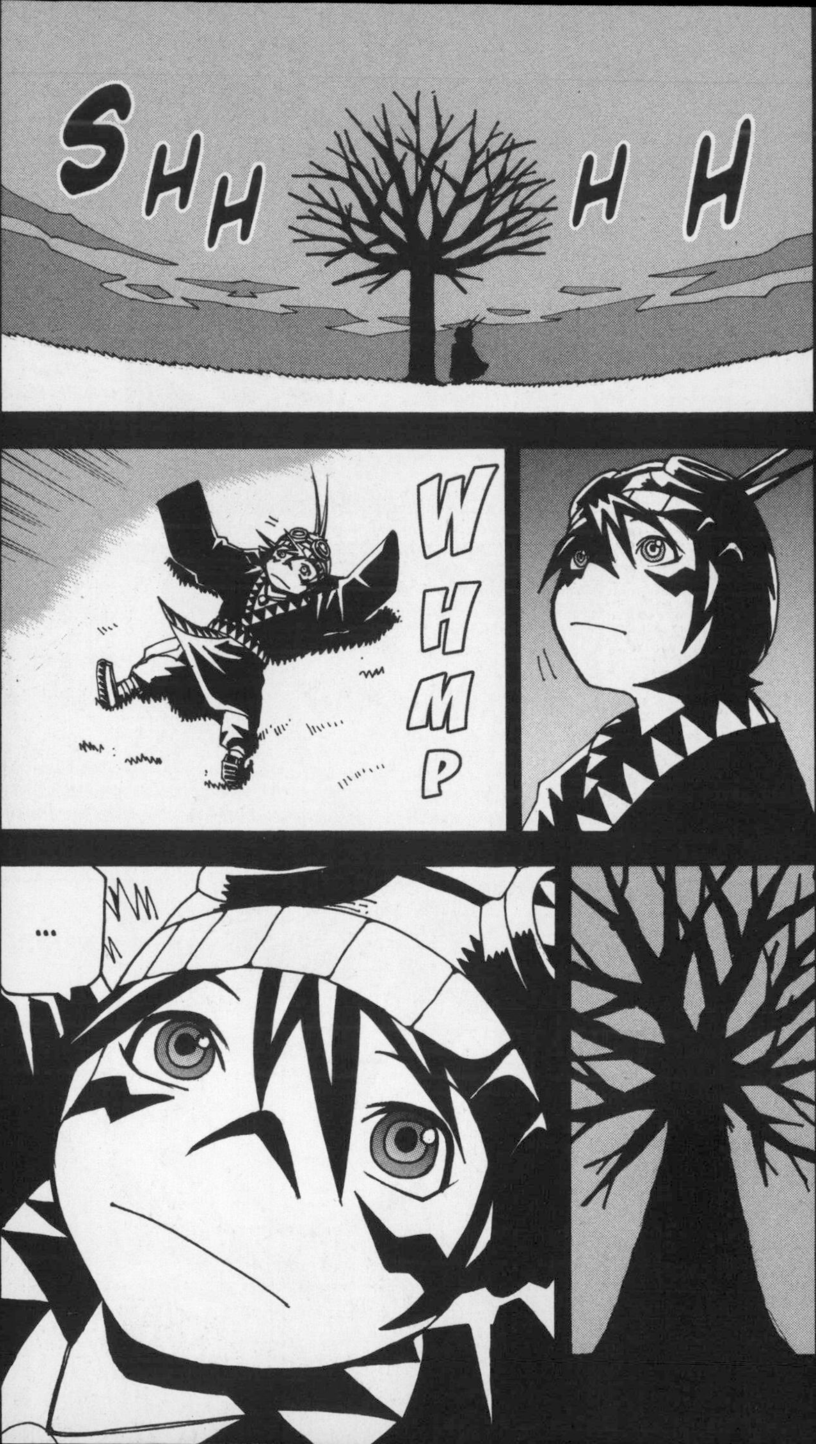
SHHHHH
WHMP
...

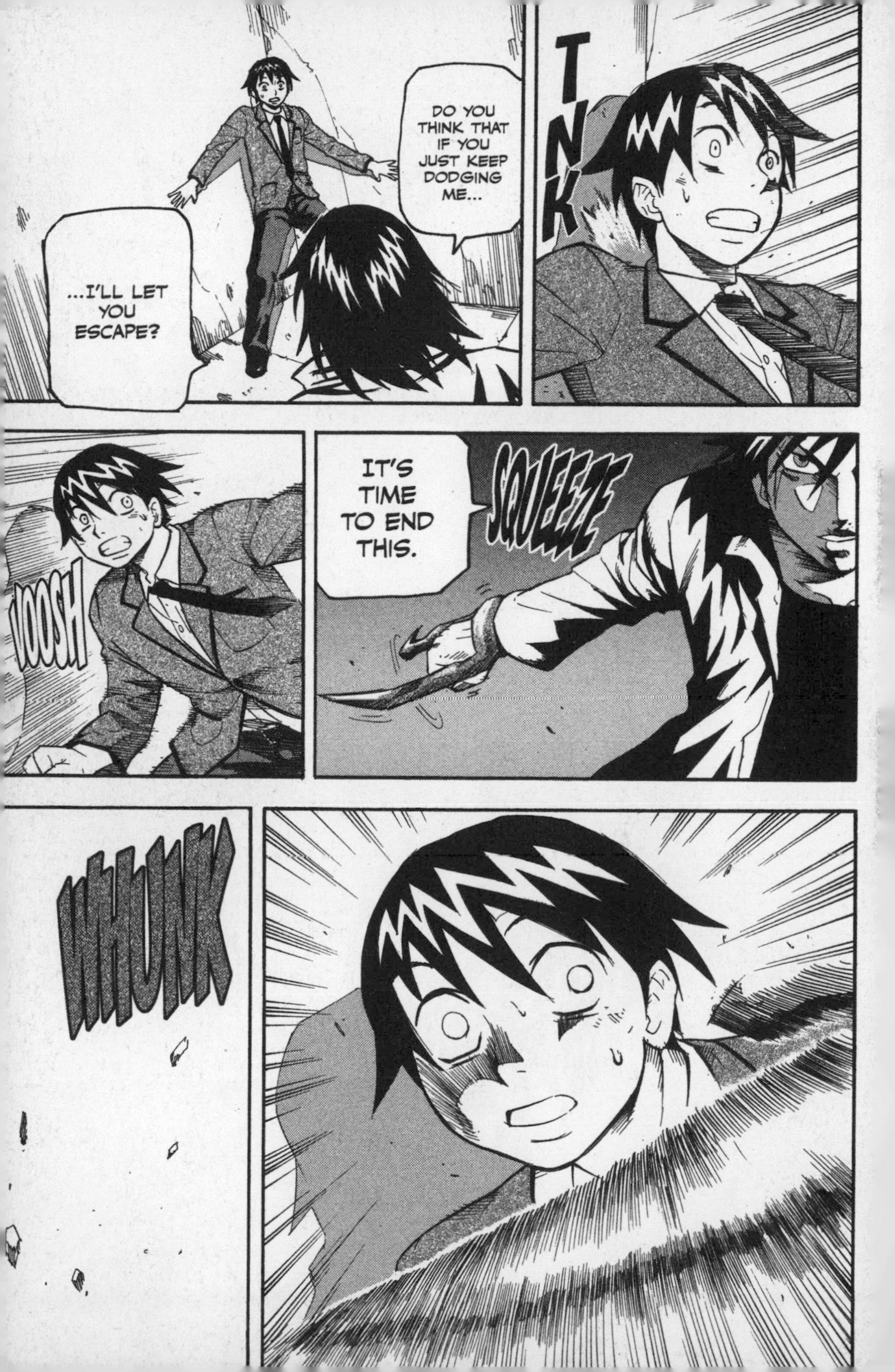
TNK
DO YOU THINK THAT IF YOU JUST KEEP DODGING ME...
...I'LL LET YOU ESCAPE?
SQUEEZE
IT'S TIME TO END THIS.
VOOSH
WHUNK

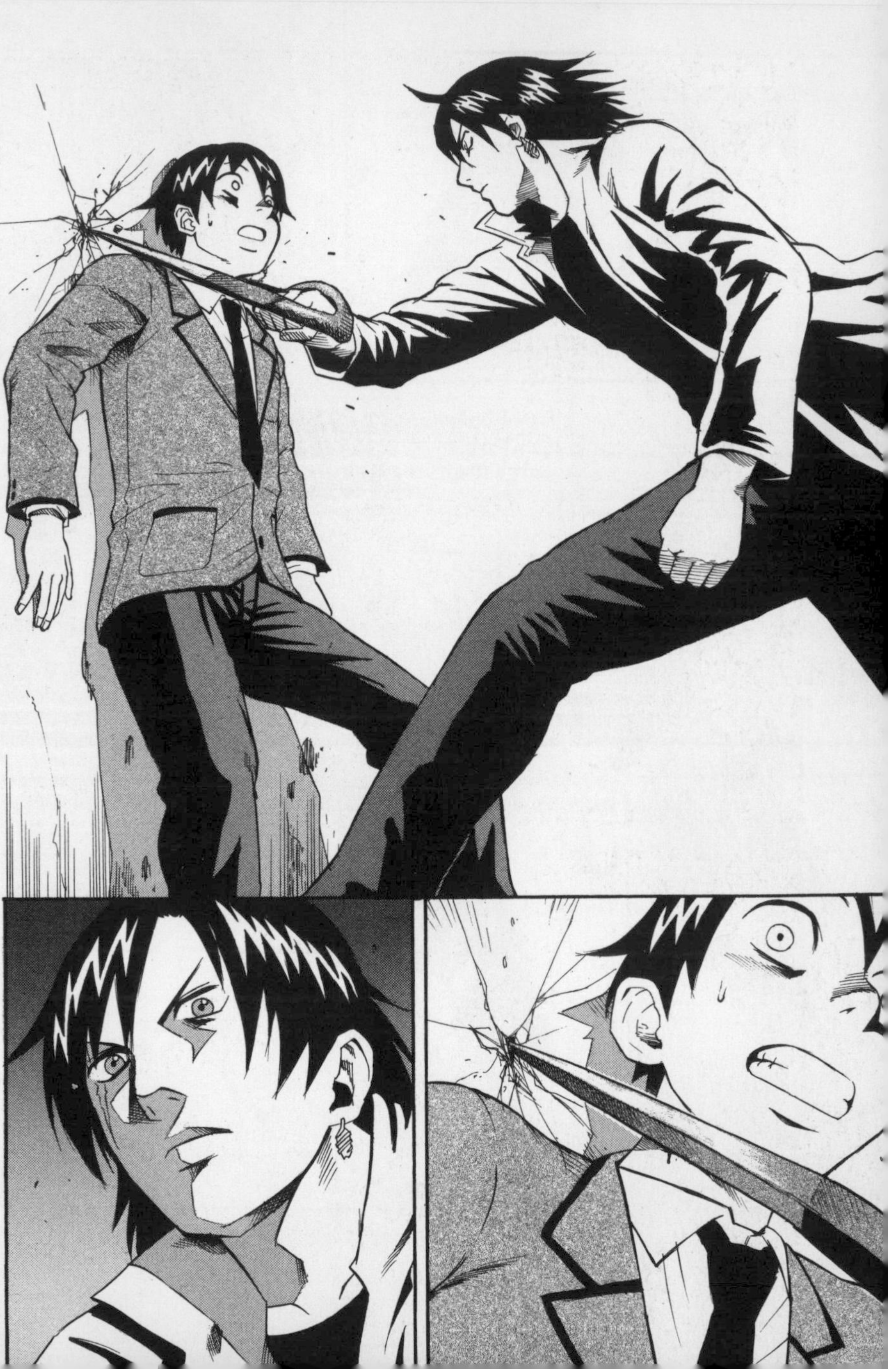

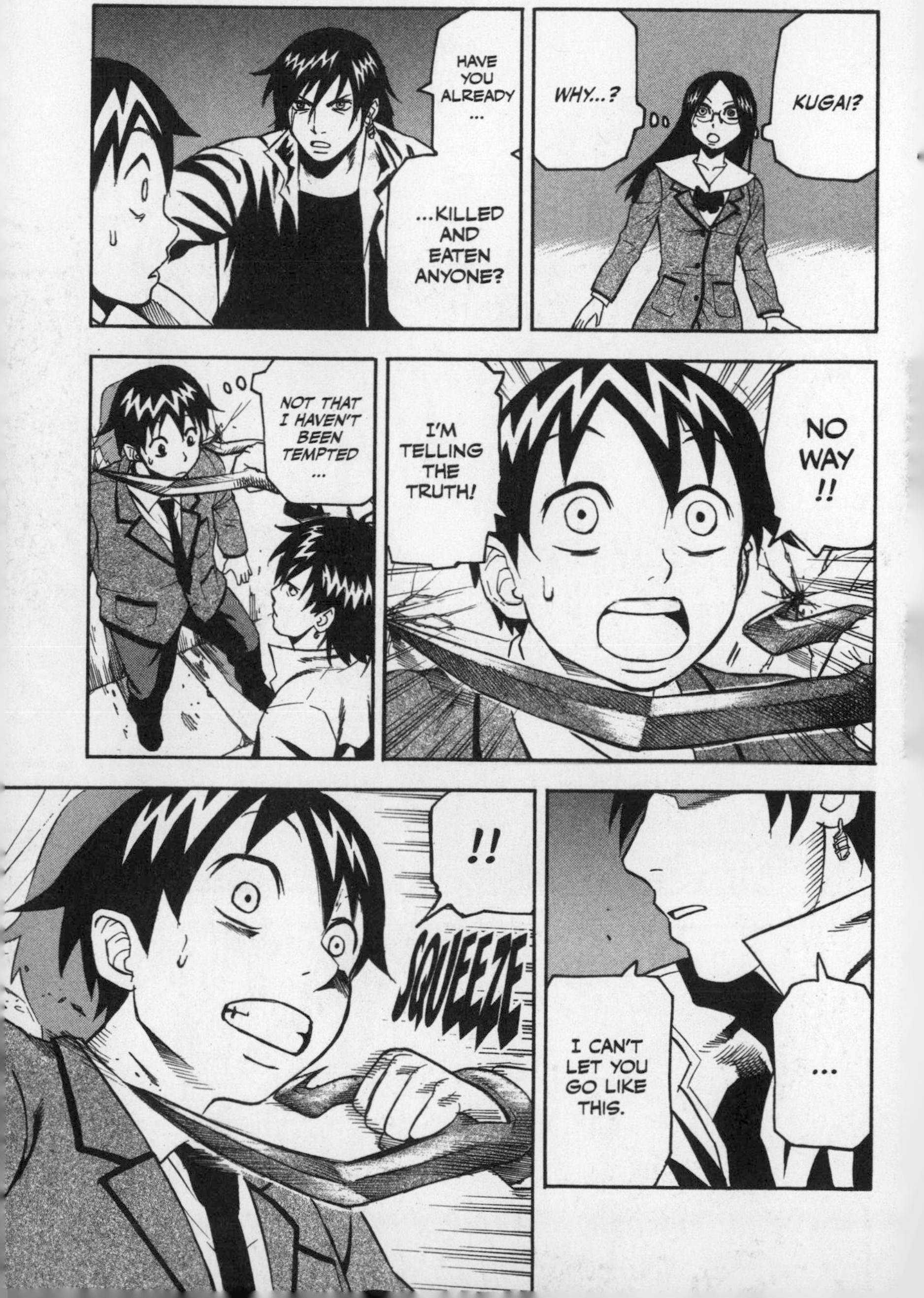
KUGAI?
WHY...?
HAVE YOU ALREADY ...
...KILLED AND EATEN ANYONE?
NO WAY !!
I'M TELLING THE TRUTH!
NOT THAT I HAVEN'T BEEN TEMPTED ...
...
I CAN'T LET YOU GO LIKE THIS.
!!
SQUEEZE

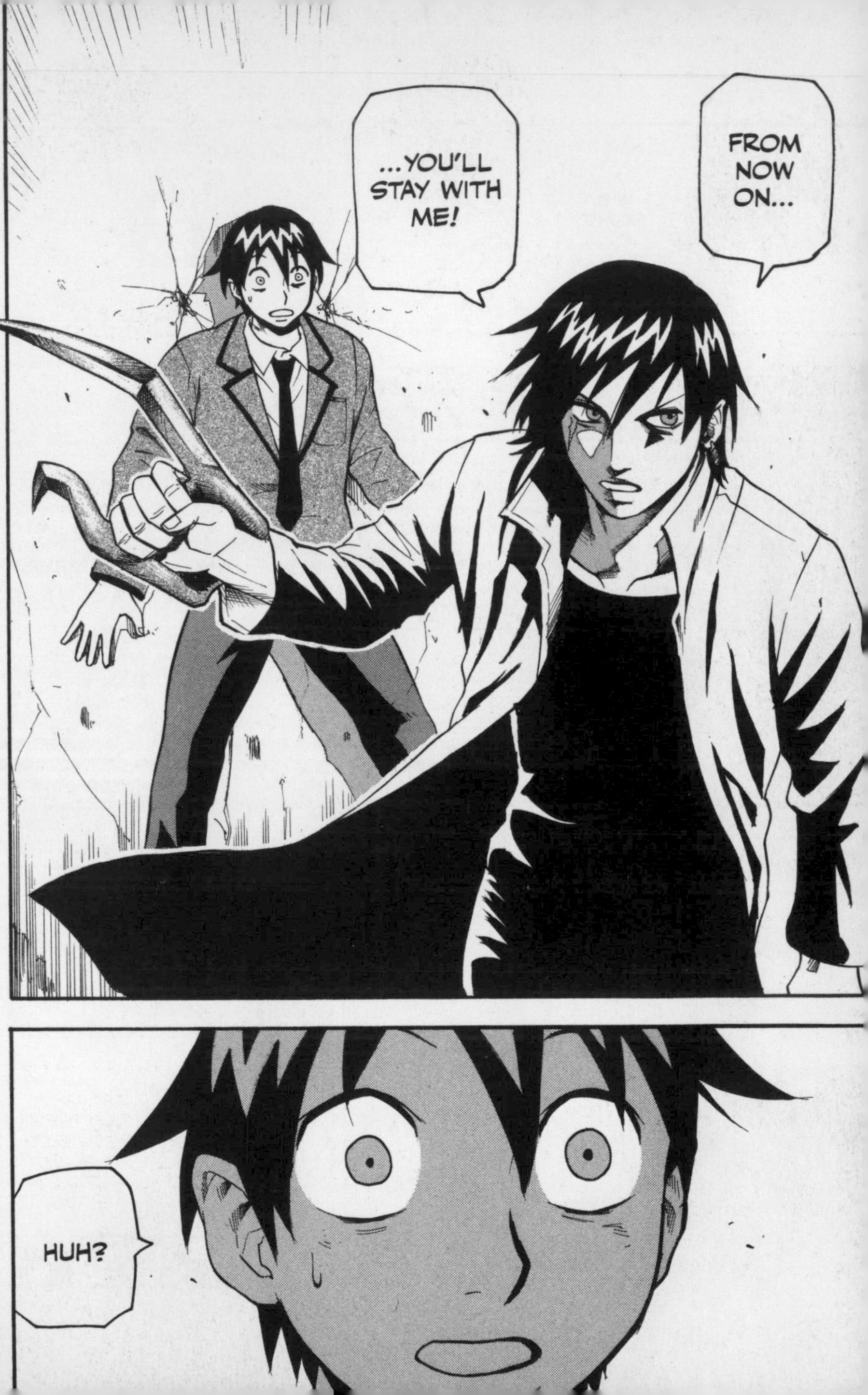
FROM NOW ON...
...YOU'LL STAY WITH ME!
HUH?

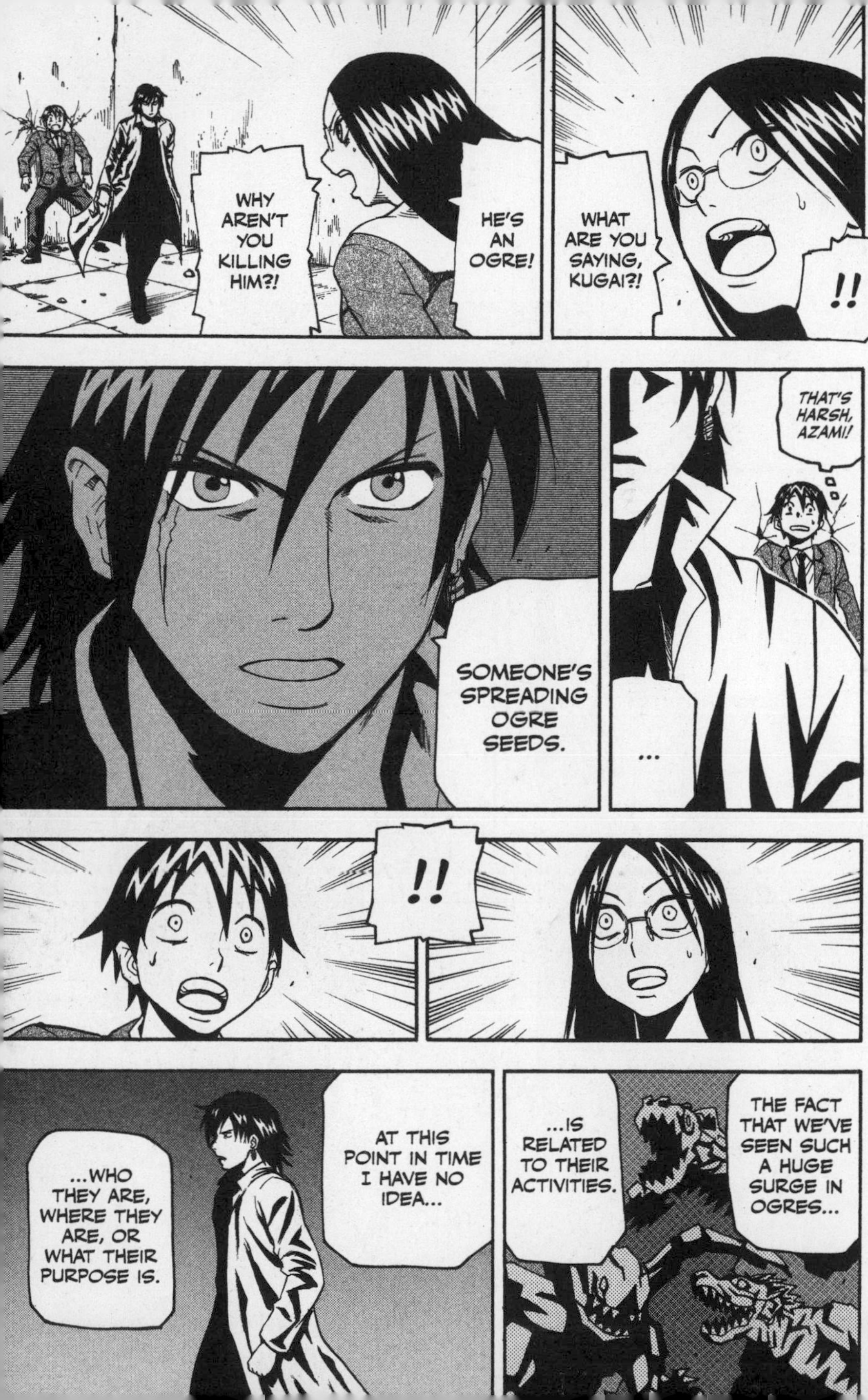
!!
WHAT ARE YOU SAYING, KUGAI?!
HE'S AN OGRE!
WHY AREN'T YOU KILLING HIM?!
THAT'S HARSH, AZAMI!
...
SOMEONE'S SPREADING OGRE SEEDS.
!!
THE FACT THAT WE'VE SEEN SUCH A HUGE SURGE IN OGRES...
...IS RELATED TO THEIR ACTIVITIES.
AT THIS POINT IN TIME I HAVE NO IDEA...
...WHO THEY ARE, WHERE THEY ARE, OR WHAT THEIR PURPOSE IS.

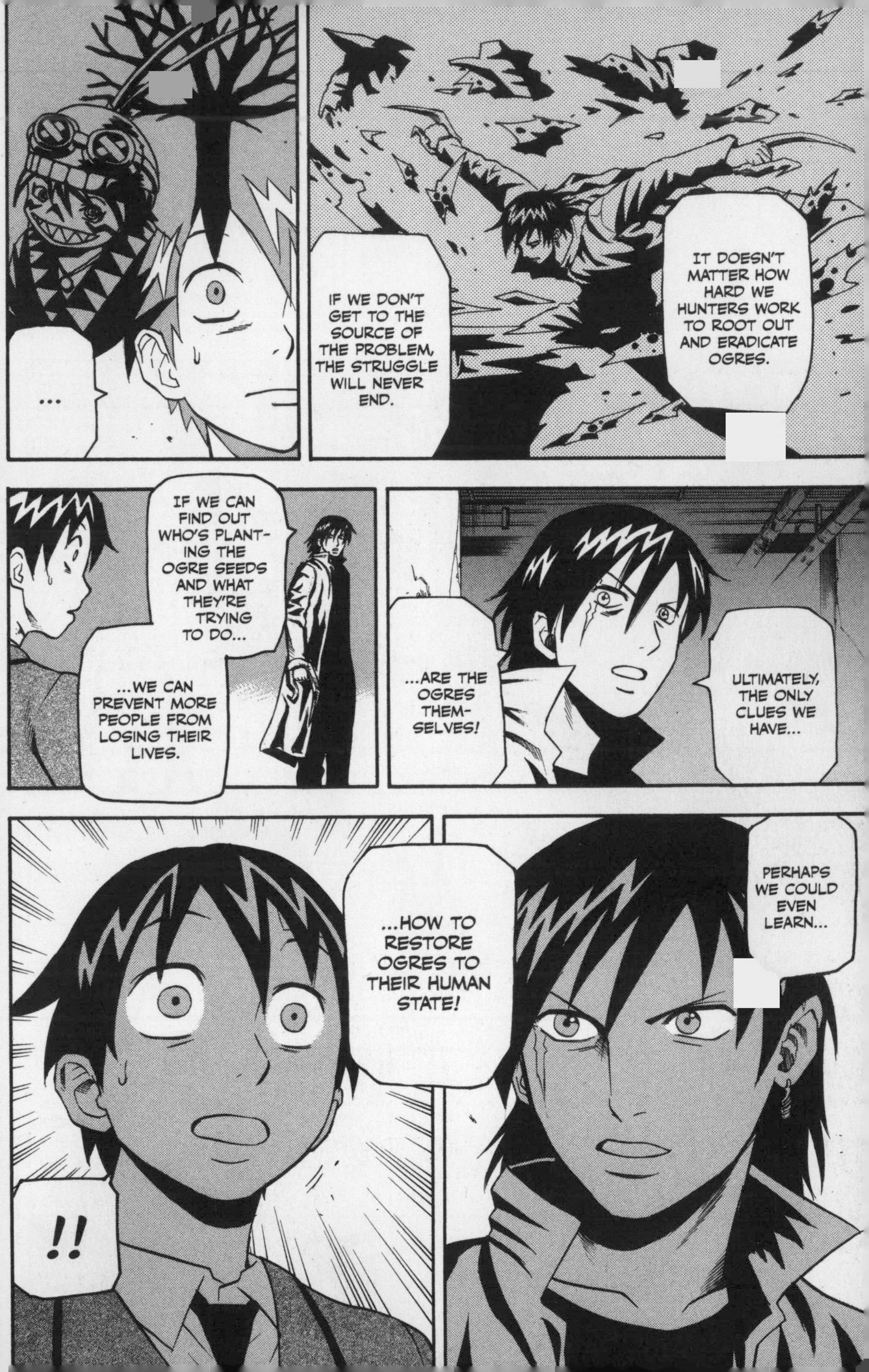
IT DOESN'T MATTER HOW HARD WE HUNTERS WORK TO ROOT OUT AND ERADICATE OGRES.
IF WE DON'T GET TO THE SOURCE OF THE PROBLEM, THE STRUGGLE WILL NEVER END.
...
ULTIMATELY, THE ONLY CLUES WE HAVE...
...ARE THE OGRES THEMSELVES!
IF WE CAN FIND OUT WHO'S PLANTING THE OGRE SEEDS AND WHAT THEY'RE TRYING TO DO...
...WE CAN PREVENT MORE PEOPLE FROM LOSING THEIR LIVES.
PERHAPS WE COULD EVEN LEARN...
...HOW TO RESTORE OGRES TO THEIR HUMAN STATE!
!!

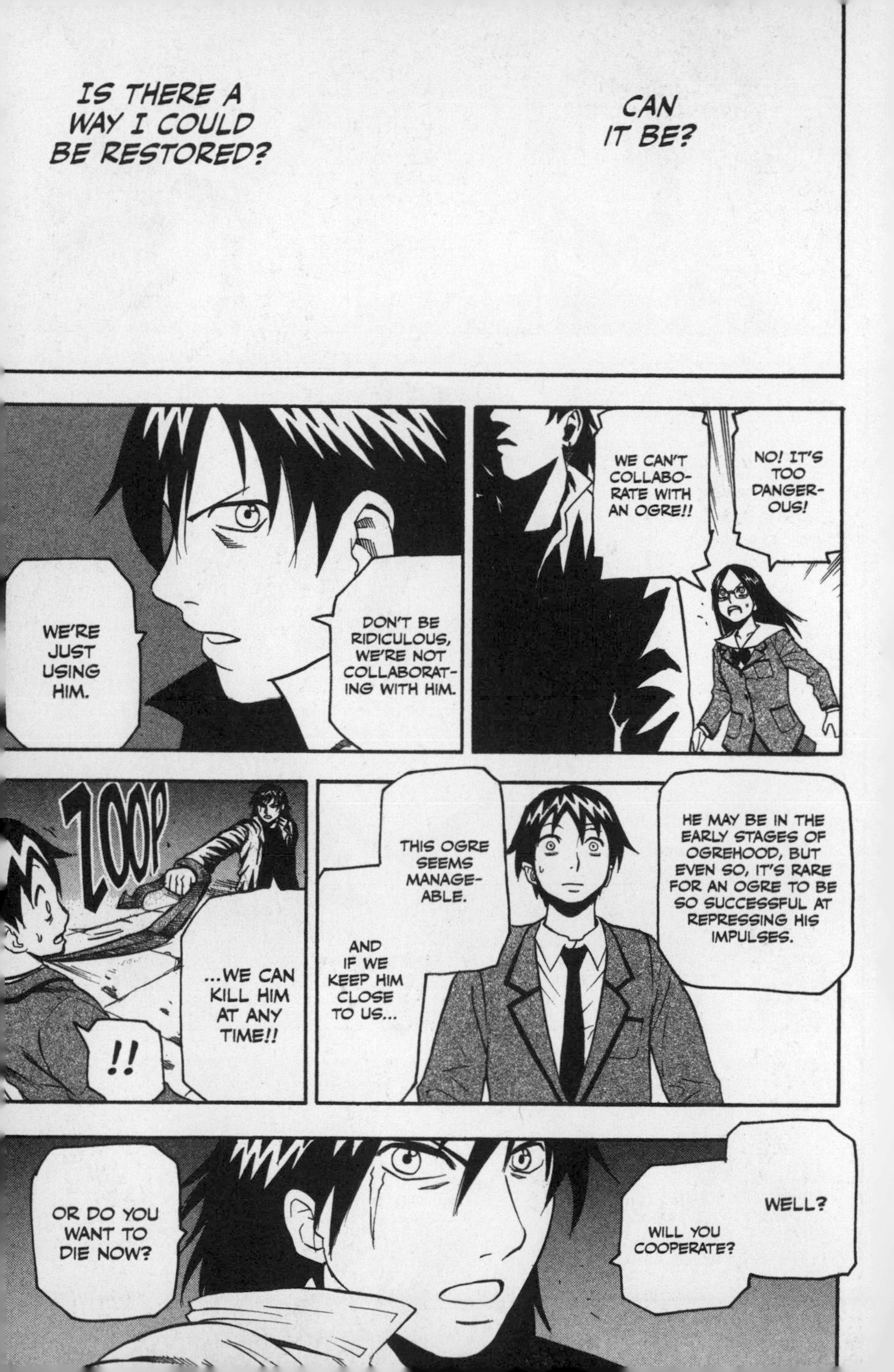
CAN IT BE?
IS THERE A WAY I COULD BE RESTORED?
NO! IT'S TOO DANGER-OUS!
WE CAN'T COLLABO-RATE WITH AN OGRE!!
DON'T BE RIDICULOUS, WE'RE NOT COLLABORAT-ING WITH HIM.
WE'RE JUST USING HIM.
HE MAY BE IN THE EARLY STAGES OF OGREHOOD, BUT EVEN SO, IT'S RARE FOR AN OGRE TO BE SO SUCCESSFUL AT REPRESSING HIS IMPULSES.
THIS OGRE SEEMS MANAGE-ABLE.
AND IF WE KEEP HIM CLOSE TO US...
ZOOP
...WE CAN KILL HIM AT ANY TIME!!
!!
WELL?
WILL YOU COOPERATE?
OR DO YOU WANT TO DIE NOW?

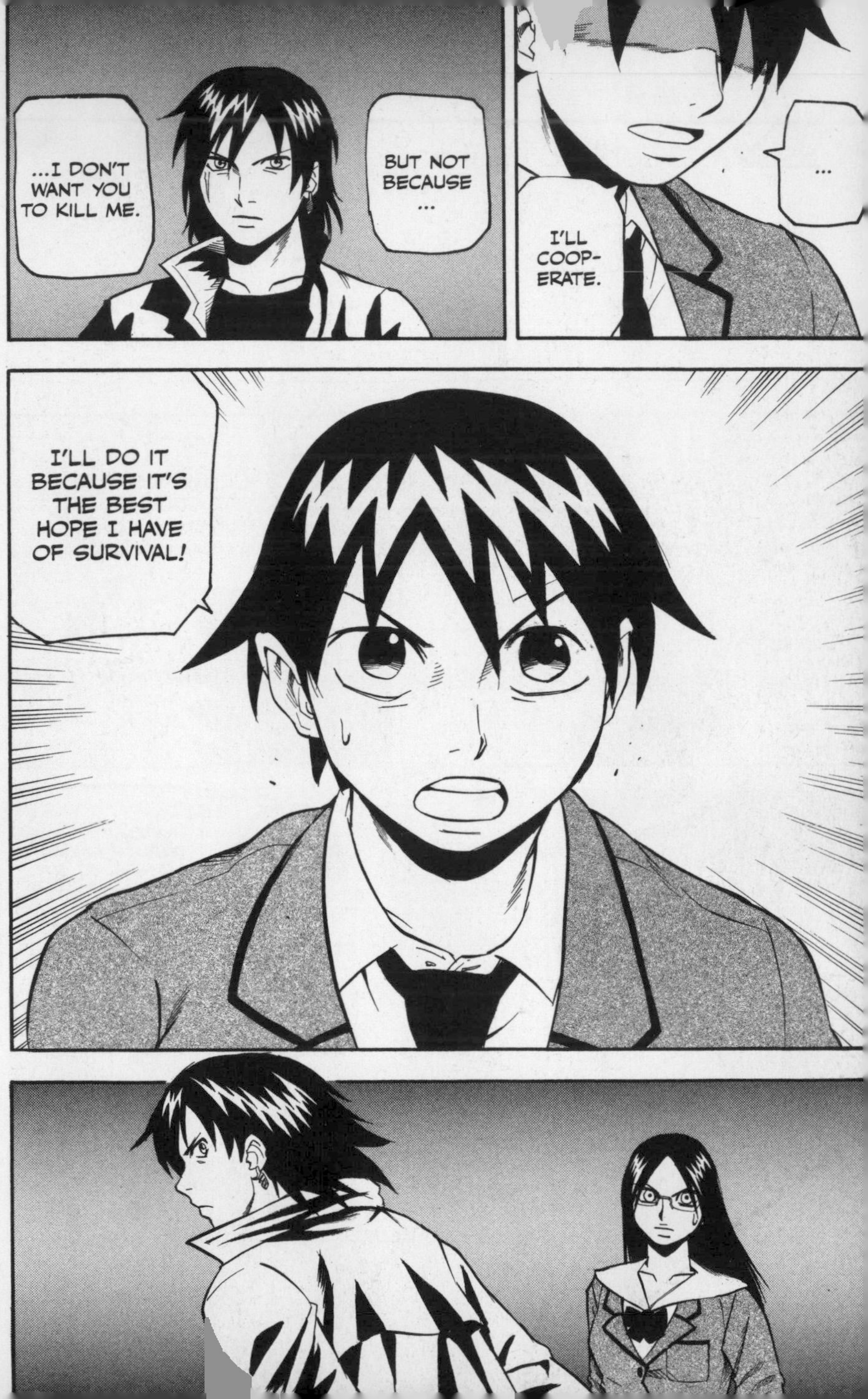
...
I'LL COOPERATE.
...I DON'T WANT YOU TO KILL ME.
BUT NOT BECAUSE ...
I'LL DO IT BECAUSE IT'S THE BEST HOPE I HAVE OF SURVIVAL!

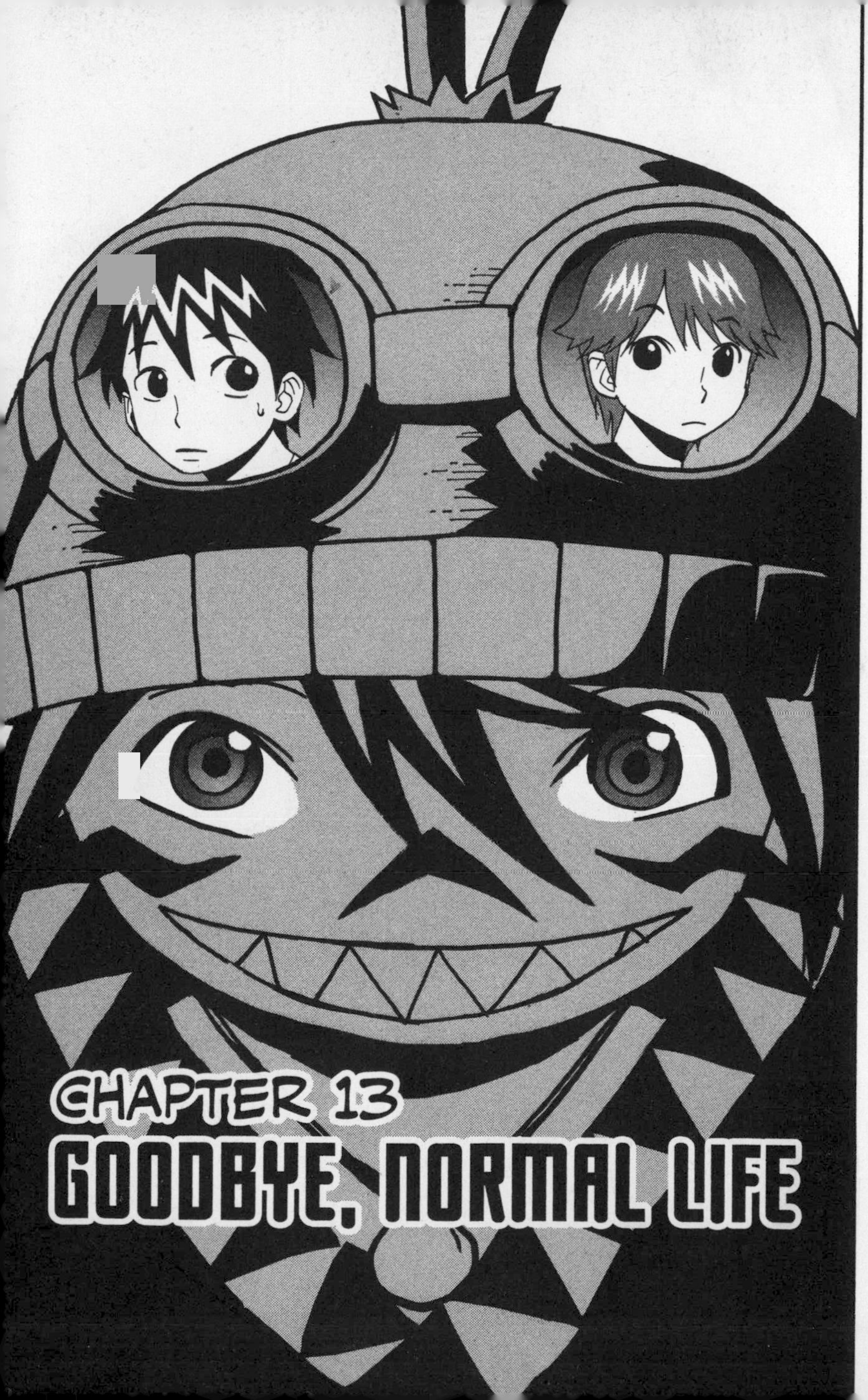
CHAPTER 13
GOODBYE, NORMAL LIFE

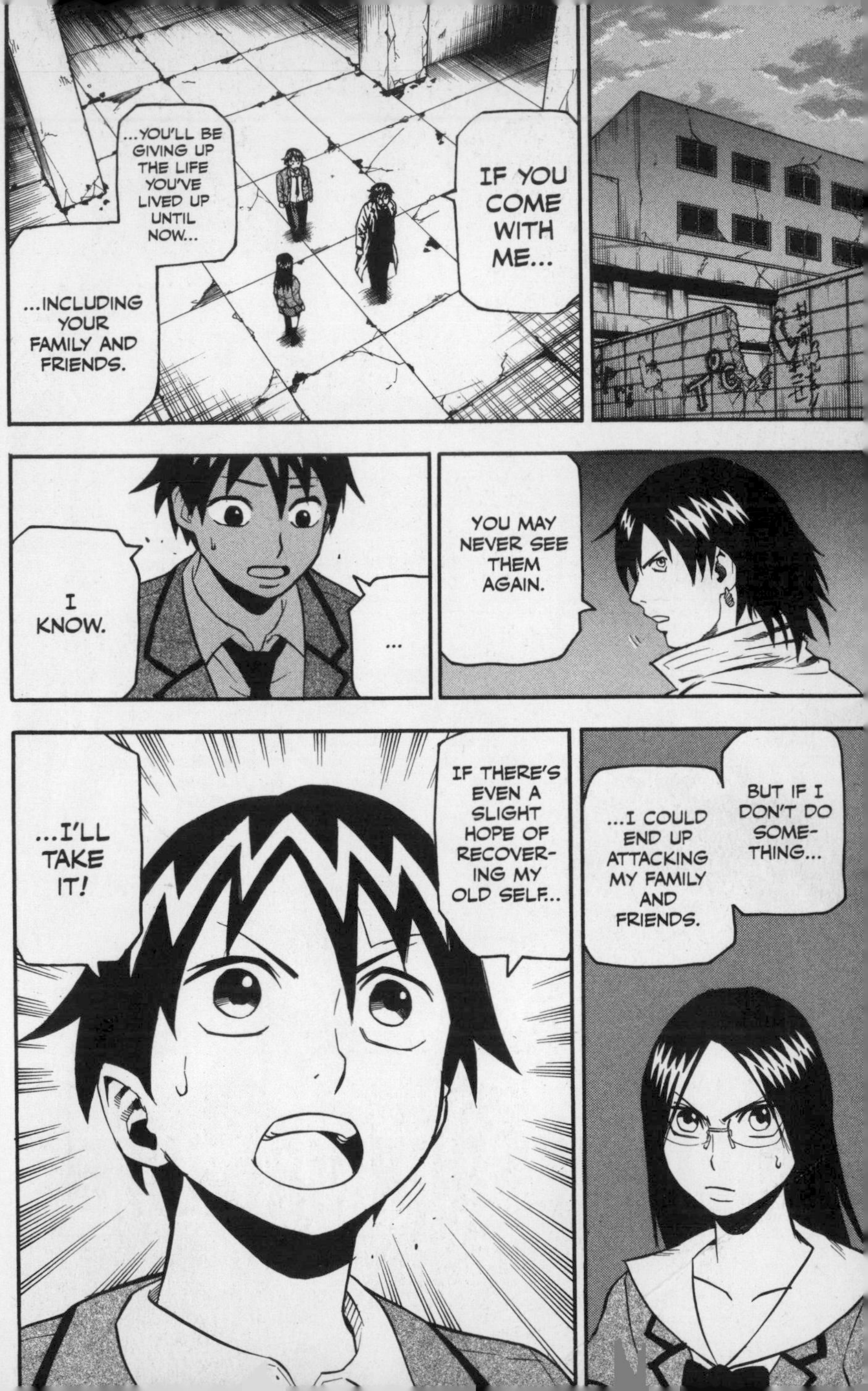
IF YOU COME WITH ME...
...YOU'LL BE GIVING UP THE LIFE YOU'VE LIVED UP UNTIL NOW...
...INCLUDING YOUR FAMILY AND FRIENDS.
YOU MAY NEVER SEE THEM AGAIN.
...
I KNOW.
BUT IF I DON'T DO SOME-THING...
...I COULD END UP ATTACKING MY FAMILY AND FRIENDS.
IF THERE'S EVEN A SLIGHT HOPE OF RECOVER-ING MY OLD SELF...
...I'LL TAKE IT!

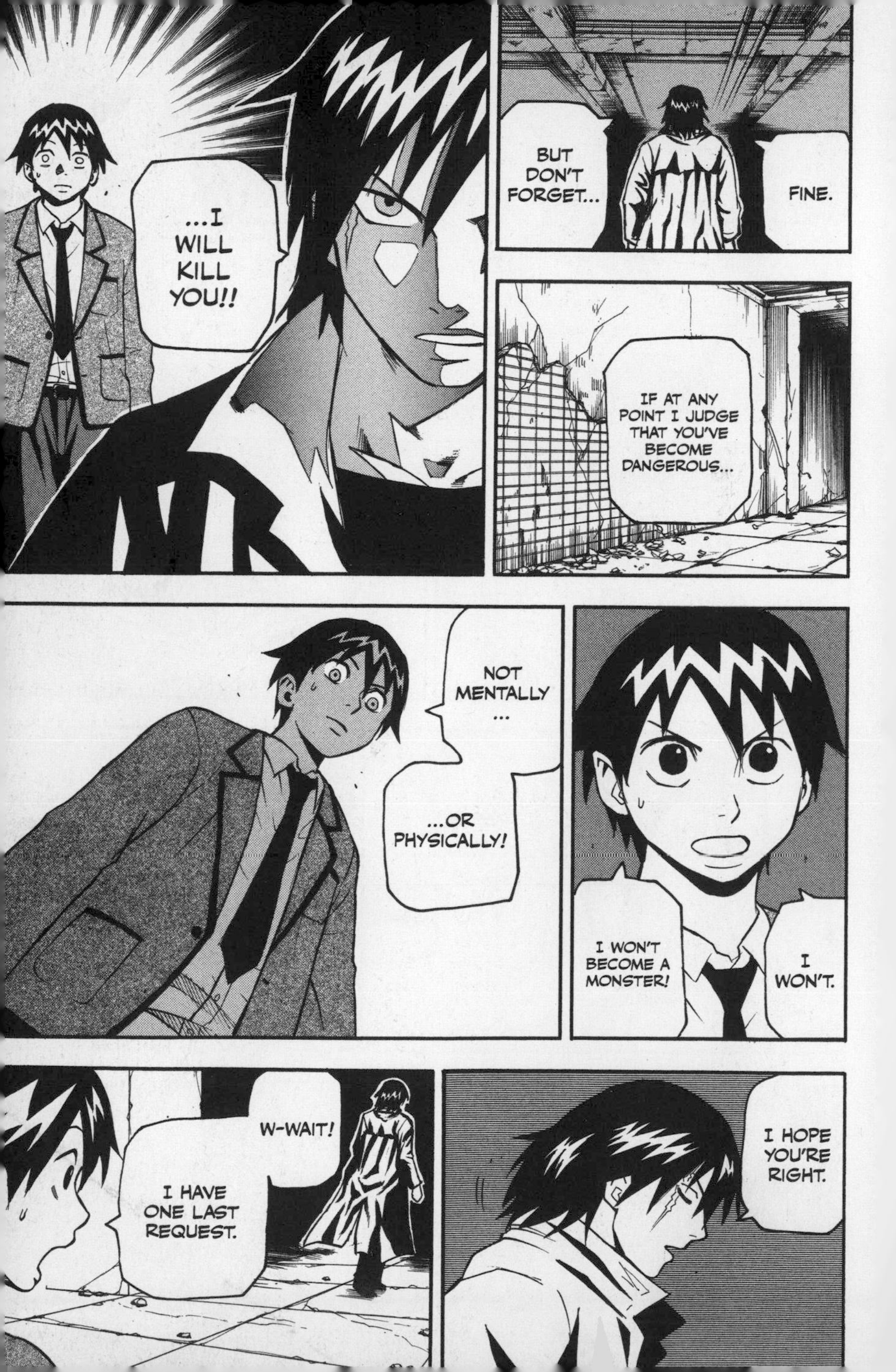
FINE.
BUT DON'T FORGET...
IF AT ANY POINT I JUDGE THAT YOU'VE BECOME DANGEROUS...
...I WILL KILL YOU!!
I WON'T.
I WON'T BECOME A MONSTER!
NOT MENTALLY ...
...OR PHYSICALLY!
I HOPE YOU'RE RIGHT.
W-WAIT!
I HAVE ONE LAST REQUEST.

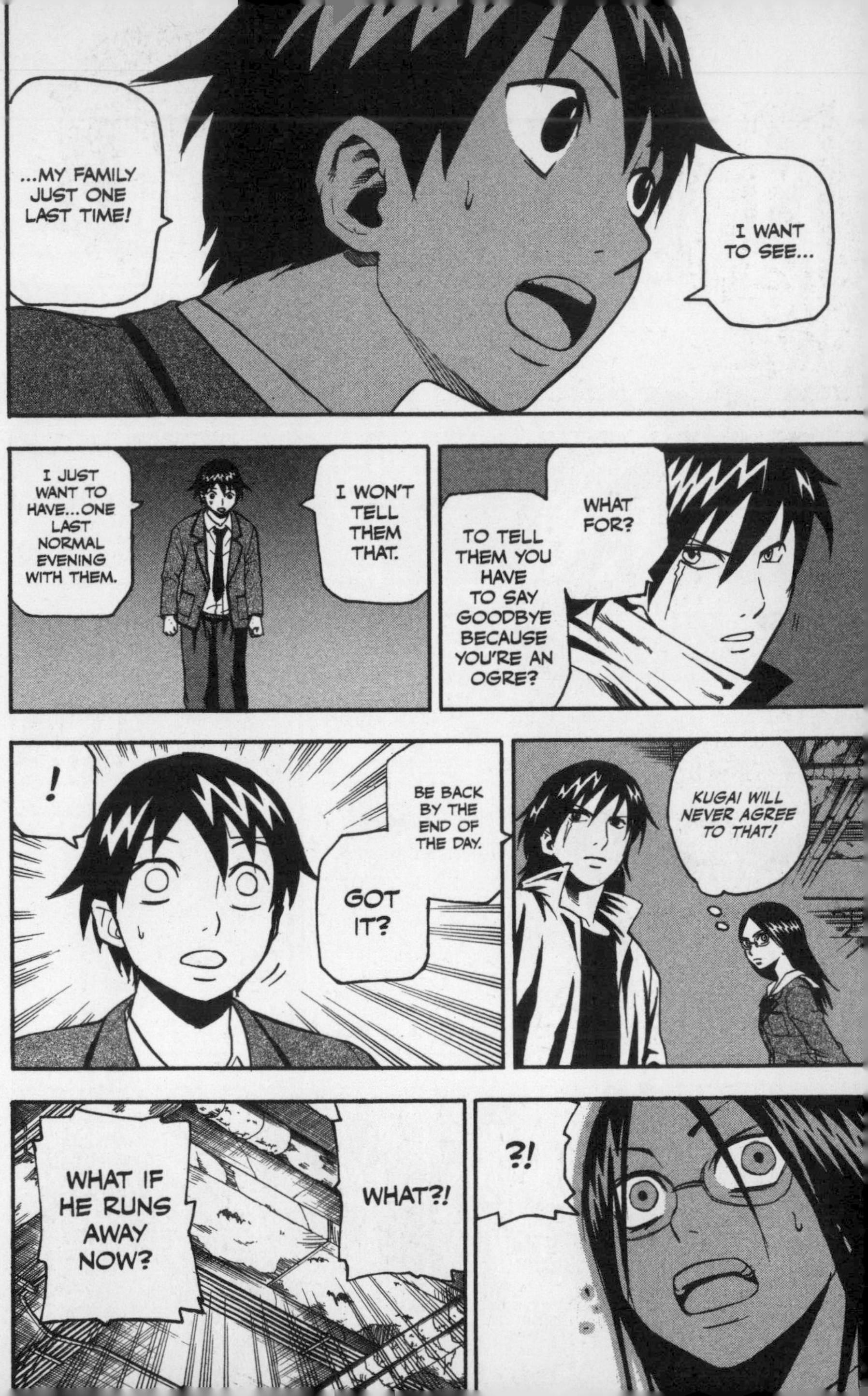
I WANT TO SEE...
...MY FAMILY JUST ONE LAST TIME!
WHAT FOR?
TO TELL THEM YOU HAVE TO SAY GOODBYE BECAUSE YOU'RE AN OGRE?
I WON'T TELL THEM THAT.
I JUST WANT TO HAVE...ONE LAST NORMAL EVENING WITH THEM.
KUGAI WILL NEVER AGREE TO THAT!
BE BACK BY THE END OF THE DAY.
GOT IT?
!
?!
WHAT?!
WHAT IF HE RUNS AWAY NOW?

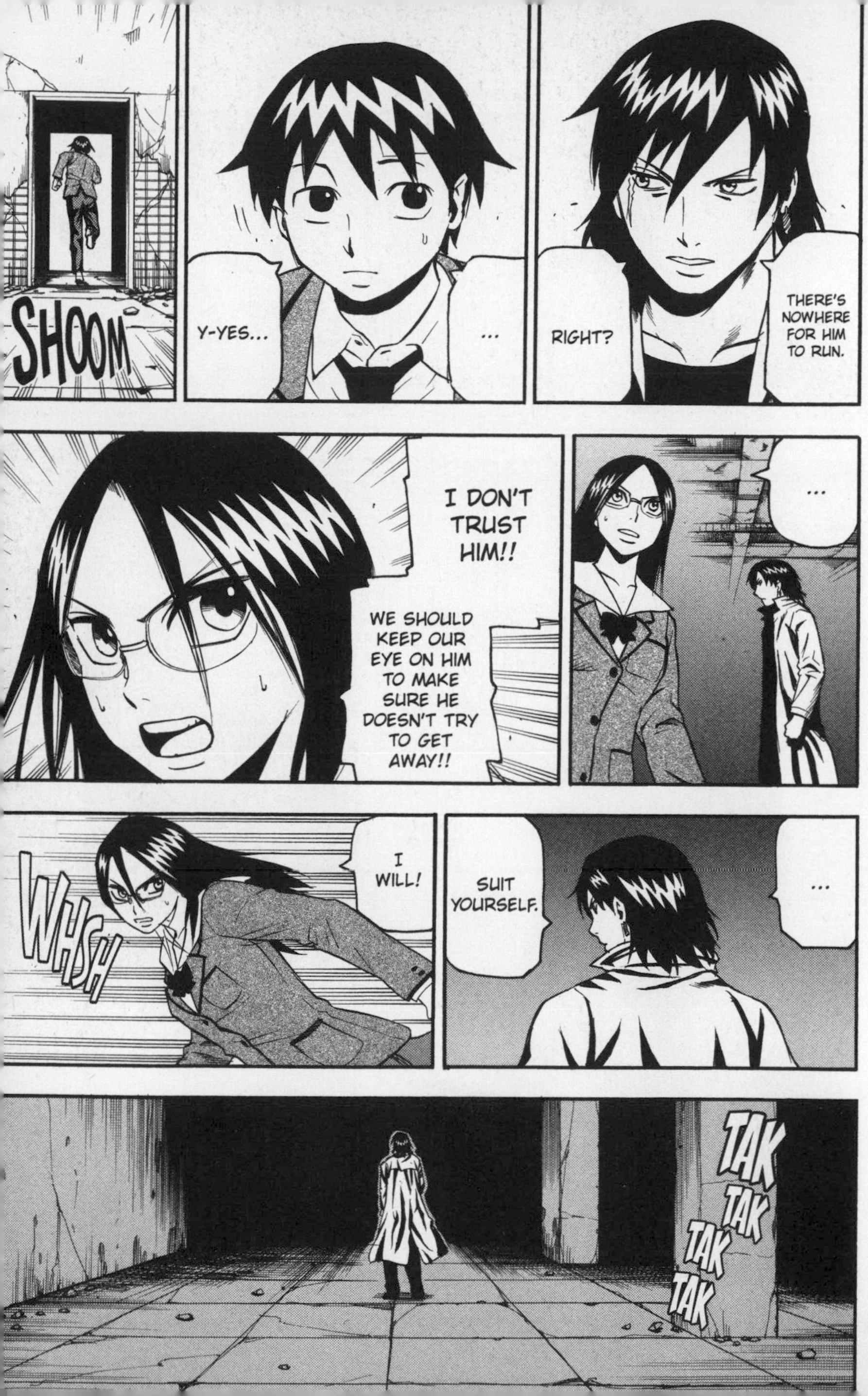
THERE'S NOWHERE FOR HIM TO RUN.
RIGHT?
...
Y-YES...
SHOOM
...
I DON'T TRUST HIM!!
WE SHOULD KEEP OUR EYE ON HIM TO MAKE SURE HE DOESN'T TRY TO GET AWAY!!
...
SUIT YOURSELF.
I WILL!
WHSH
TAK
TAK
TAK
TAK

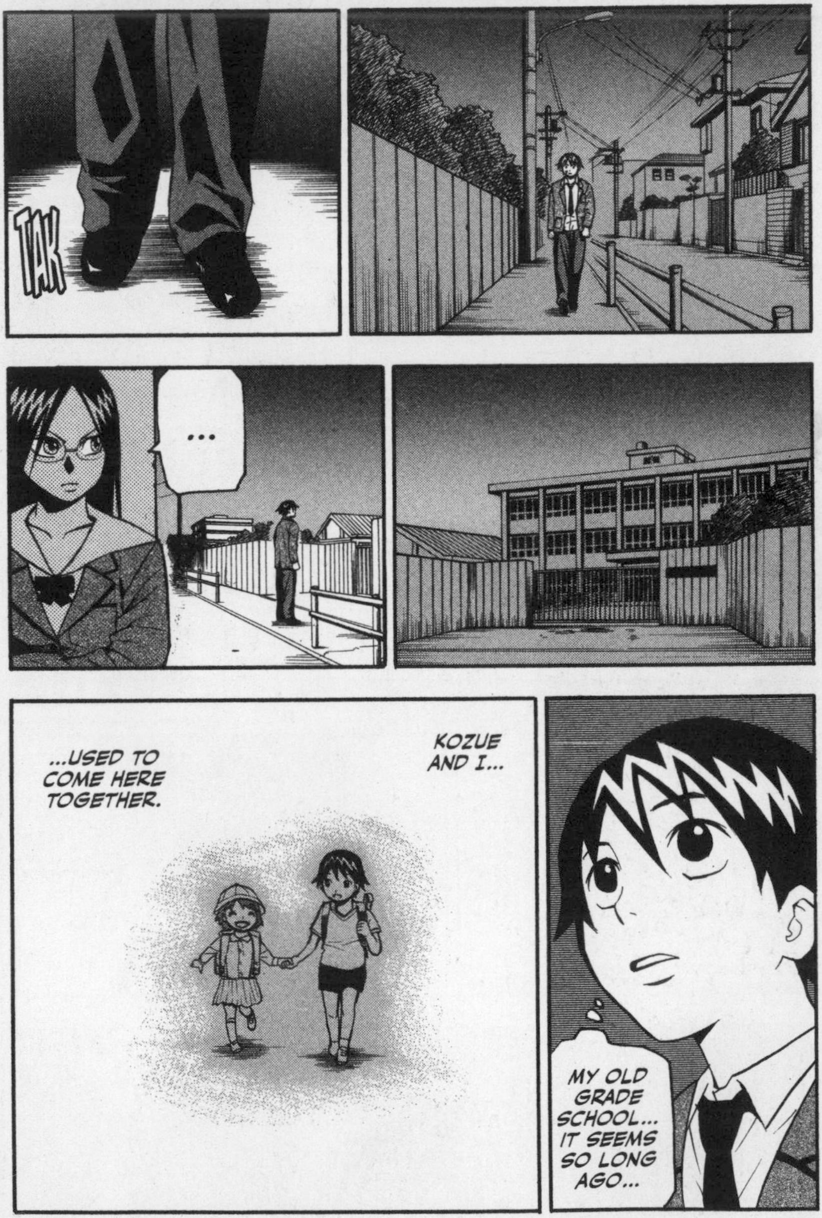
TAK
...
MY OLD GRADE SCHOOL... IT SEEMS SO LONG AGO...
KOZUE AND I...
...USED TO COME HERE TOGETHER.

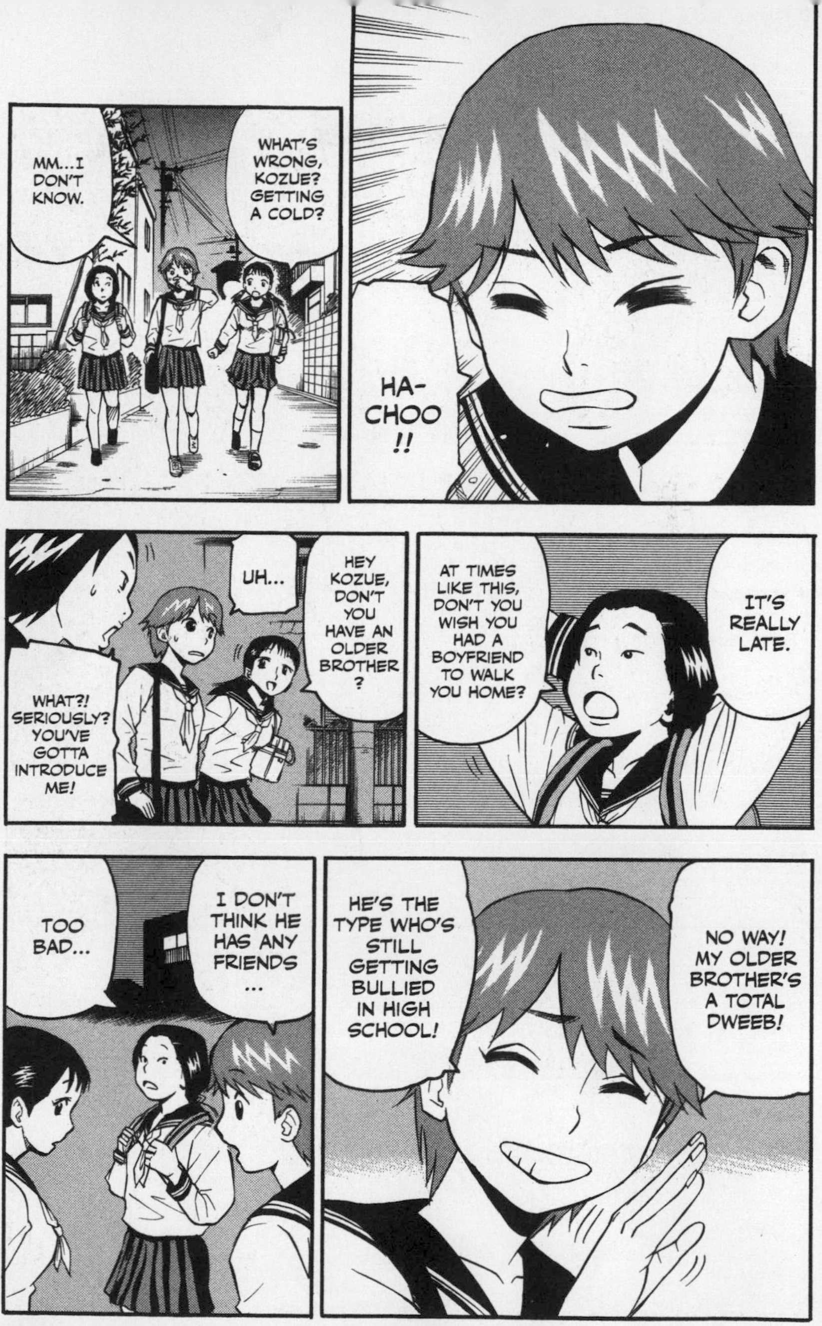
HA-CHOO!!
WHAT'S WRONG, KOZUE? GETTING A COLD?
MM...I DON'T KNOW.
IT'S REALLY LATE.
AT TIMES LIKE THIS, DON'T YOU WISH YOU HAD A BOYFRIEND TO WALK YOU HOME?
HEY KOZUE, DON'T YOU HAVE AN OLDER BROTHER?
UH...
WHAT?! SERIOUSLY? YOU'VE GOTTA INTRODUCE ME!
NO WAY! MY OLDER BROTHER'S A TOTAL DWEEB!
HE'S THE TYPE WHO'S STILL GETTING BULLIED IN HIGH SCHOOL!
I DON'T THINK HE HAS ANY FRIENDS...
TOO BAD...

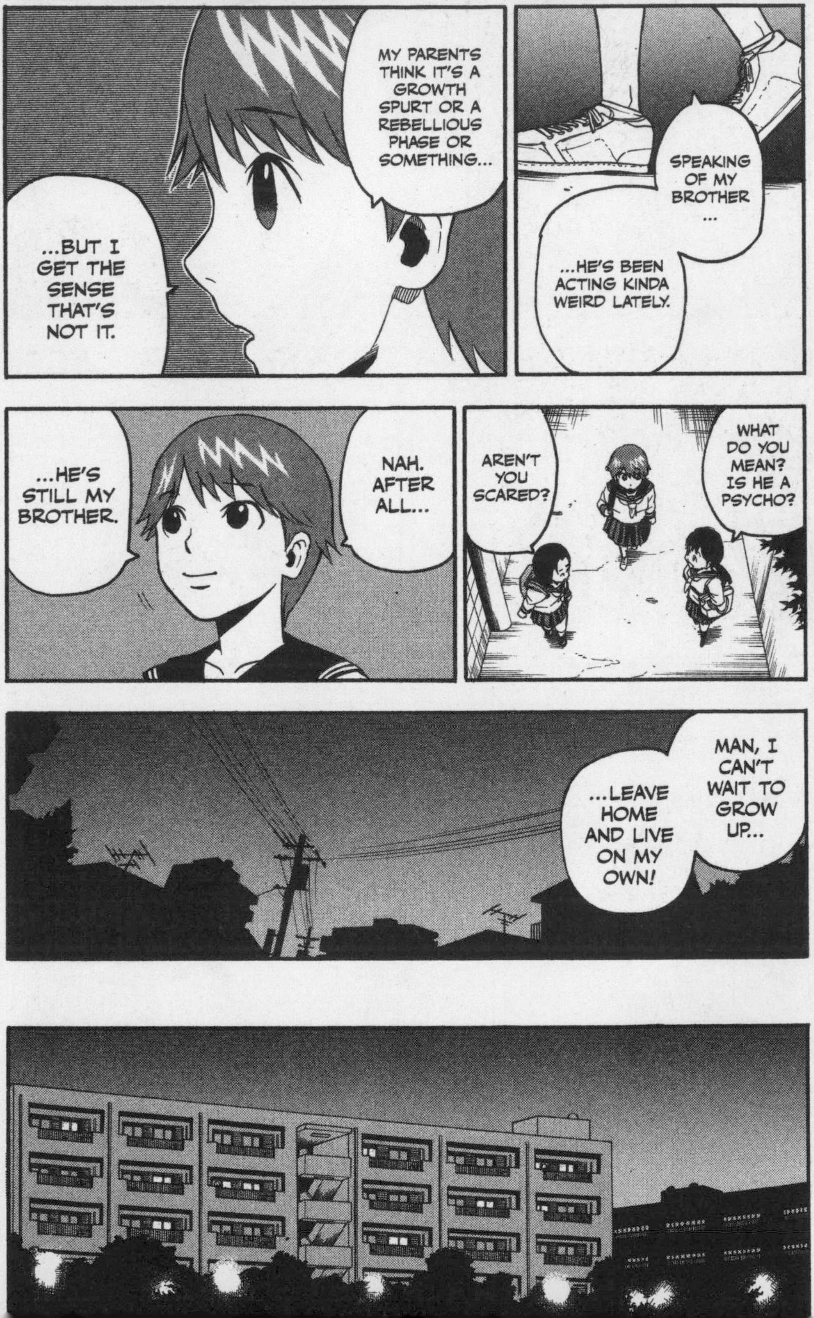
SPEAKING OF MY BROTHER ...
...HE'S BEEN ACTING KINDA WEIRD LATELY.
MY PARENTS THINK IT'S A GROWTH SPURT OR A REBELLIOUS PHASE OR SOMETHING...
...BUT I GET THE SENSE THAT'S NOT IT.
WHAT DO YOU MEAN? IS HE A PSYCHO?
AREN'T YOU SCARED?
NAH. AFTER ALL...
...HE'S STILL MY BROTHER.
MAN, I CAN'T WAIT TO GROW UP...
...LEAVE HOME AND LIVE ON MY OWN!

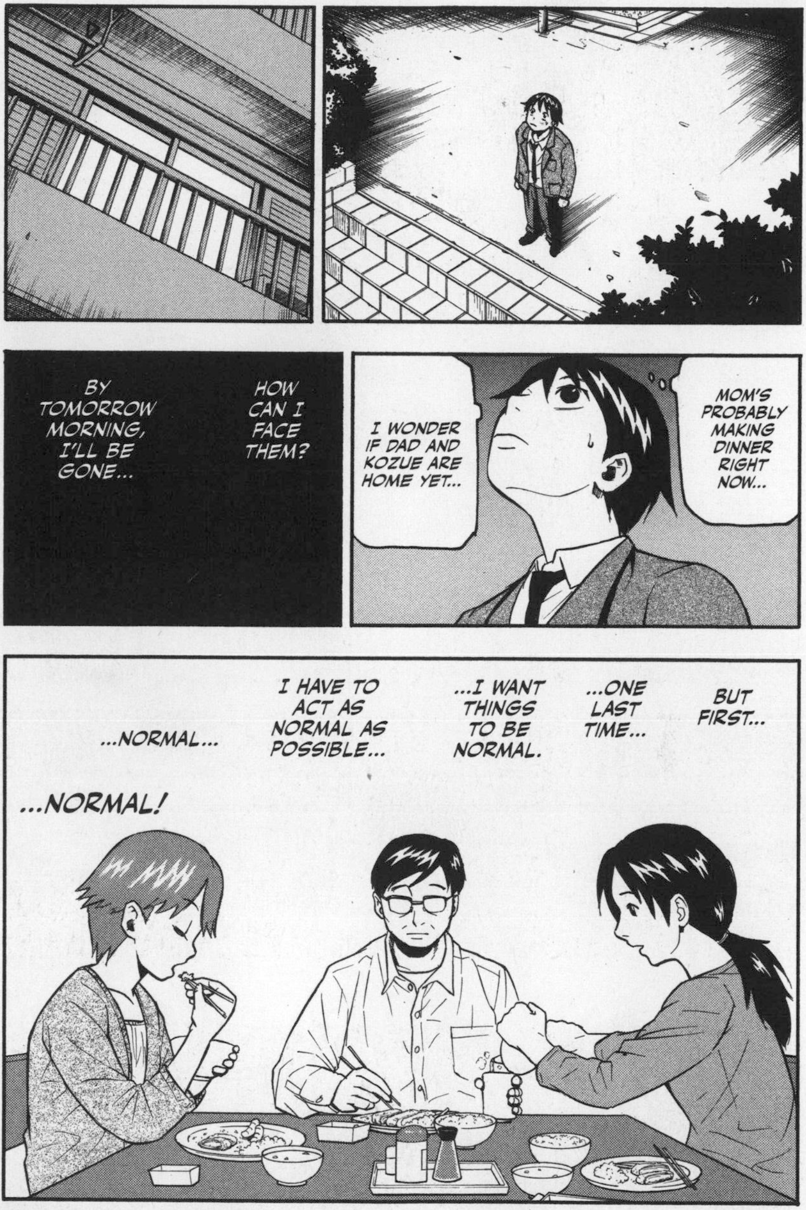
MOM'S PROBABLY MAKING DINNER RIGHT NOW...
I WONDER IF DAD AND KOZUE ARE HOME YET...
HOW CAN I FACE THEM?
BY TOMORROW MORNING, I'LL BE GONE...
BUT FIRST...
...ONE LAST TIME...
...I WANT THINGS TO BE NORMAL.
I HAVE TO ACT AS NORMAL AS POSSIBLE...
...NORMAL...
...NORMAL!

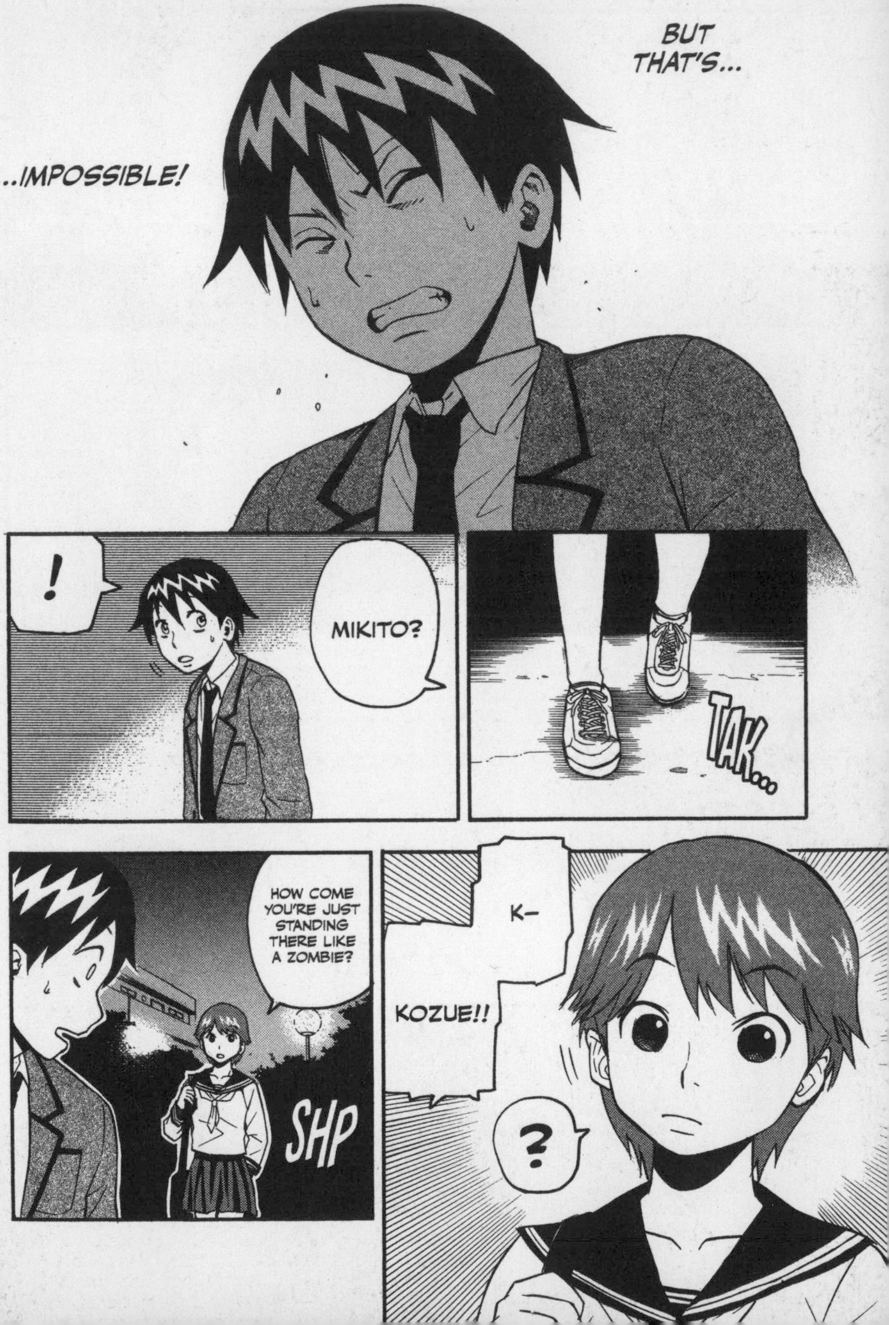
BUT THAT'S...
...IMPOSSIBLE!
TAK...
MIKITO?
!
K-
KOZUE!!
?
HOW COME YOU'RE JUST STANDING THERE LIKE A ZOMBIE?
SHP

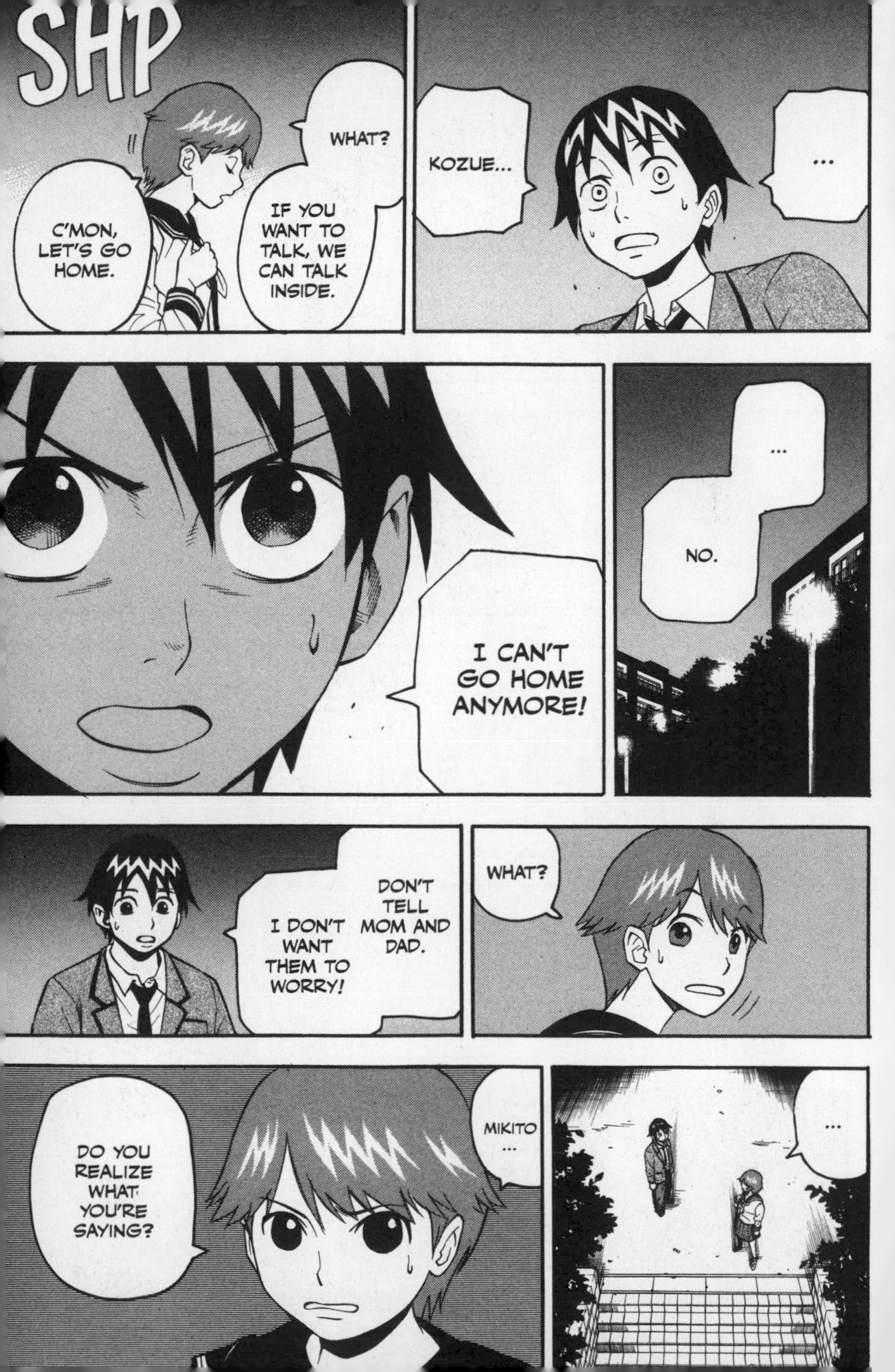
...
KOZUE...
SHP
WHAT?
IF YOU WANT TO TALK, WE CAN TALK INSIDE.
C'MON, LET'S GO HOME.
...
NO.
I CAN'T GO HOME ANYMORE!
WHAT?
DON'T TELL MOM AND DAD.
I DON'T WANT THEM TO WORRY!
...
MIKITO ...
DO YOU REALIZE WHAT YOU'RE SAYING?

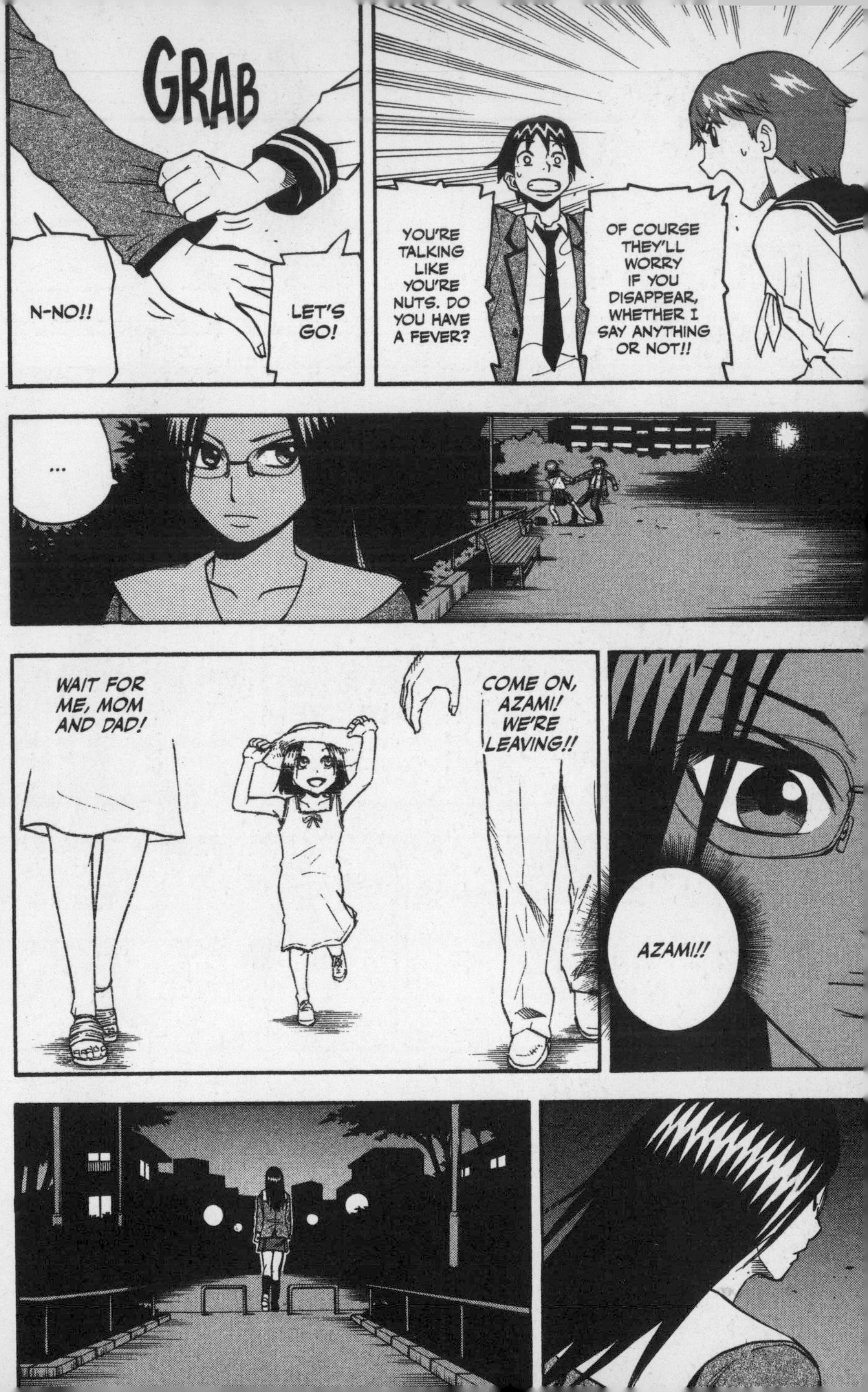
OF COURSE THEY'LL WORRY IF YOU DISAPPEAR, WHETHER I SAY ANYTHING OR NOT!!
YOU'RE TALKING LIKE YOU'RE NUTS. DO YOU HAVE A FEVER?
GRAB
LET'S GO!
N-NO!!
...
AZAMI!!
COME ON, AZAMI! WE'RE LEAVING!!
WAIT FOR ME, MOM AND DAD!

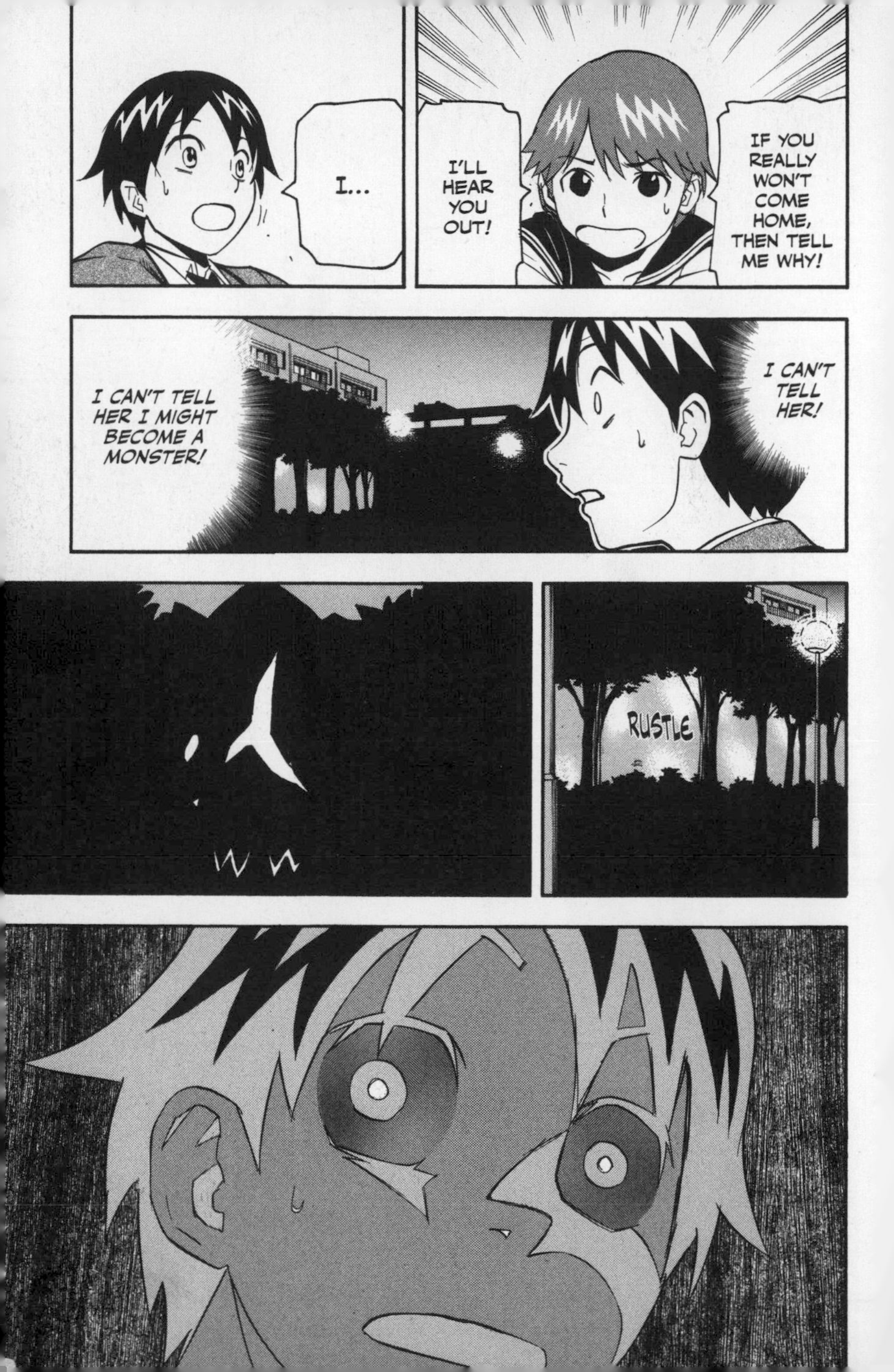
IF YOU REALLY WON'T COME HOME, THEN TELL ME WHY!
I'LL HEAR YOU OUT!
I...
I CAN'T TELL HER!
I CAN'T TELL HER I MIGHT BECOME A MONSTER!
RUSTLE

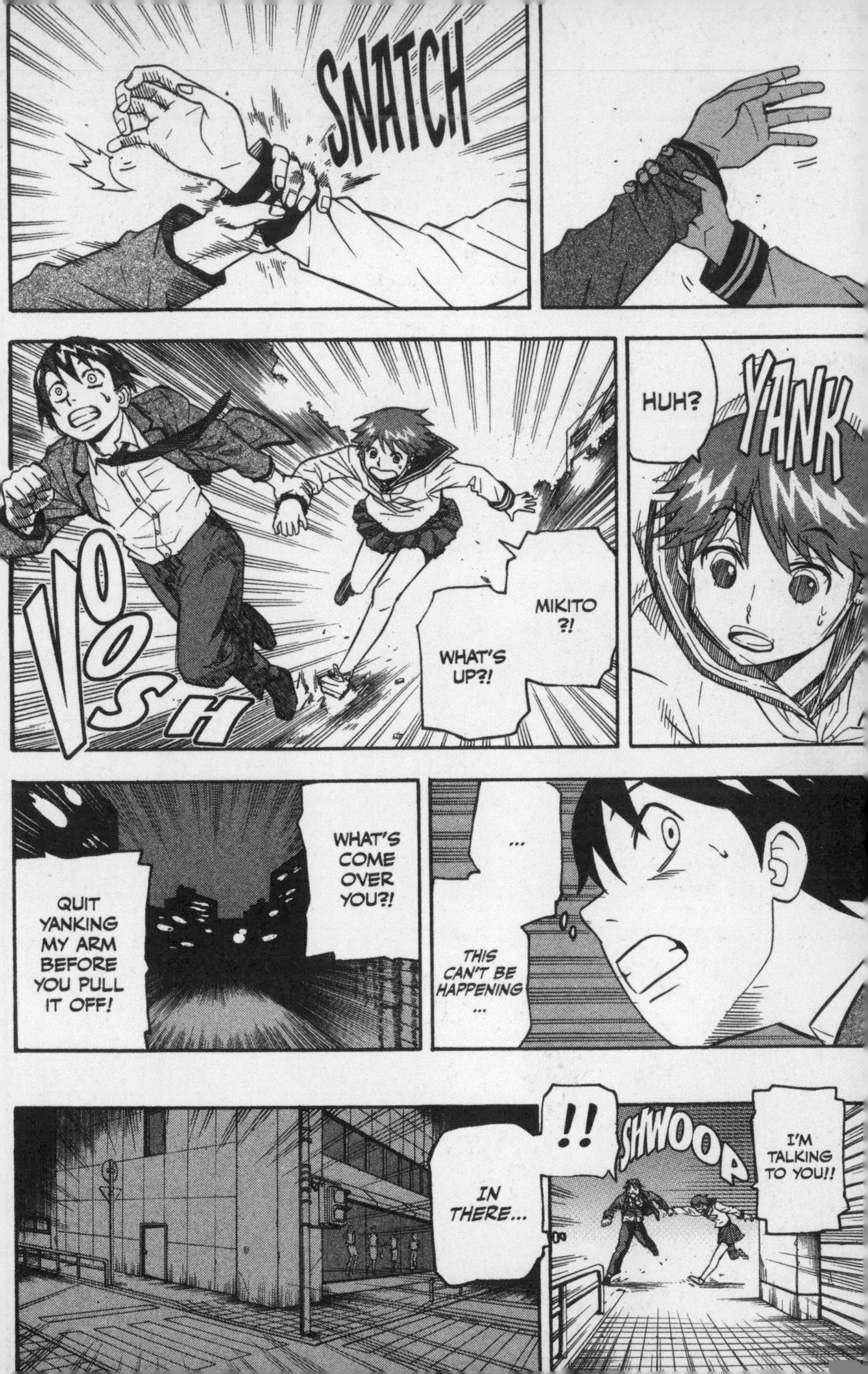
SNATCH
HUH?
YANK
MIKITO?!
WHAT'S UP?!
VOOSH
...
THIS CAN'T BE HAPPENING...
WHAT'S COME OVER YOU?!
QUIT YANKING MY ARM BEFORE YOU PULL IT OFF!
I'M TALKING TO YOU!!
SHWOOP
!!
IN THERE...

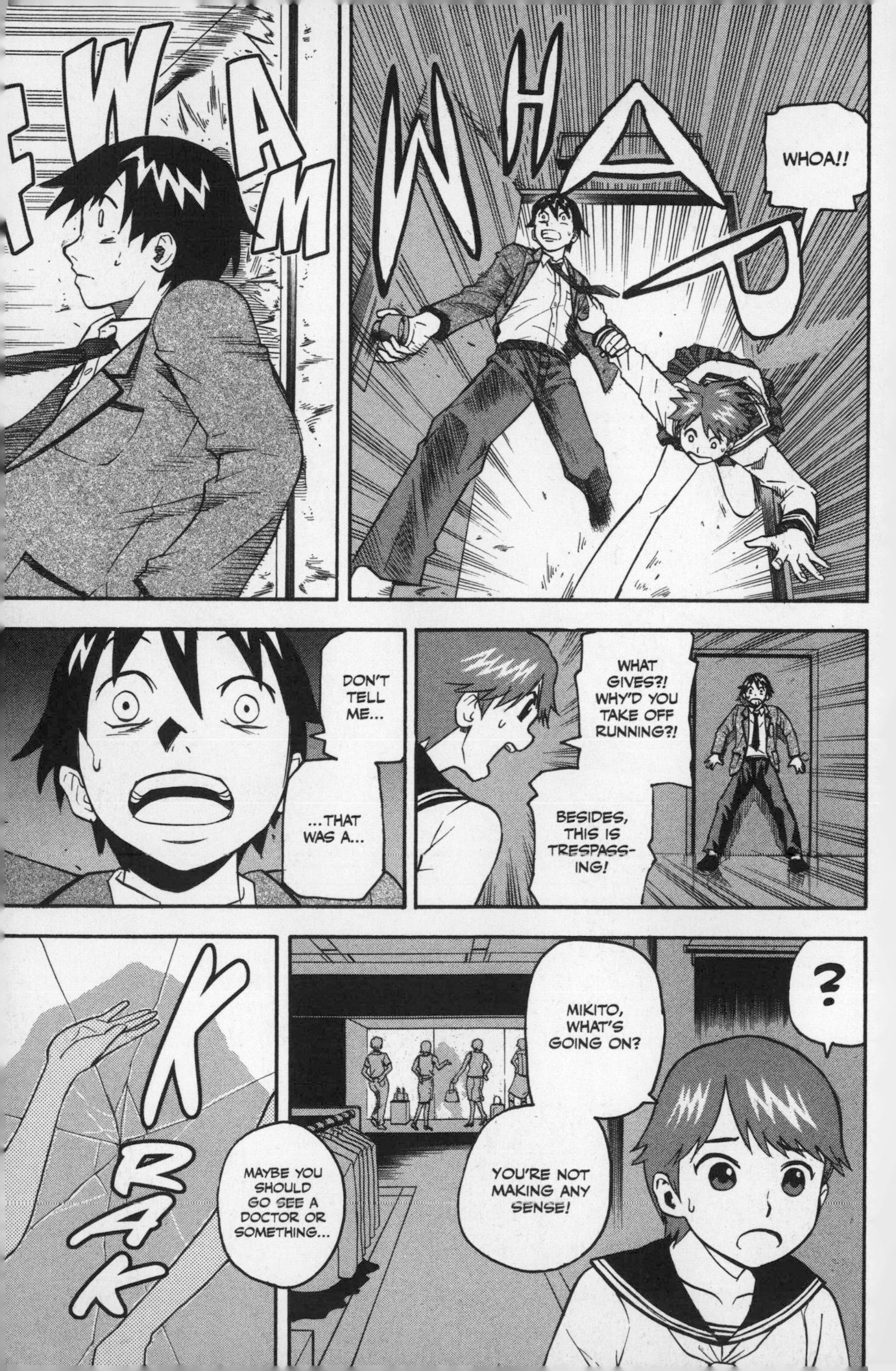
WHAP
WHOA!!
FWAM
WHAT GIVES?! WHY'D YOU TAKE OFF RUNNING?!
BESIDES, THIS IS TRESPASSING!
DON'T TELL ME...
...THAT WAS A...
?
MIKITO, WHAT'S GOING ON?
YOU'RE NOT MAKING ANY SENSE!
MAYBE YOU SHOULD GO SEE A DOCTOR OR SOMETHING...
KRAK

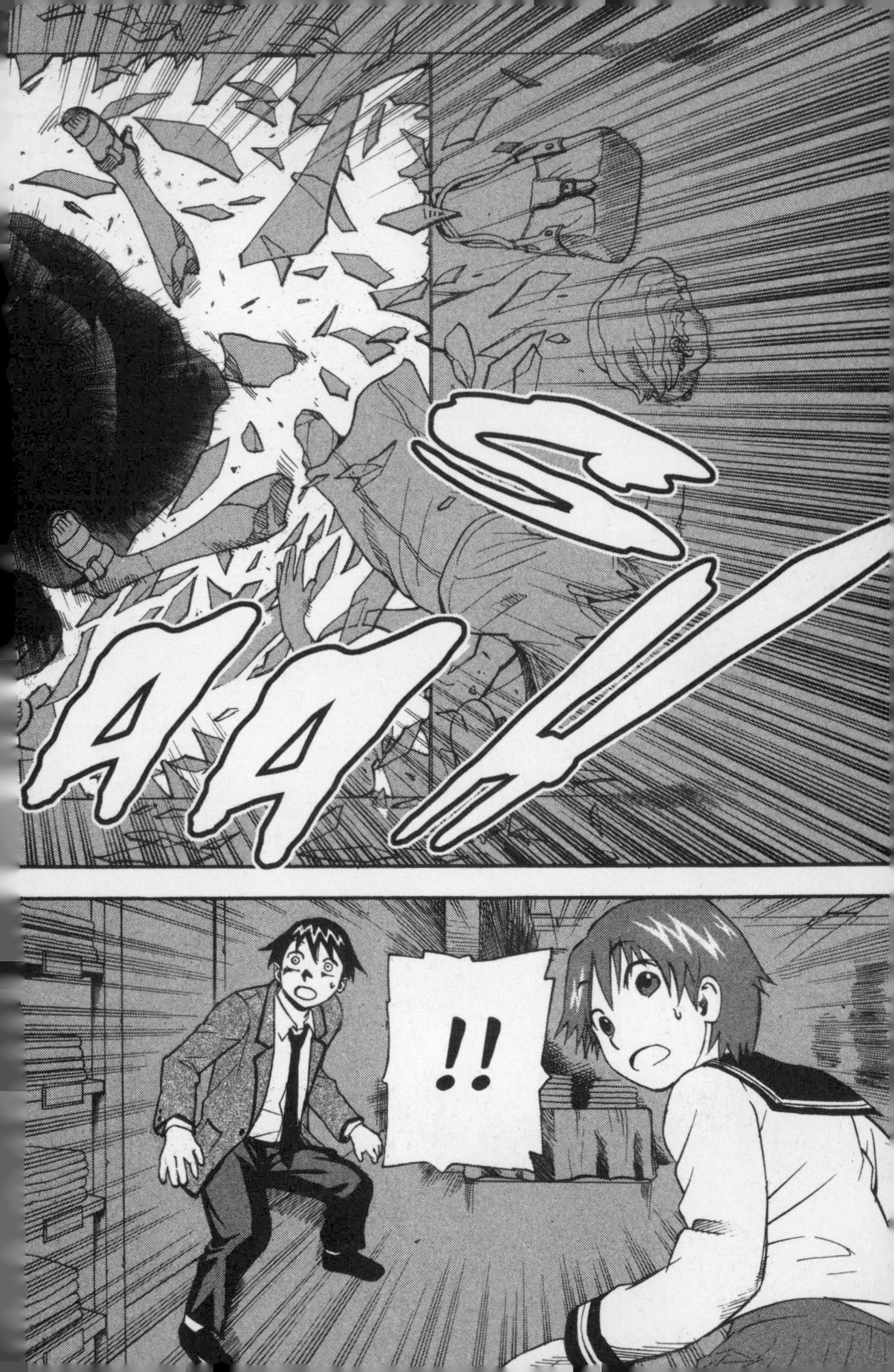
GWAAAAA!
!!

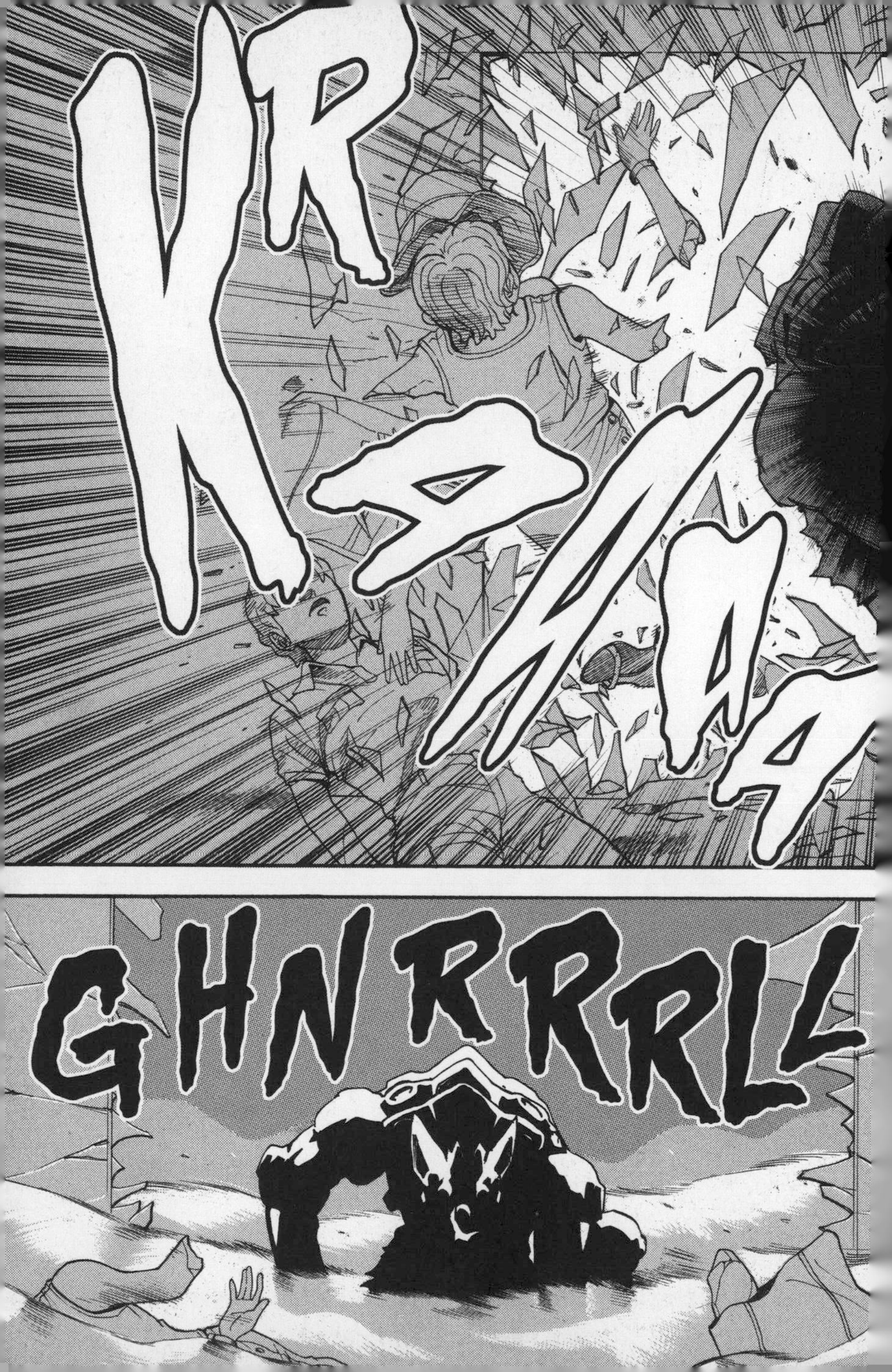
VRKAAAA
GHNRRRLL

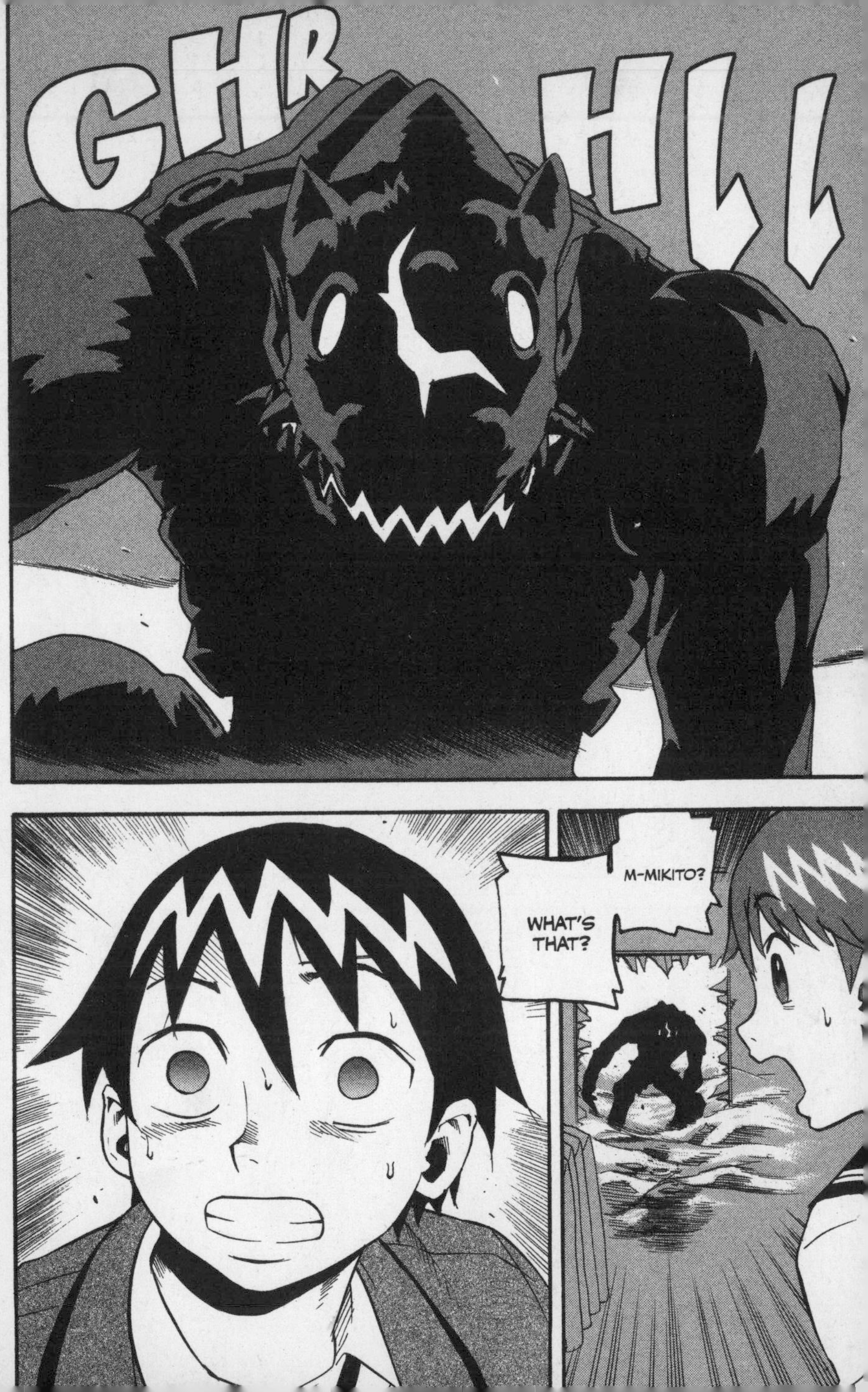
GHRHLL
M-MIKITO?
WHAT'S THAT?

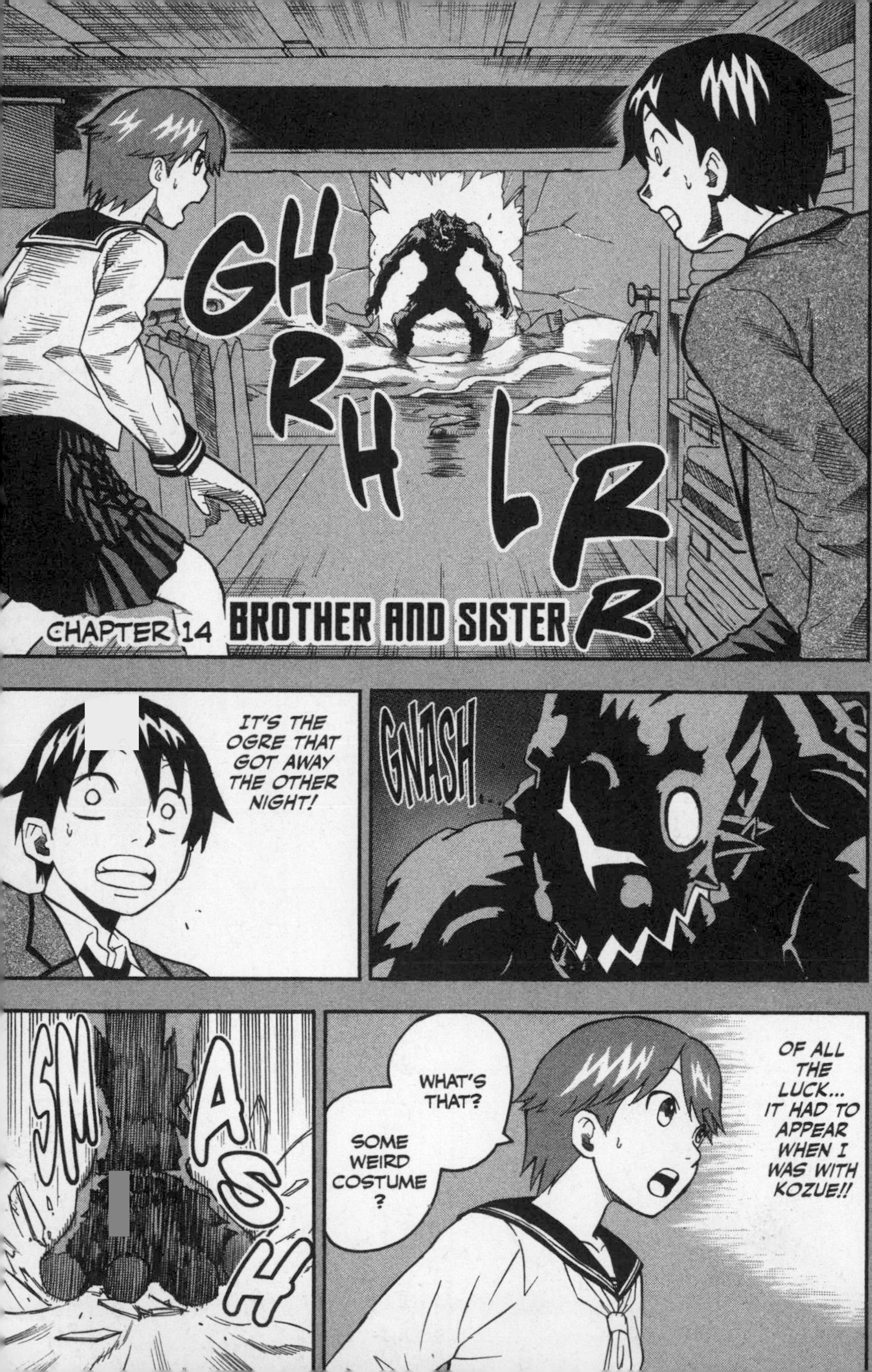
GHRHLRR
CHAPTER 14 BROTHER AND SISTER
GNASH
IT'S THE OGRE THAT GOT AWAY THE OTHER NIGHT!
OF ALL THE LUCK... IT HAD TO APPEAR WHEN I WAS WITH KOZUE!!
WHAT'S THAT?
SOME WEIRD COSTUME?
SMASH

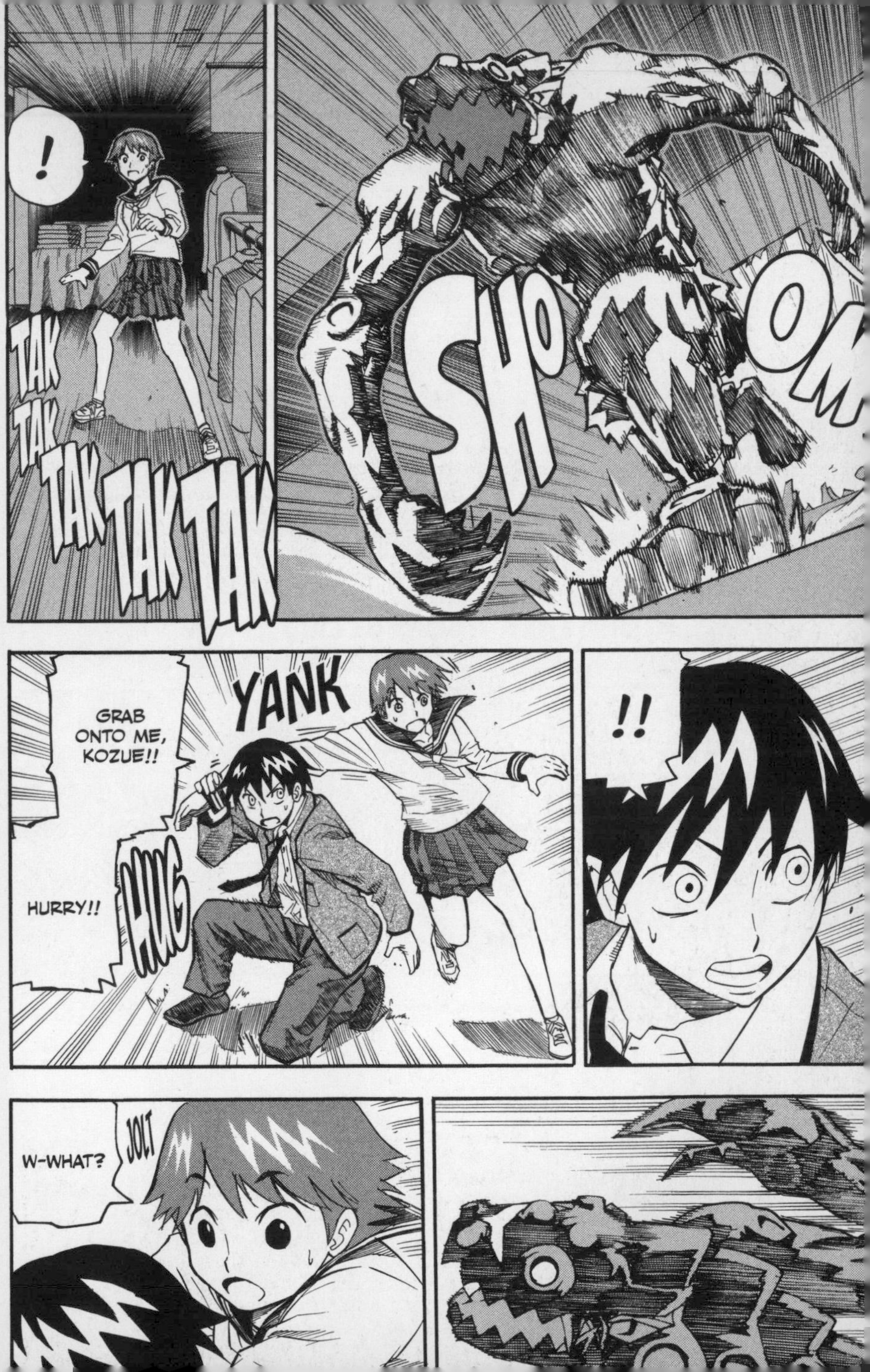
SHOOM
!
TAK TAK TAK TAK TAK
!!
YANK
GRAB ONTO ME, KOZUE!!
THUG
HURRY!!
JOLT
W-WHAT?

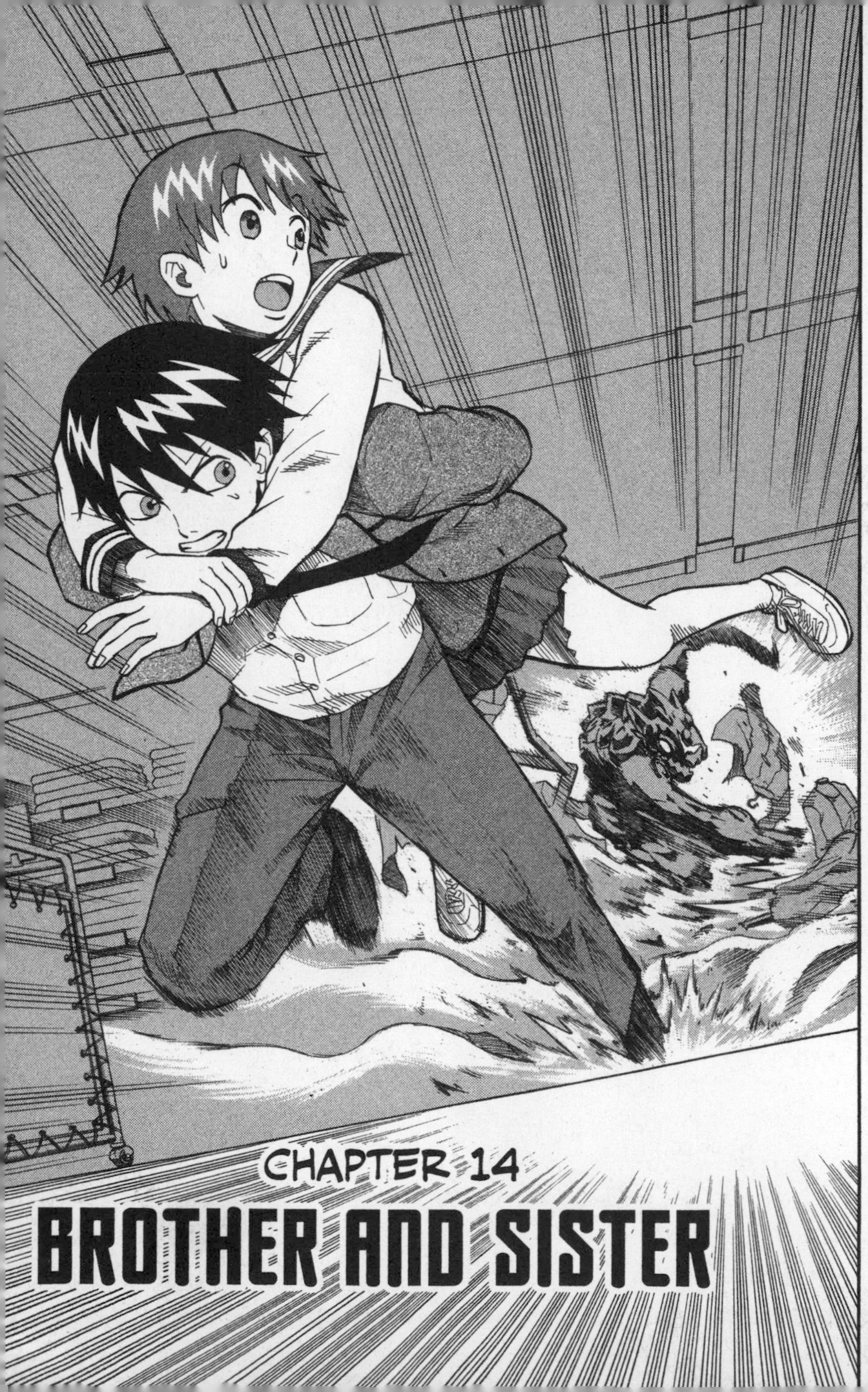
CHAPTER 14
BROTHER AND SISTER

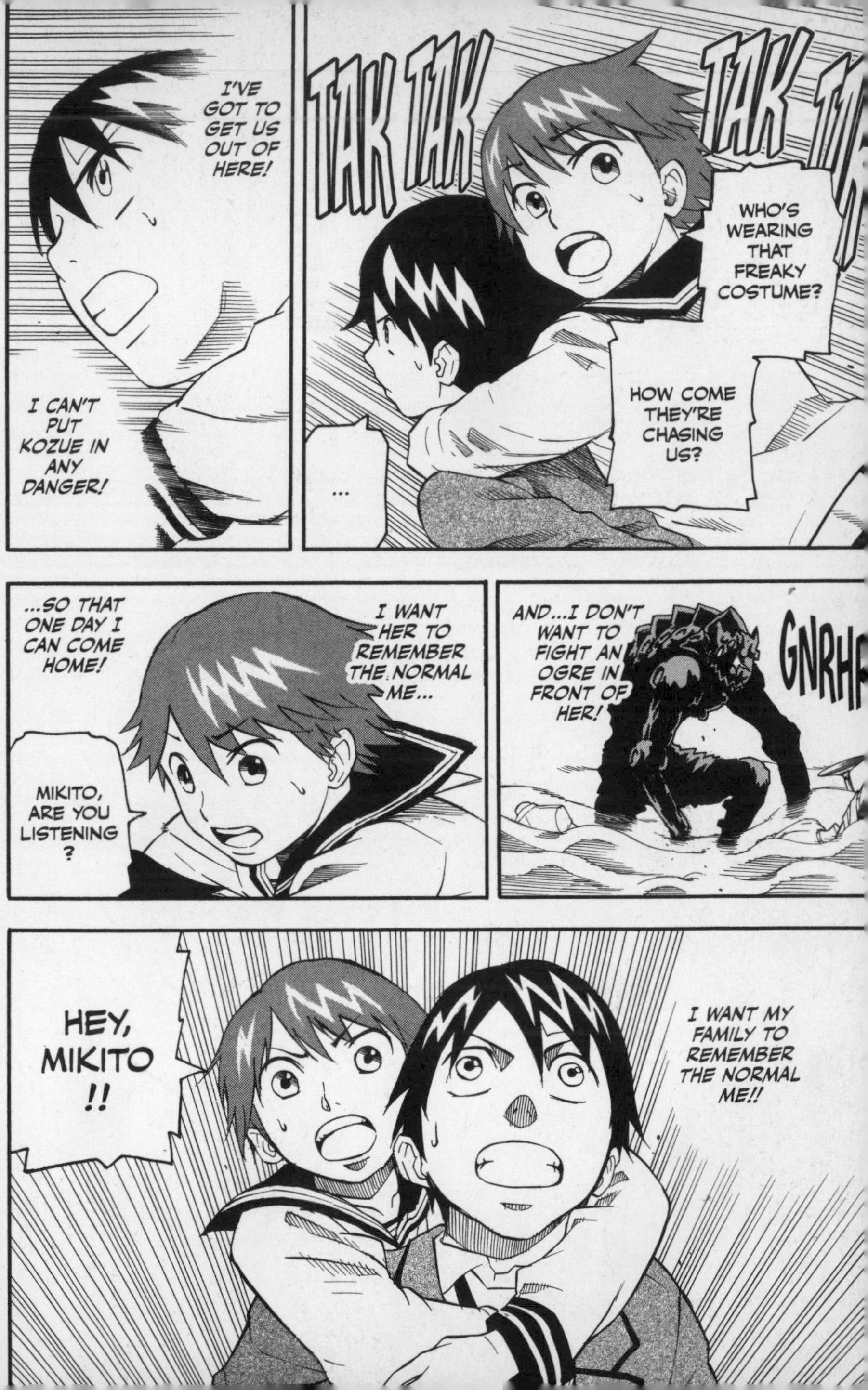
TAK TAK
TAK TA
WHO'S WEARING THAT FREAKY COSTUME?
HOW COME THEY'RE CHASING US?
...
I'VE GOT TO GET US OUT OF HERE!
I CAN'T PUT KOZUE IN ANY DANGER!
AND...I DON'T WANT TO FIGHT AN OGRE IN FRONT OF HER!
GNRH
I WANT HER TO REMEMBER THE NORMAL ME...
...SO THAT ONE DAY I CAN COME HOME!
MIKITO, ARE YOU LISTENING?
I WANT MY FAMILY TO REMEMBER THE NORMAL ME!!
HEY, MIKITO!!

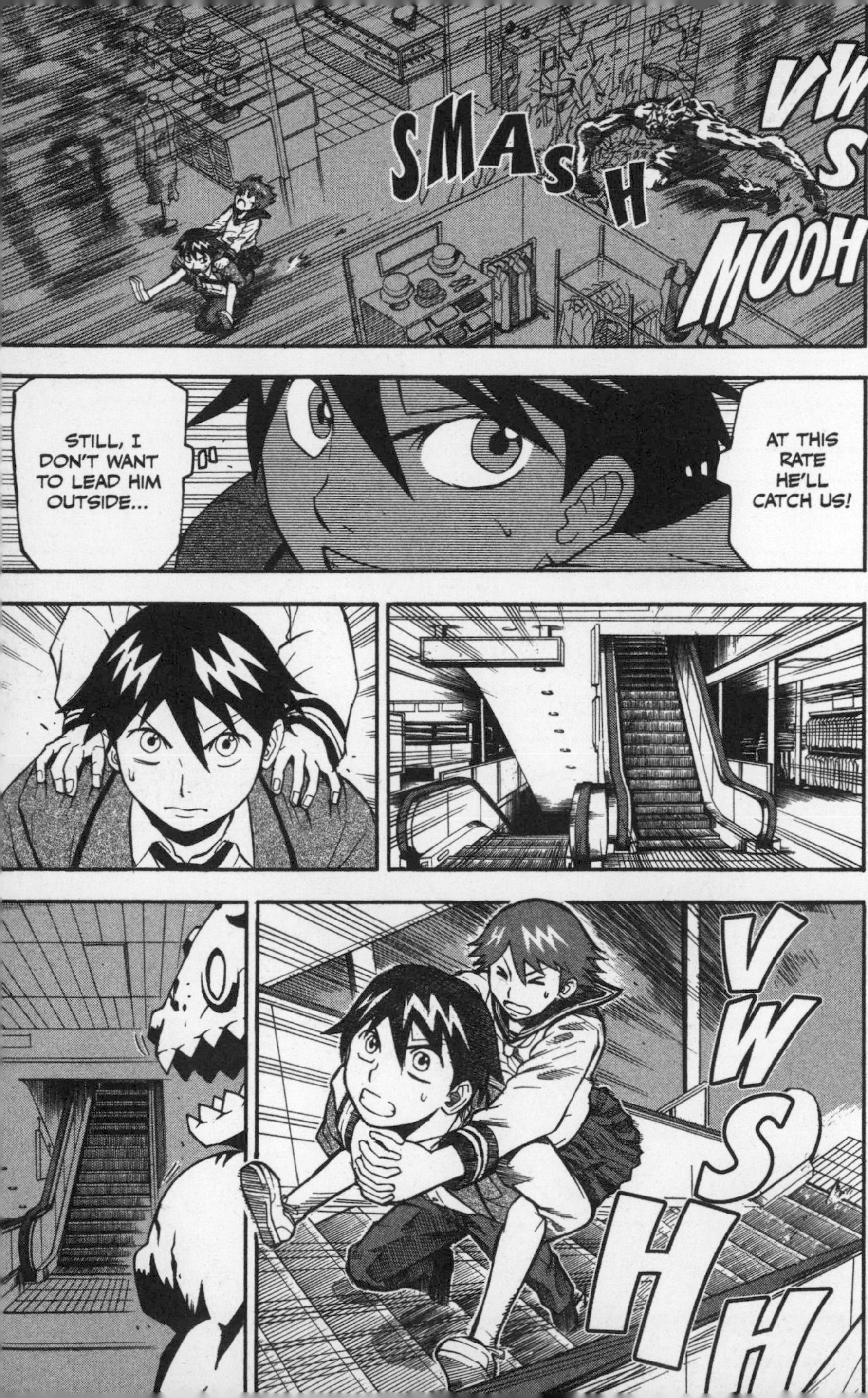
VWS
SMASH
MOOH
AT THIS RATE HE'LL CATCH US!
STILL, I DON'T WANT TO LEAD HIM OUTSIDE...
VWSHH

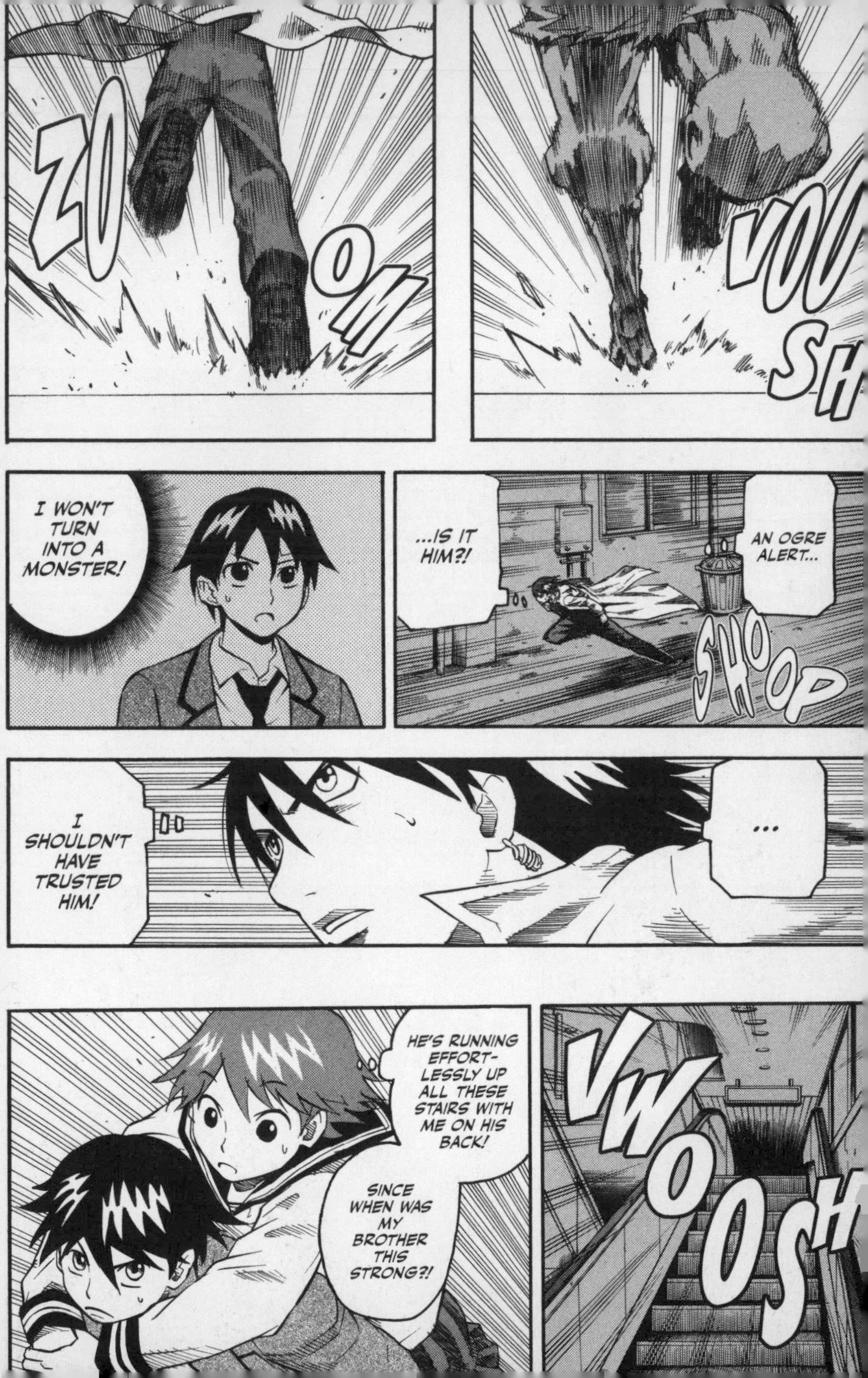
VOOSH
ZOOM
AN OGRE ALERT...
...IS IT HIM?!
SHOOP
I WON'T TURN INTO A MONSTER!
...
I SHOULDN'T HAVE TRUSTED HIM!
VWOOSH
HE'S RUNNING EFFORT-LESSLY UP ALL THESE STAIRS WITH ME ON HIS BACK!
SINCE WHEN WAS MY BROTHER THIS STRONG?!

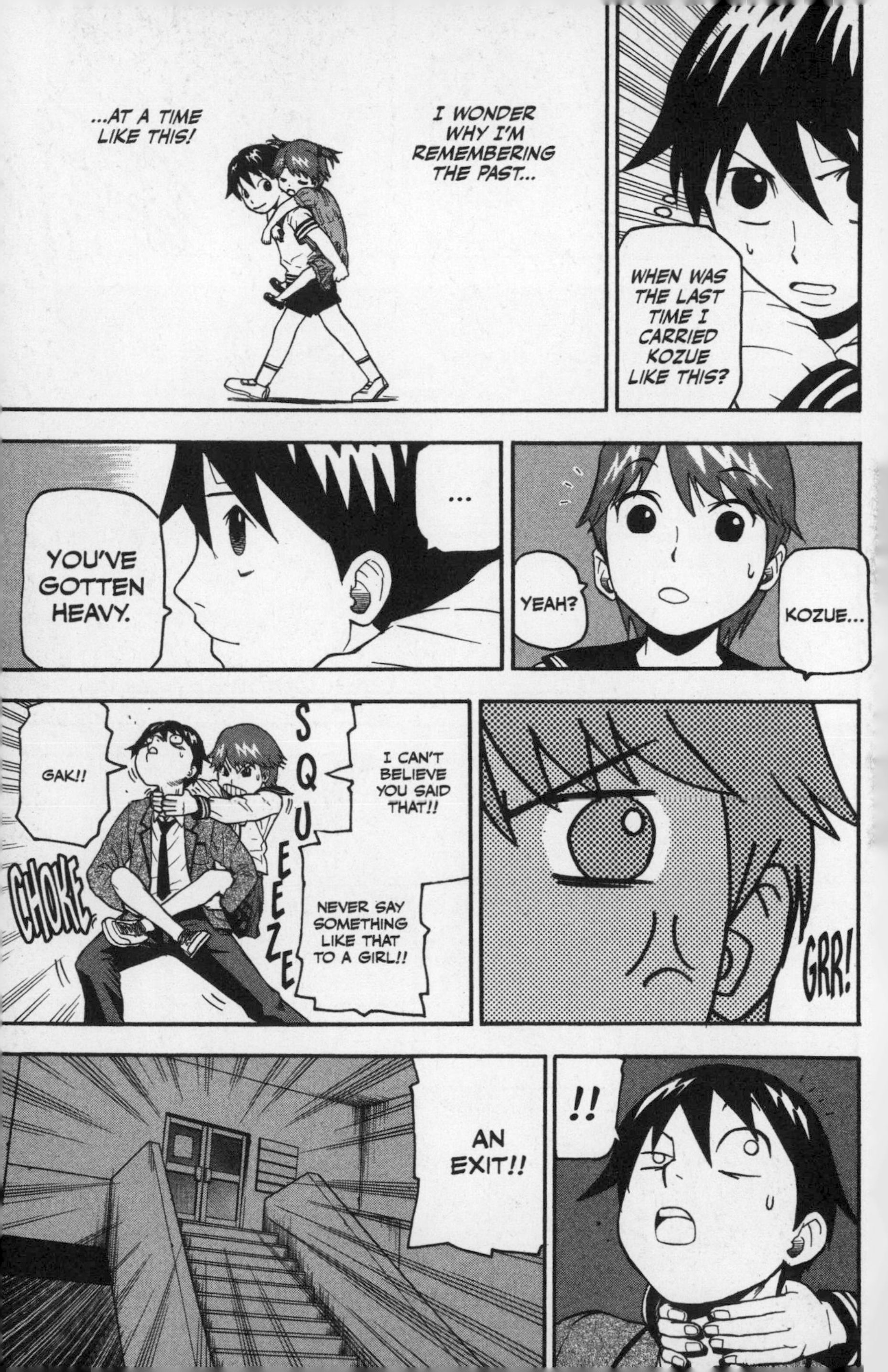
WHEN WAS THE LAST TIME I CARRIED KOZUE LIKE THIS?
I WONDER WHY I'M REMEMBERING THE PAST...
...AT A TIME LIKE THIS!
KOZUE...
YEAH?
...
YOU'VE GOTTEN HEAVY.
GRR!
I CAN'T BELIEVE YOU SAID THAT!!
NEVER SAY SOMETHING LIKE THAT TO A GIRL!!
SQUEEZE
GAK!!
CHOKE
!!
AN EXIT!!

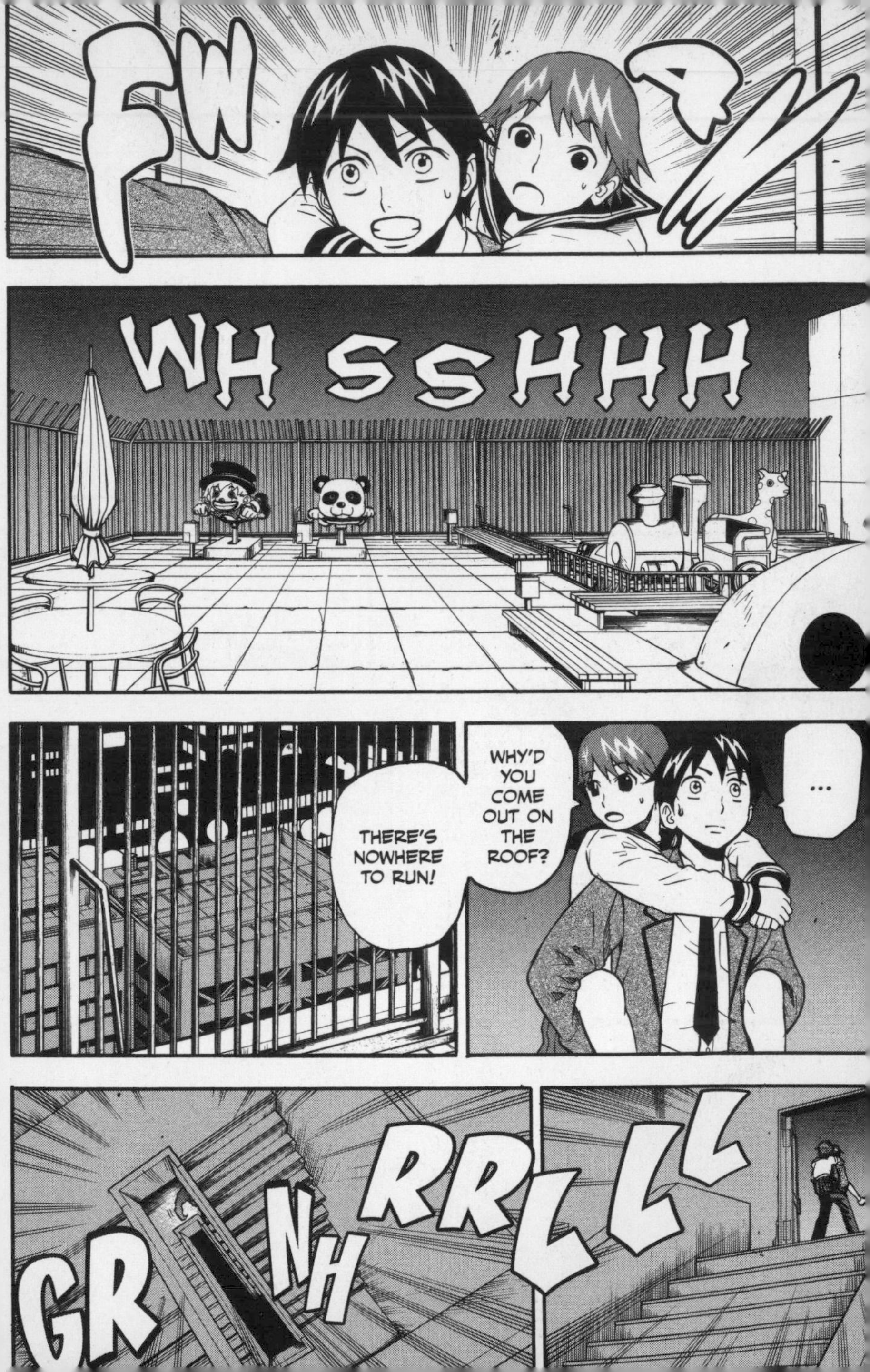
FWAY
WH SSHHH
...
WHY'D YOU COME OUT ON THE ROOF?
THERE'S NOWHERE TO RUN!
GRNH RRLLL

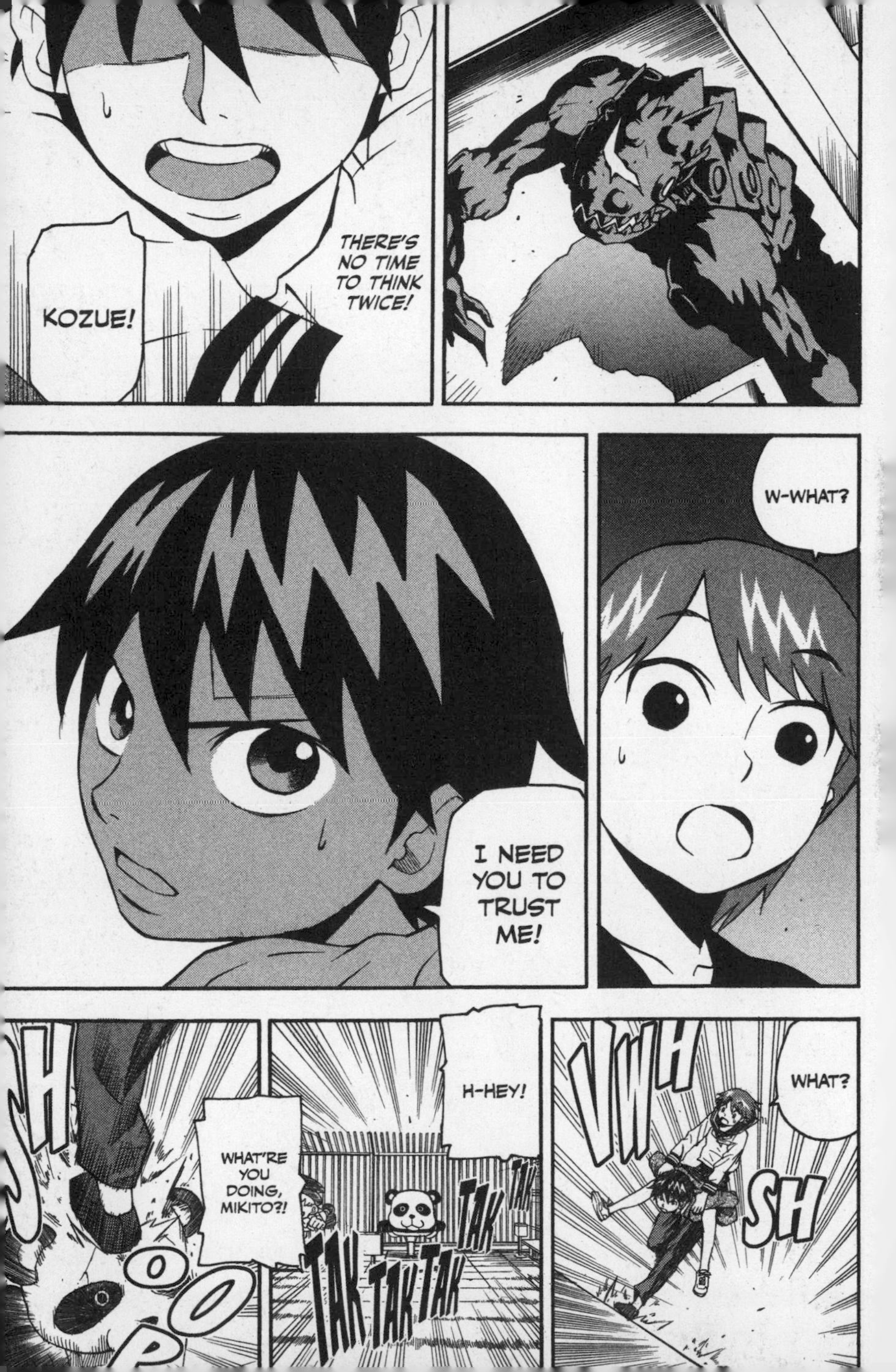
THERE'S NO TIME TO THINK TWICE!
KOZUE!
W-WHAT?
I NEED YOU TO TRUST ME!
WHAT?
VWH
SH
H-HEY!
TAK TAK
WHAT'RE YOU DOING, MIKITO?!
TAK TAK TAK TAK

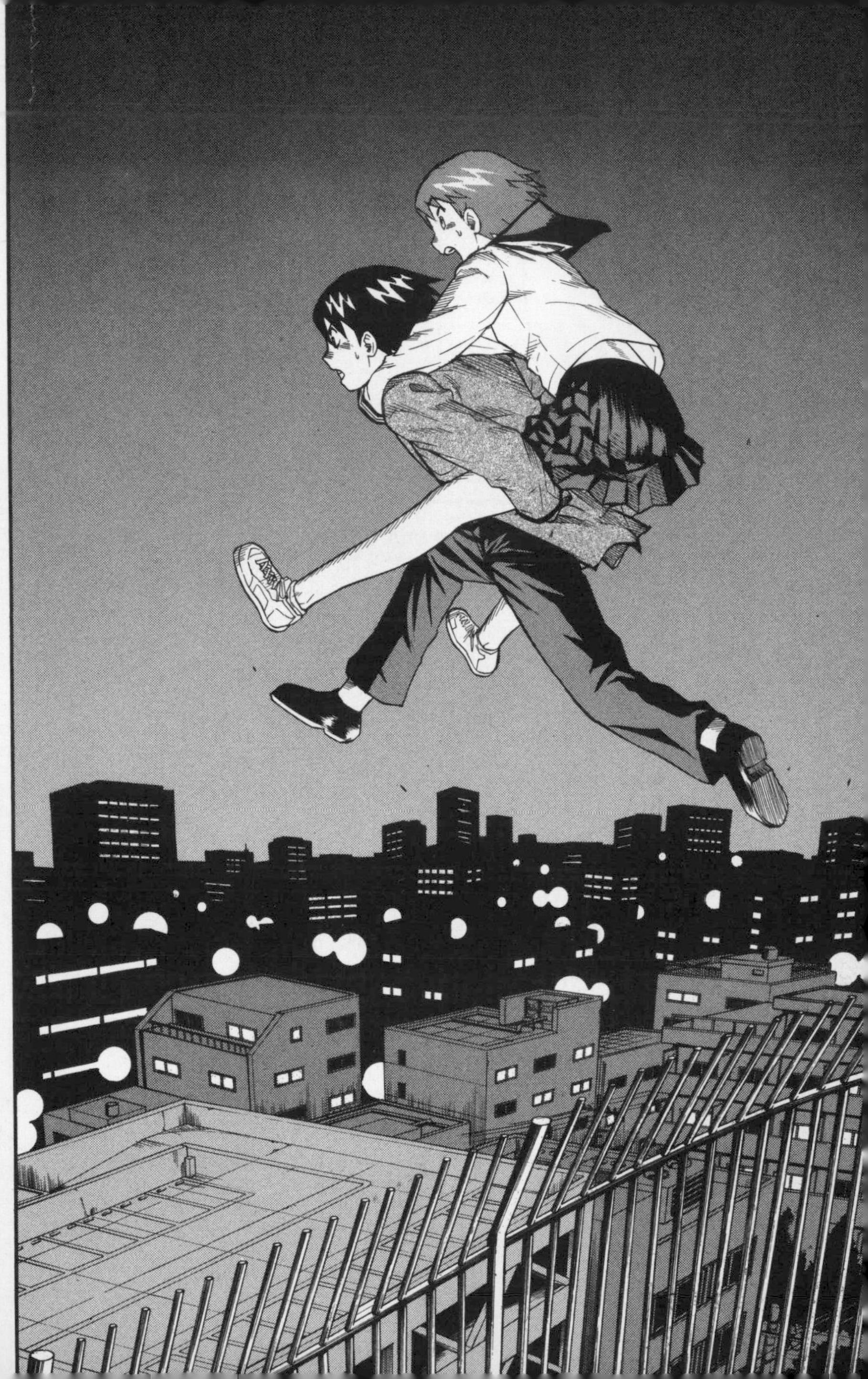

EEEEEEK!!
WHUMP!

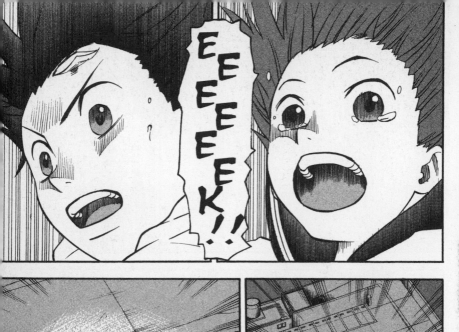

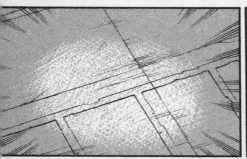

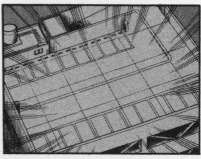

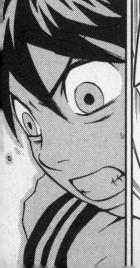

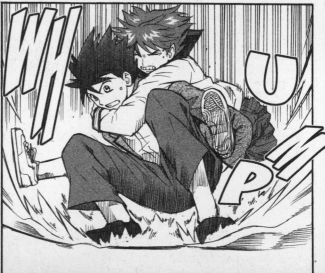

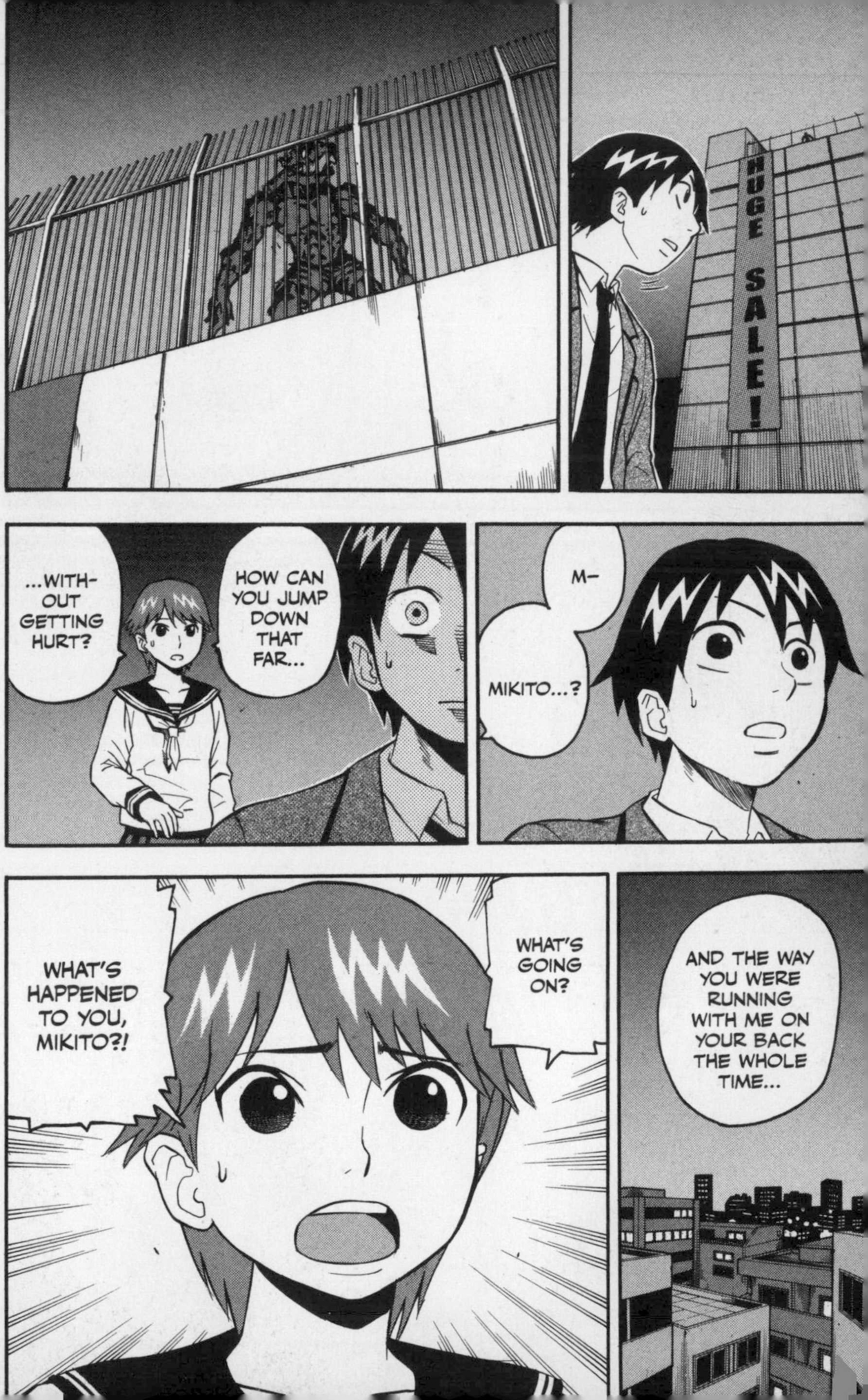
HUGE SALE!
M—
MIKITO...?
HOW CAN YOU JUMP DOWN THAT FAR...
...WITH-OUT GETTING HURT?
AND THE WAY YOU WERE RUNNING WITH ME ON YOUR BACK THE WHOLE TIME...
WHAT'S GOING ON?
WHAT'S HAPPENED TO YOU, MIKITO?!

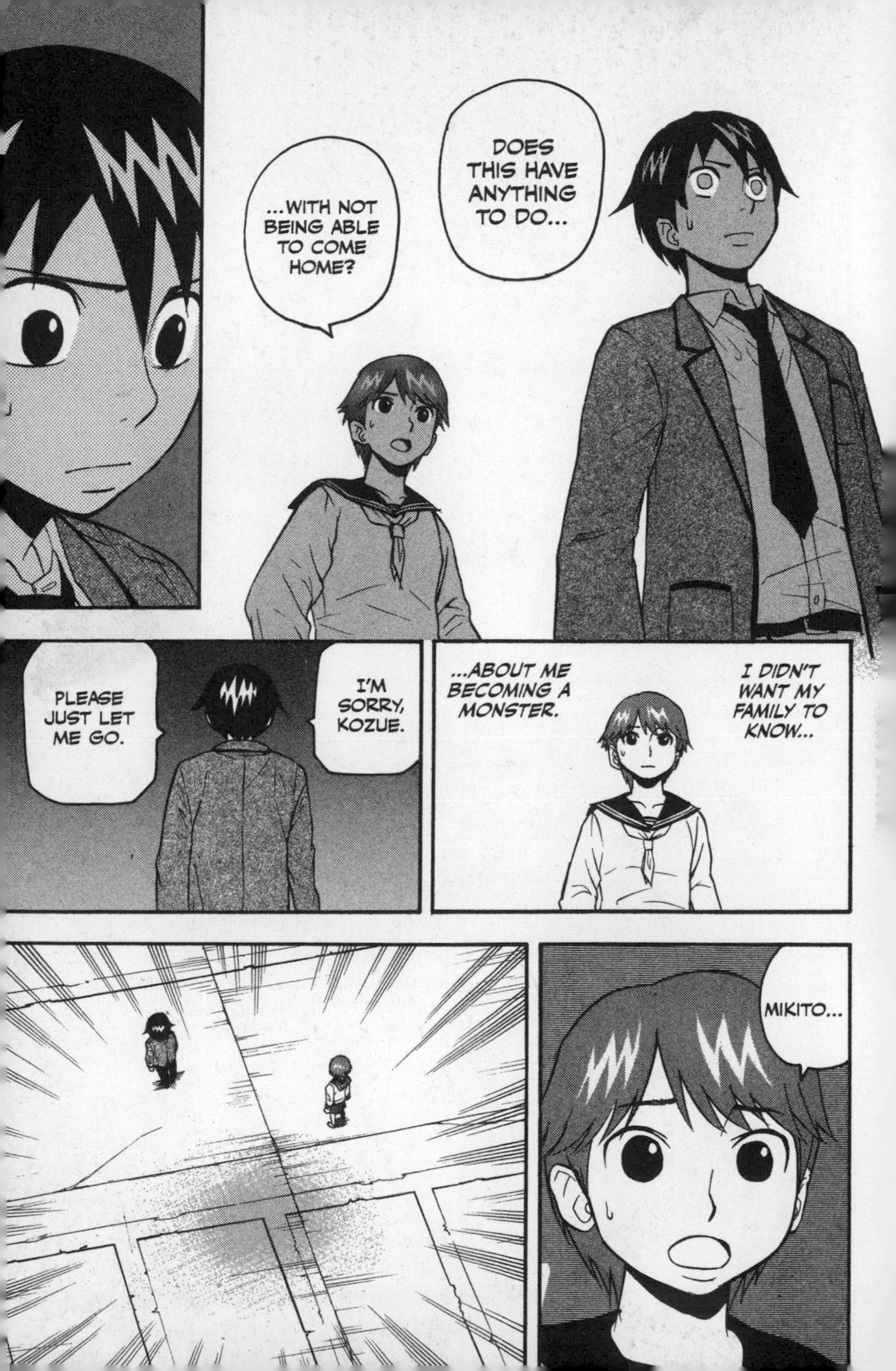
DOES THIS HAVE ANYTHING TO DO...
...WITH NOT BEING ABLE TO COME HOME?
I DIDN'T WANT MY FAMILY TO KNOW...
...ABOUT ME BECOMING A MONSTER.
I'M SORRY, KOZUE.
PLEASE JUST LET ME GO.
MIKITO...

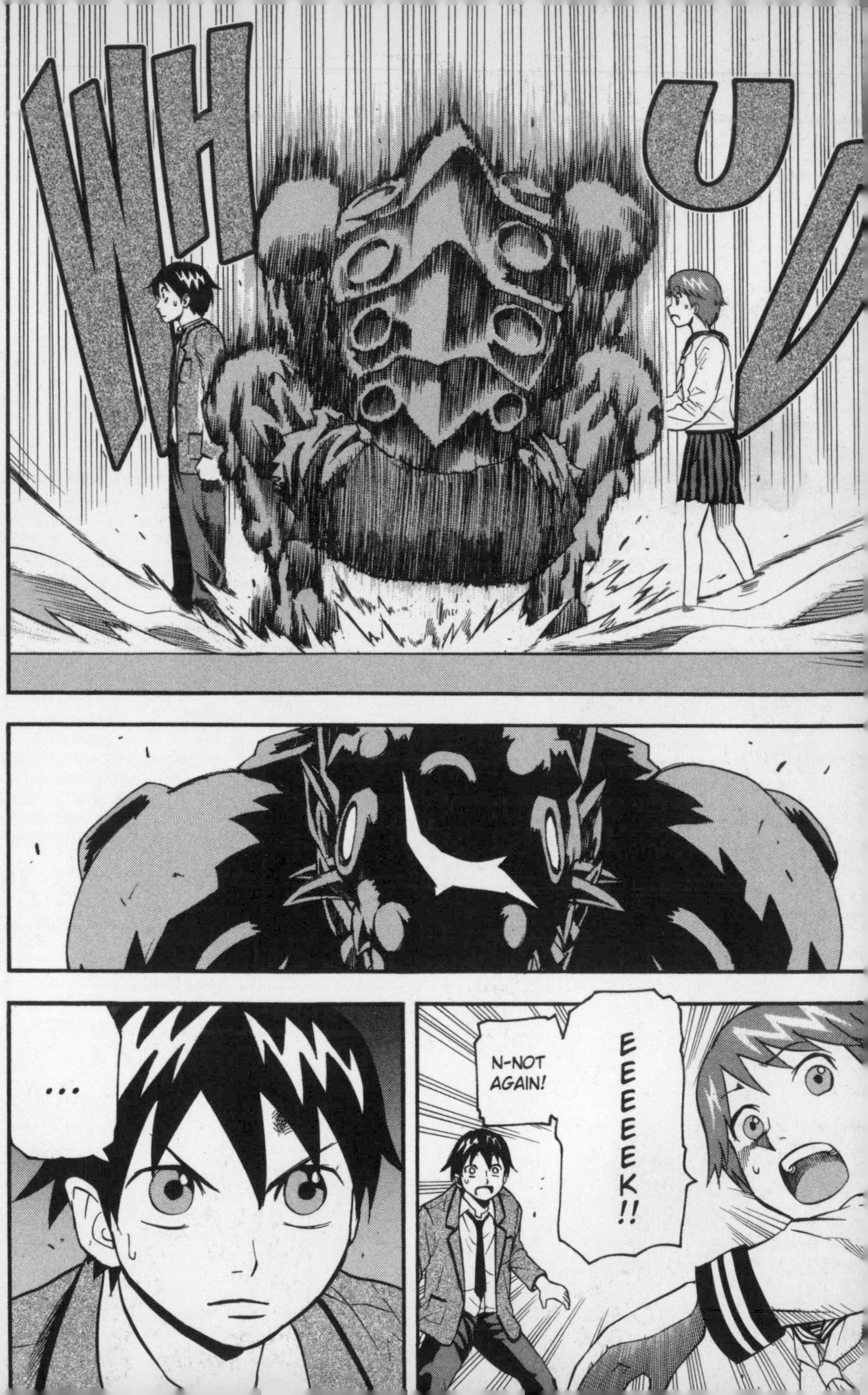
WHUV
N-NOT AGAIN!
EEEEEEK!!
...

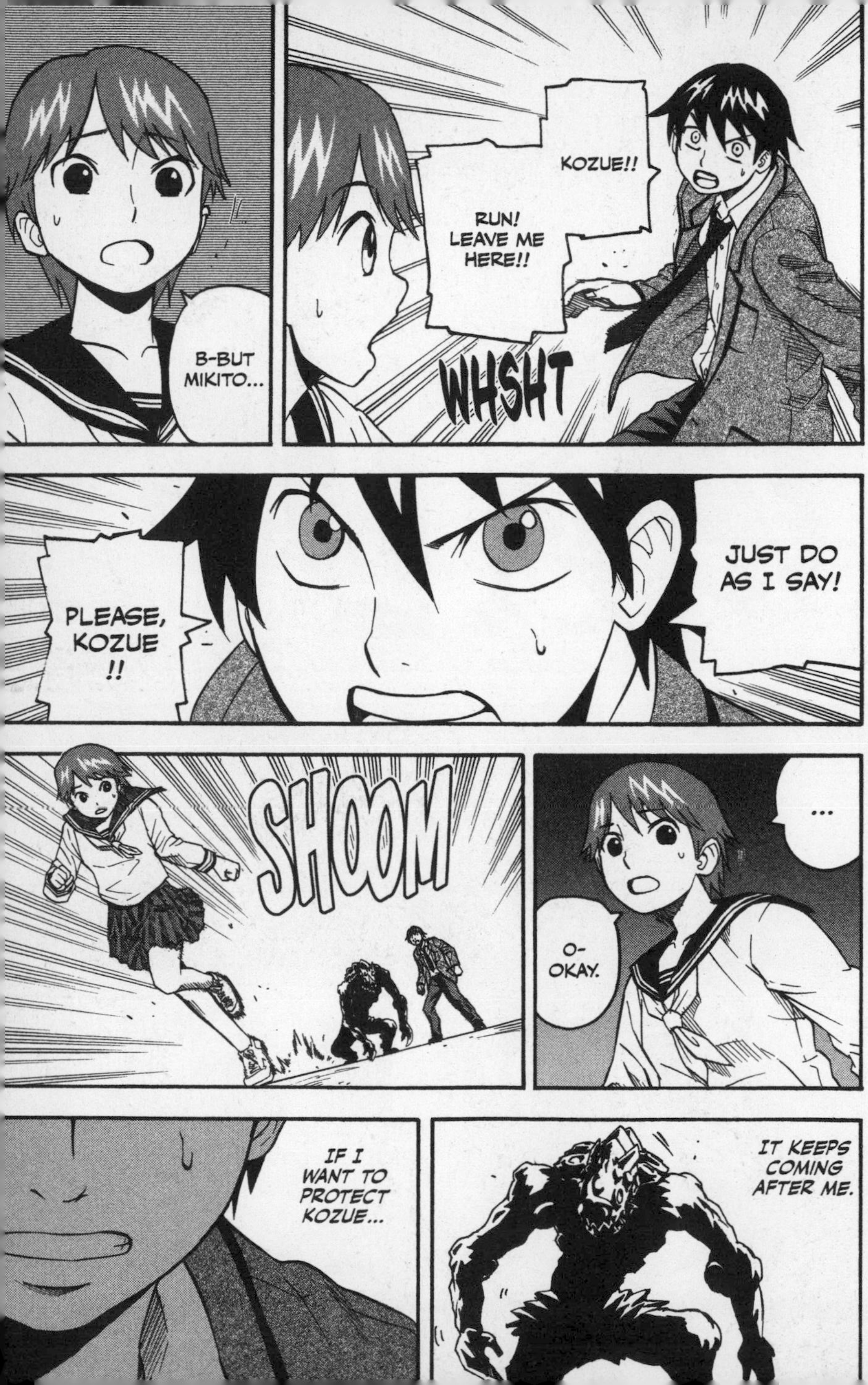
KOZUE!!
RUN! LEAVE ME HERE!!
WHSHT
B-BUT MIKITO...
JUST DO AS I SAY!
PLEASE, KOZUE !!
...
O-OKAY.
SHOOM
IT KEEPS COMING AFTER ME.
IF I WANT TO PROTECT KOZUE...

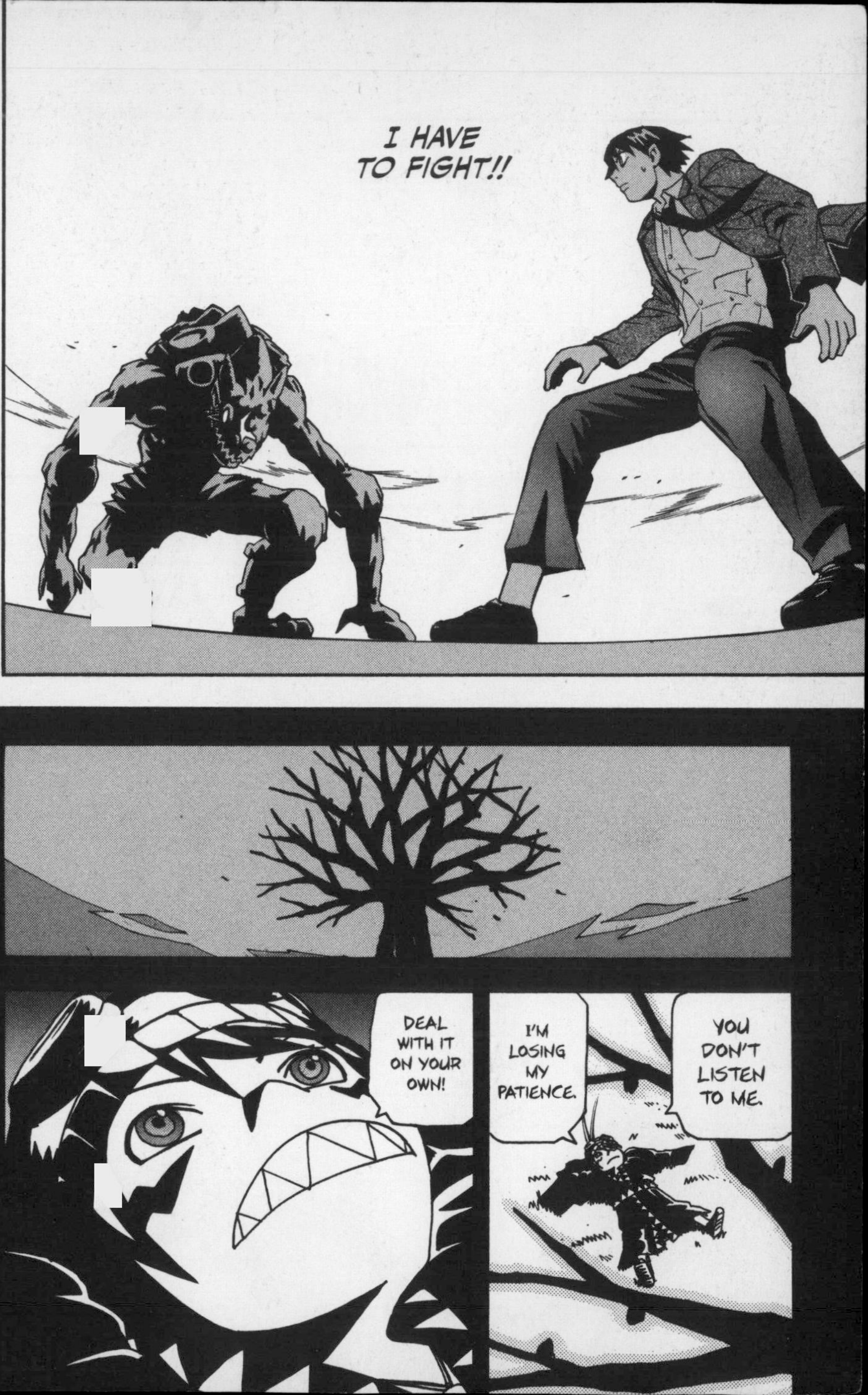
I HAVE TO FIGHT!!
YOU DON'T LISTEN TO ME.
I'M LOSING MY PATIENCE.
DEAL WITH IT ON YOUR OWN!

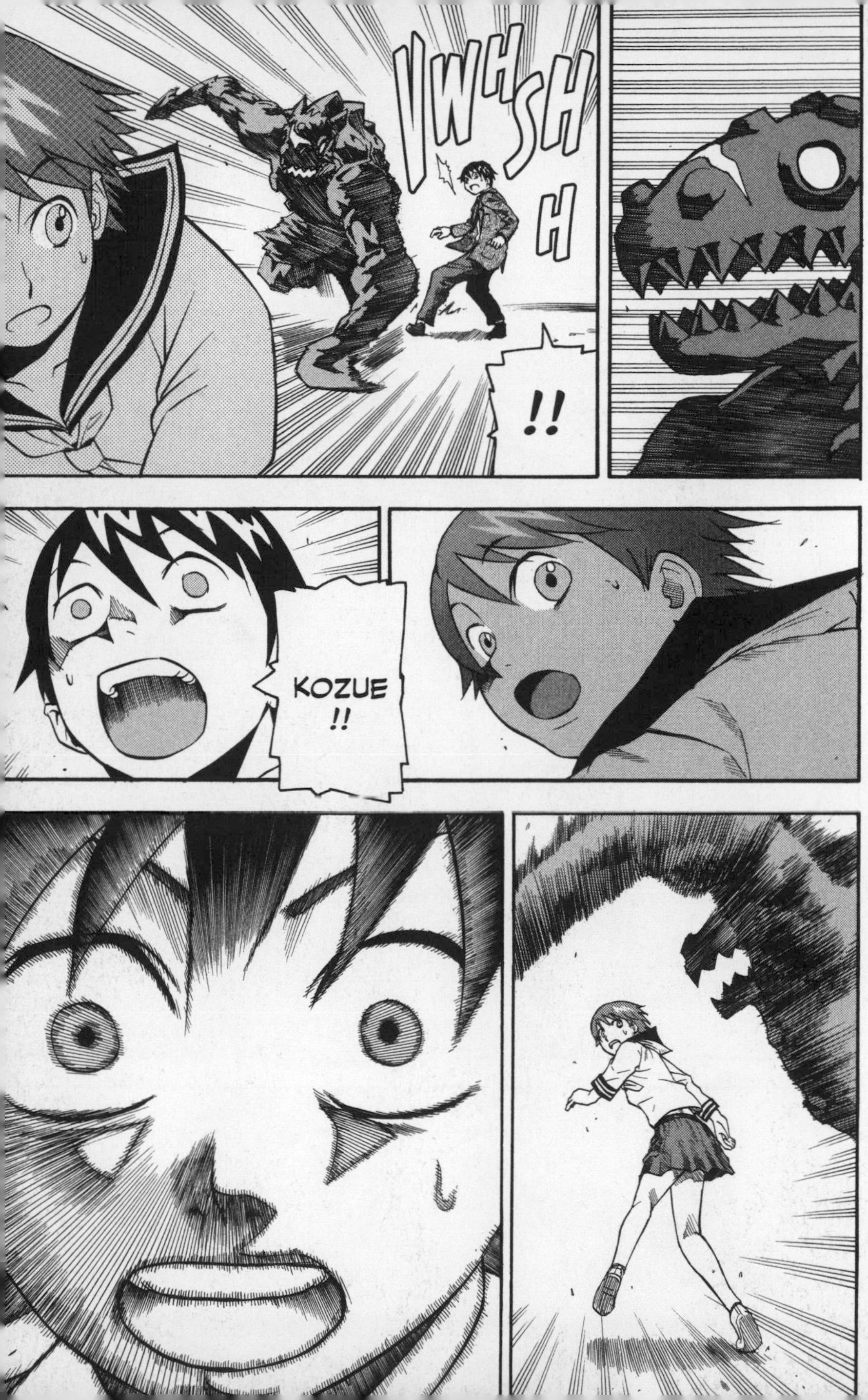
!!
VWHSH
H
KOZUE !!

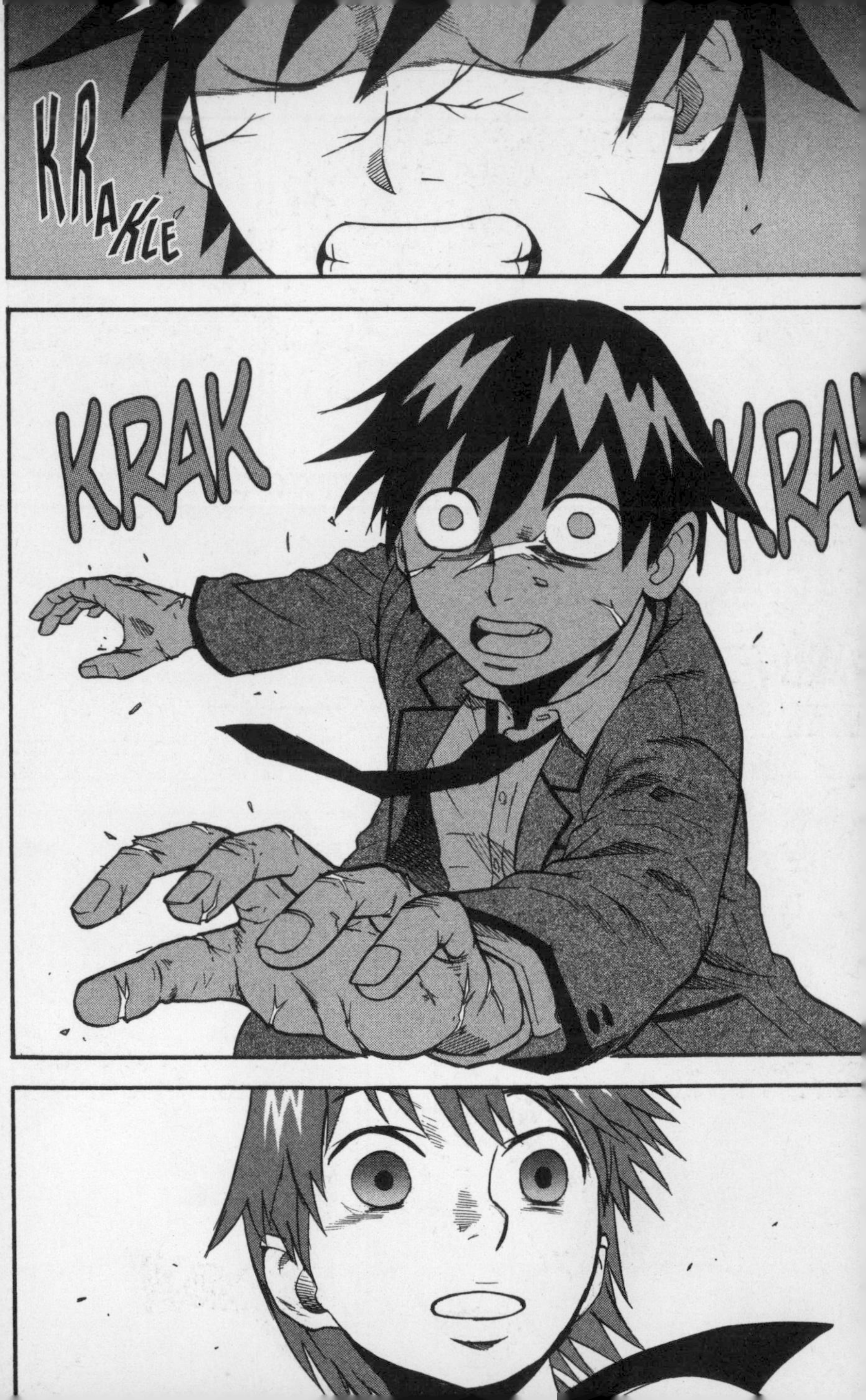
KRAKLE
KRA
KRAK

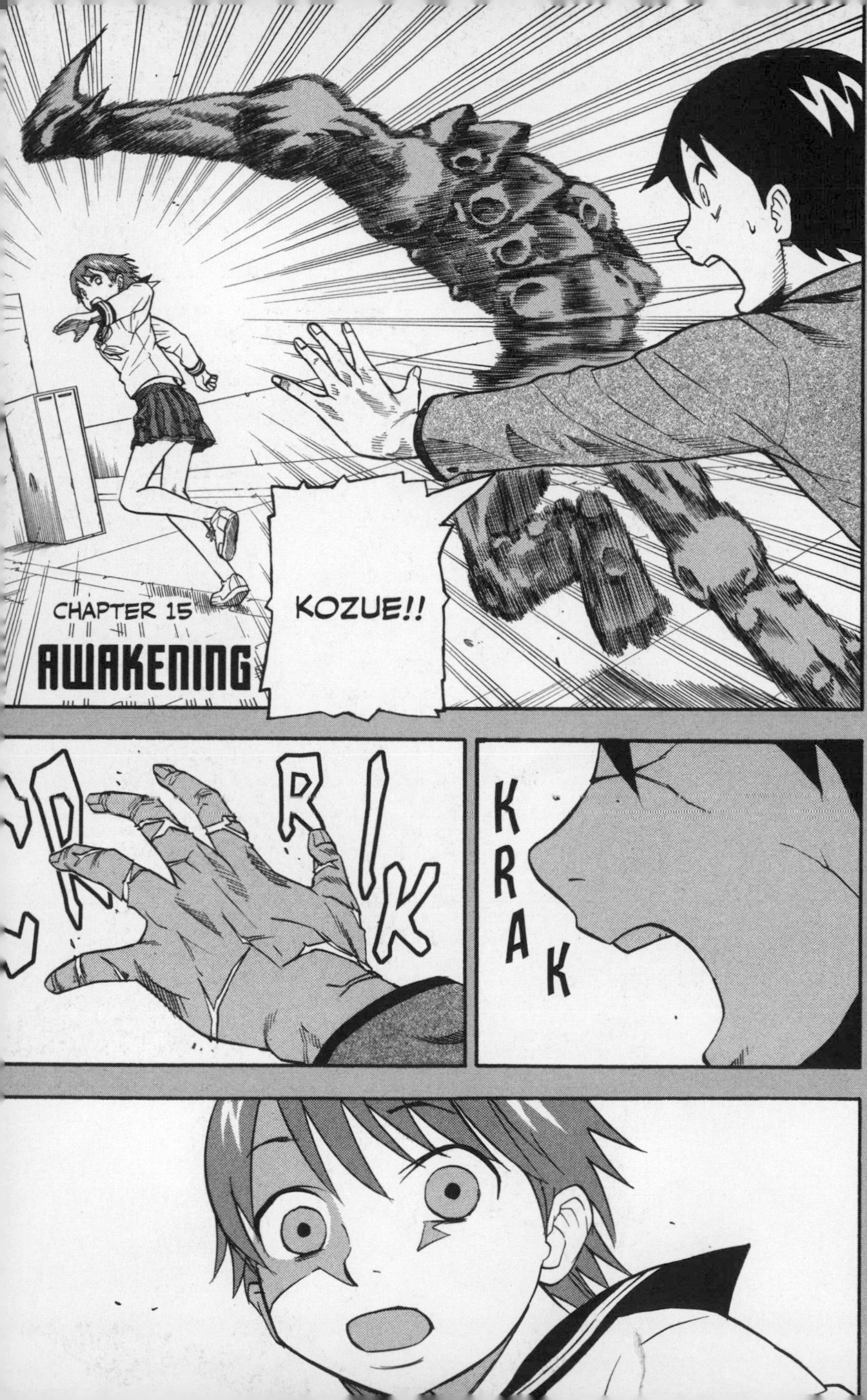
KOZUE!!
CHAPTER 15
AWAKENING
KRAK
CRIK

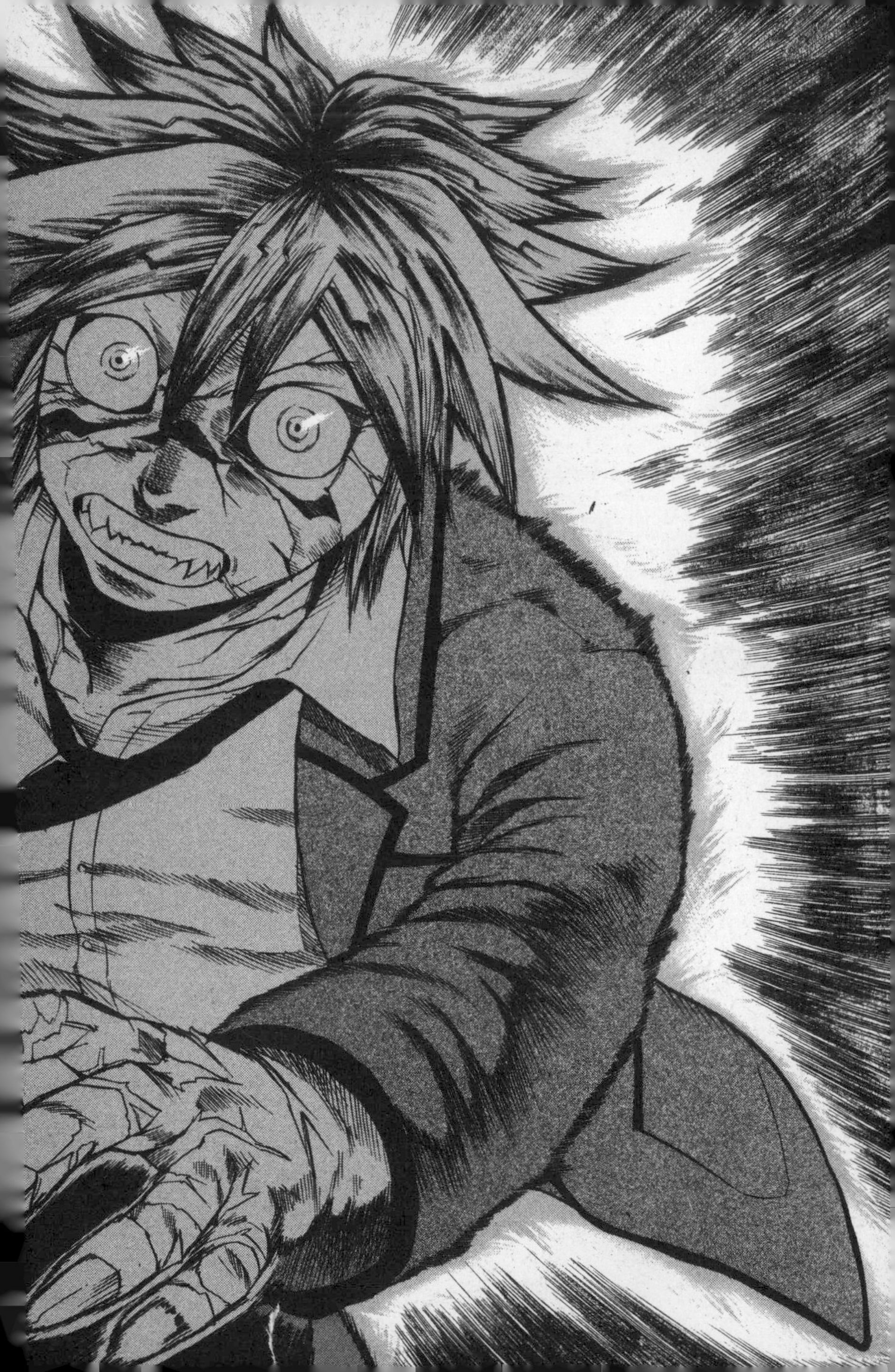

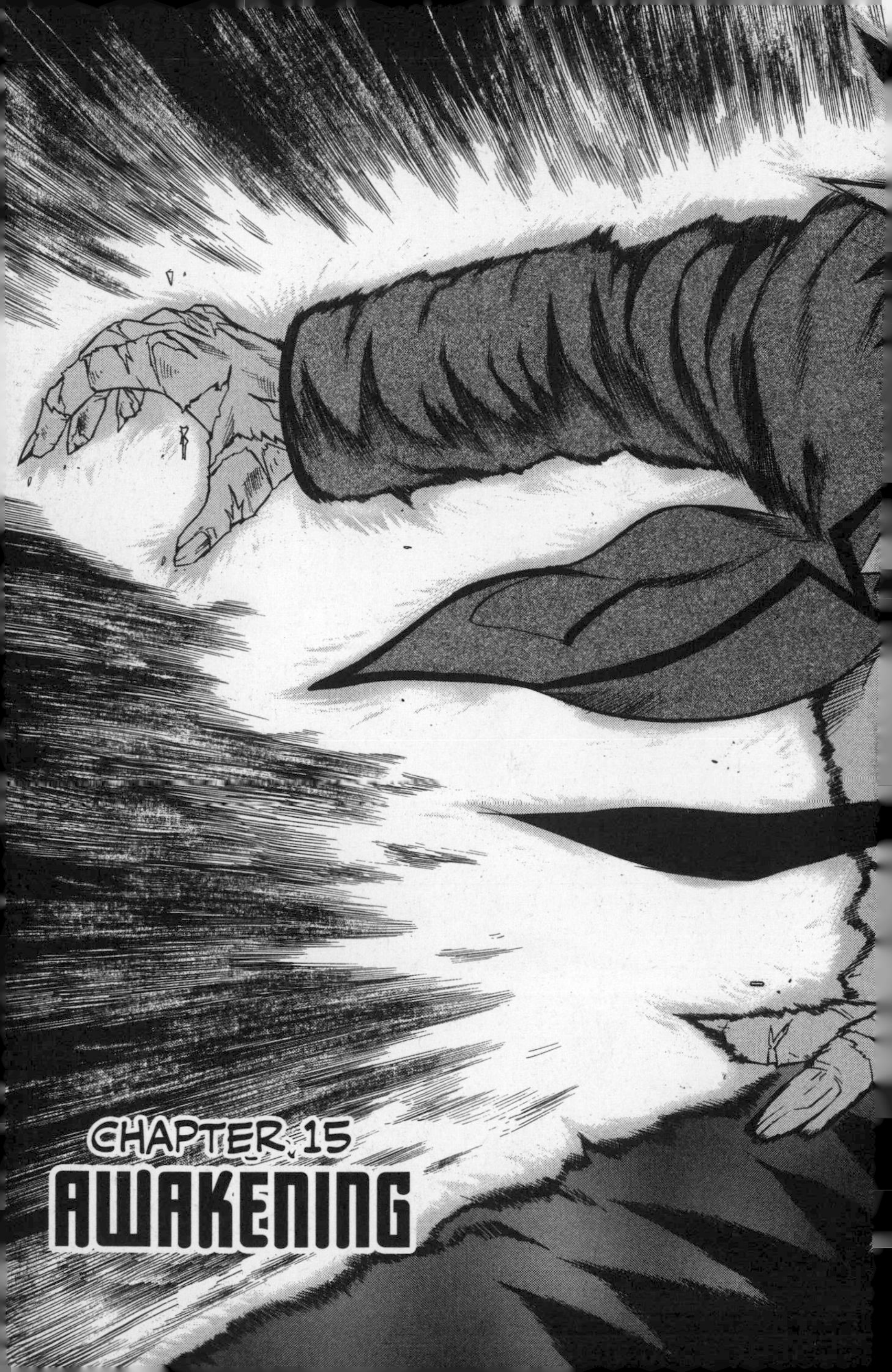

CHAPTER 15
AWAKENING

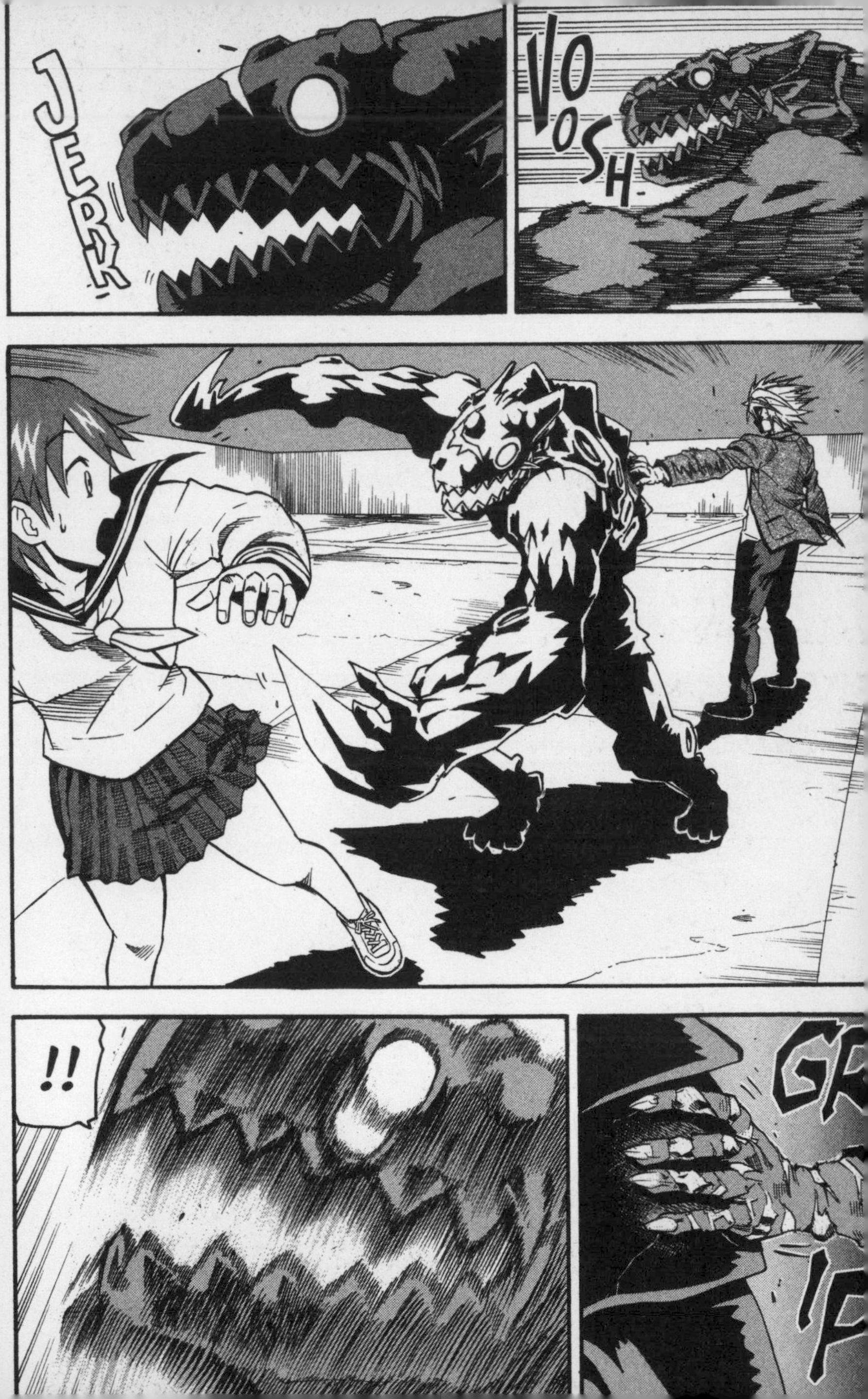
VOOSH
JERK
!!

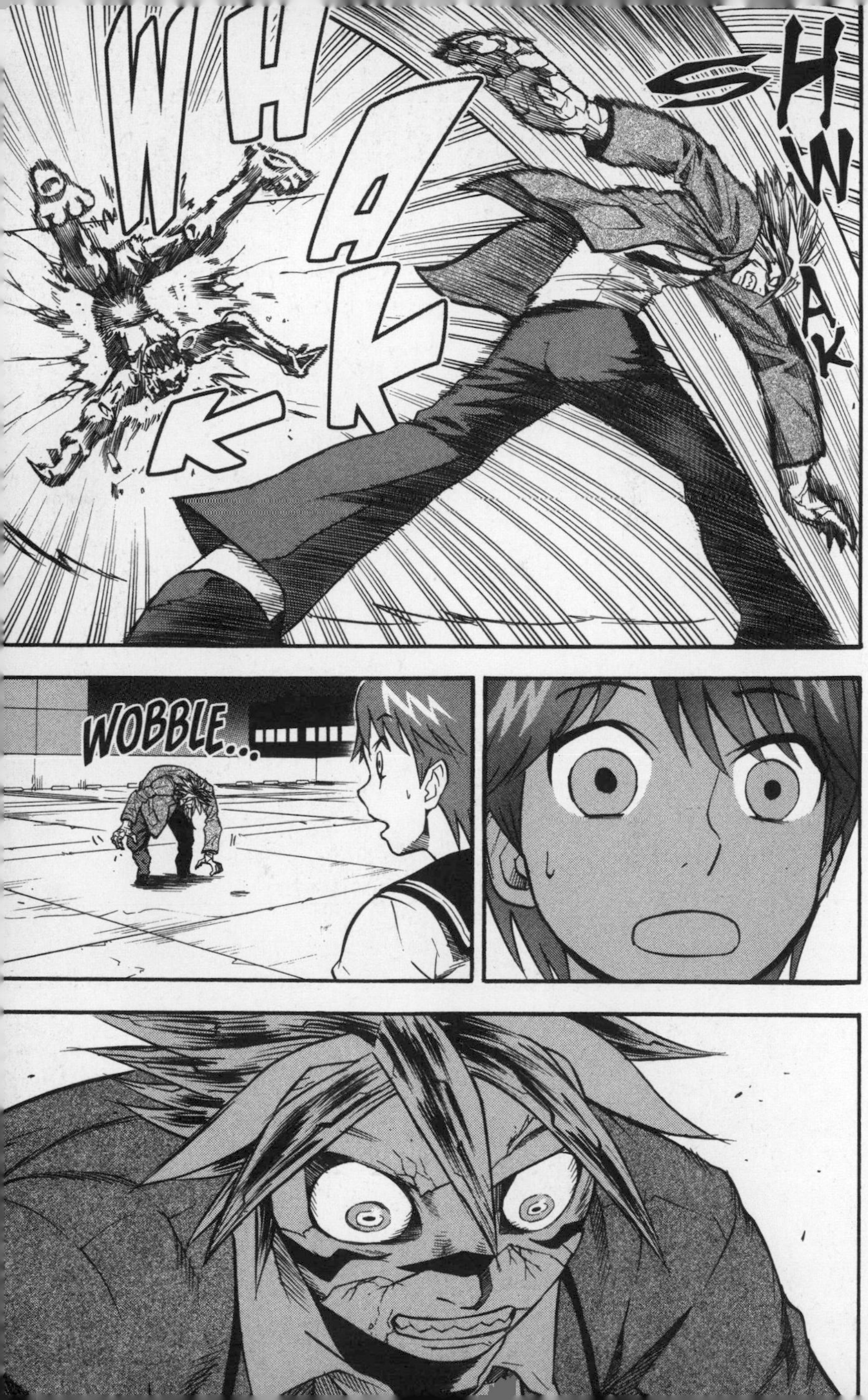
SHWAK
WHAKK
WOBBLE...

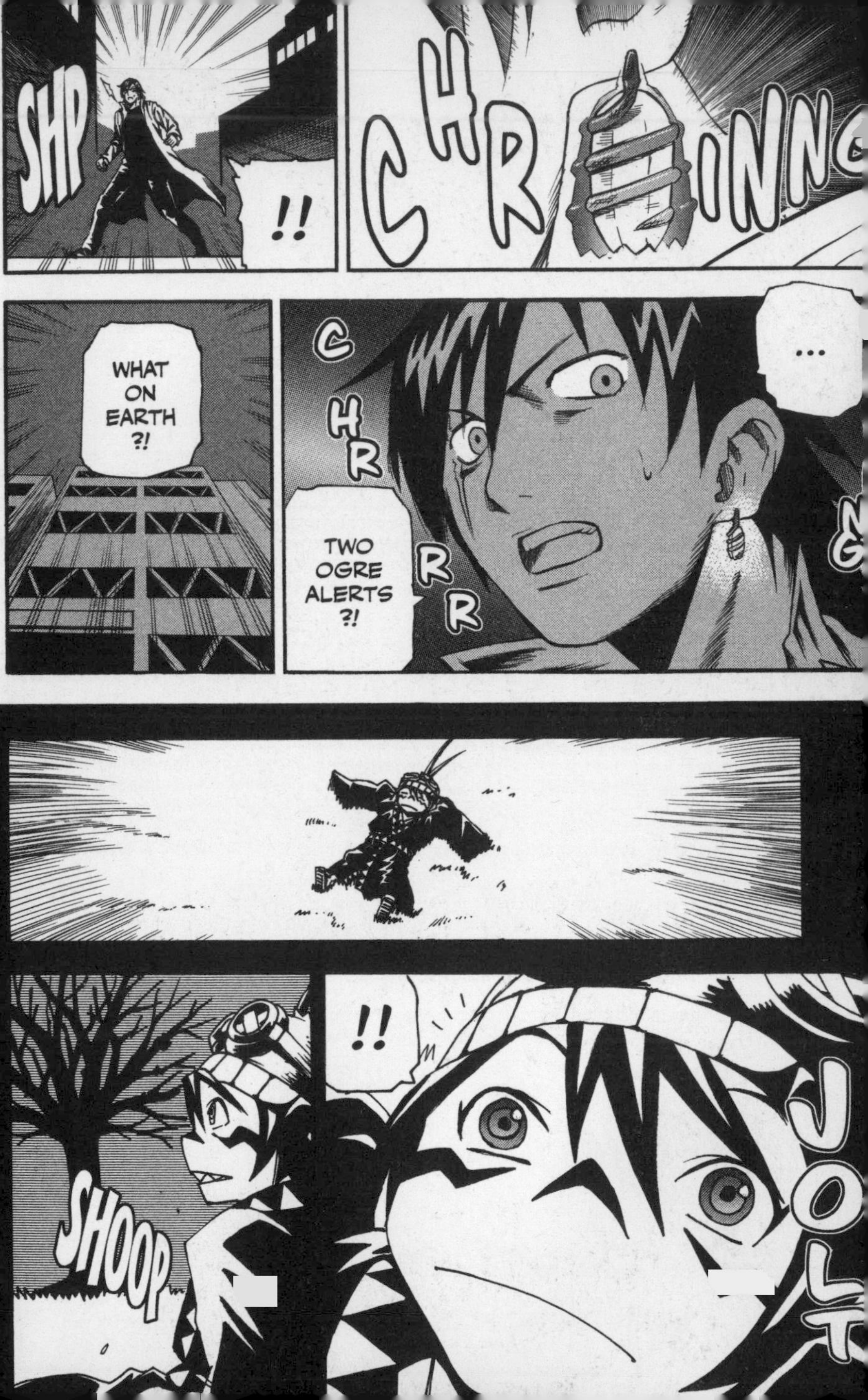
CHRINNG
!!
SHP
...
TWO OGRE ALERTS ?!
CHRRR
NG
WHAT ON EARTH ?!
!!
JOLT
SHOOP

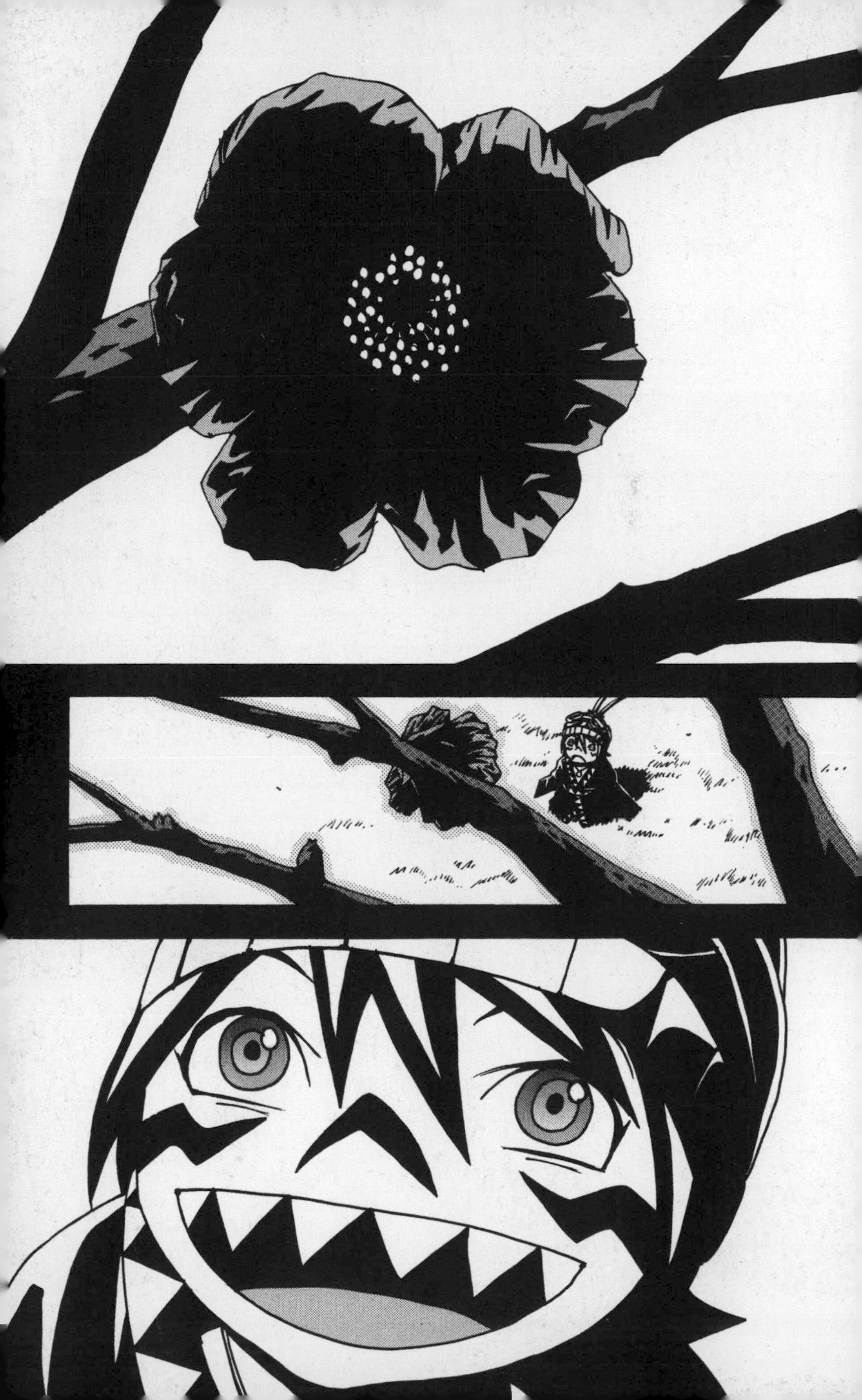

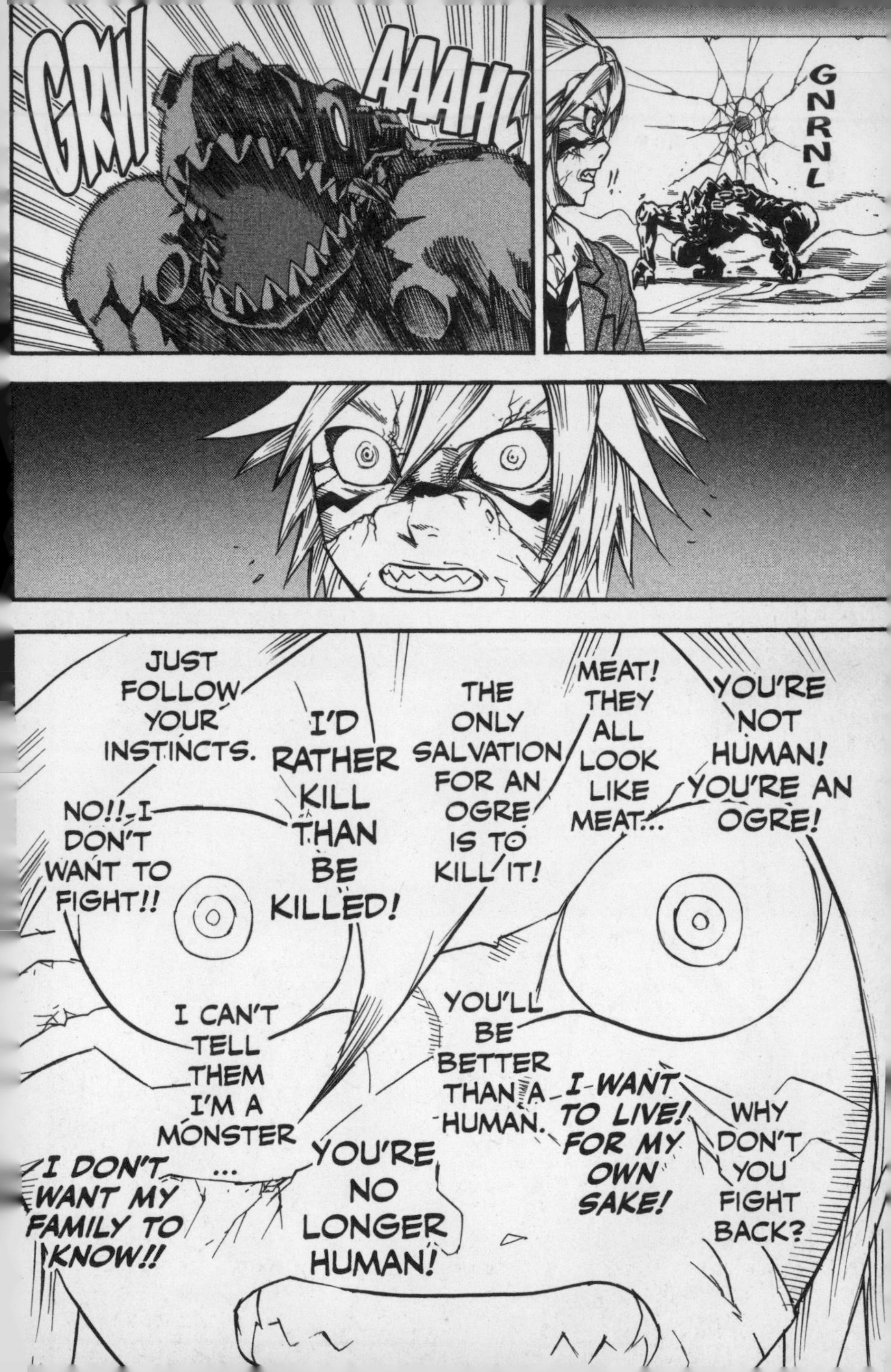
GNRNL
GRW
AAAHL
YOU'RE NOT HUMAN! YOU'RE AN OGRE!
MEAT! THEY ALL LOOK LIKE MEAT...
THE ONLY SALVATION FOR AN OGRE IS TO KILL IT!
I'D RATHER KILL THAN BE KILLED!
JUST FOLLOW YOUR INSTINCTS.
NO!! I DON'T WANT TO FIGHT!!
WHY DON'T YOU FIGHT BACK?
I WANT TO LIVE! FOR MY OWN SAKE!
YOU'LL BE BETTER THAN A HUMAN.
YOU'RE NO LONGER HUMAN!
I CAN'T TELL THEM I'M A MONSTER ...
I DON'T WANT MY FAMILY TO KNOW!!

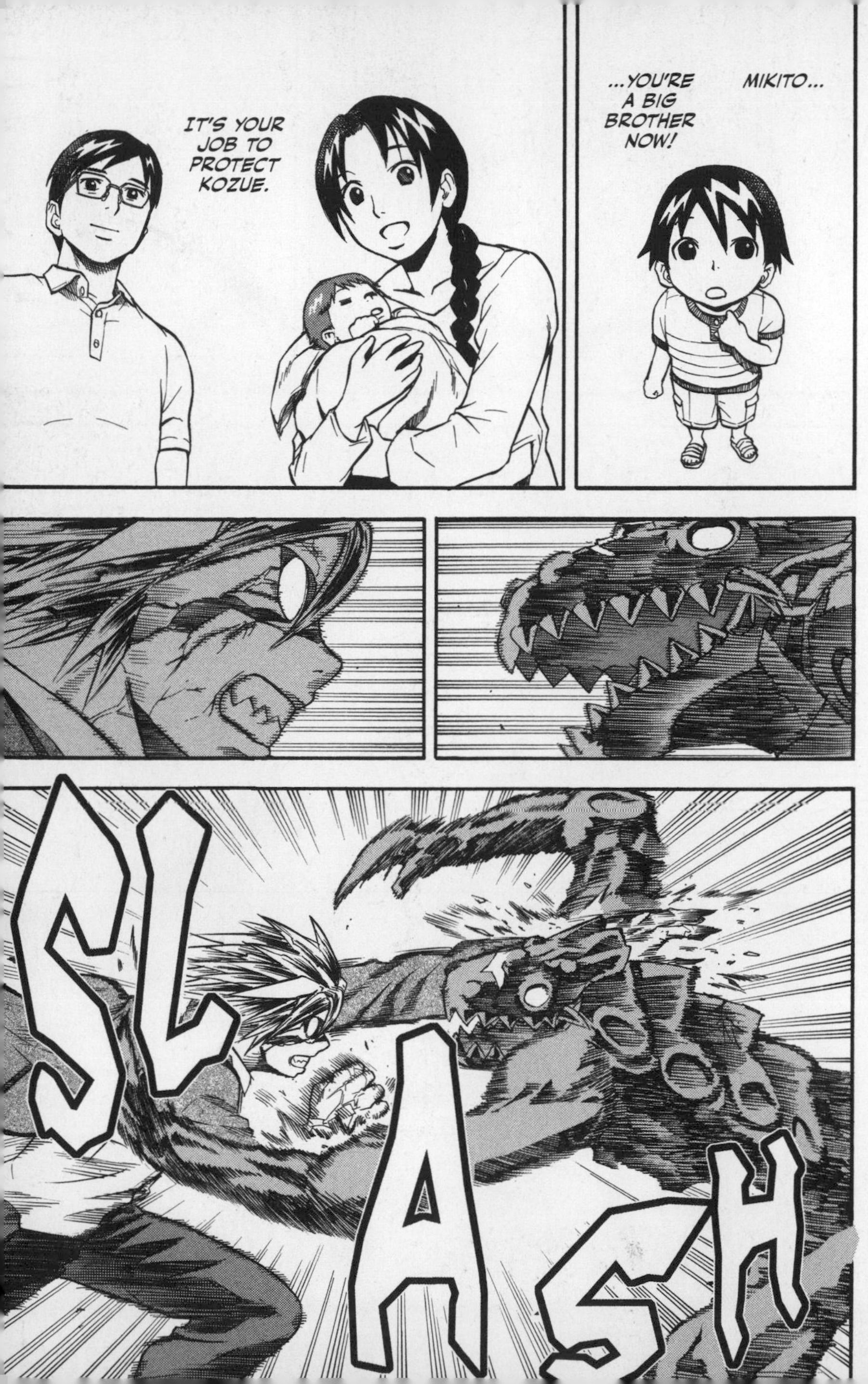
MIKITO...
...YOU'RE A BIG BROTHER NOW!
IT'S YOUR JOB TO PROTECT KOZUE.
SLASH

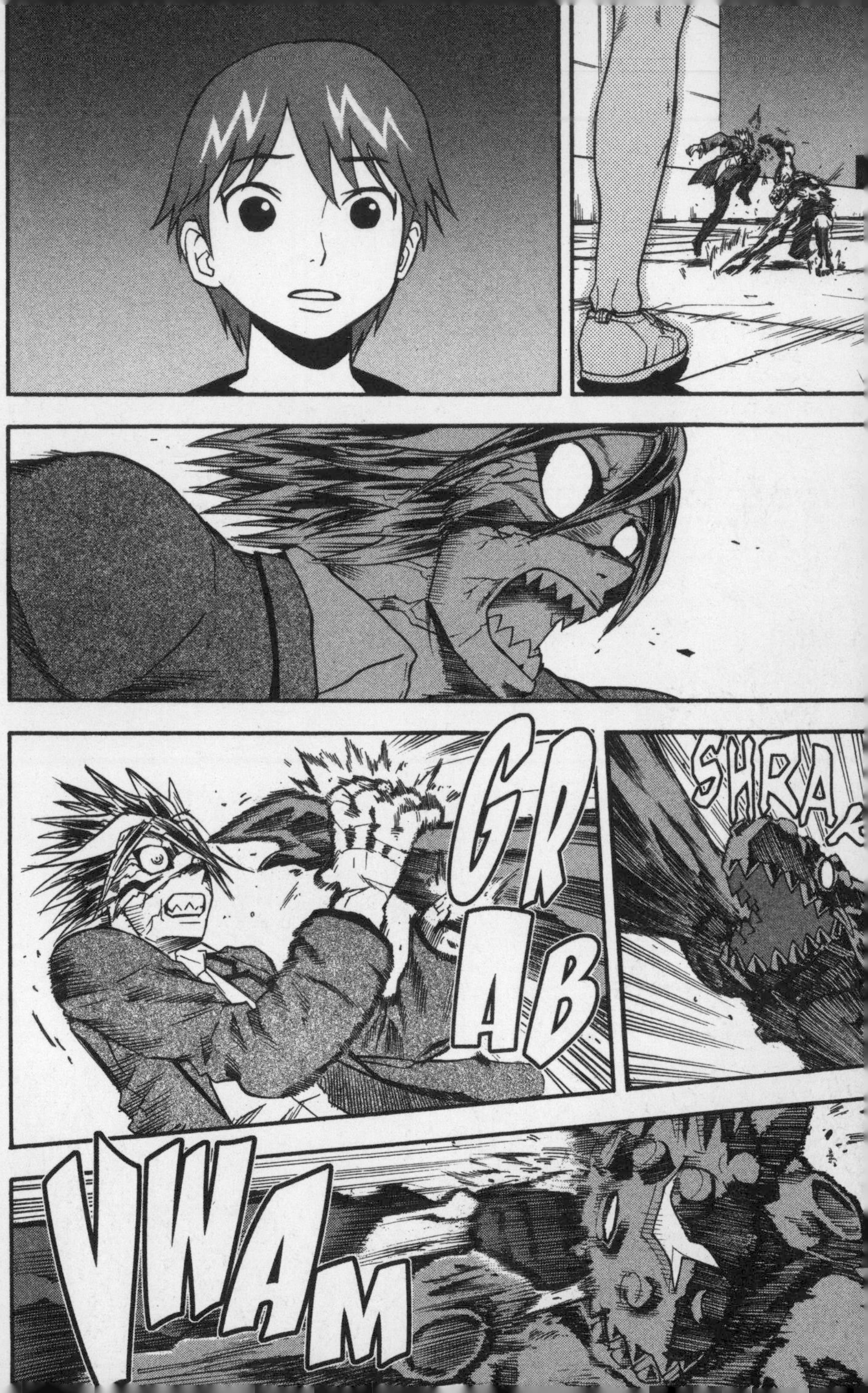
SHRA
GRAB
VWAM

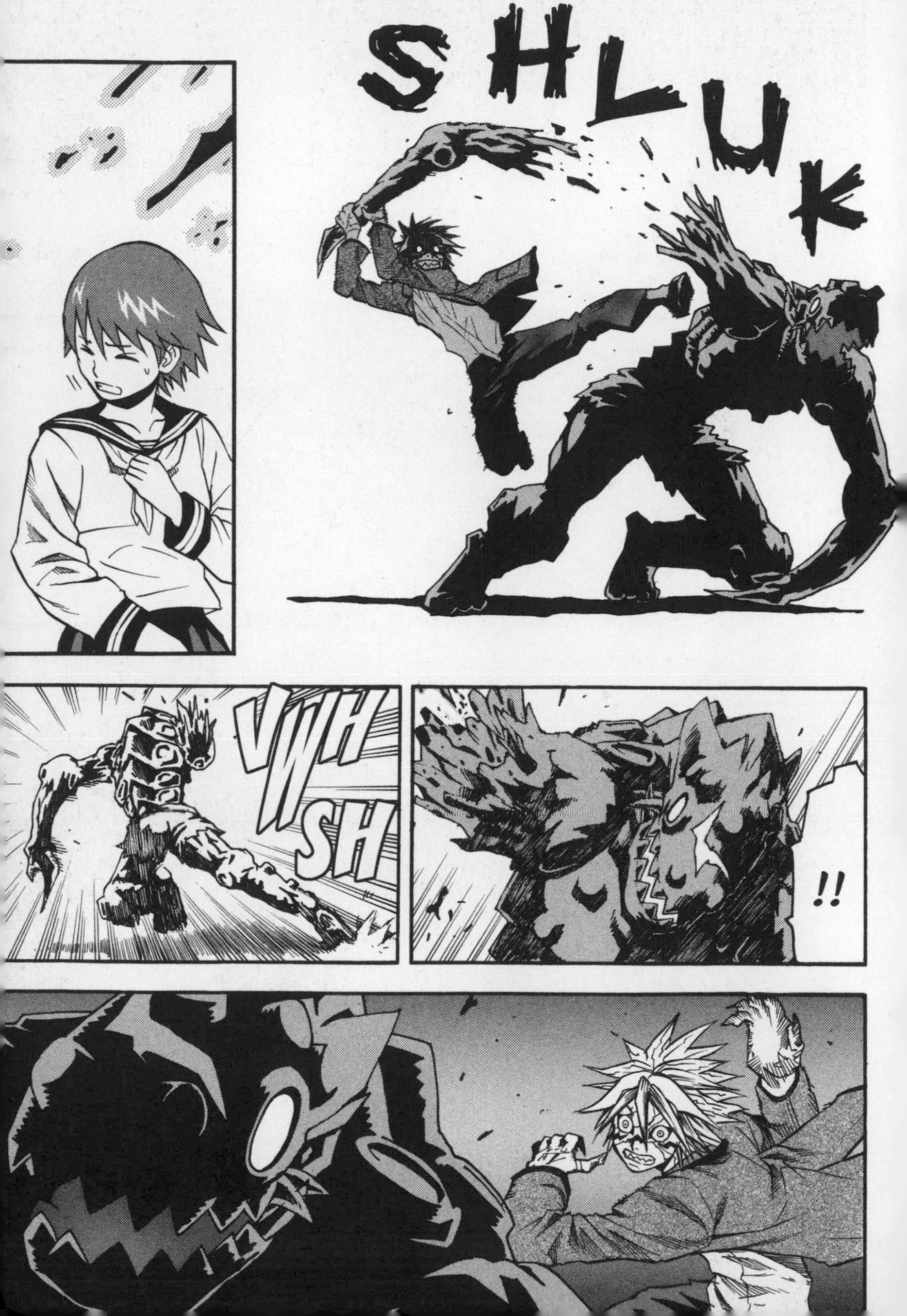
SHLUK
!!
VWHISH

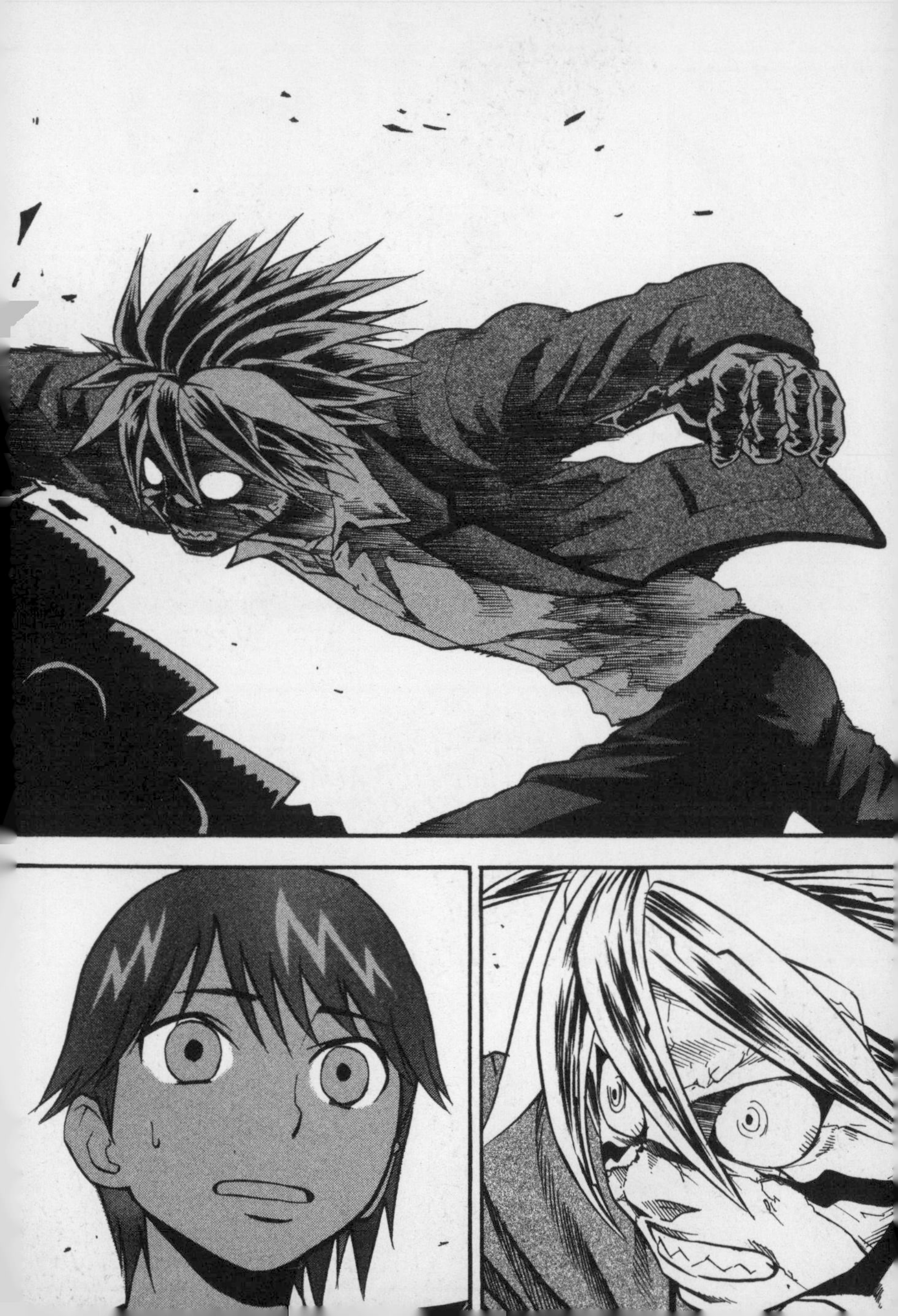

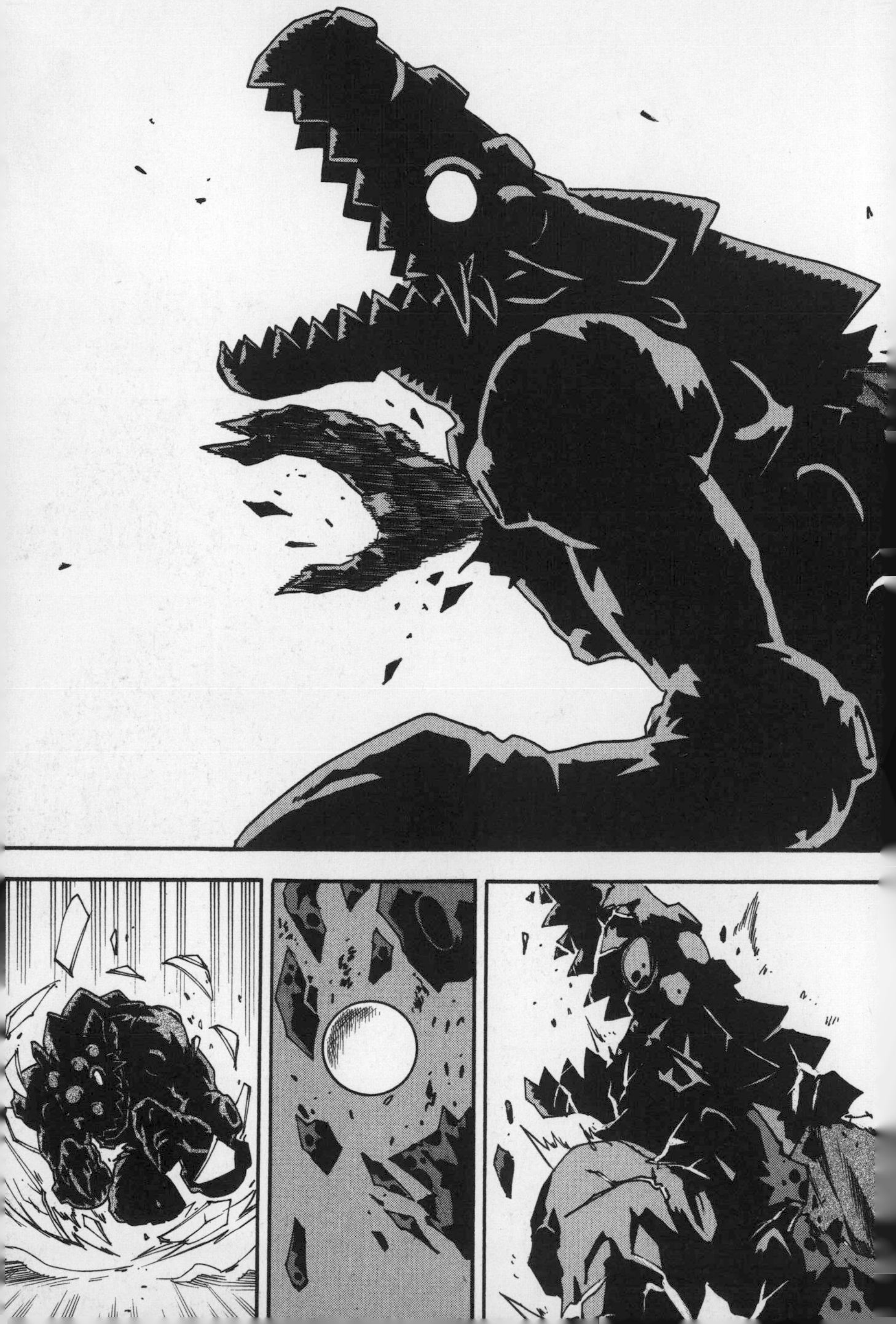

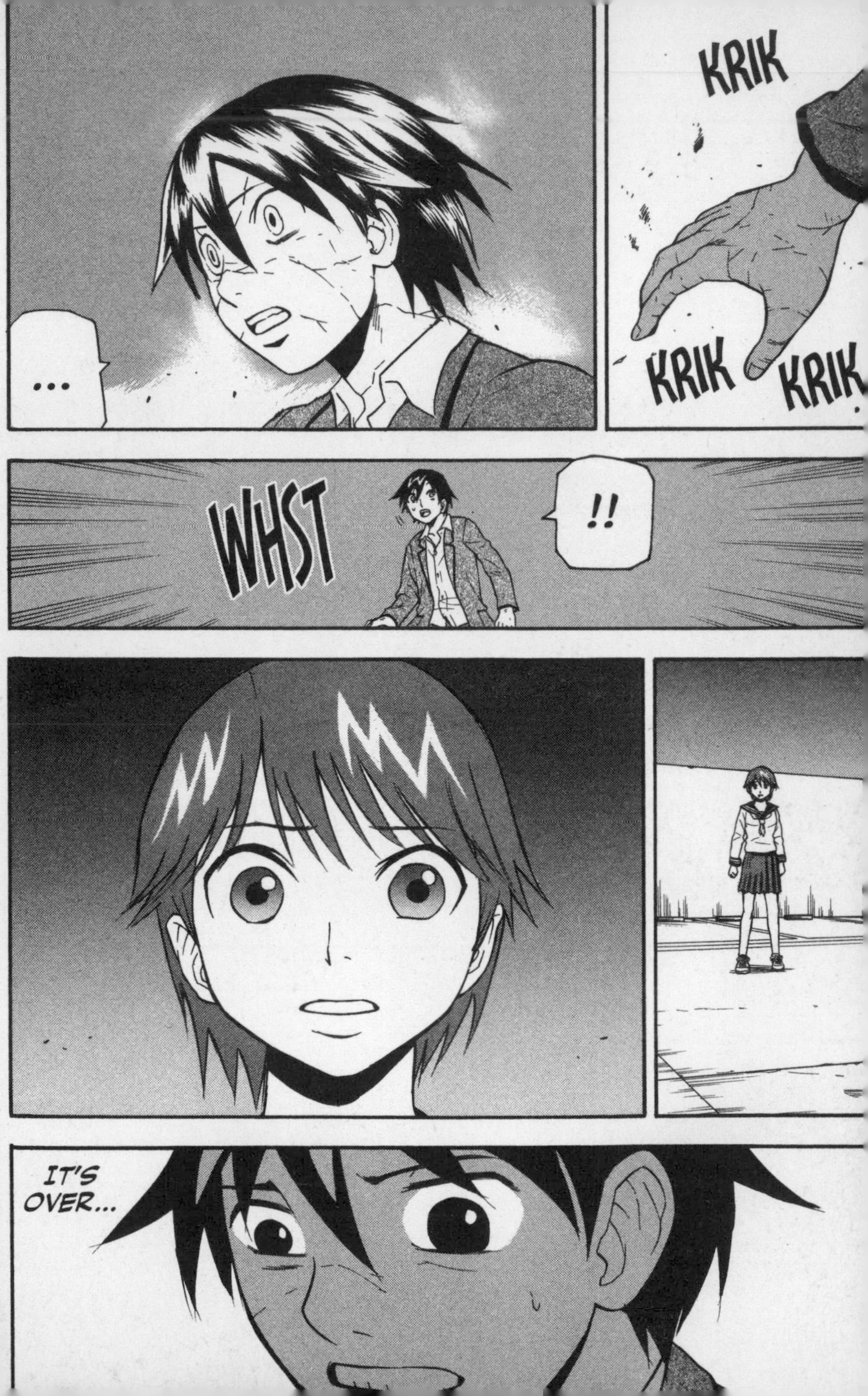
KRIK
KRIK
KRIK
...
!!
WHST
IT'S OVER...

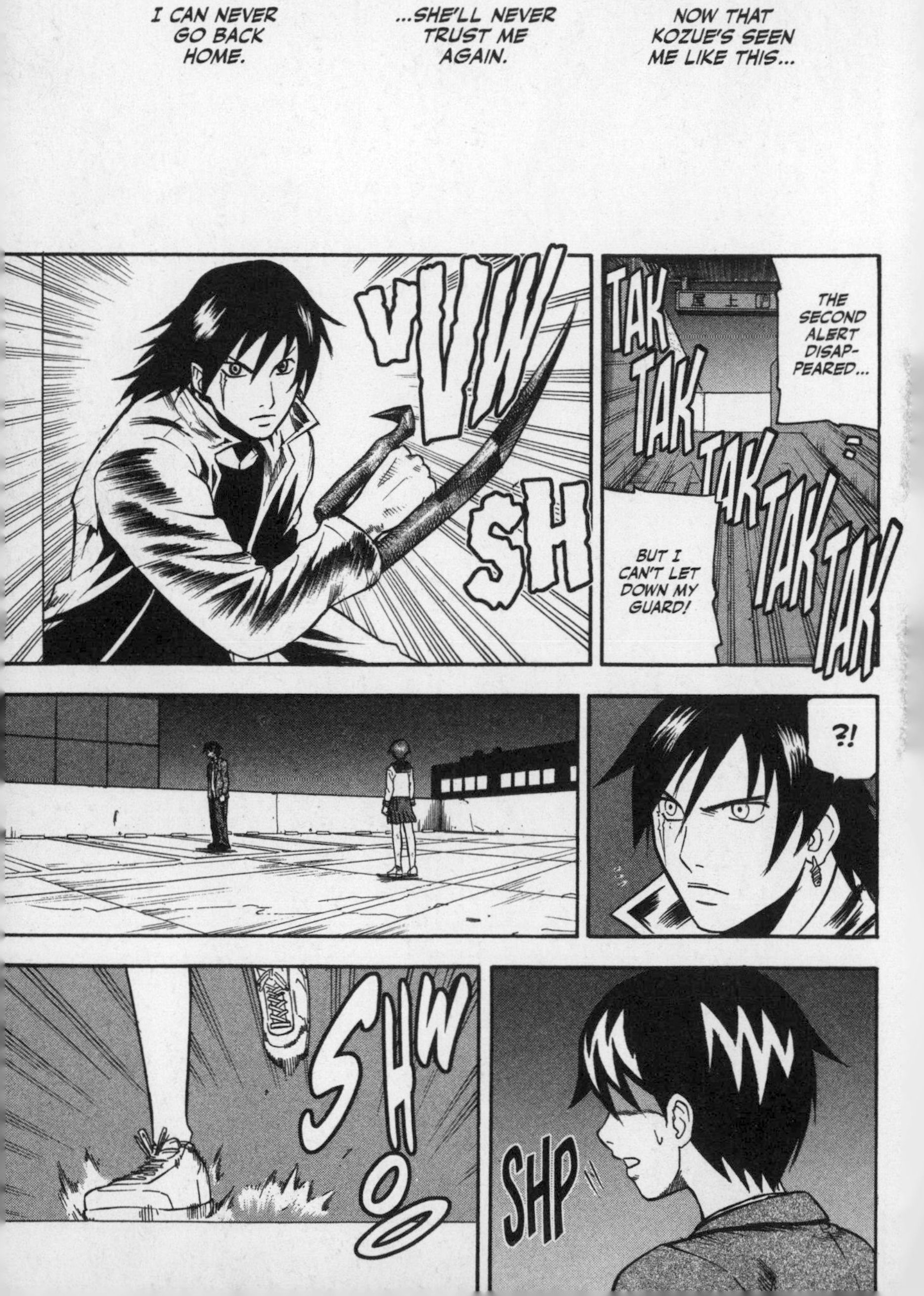
NOW THAT KOZUE'S SEEN ME LIKE THIS...
...SHE'LL NEVER TRUST ME AGAIN.
I CAN NEVER GO BACK HOME.
TAK TAK TAK TAK TAK
THE SECOND ALERT DISAPPEARED...
BUT I CAN'T LET DOWN MY GUARD!
VUW
SH
?!
SHP
SHWOO

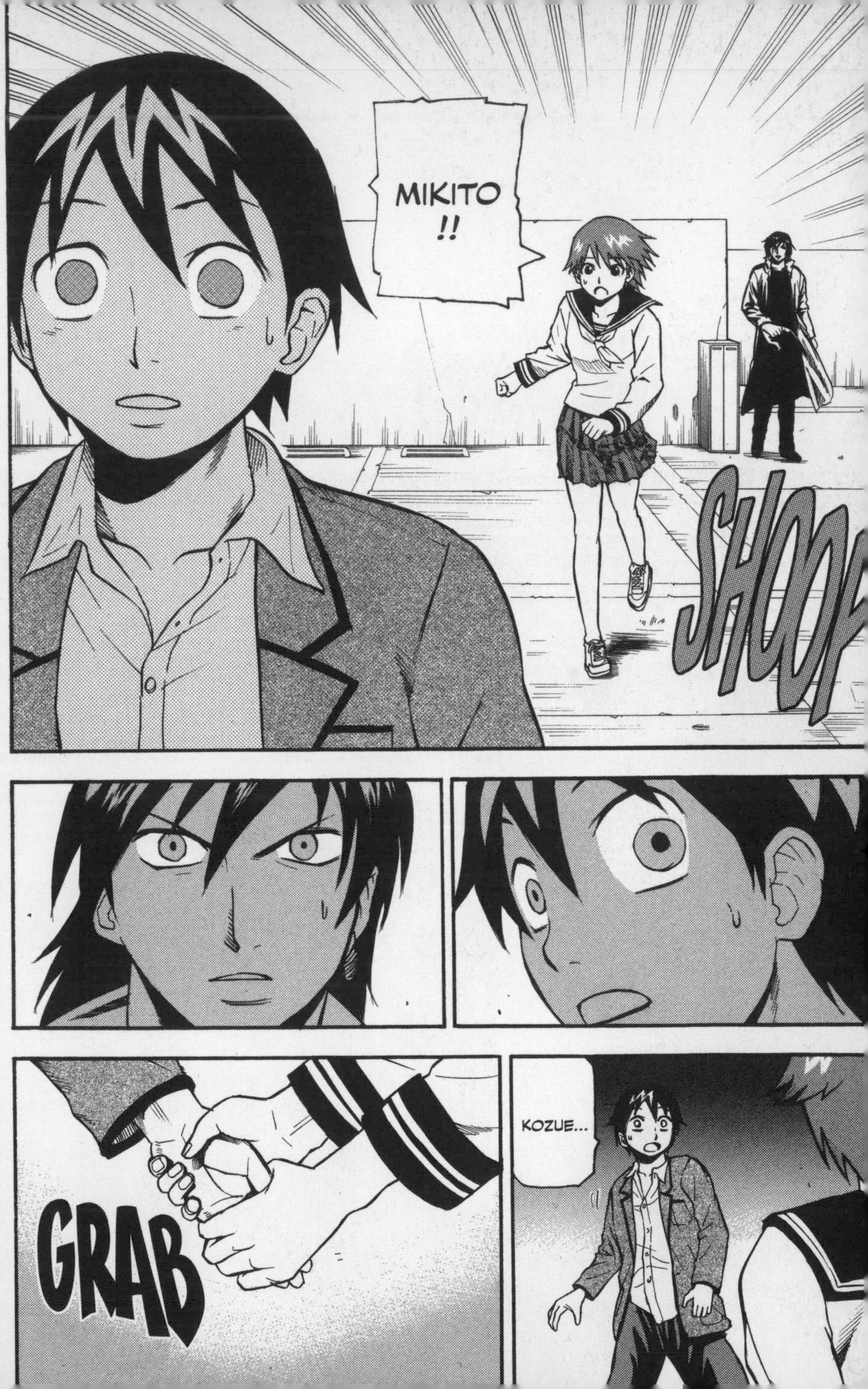
MIKITO !!
KOZUE...
GRAB

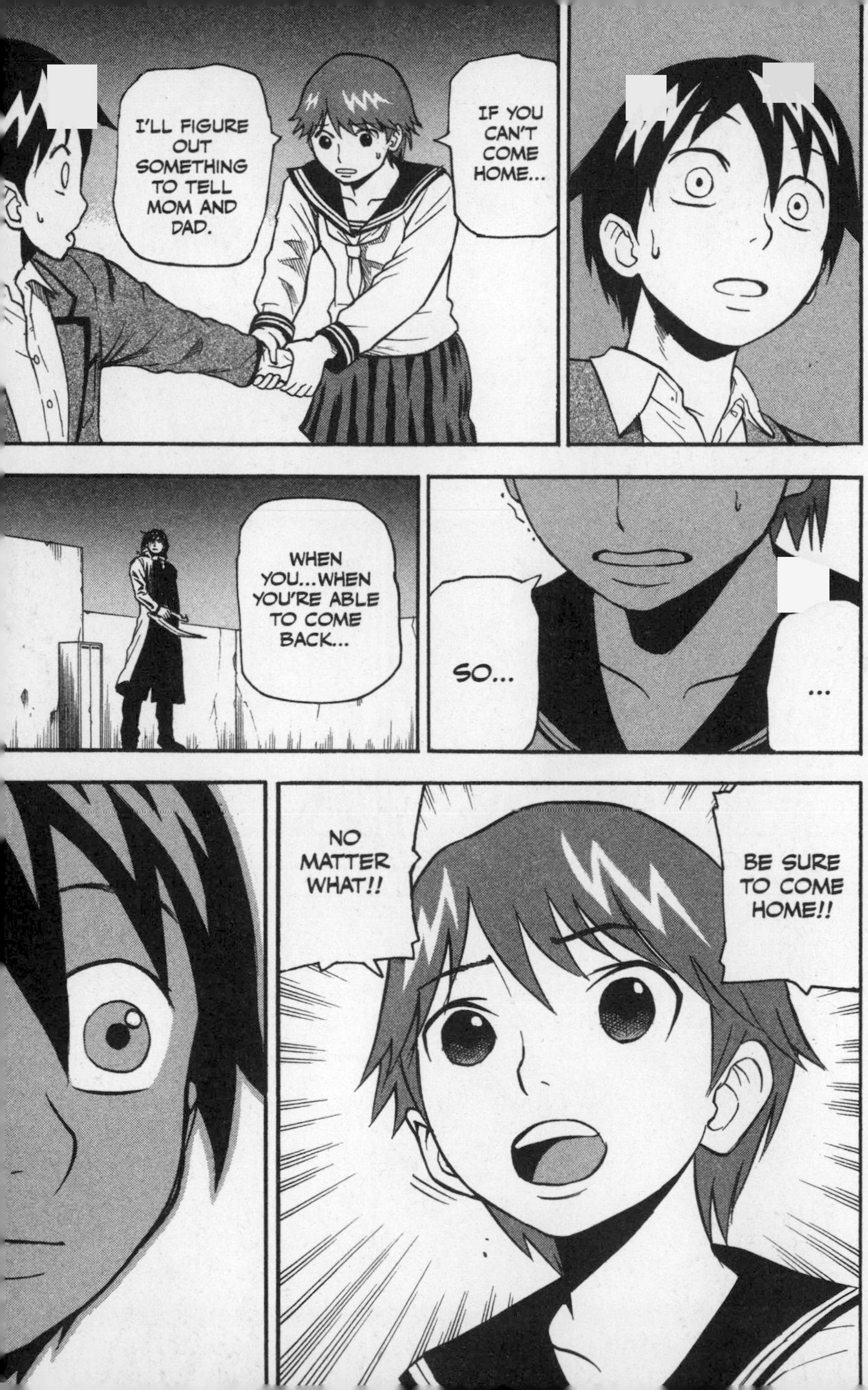
IF YOU CAN'T COME HOME...
I'LL FIGURE OUT SOMETHING TO TELL MOM AND DAD.
...
SO...
WHEN YOU...WHEN YOU'RE ABLE TO COME BACK...
BE SURE TO COME HOME!!
NO MATTER WHAT!!

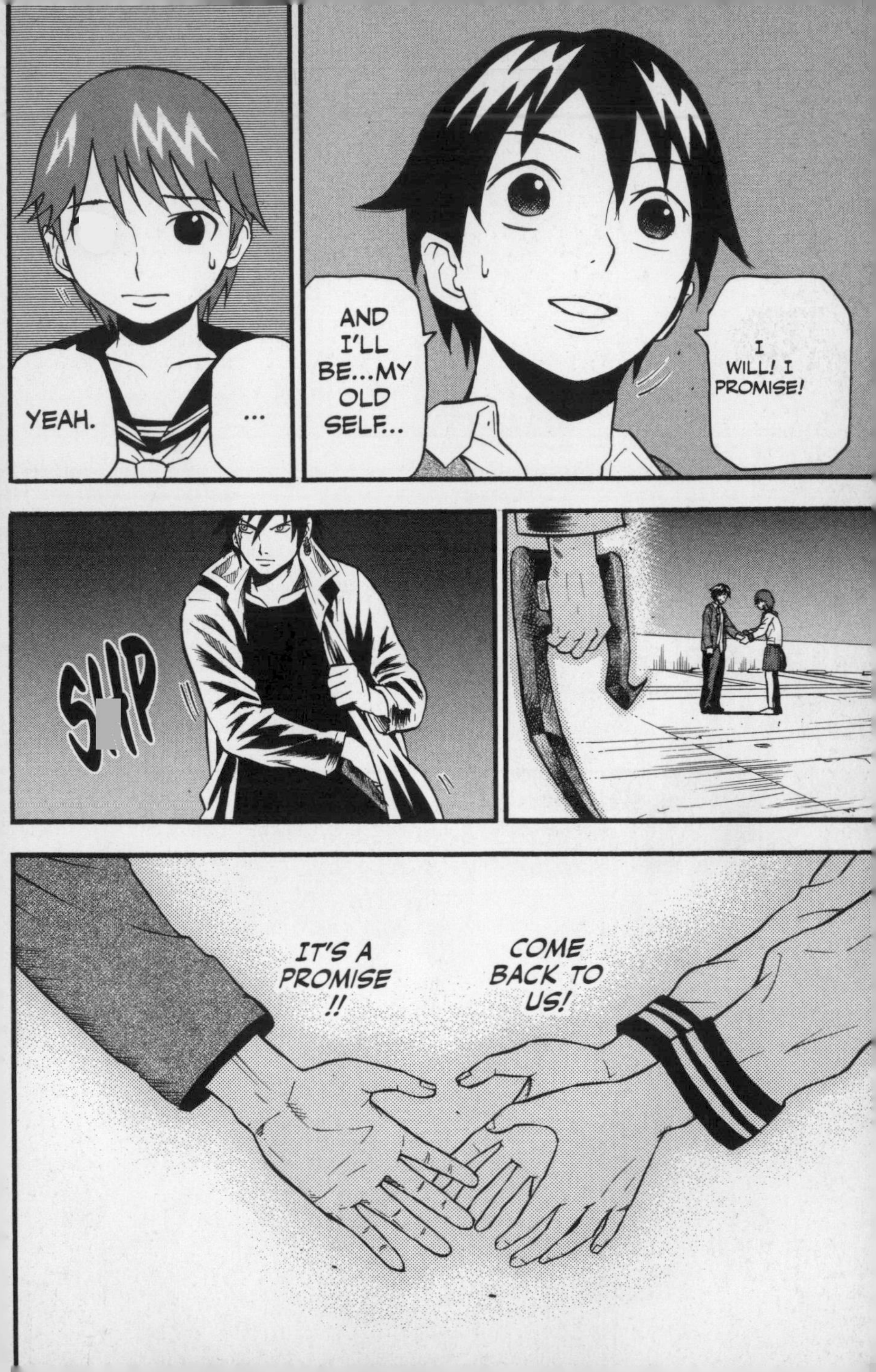
I WILL! I PROMISE!
AND I'LL BE...MY OLD SELF...
...
YEAH.
COME BACK TO US!
IT'S A PROMISE !!

CHAPTER 16 DEPARTURE

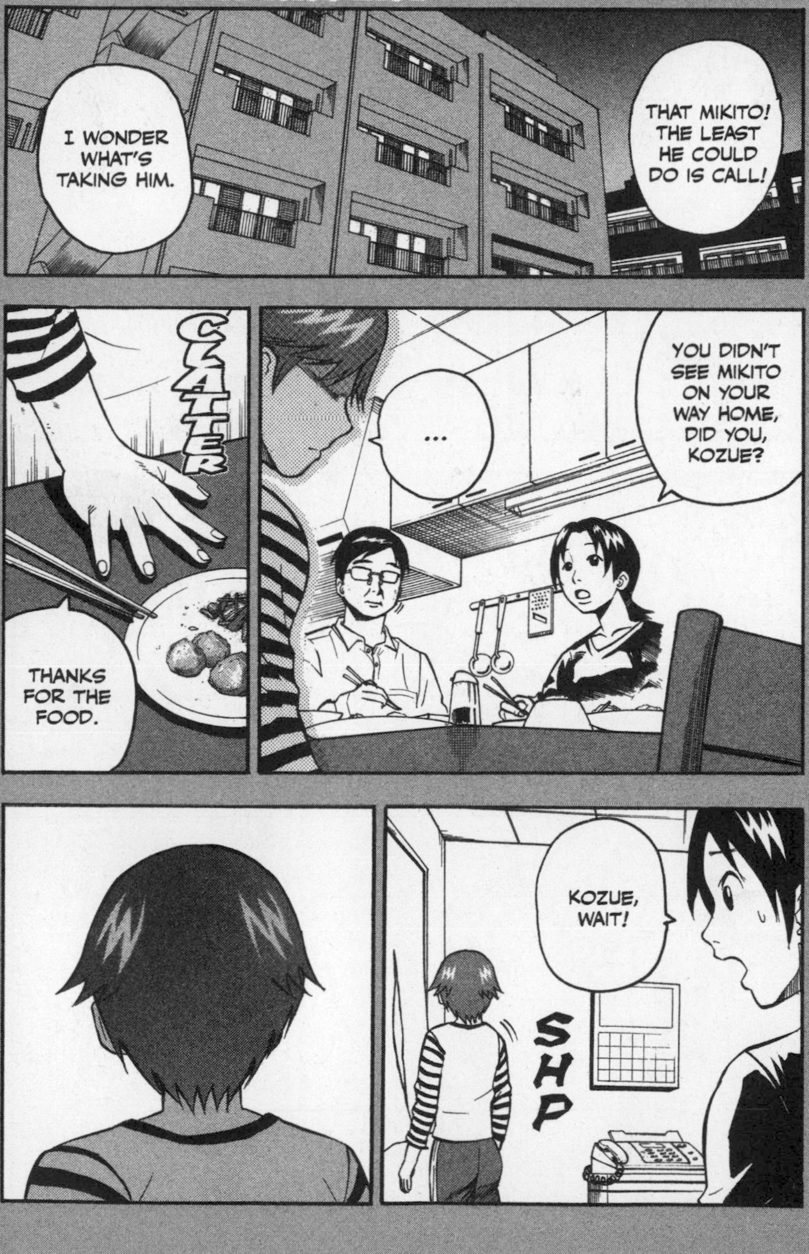
THAT MIKITO! THE LEAST HE COULD DO IS CALL!
I WONDER WHAT'S TAKING HIM.
YOU DIDN'T SEE MIKITO ON YOUR WAY HOME, DID YOU, KOZUE?
...
CLATTER
THANKS FOR THE FOOD.
KOZUE, WAIT!
SHP

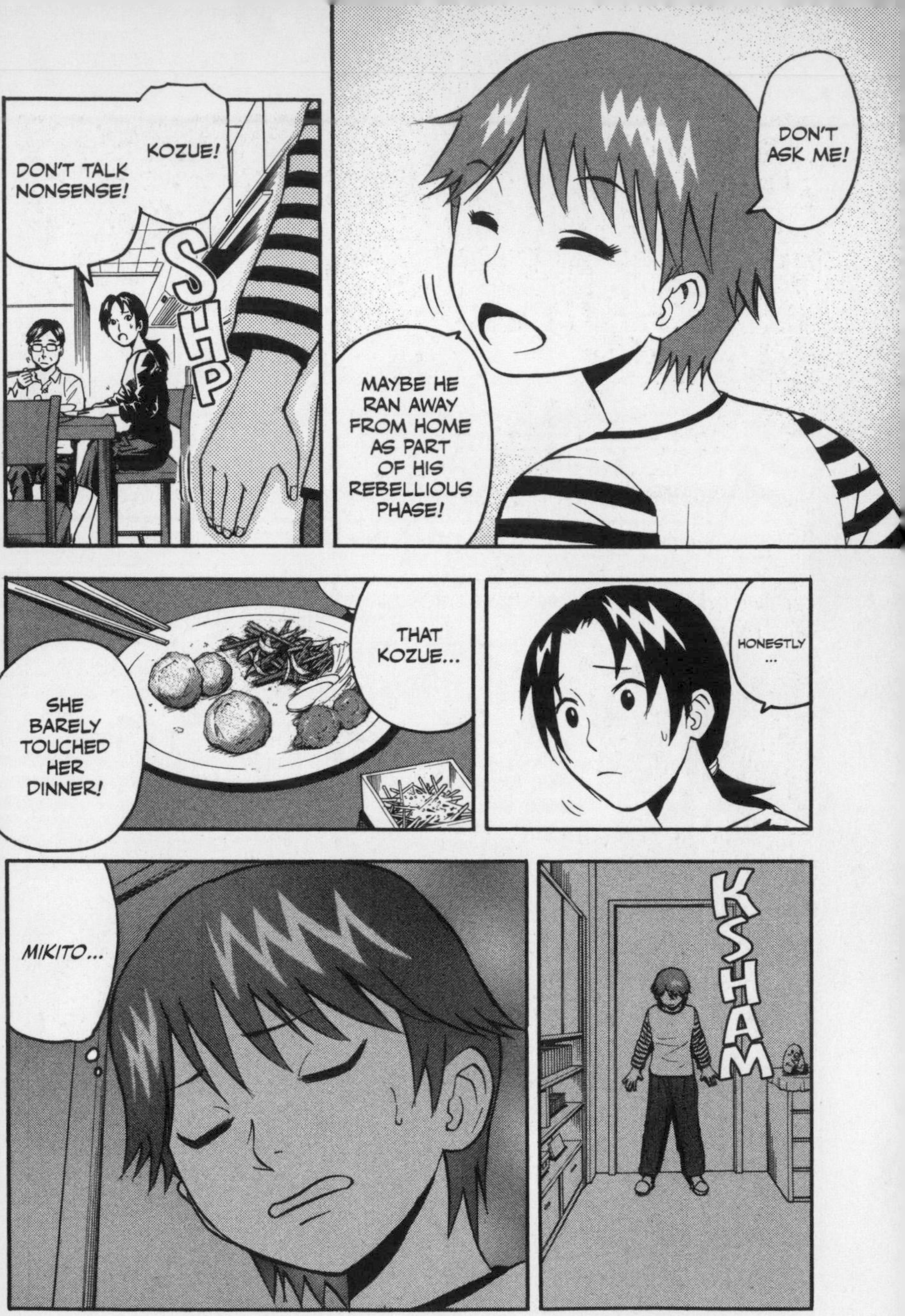
DON'T ASK ME!
MAYBE HE RAN AWAY FROM HOME AS PART OF HIS REBELLIOUS PHASE!
KOZUE!
DON'T TALK NONSENSE!
SHP
HONESTLY ...
THAT KOZUE...
SHE BARELY TOUCHED HER DINNER!
KSHAM
MIKITO...

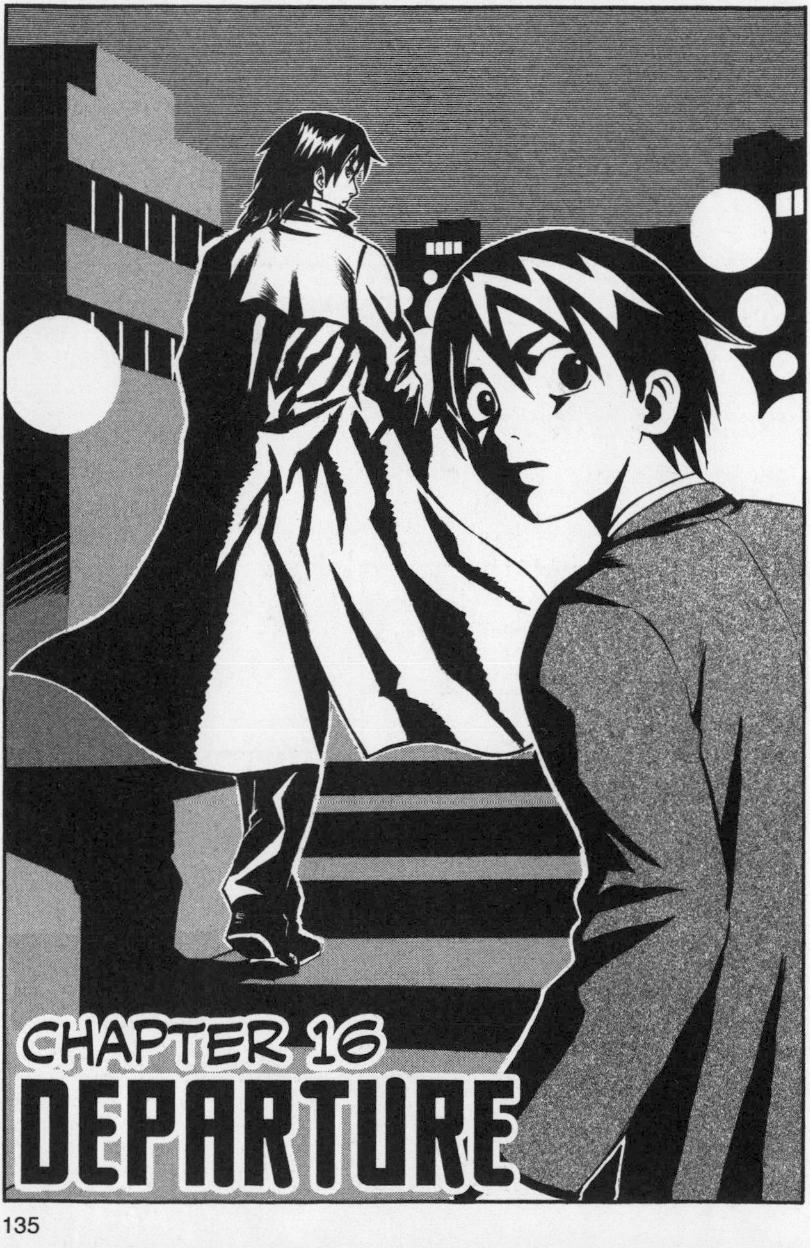
CHAPTER 16
DEPARTURE

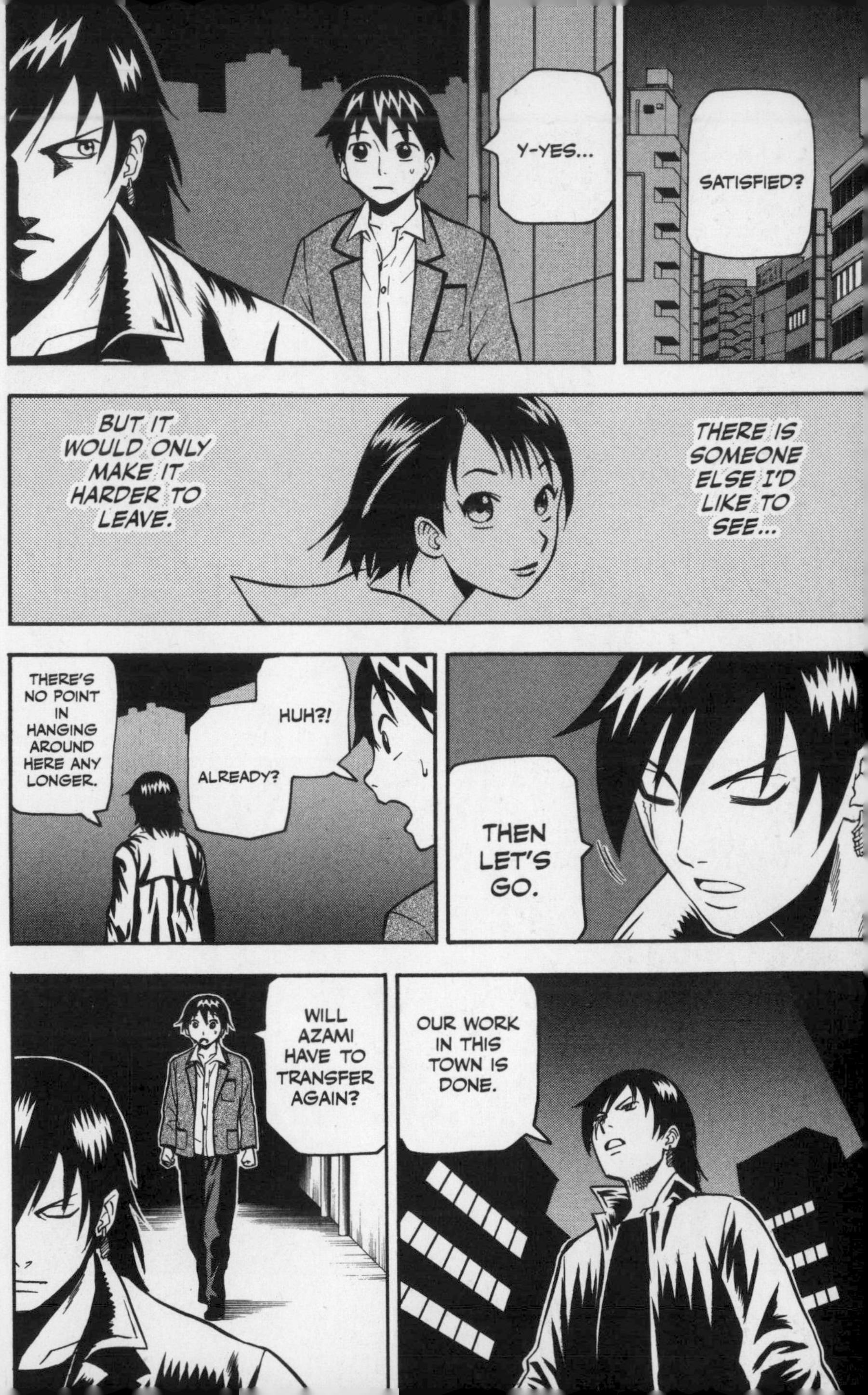
SATISFIED?
Y-YES...
THERE IS SOMEONE ELSE I'D LIKE TO SEE...
BUT IT WOULD ONLY MAKE IT HARDER TO LEAVE.
THEN LET'S GO.
HUH?!
ALREADY?
THERE'S NO POINT IN HANGING AROUND HERE ANY LONGER.
OUR WORK IN THIS TOWN IS DONE.
WILL AZAMI HAVE TO TRANSFER AGAIN?

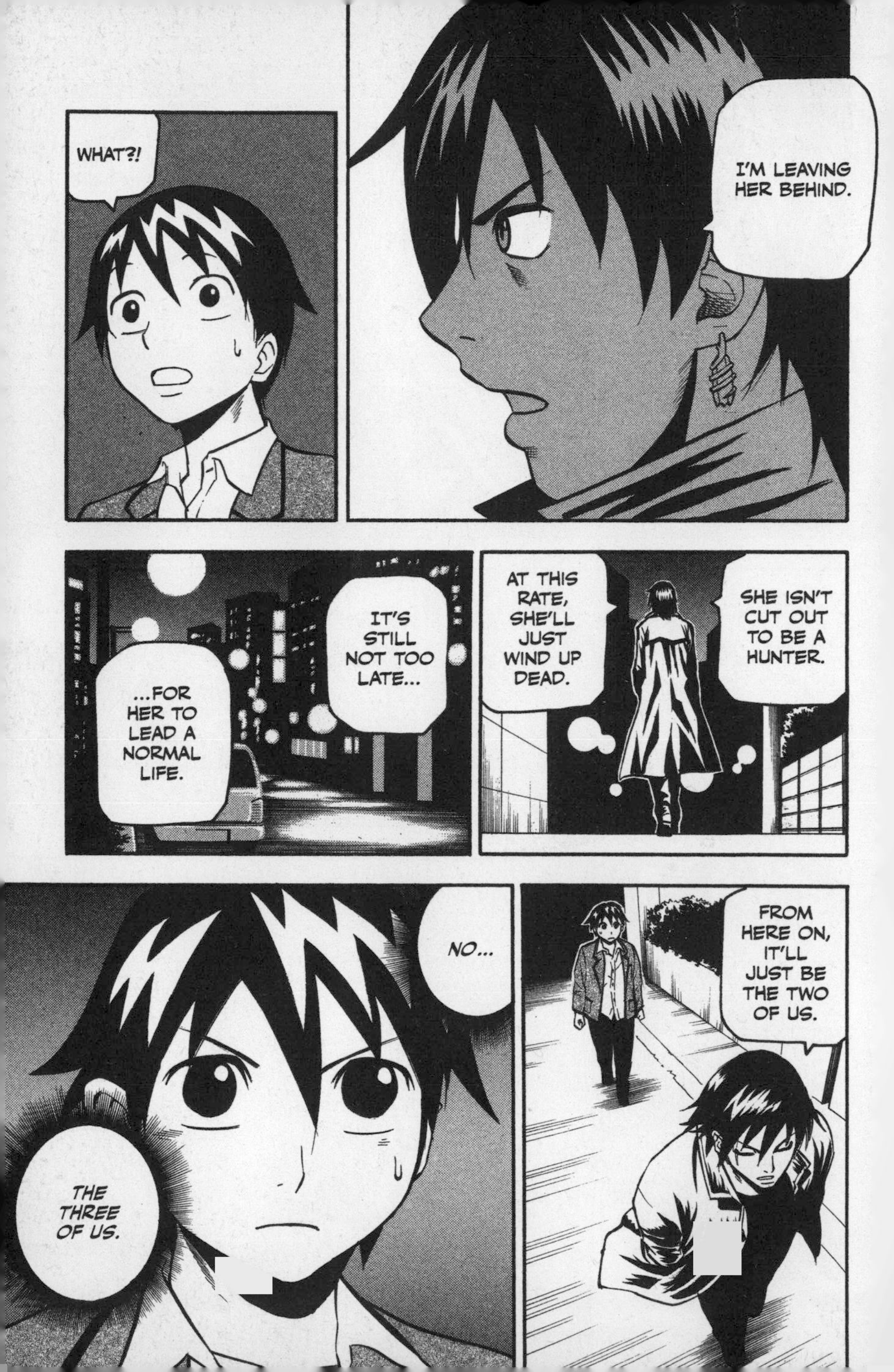
I'M LEAVING HER BEHIND.
WHAT?!
SHE ISN'T CUT OUT TO BE A HUNTER.
AT THIS RATE, SHE'LL JUST WIND UP DEAD.
IT'S STILL NOT TOO LATE...
...FOR HER TO LEAD A NORMAL LIFE.
FROM HERE ON, IT'LL JUST BE THE TWO OF US.
NO...
THE THREE OF US.

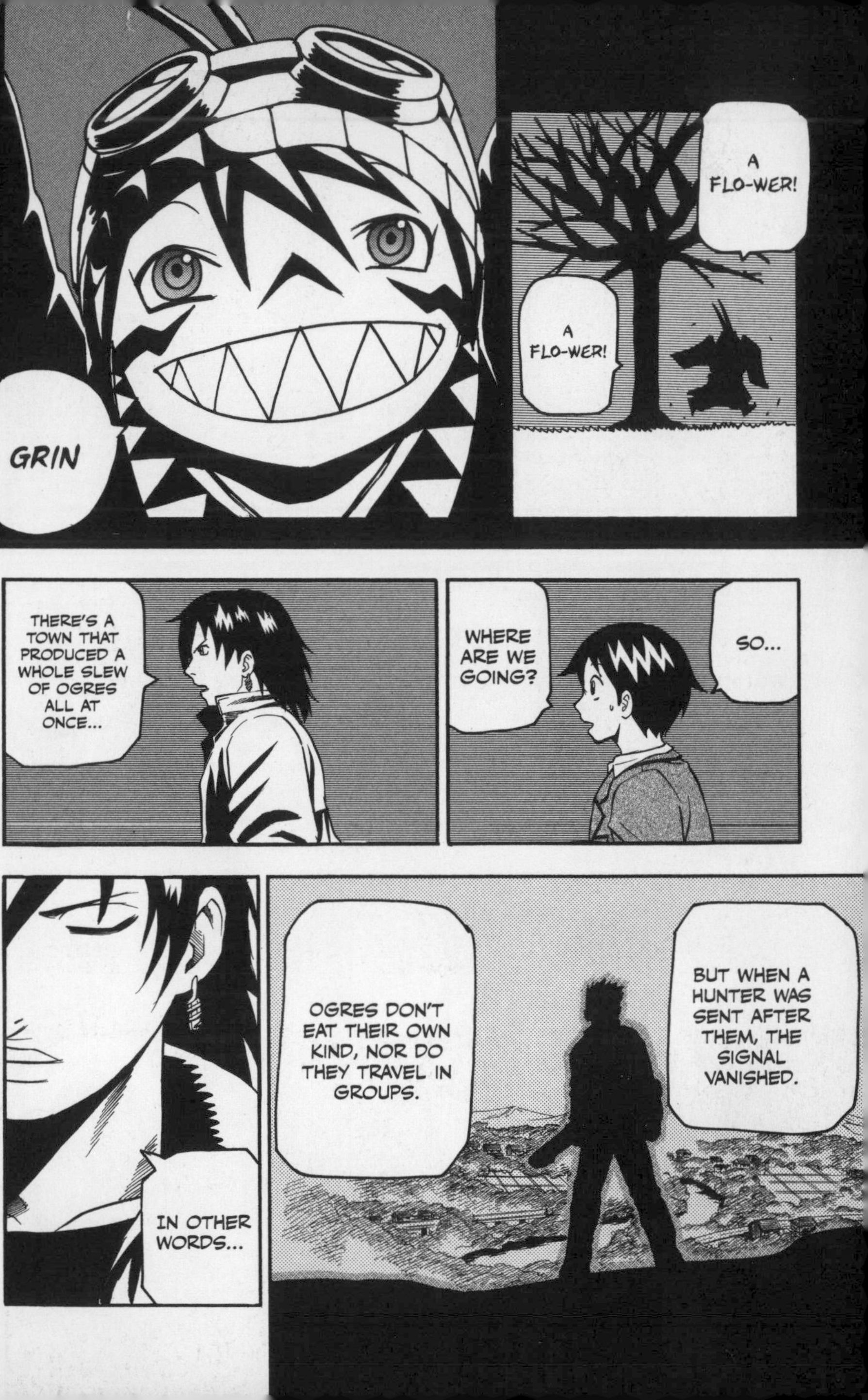
A FLO-WER!
A FLO-WER!
GRIN
SO...
WHERE ARE WE GOING?
THERE'S A TOWN THAT PRODUCED A WHOLE SLEW OF OGRES ALL AT ONCE...
BUT WHEN A HUNTER WAS SENT AFTER THEM, THE SIGNAL VANISHED.
OGRES DON'T EAT THEIR OWN KIND, NOR DO THEY TRAVEL IN GROUPS.
IN OTHER WORDS...

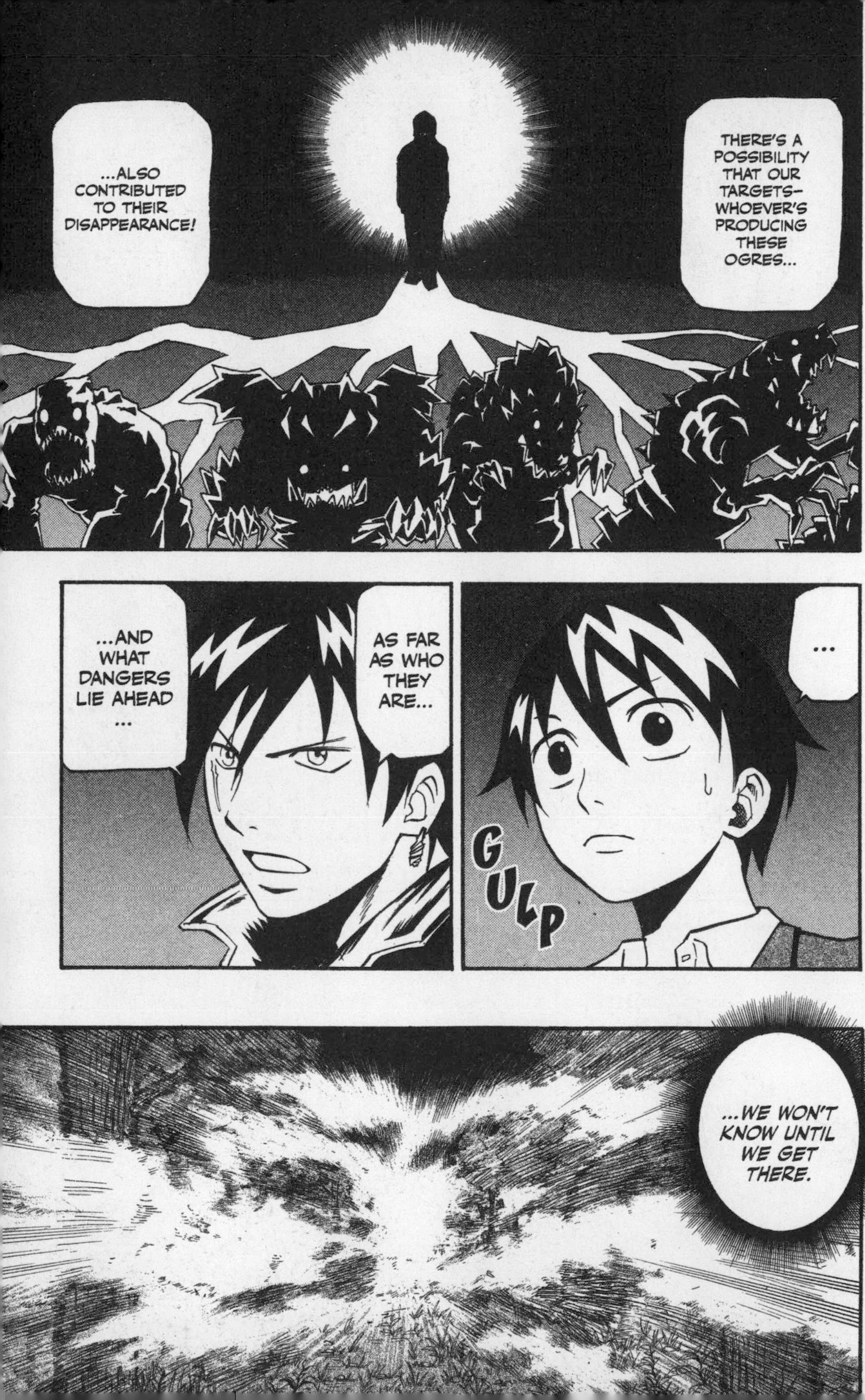
THERE'S A POSSIBILITY THAT OUR TARGETS- WHOEVER'S PRODUCING THESE OGRES...
...ALSO CONTRIBUTED TO THEIR DISAPPEARANCE!
...
GULP
AS FAR AS WHO THEY ARE...
...AND WHAT DANGERS LIE AHEAD ...
...WE WON'T KNOW UNTIL WE GET THERE.

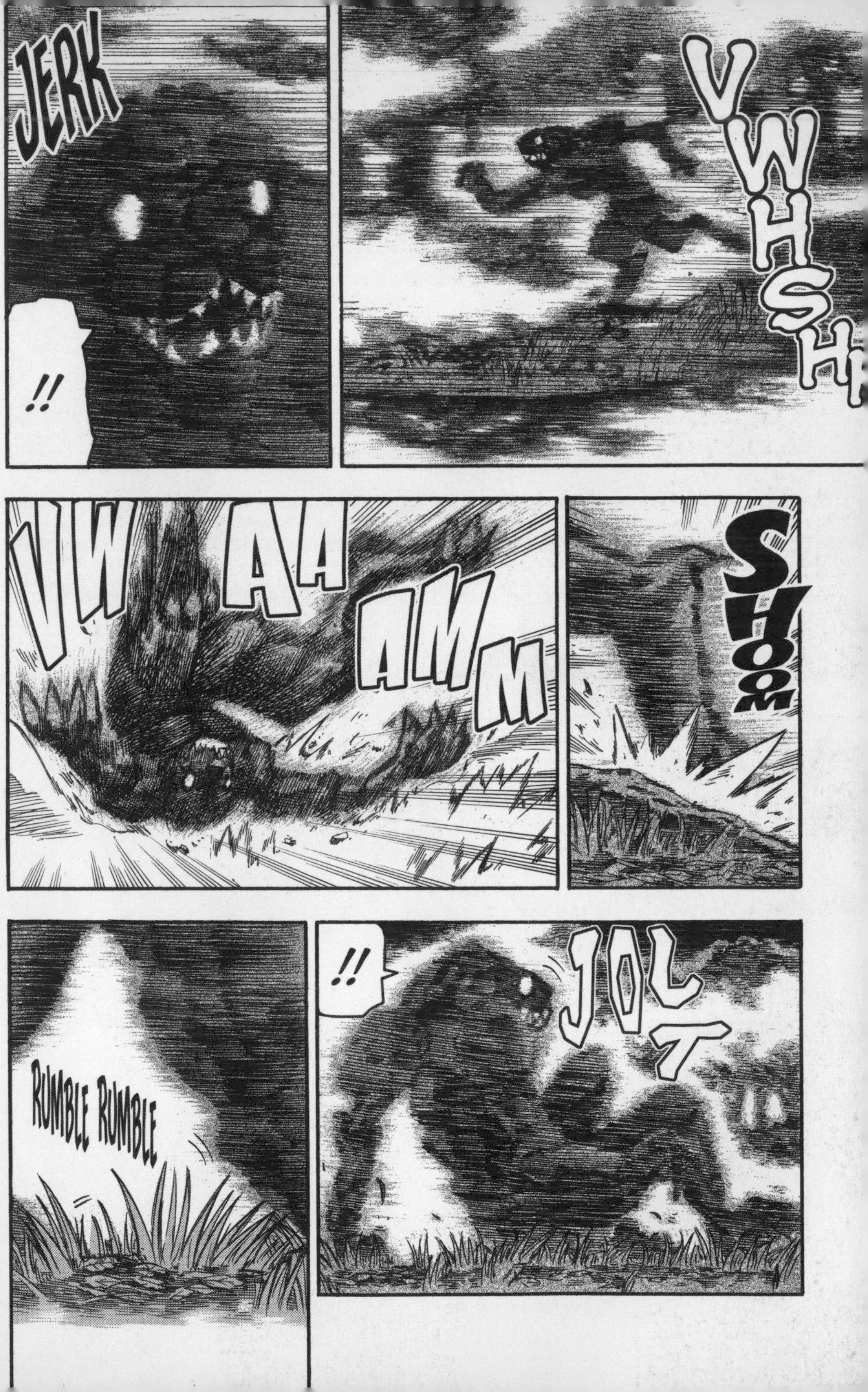
VWHSHH
JERK
!!
SHOOM
VWAAAMM
JOLT
!!
RUMBLE RUMBLE

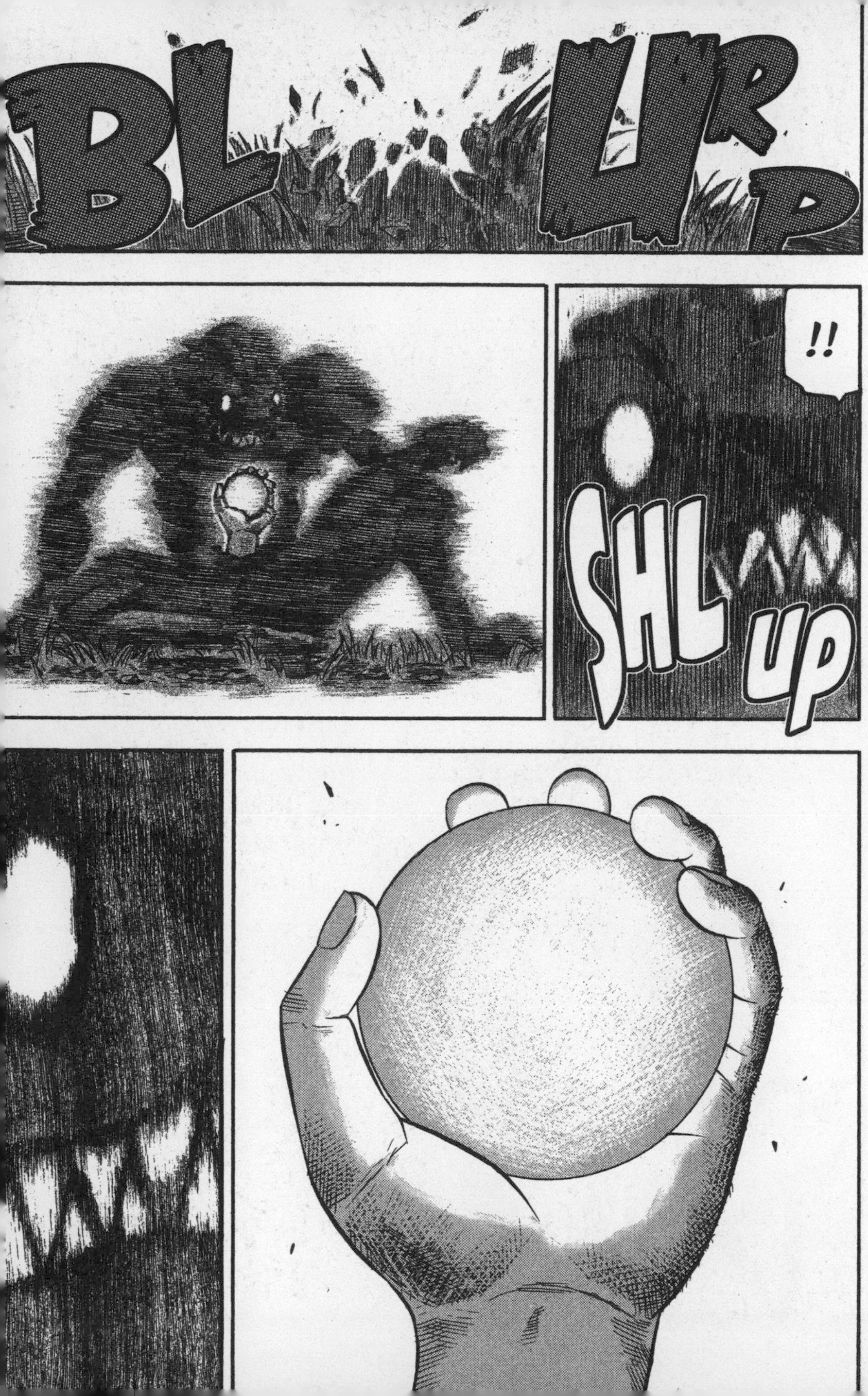
BL URP
!!
SHL UP

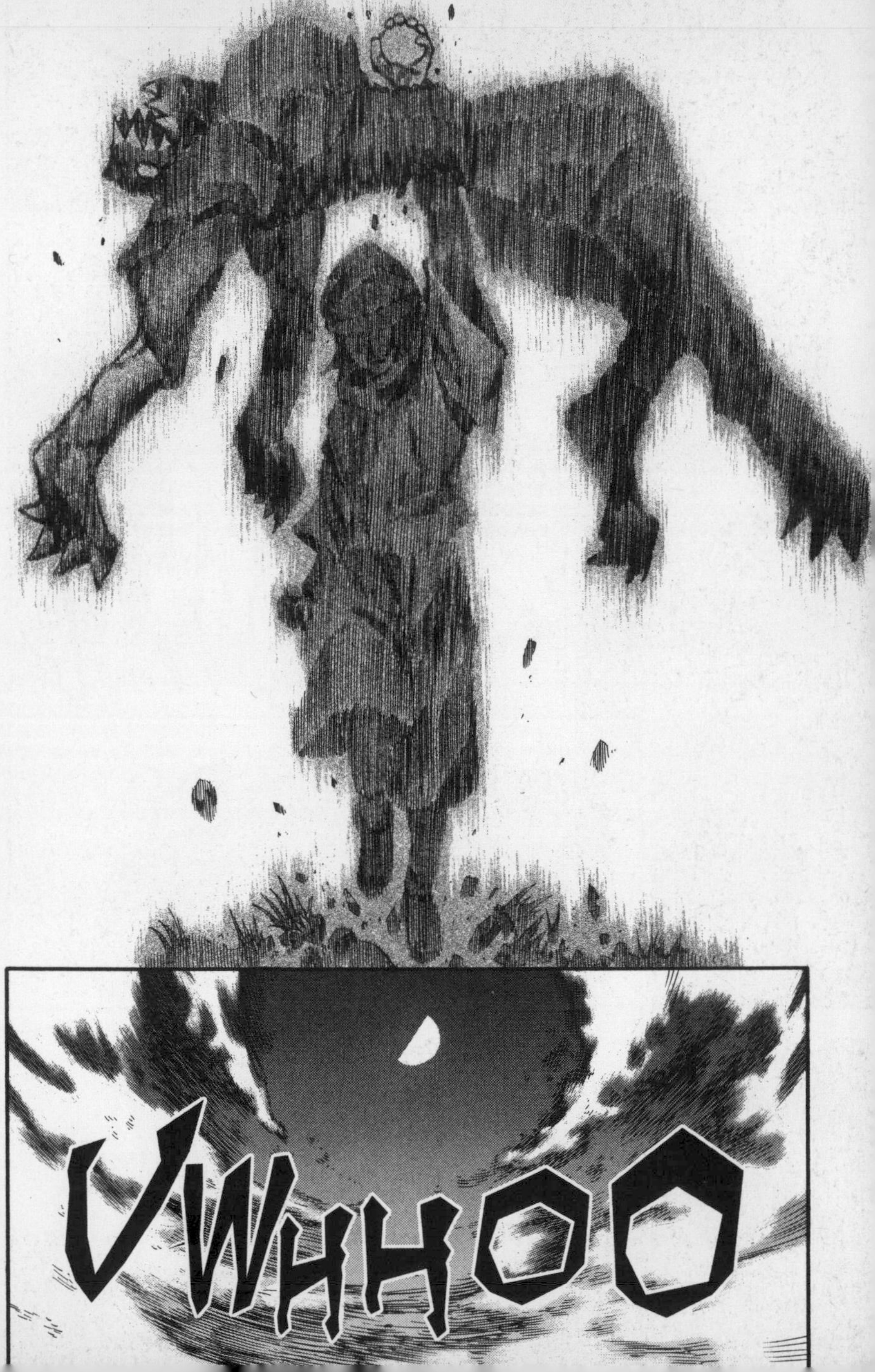
VWHOO

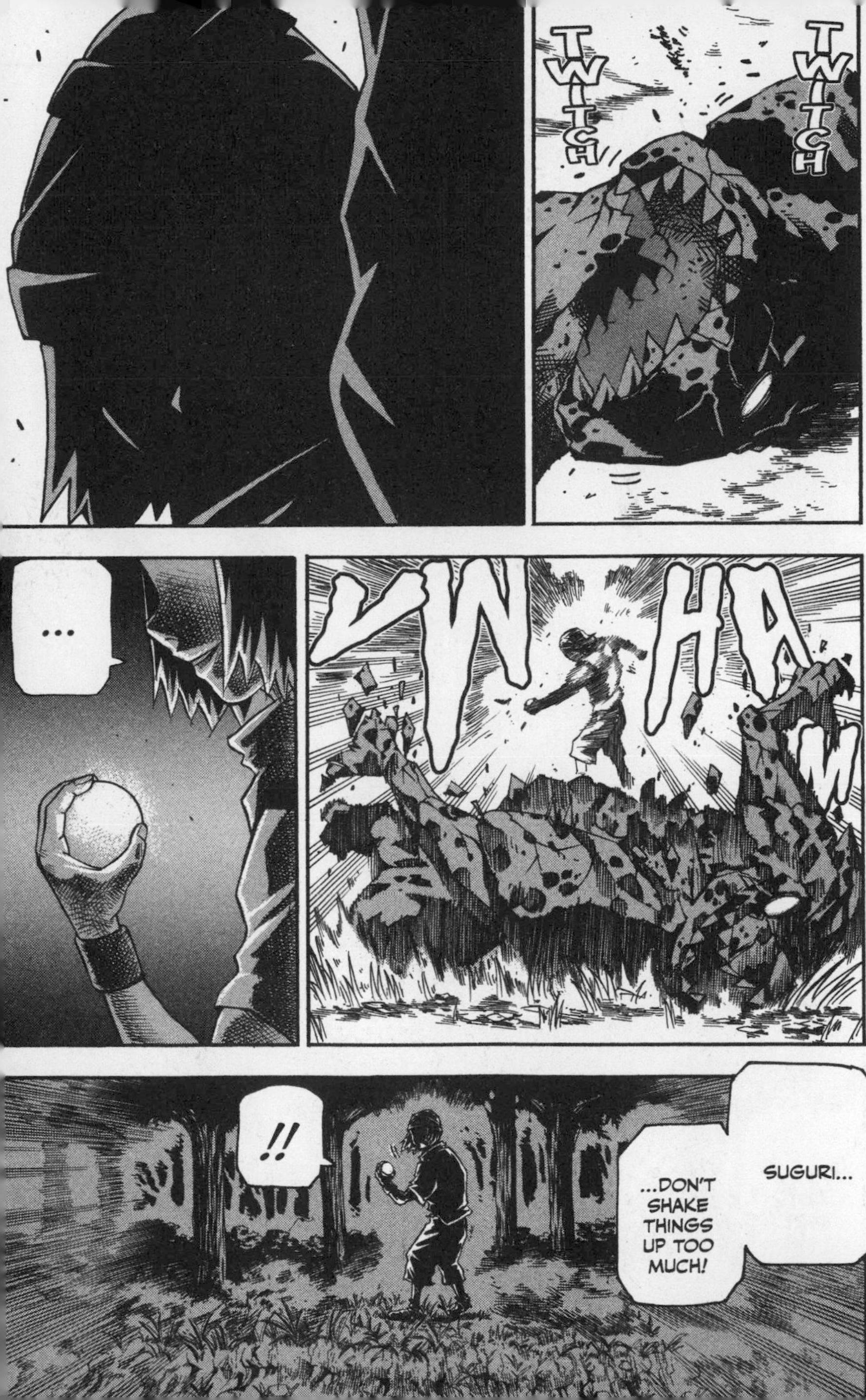

TWITCH
TWITCH
WHAM
...
SUGURI...
...DON'T SHAKE THINGS UP TOO MUCH!
!!

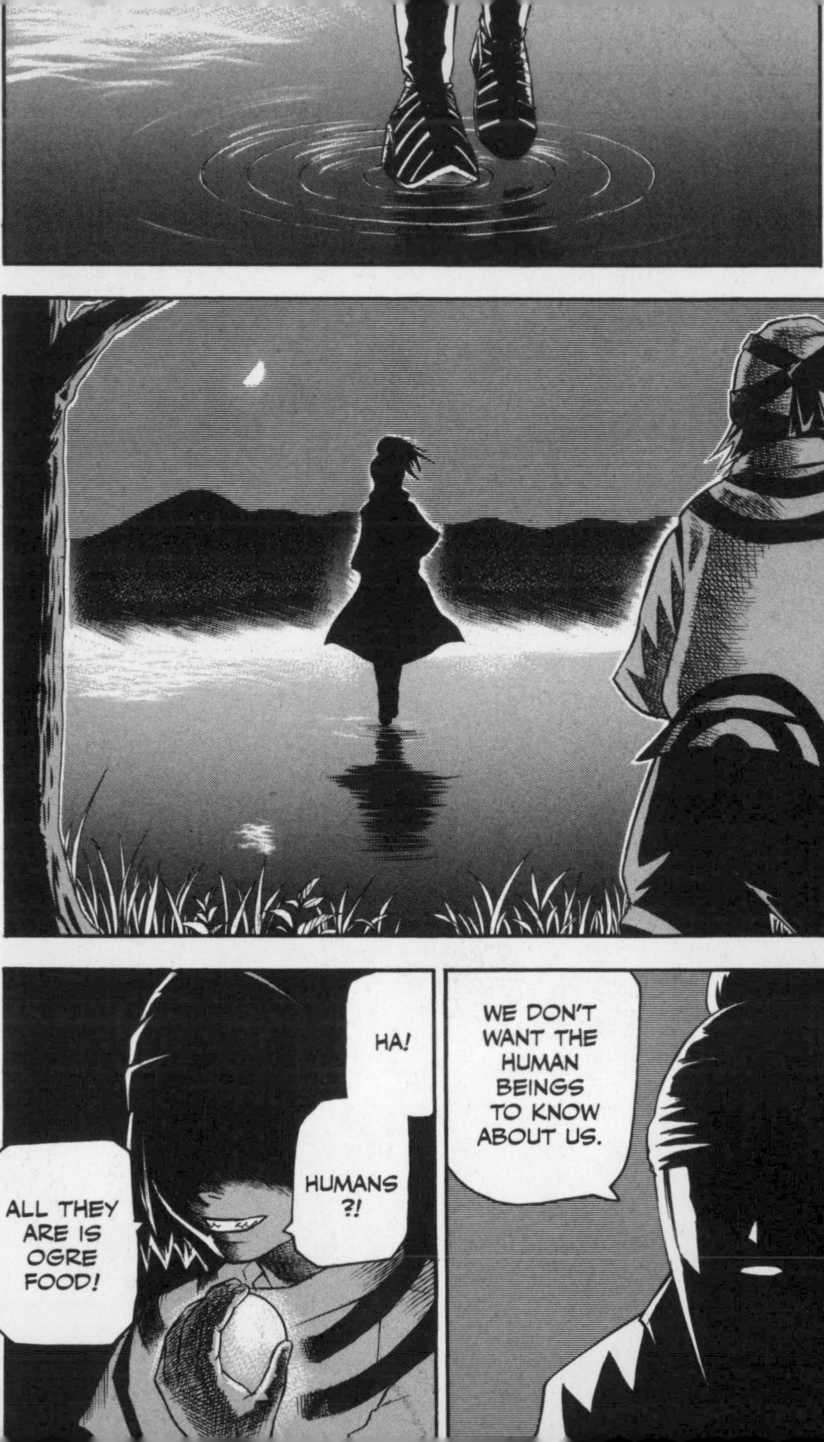
WE DON'T WANT THE HUMAN BEINGS TO KNOW ABOUT US.
HA!
HUMANS ?!
ALL THEY ARE IS OGRE FOOD!

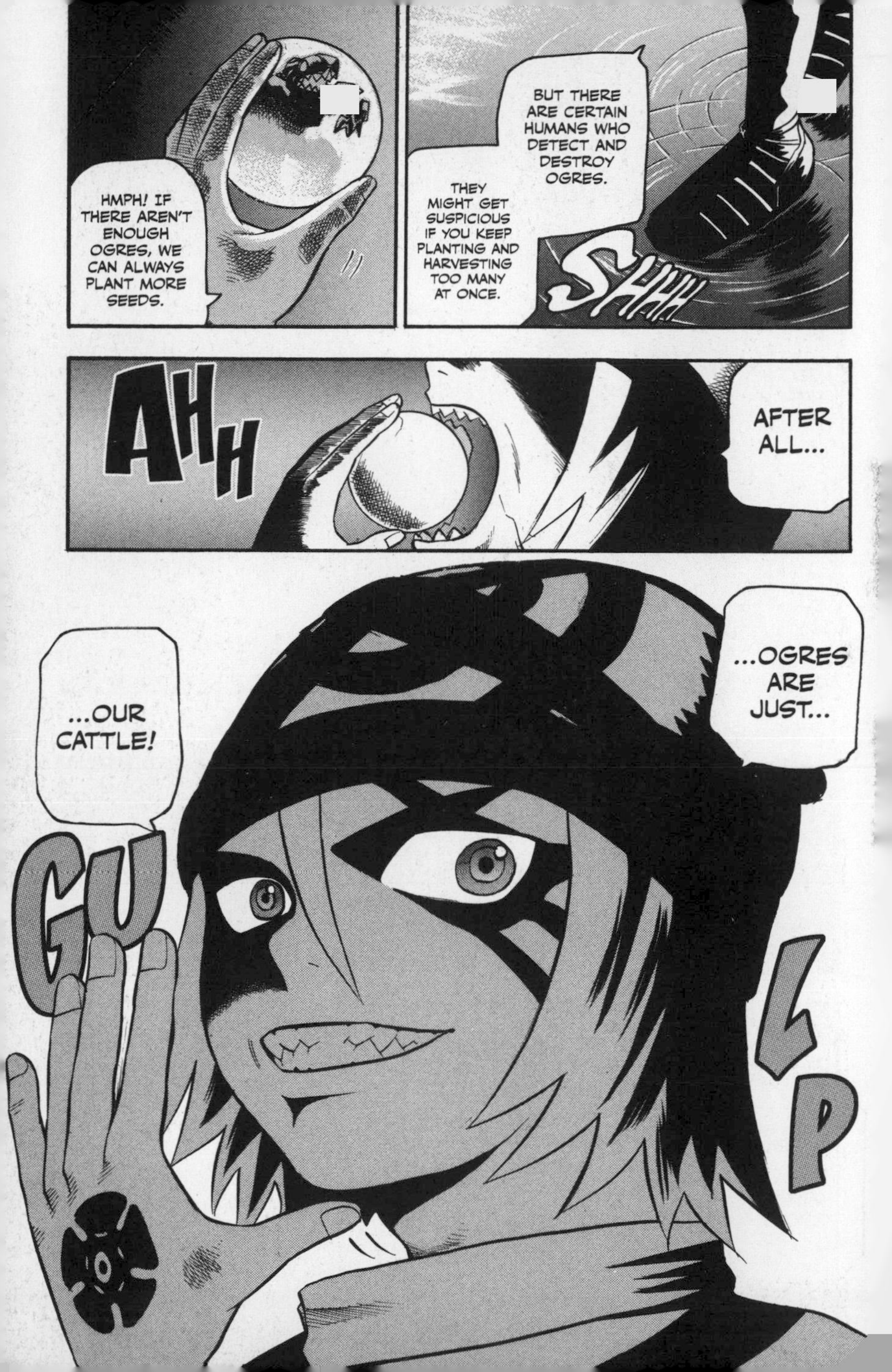
BUT THERE ARE CERTAIN HUMANS WHO DETECT AND DESTROY OGRES.
THEY MIGHT GET SUSPICIOUS IF YOU KEEP PLANTING AND HARVESTING TOO MANY AT ONCE.
SHHH
HMPH! IF THERE AREN'T ENOUGH OGRES, WE CAN ALWAYS PLANT MORE SEEDS.
AFTER ALL...
AHHH
...OGRES ARE JUST...
...OUR CATTLE!
GULP

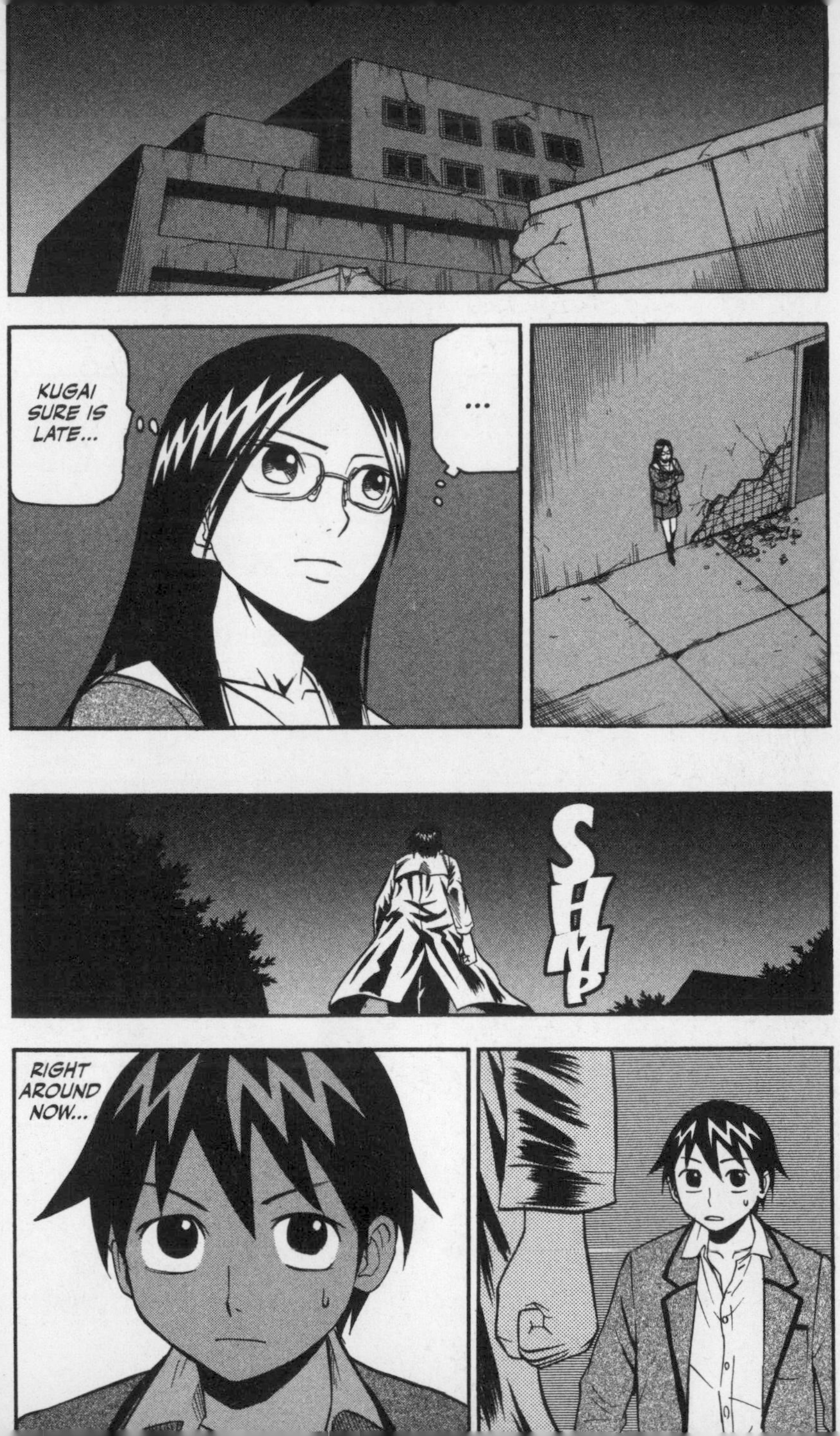
...
KUGAI SURE IS LATE...
SHMP
RIGHT AROUND NOW...

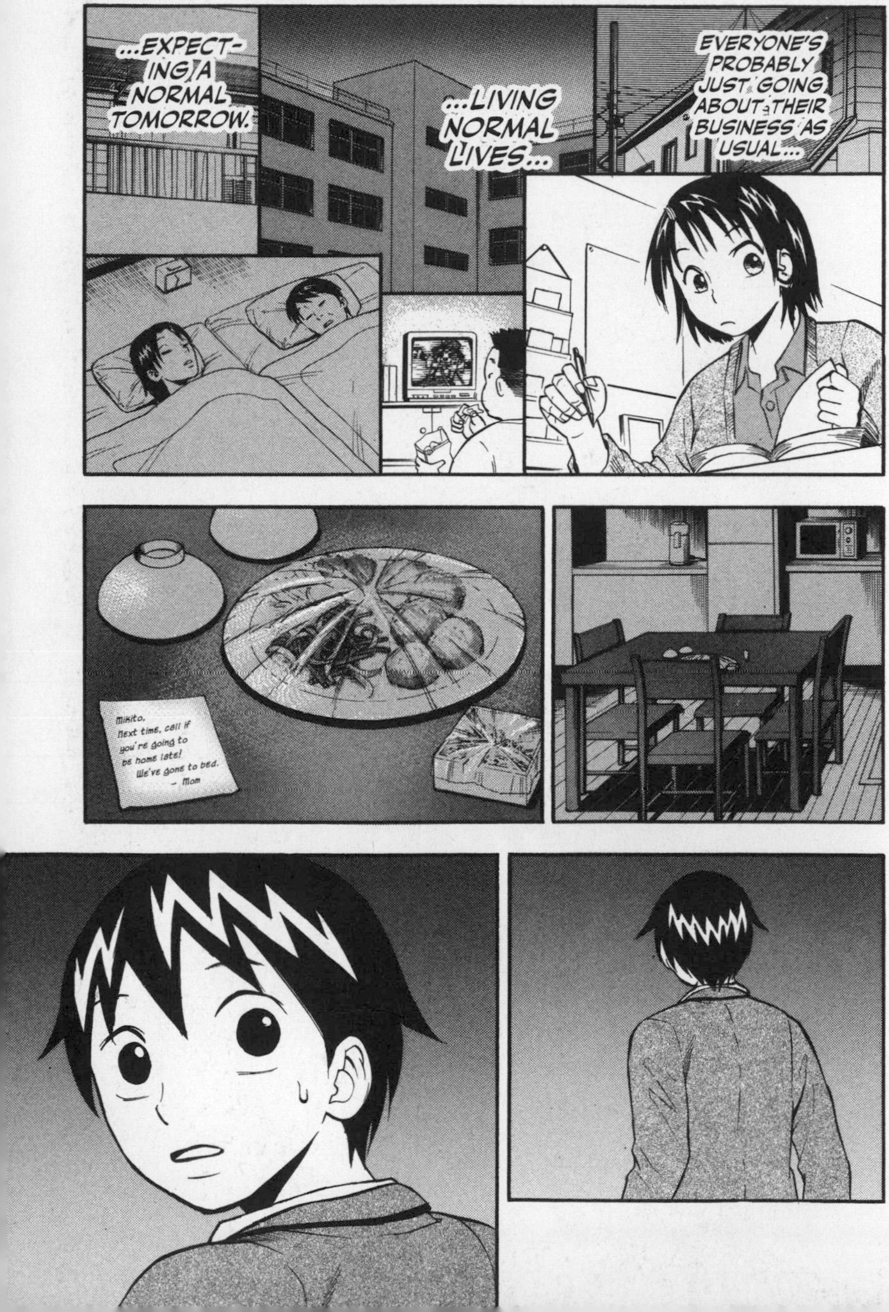
EVERYONE'S PROBABLY JUST GOING ABOUT THEIR BUSINESS AS USUAL...
...LIVING NORMAL LIVES...
...EXPECT-ING A NORMAL TOMORROW.
Mikito,
Next time, call if you're going to be home late!
We've gone to bed.
– Mom

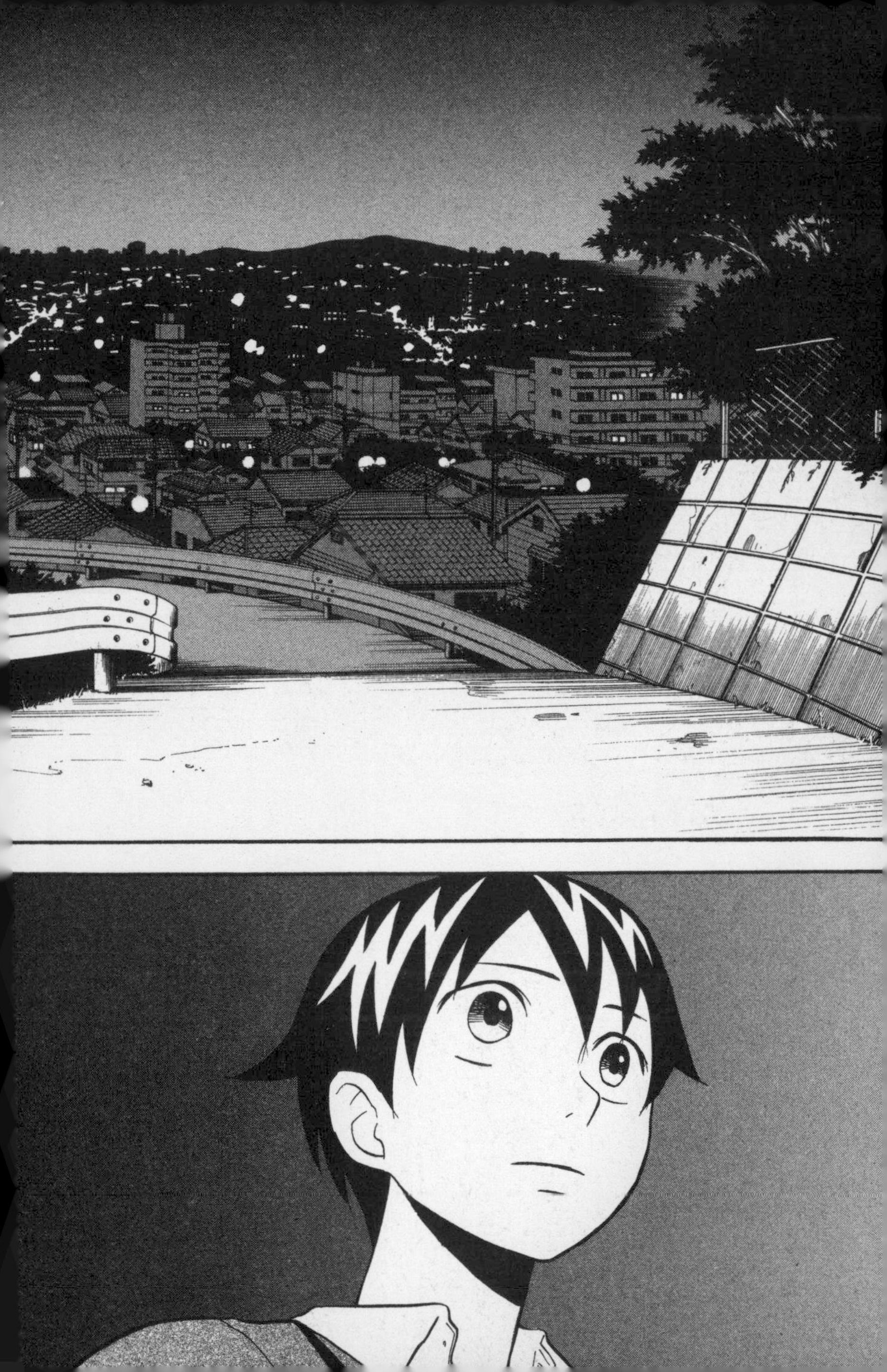

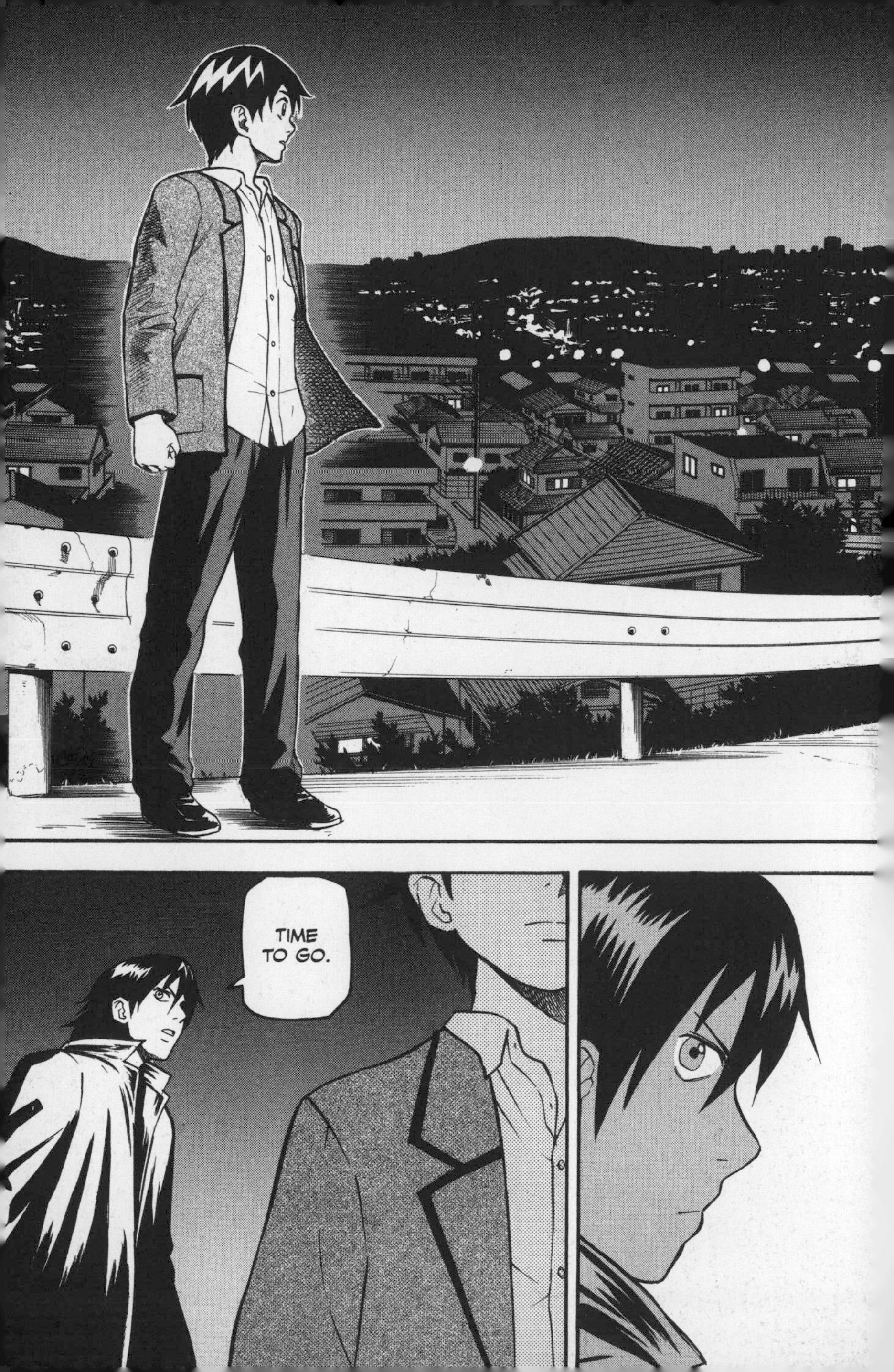
TIME TO GO.

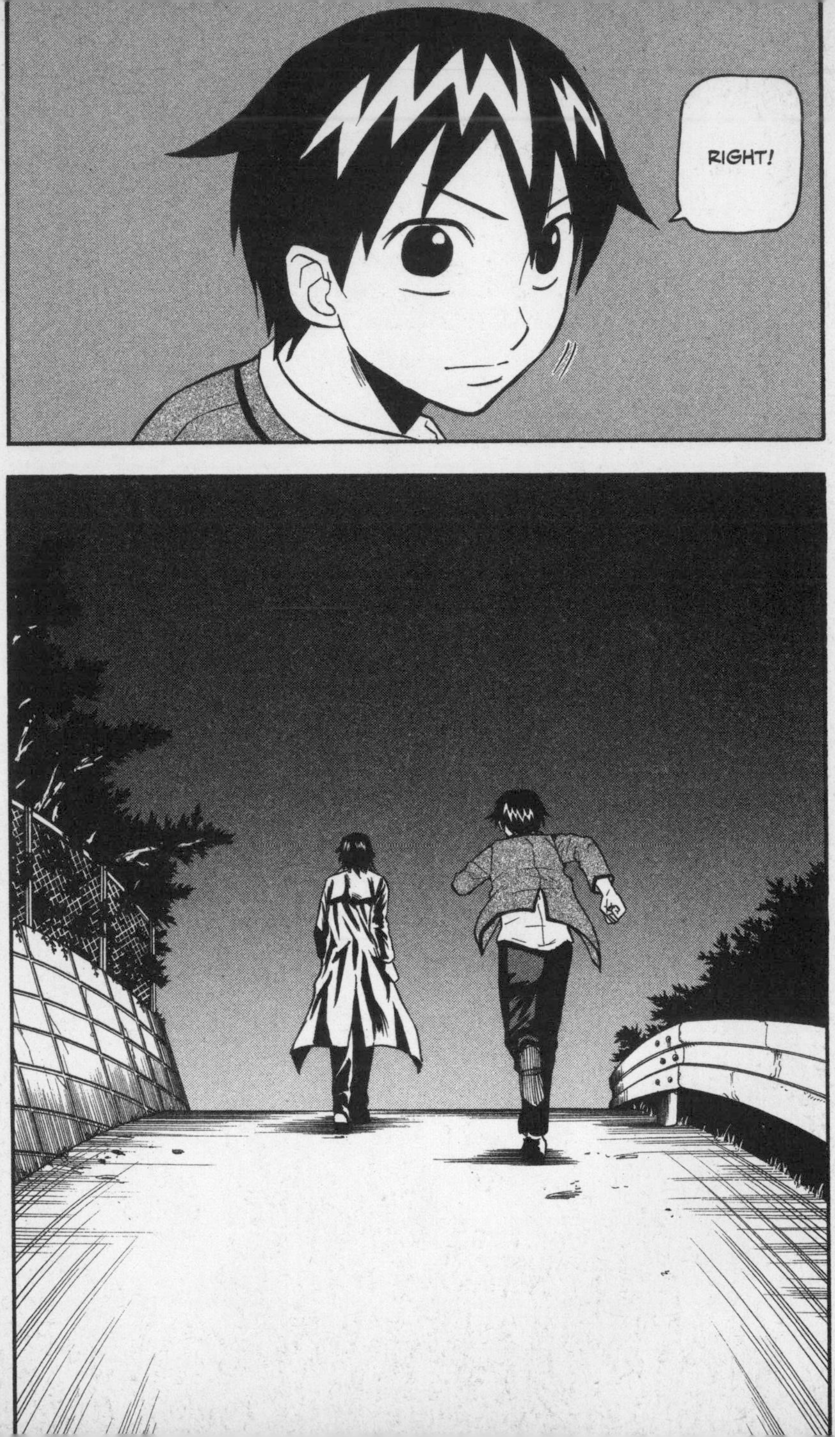
RIGHT!

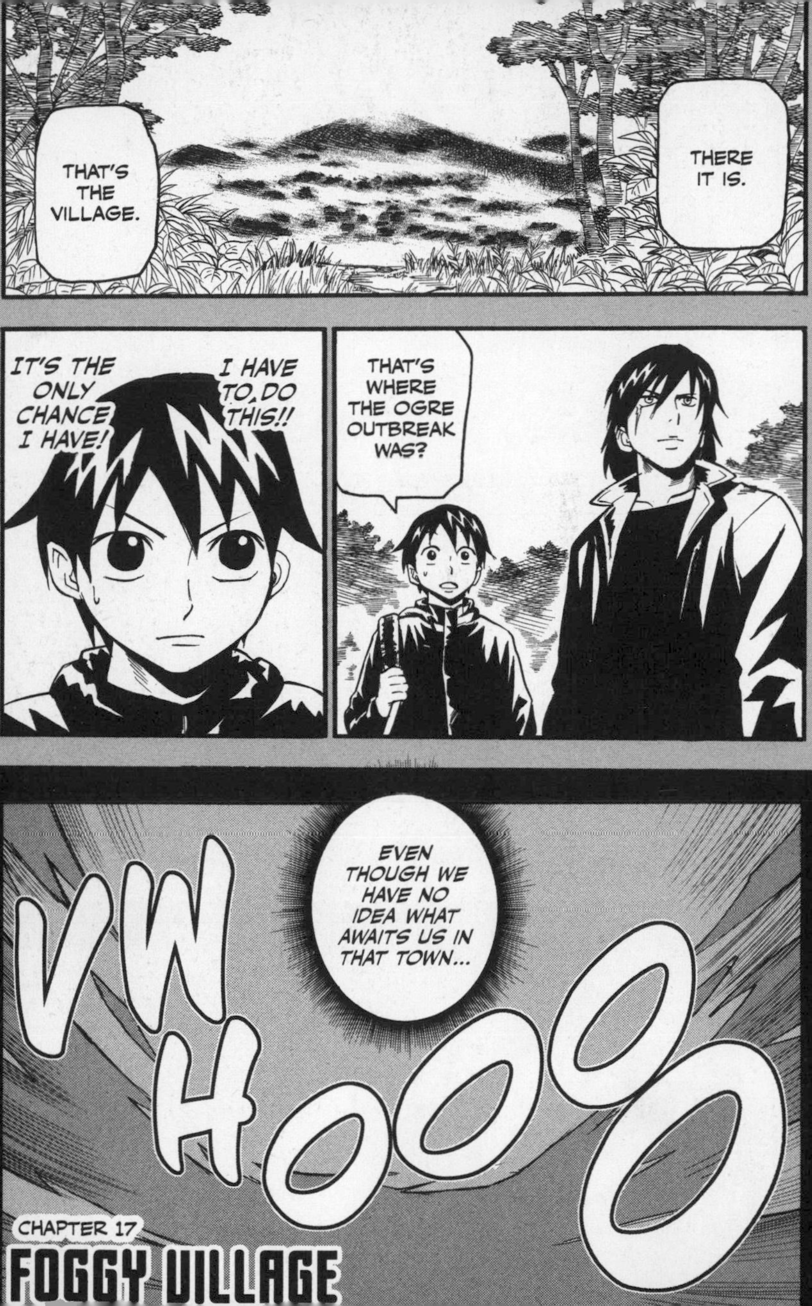
THERE IT IS.
THAT'S THE VILLAGE.
THAT'S WHERE THE OGRE OUTBREAK WAS?
I HAVE TO DO THIS!!
IT'S THE ONLY CHANCE I HAVE!
EVEN THOUGH WE HAVE NO IDEA WHAT AWAITS US IN THAT TOWN...
VWHOOOO
CHAPTER 17
FOGGY VILLAGE

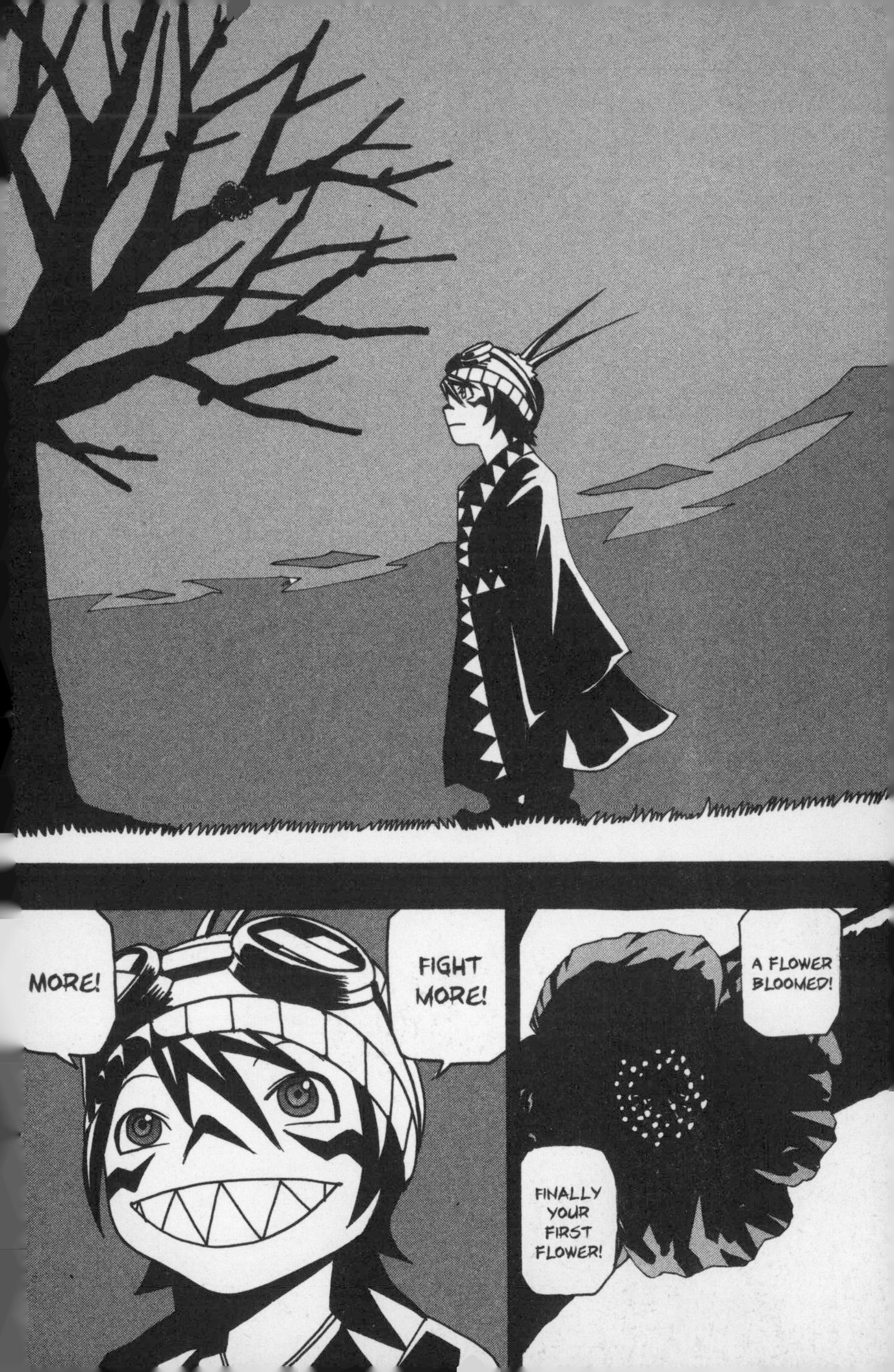
A FLOWER BLOOMED!
FINALLY YOUR FIRST FLOWER!
FIGHT MORE!
MORE!

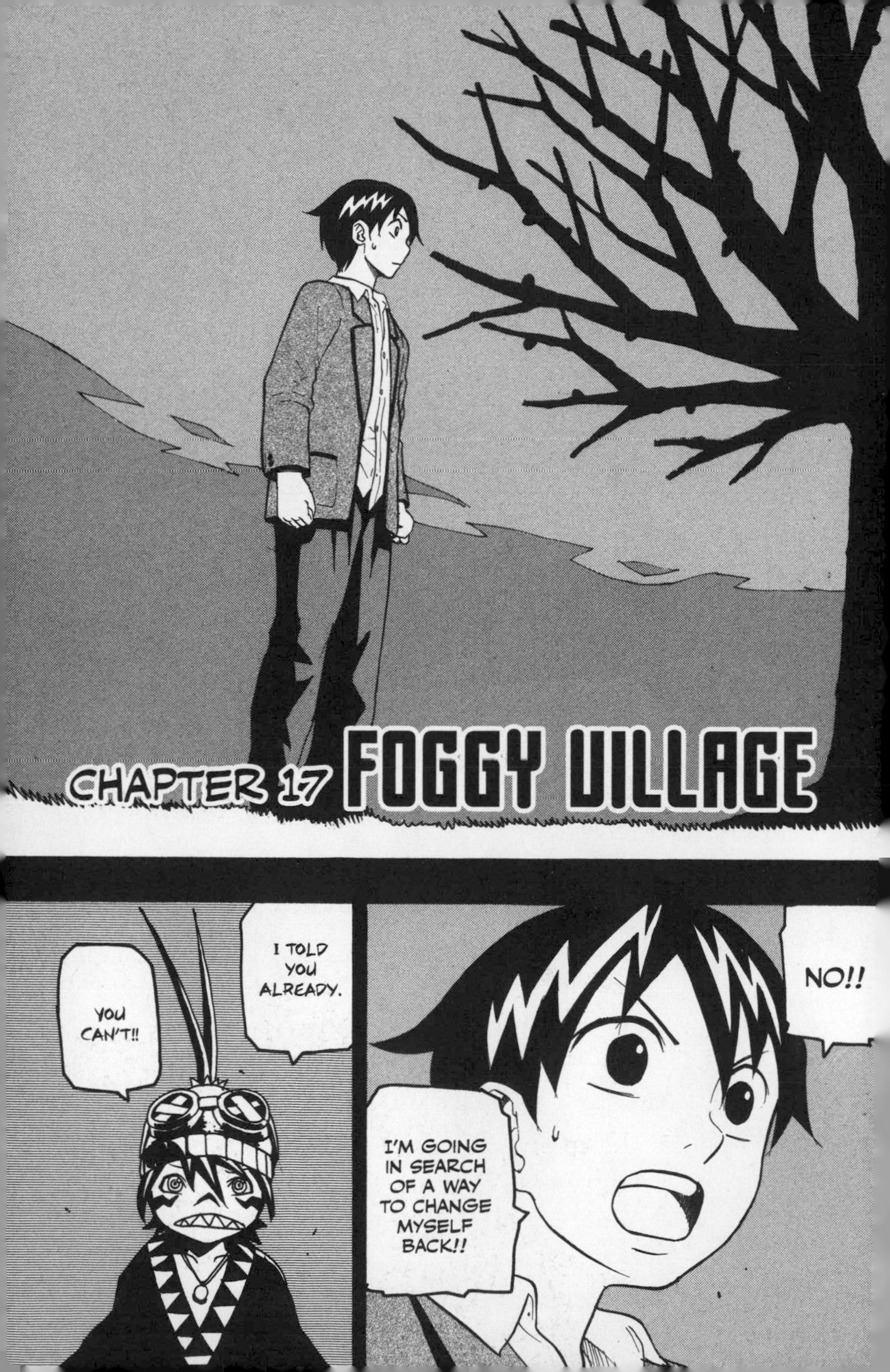
CHAPTER 17 FOGGY VILLAGE
NO!!
I'M GOING IN SEARCH OF A WAY TO CHANGE MYSELF BACK!!
I TOLD YOU ALREADY.
YOU CAN'T!!

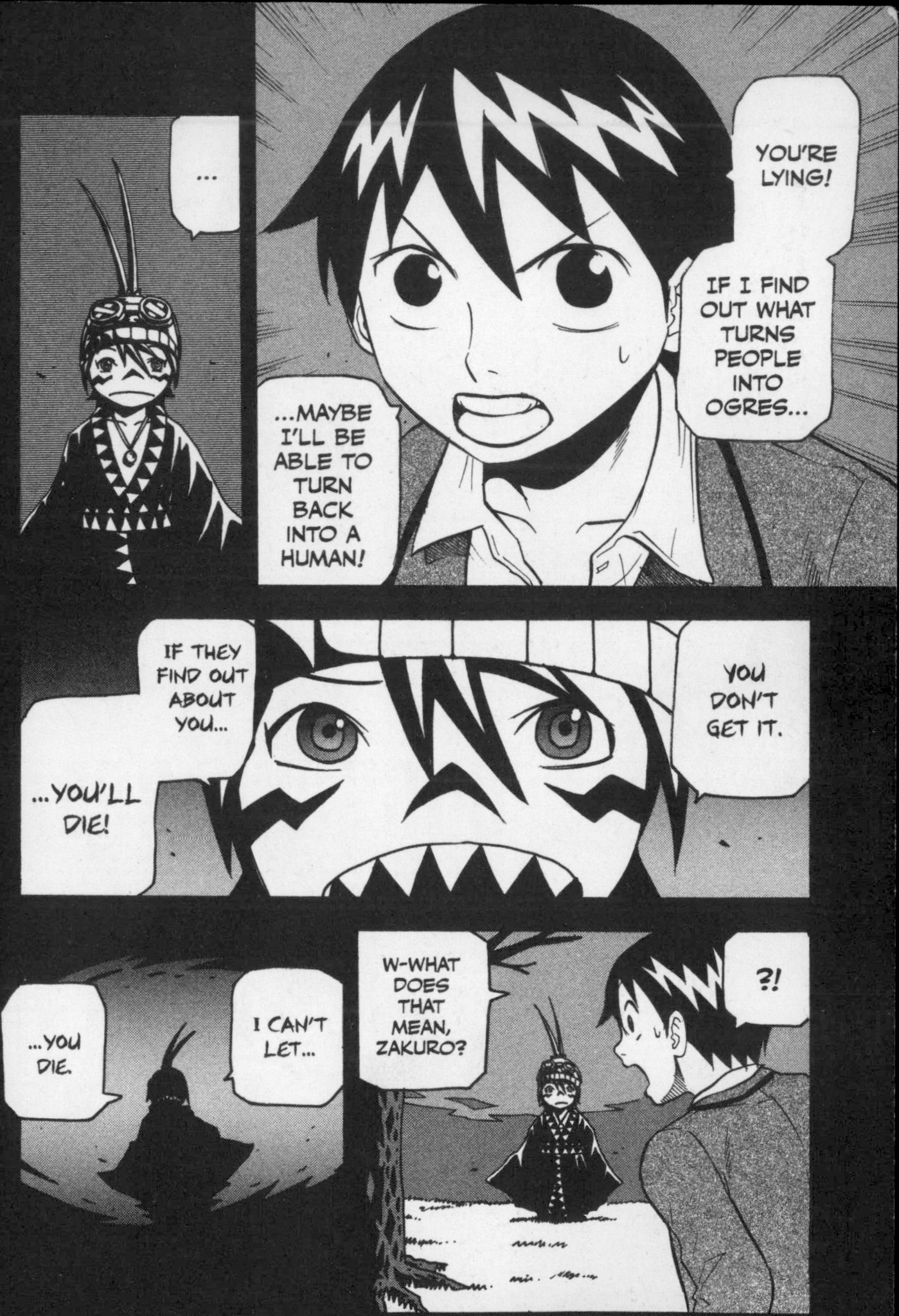
YOU'RE LYING!
IF I FIND OUT WHAT TURNS PEOPLE INTO OGRES...
...MAYBE I'LL BE ABLE TO TURN BACK INTO A HUMAN!
...
YOU DON'T GET IT.
IF THEY FIND OUT ABOUT YOU...
...YOU'LL DIE!
?!
W-WHAT DOES THAT MEAN, ZAKURO?
I CAN'T LET...
...YOU DIE.

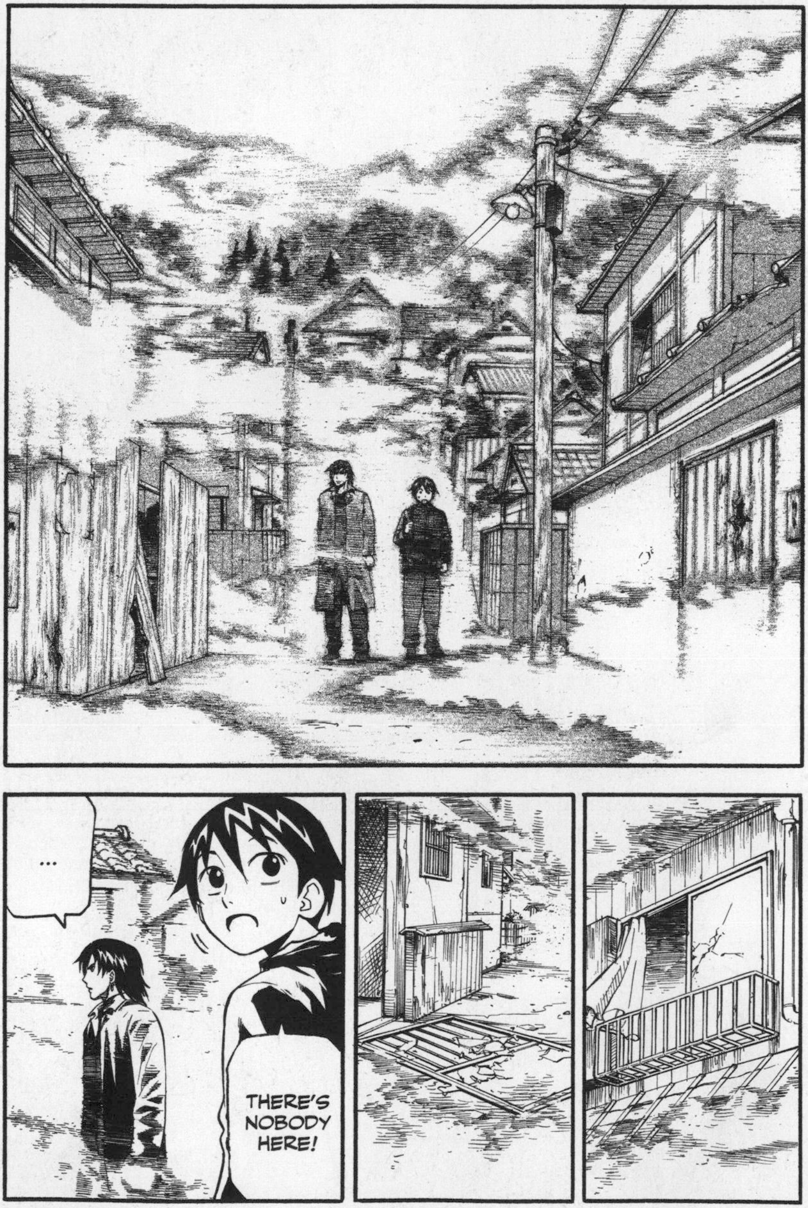
THERE'S NOBODY HERE!
...

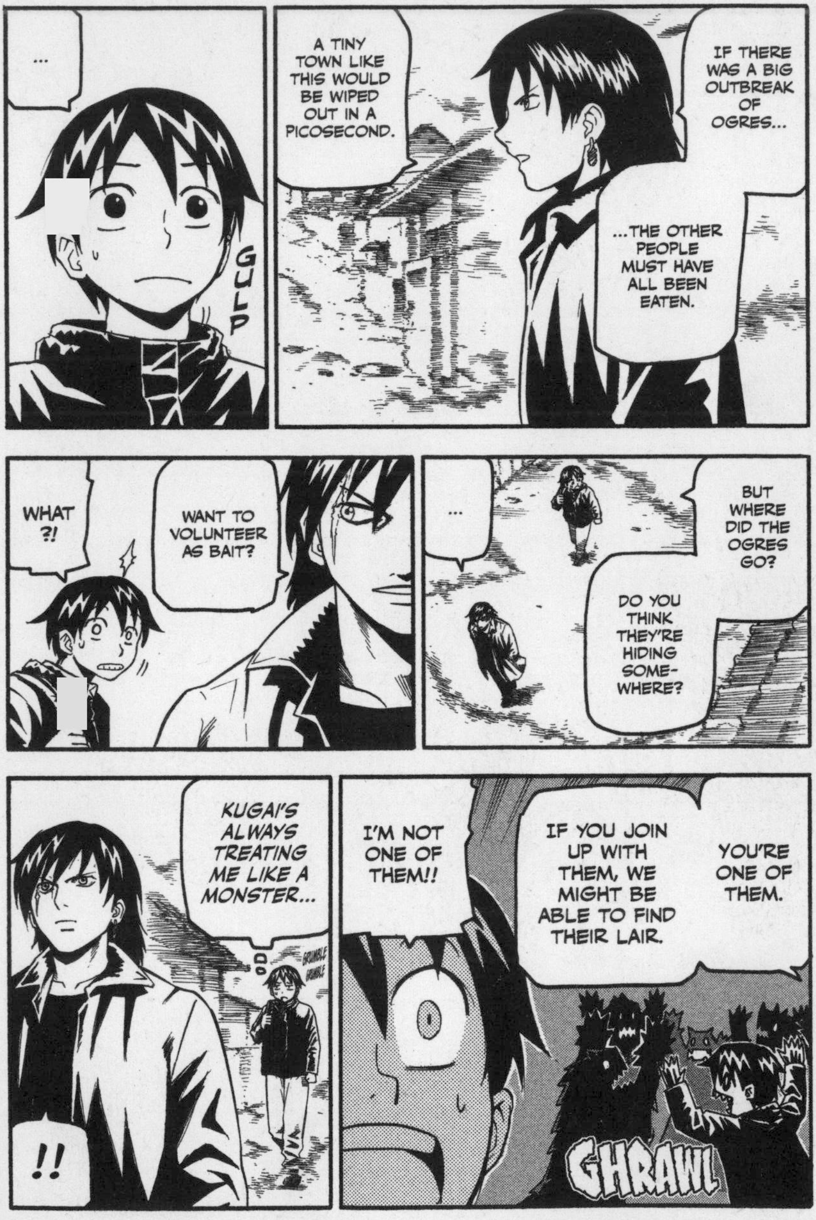
IF THERE WAS A BIG OUTBREAK OF OGRES...
...THE OTHER PEOPLE MUST HAVE ALL BEEN EATEN.
A TINY TOWN LIKE THIS WOULD BE WIPED OUT IN A PICOSECOND.
...
GULP
BUT WHERE DID THE OGRES GO?
DO YOU THINK THEY'RE HIDING SOME-WHERE?
...
WANT TO VOLUNTEER AS BAIT?
WHAT ?!
YOU'RE ONE OF THEM.
IF YOU JOIN UP WITH THEM, WE MIGHT BE ABLE TO FIND THEIR LAIR.
I'M NOT ONE OF THEM!!
GHRAWL
KUGAI'S ALWAYS TREATING ME LIKE A MONSTER...
GRUMBLE GRUMBLE
!!

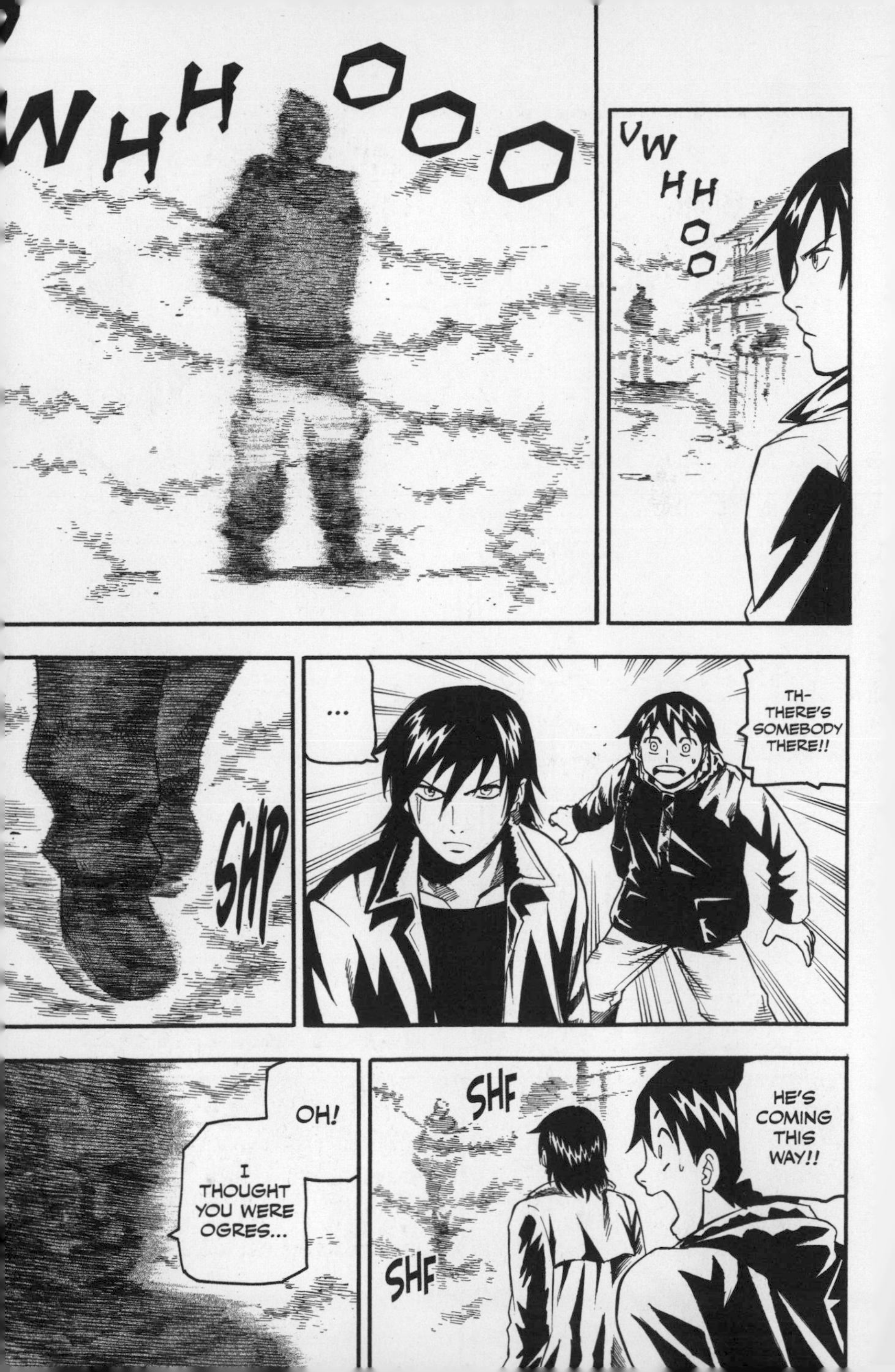
VWHHOO
WHHOOO
TH- THERE'S SOMEBODY THERE!!
...
SHP
SHF
HE'S COMING THIS WAY!!
SHF
OH!
I THOUGHT YOU WERE OGRES...

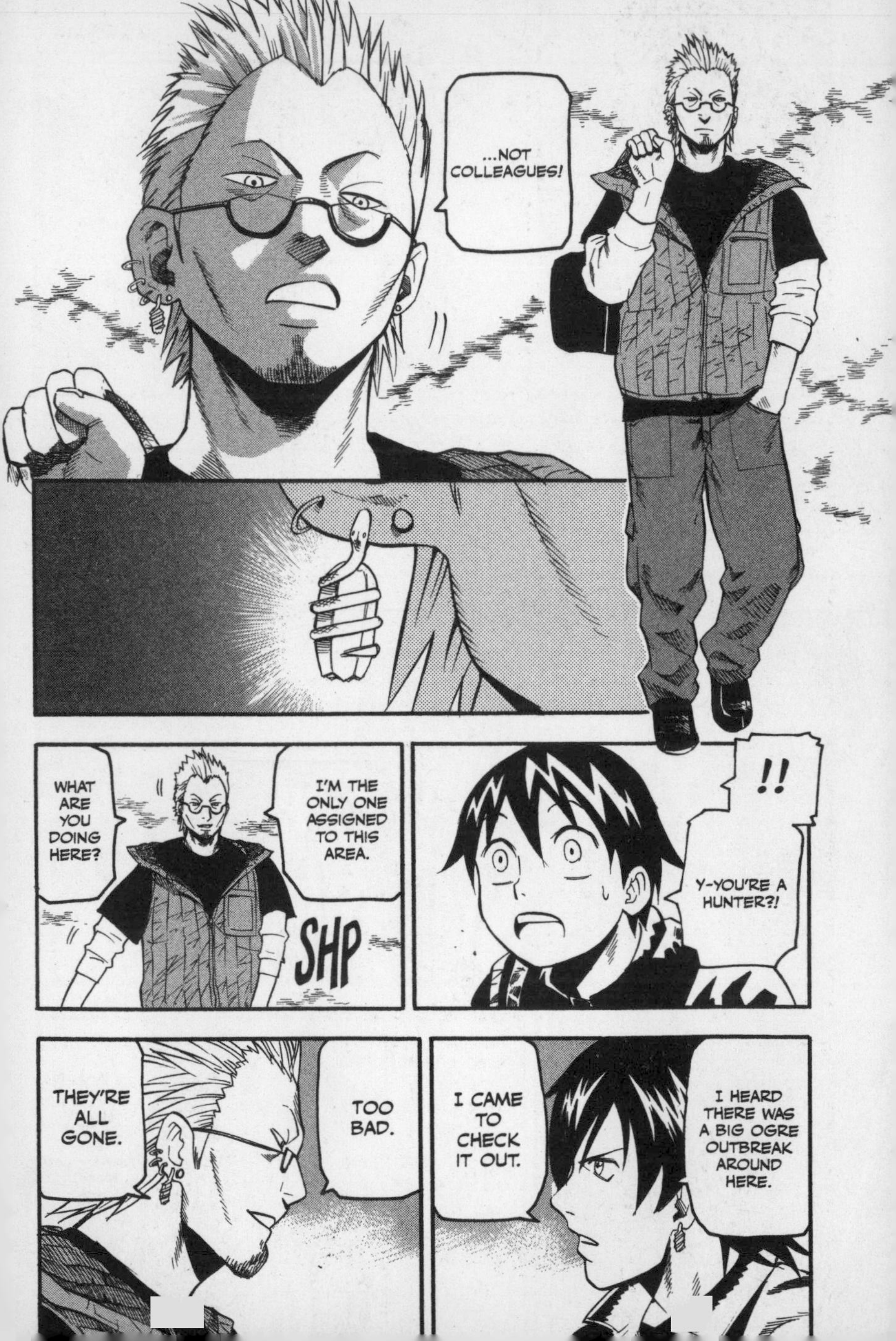
...NOT COLLEAGUES!
!!
Y-YOU'RE A HUNTER?!
I'M THE ONLY ONE ASSIGNED TO THIS AREA.
WHAT ARE YOU DOING HERE?
SHP
I HEARD THERE WAS A BIG OGRE OUTBREAK AROUND HERE.
I CAME TO CHECK IT OUT.
TOO BAD.
THEY'RE ALL GONE.

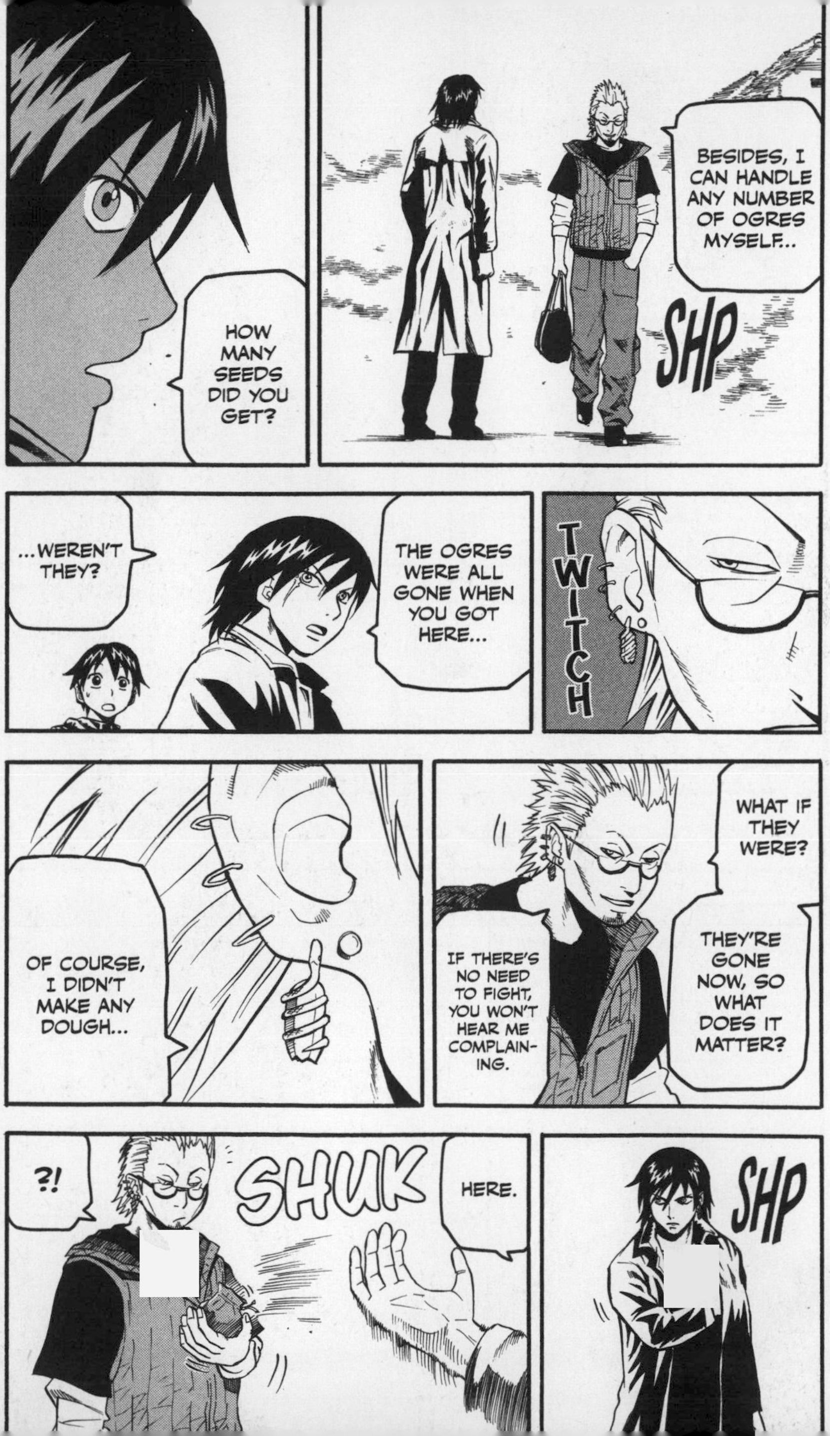
BESIDES, I CAN HANDLE ANY NUMBER OF OGRES MYSELF...
SHP
HOW MANY SEEDS DID YOU GET?
TWITCH
THE OGRES WERE ALL GONE WHEN YOU GOT HERE...
...WEREN'T THEY?
WHAT IF THEY WERE?
THEY'RE GONE NOW, SO WHAT DOES IT MATTER?
IF THERE'S NO NEED TO FIGHT, YOU WON'T HEAR ME COMPLAIN-ING.
OF COURSE, I DIDN'T MAKE ANY DOUGH...
SHP
HERE.
SHUK
?!

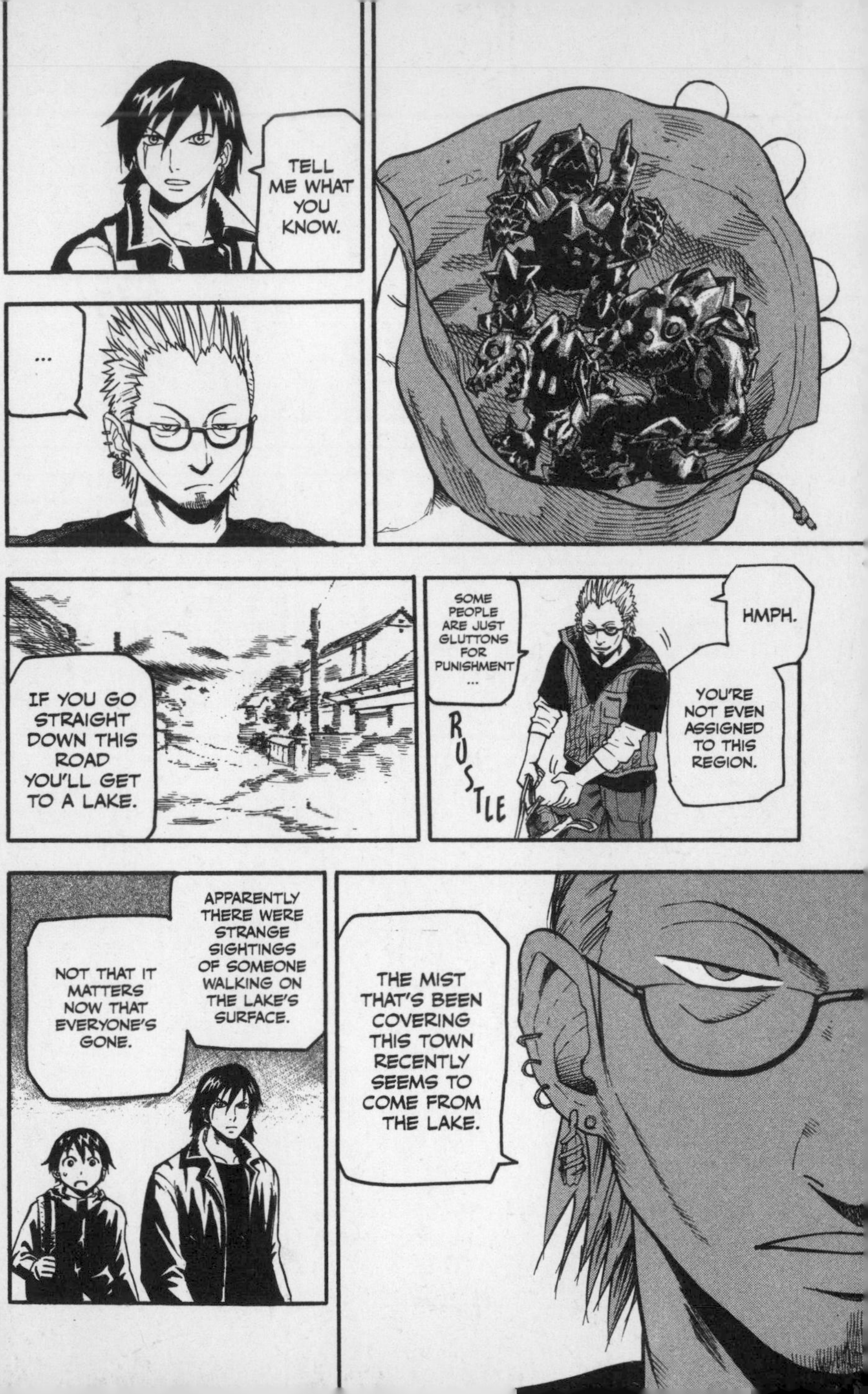

TELL ME WHAT YOU KNOW.
...
HMPH.
YOU'RE NOT EVEN ASSIGNED TO THIS REGION.
SOME PEOPLE ARE JUST GLUTTONS FOR PUNISHMENT...
RUSTLE
IF YOU GO STRAIGHT DOWN THIS ROAD YOU'LL GET TO A LAKE.
THE MIST THAT'S BEEN COVERING THIS TOWN RECENTLY SEEMS TO COME FROM THE LAKE.
APPARENTLY THERE WERE STRANGE SIGHTINGS OF SOMEONE WALKING ON THE LAKE'S SURFACE.
NOT THAT IT MATTERS NOW THAT EVERYONE'S GONE.

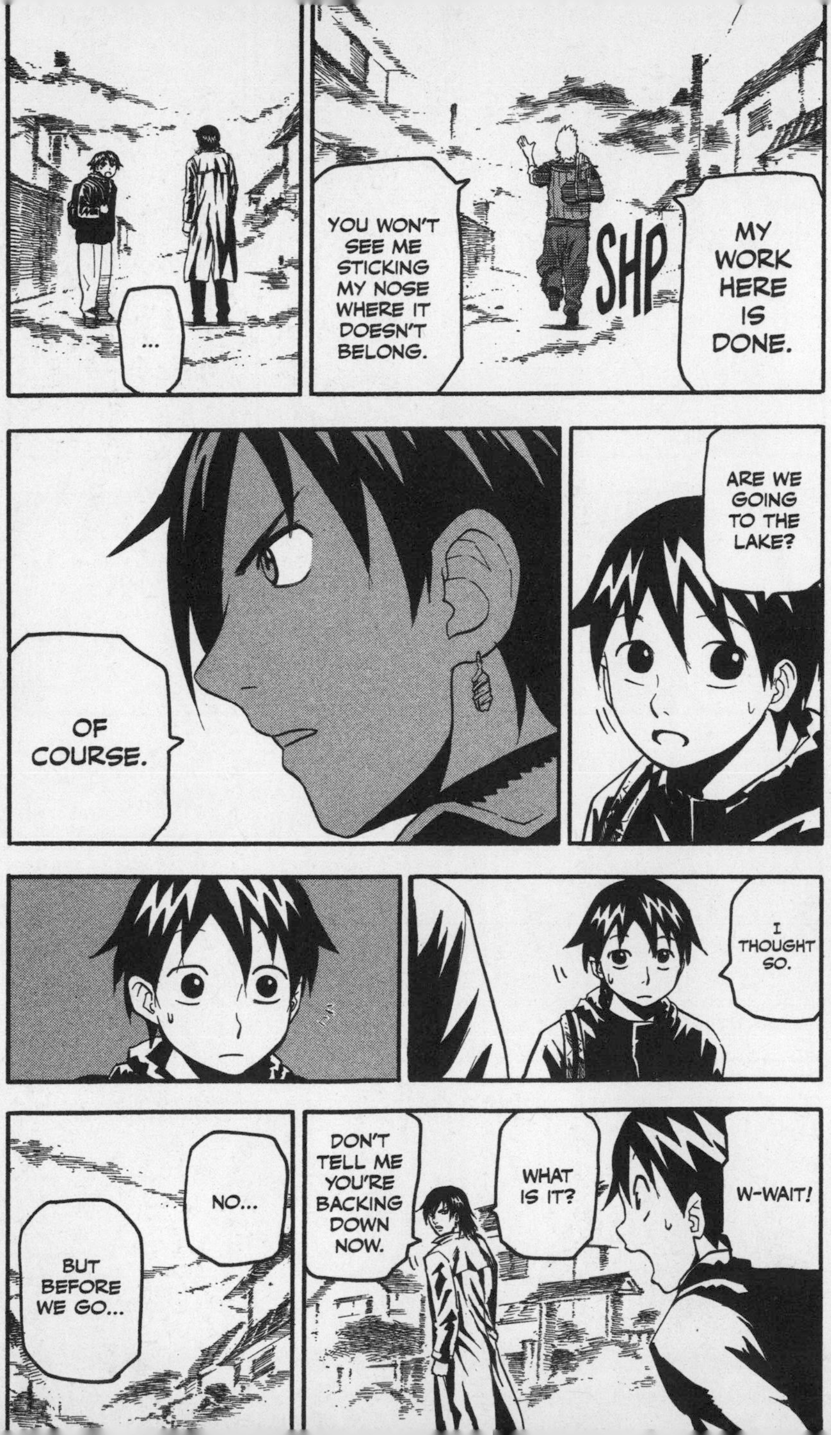
MY WORK HERE IS DONE.
SHP
YOU WON'T SEE ME STICKING MY NOSE WHERE IT DOESN'T BELONG.
...
ARE WE GOING TO THE LAKE?
OF COURSE.
I THOUGHT SO.
W-WAIT!
WHAT IS IT?
DON'T TELL ME YOU'RE BACKING DOWN NOW.
NO...
BUT BEFORE WE GO...

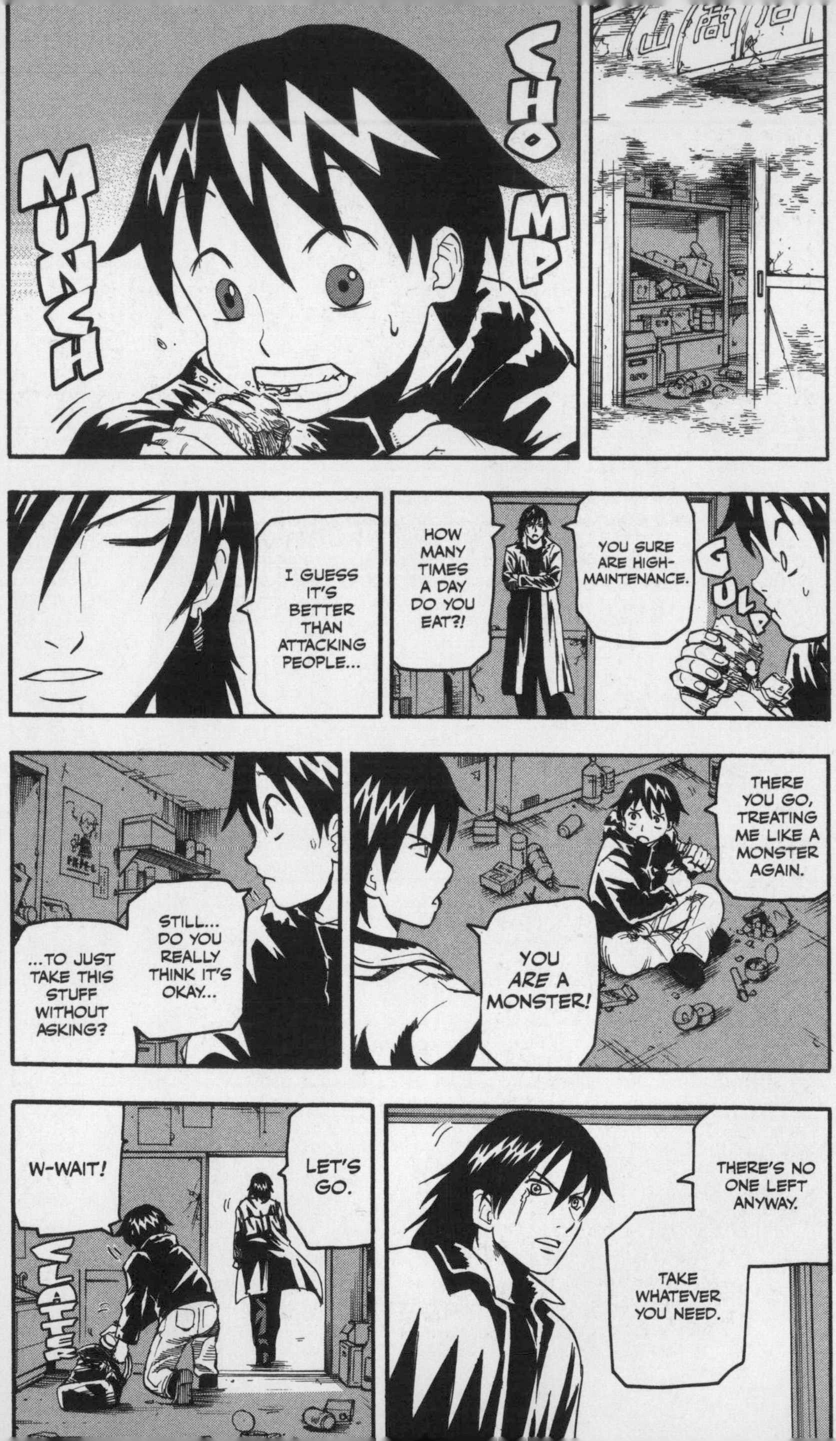
CHOMP
MUNCH
GULP
YOU SURE ARE HIGH-MAINTENANCE.
HOW MANY TIMES A DAY DO YOU EAT?!
I GUESS IT'S BETTER THAN ATTACKING PEOPLE...
THERE YOU GO, TREATING ME LIKE A MONSTER AGAIN.
YOU *ARE* A MONSTER!
STILL... DO YOU REALLY THINK IT'S OKAY...
...TO JUST TAKE THIS STUFF WITHOUT ASKING?
THERE'S NO ONE LEFT ANYWAY.
TAKE WHATEVER YOU NEED.
LET'S GO.
W-WAIT!
CLATTER

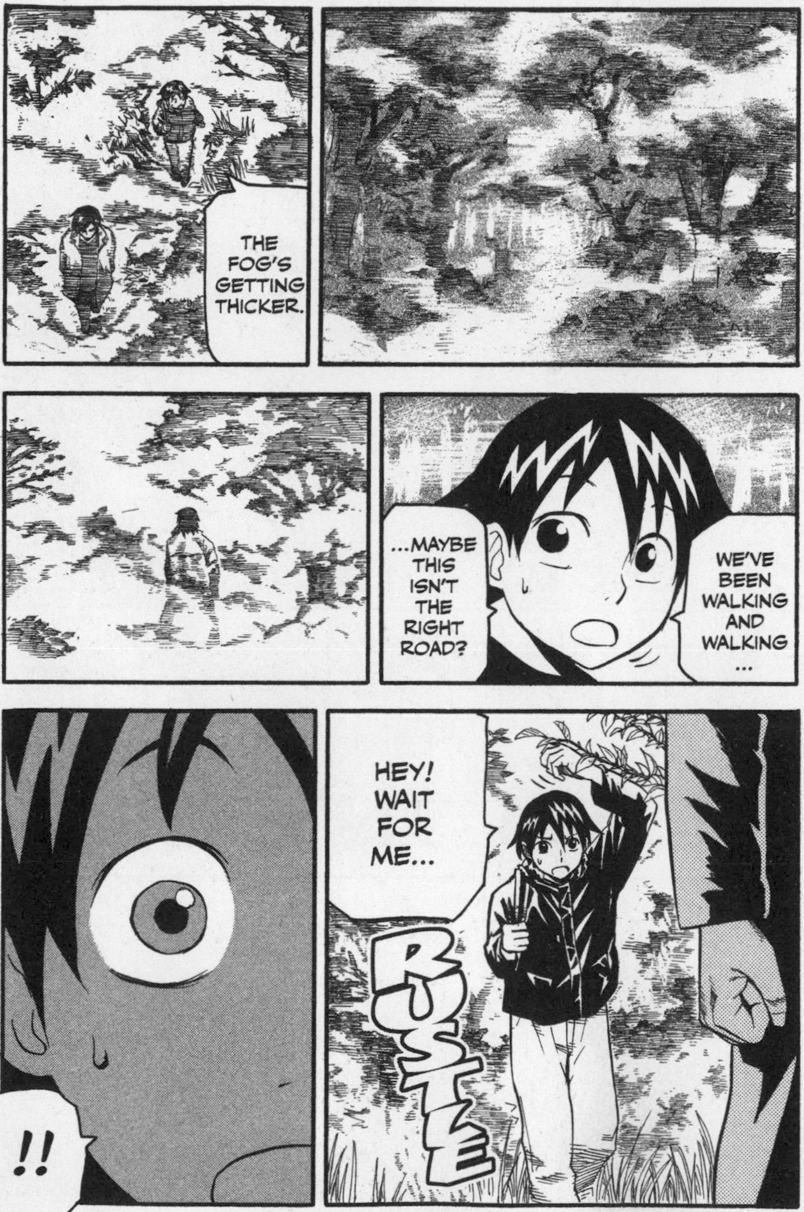
THE FOG'S GETTING THICKER.
WE'VE BEEN WALKING AND WALKING ...
...MAYBE THIS ISN'T THE RIGHT ROAD?
HEY! WAIT FOR ME...
RUSTLE
!!

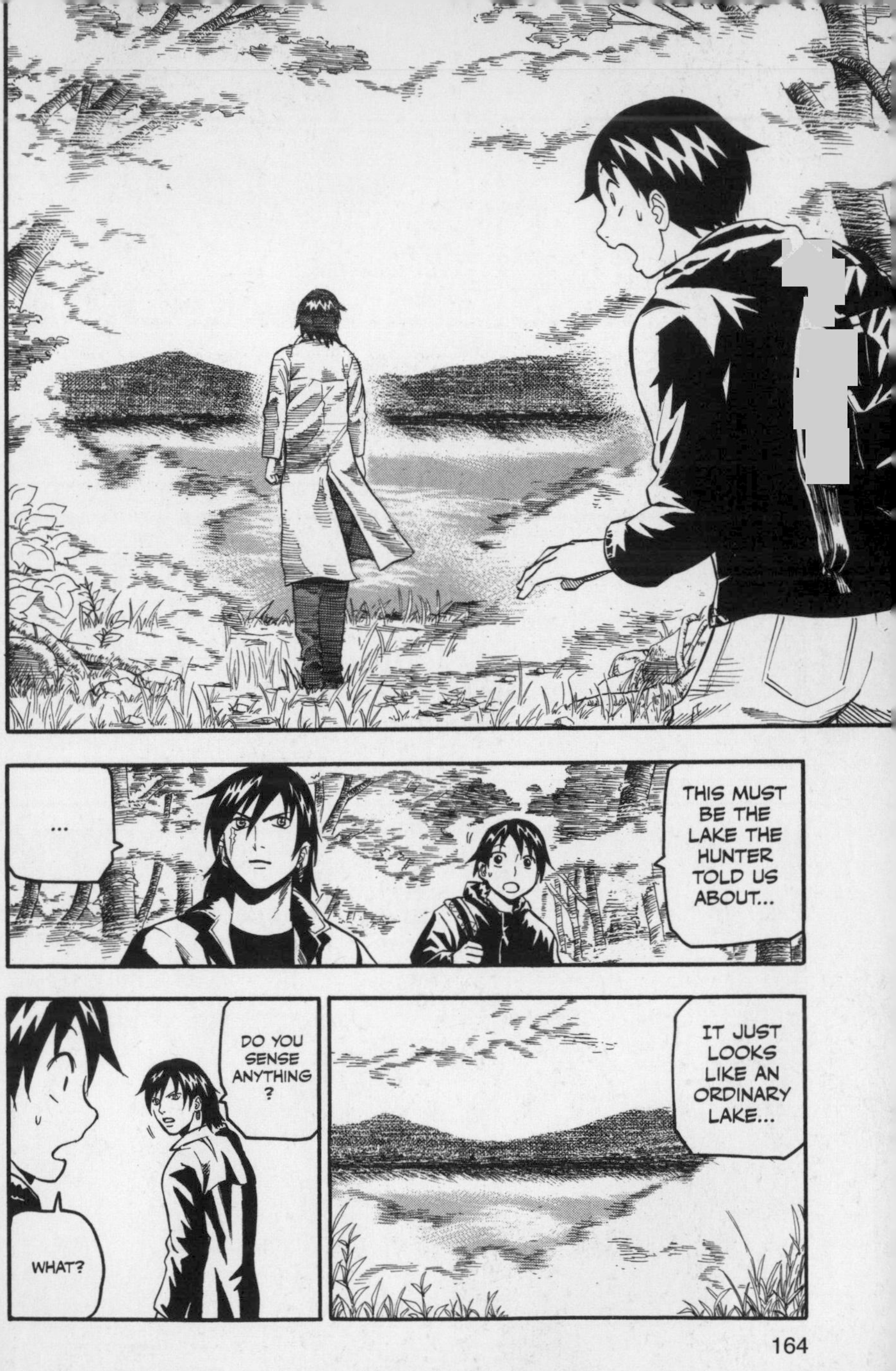
THIS MUST BE THE LAKE THE HUNTER TOLD US ABOUT...
...
IT JUST LOOKS LIKE AN ORDINARY LAKE...
DO YOU SENSE ANYTHING ?
WHAT?

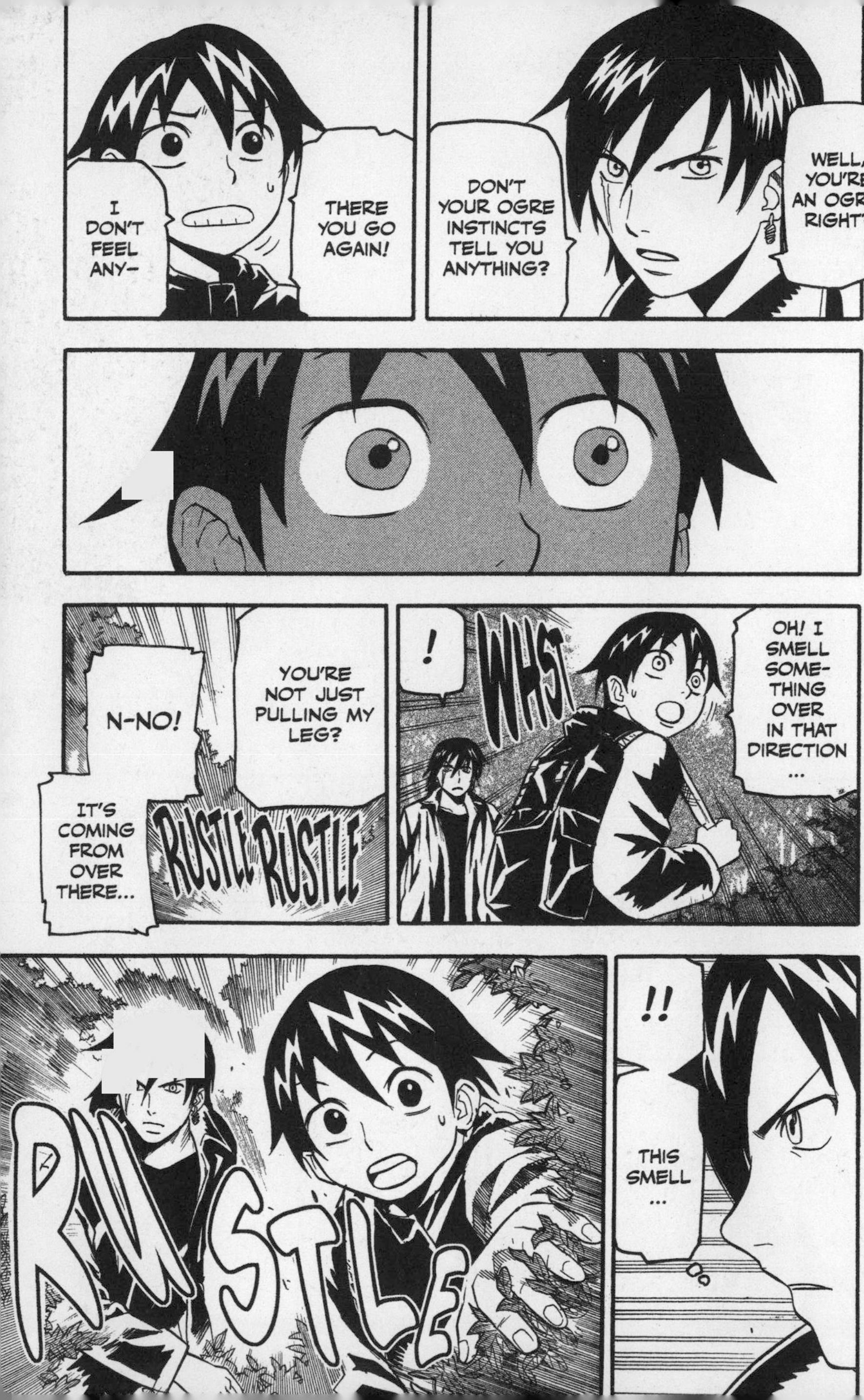
WELL, YOU'RE AN OGRE, RIGHT?
DON'T YOUR OGRE INSTINCTS TELL YOU ANYTHING?
THERE YOU GO AGAIN!
I DON'T FEEL ANY–
OH! I SMELL SOME-THING OVER IN THAT DIRECTION ...
WHST
!
YOU'RE NOT JUST PULLING MY LEG?
N-NO!
IT'S COMING FROM OVER THERE...
RUSTLE RUSTLE
!!
THIS SMELL ...
RUSTLE

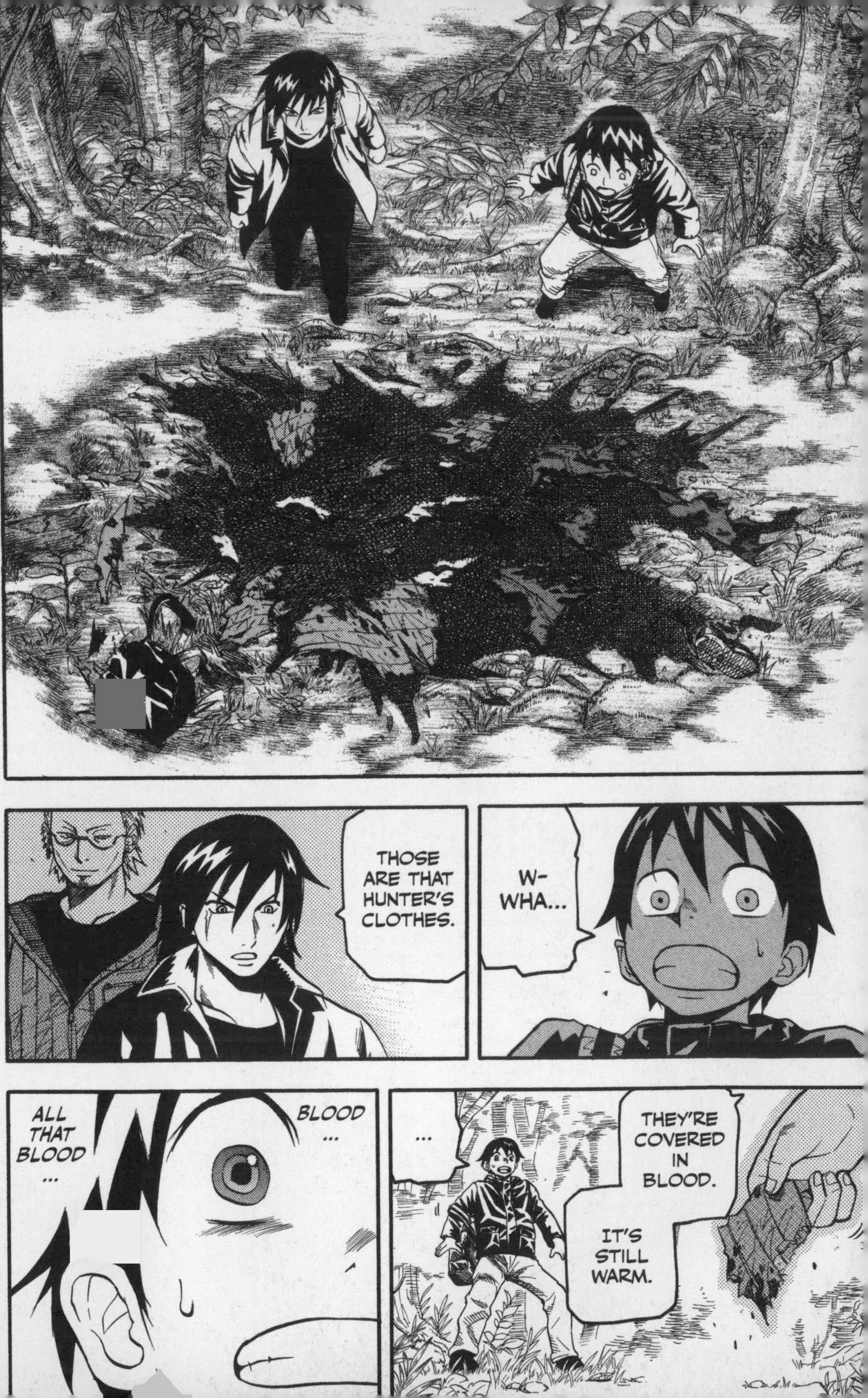
W- WHA...
THOSE ARE THAT HUNTER'S CLOTHES.
THEY'RE COVERED IN BLOOD.
...
IT'S STILL WARM.
BLOOD ...
ALL THAT BLOOD ...

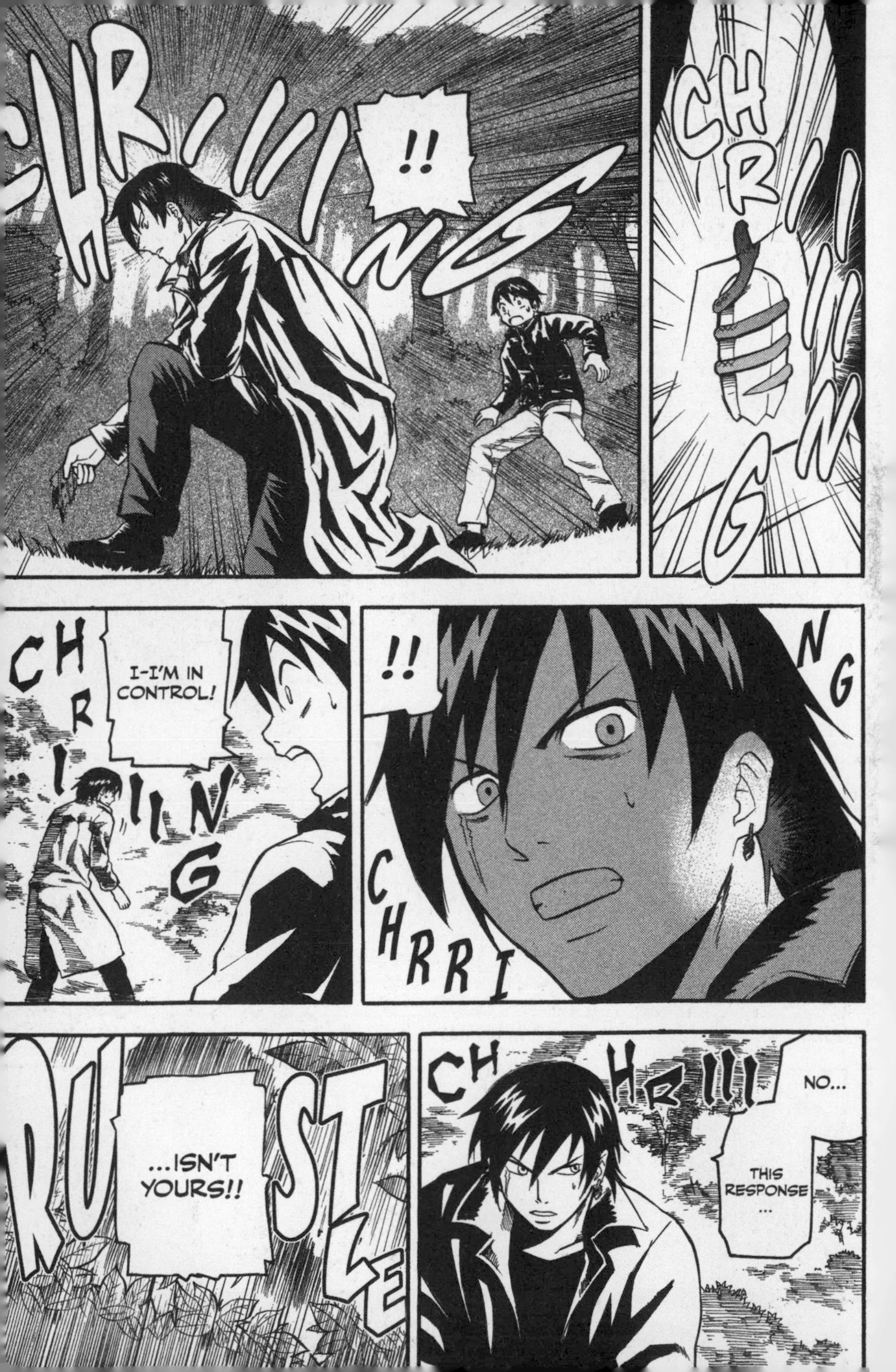
CHRIIIING
CHRIIIING
!!
!!
CHRRI
NG
I-I'M IN CONTROL!
CHRIIING
CH
HRIII
NO...
THIS RESPONSE ...
...ISN'T YOURS!!
RUSTLE

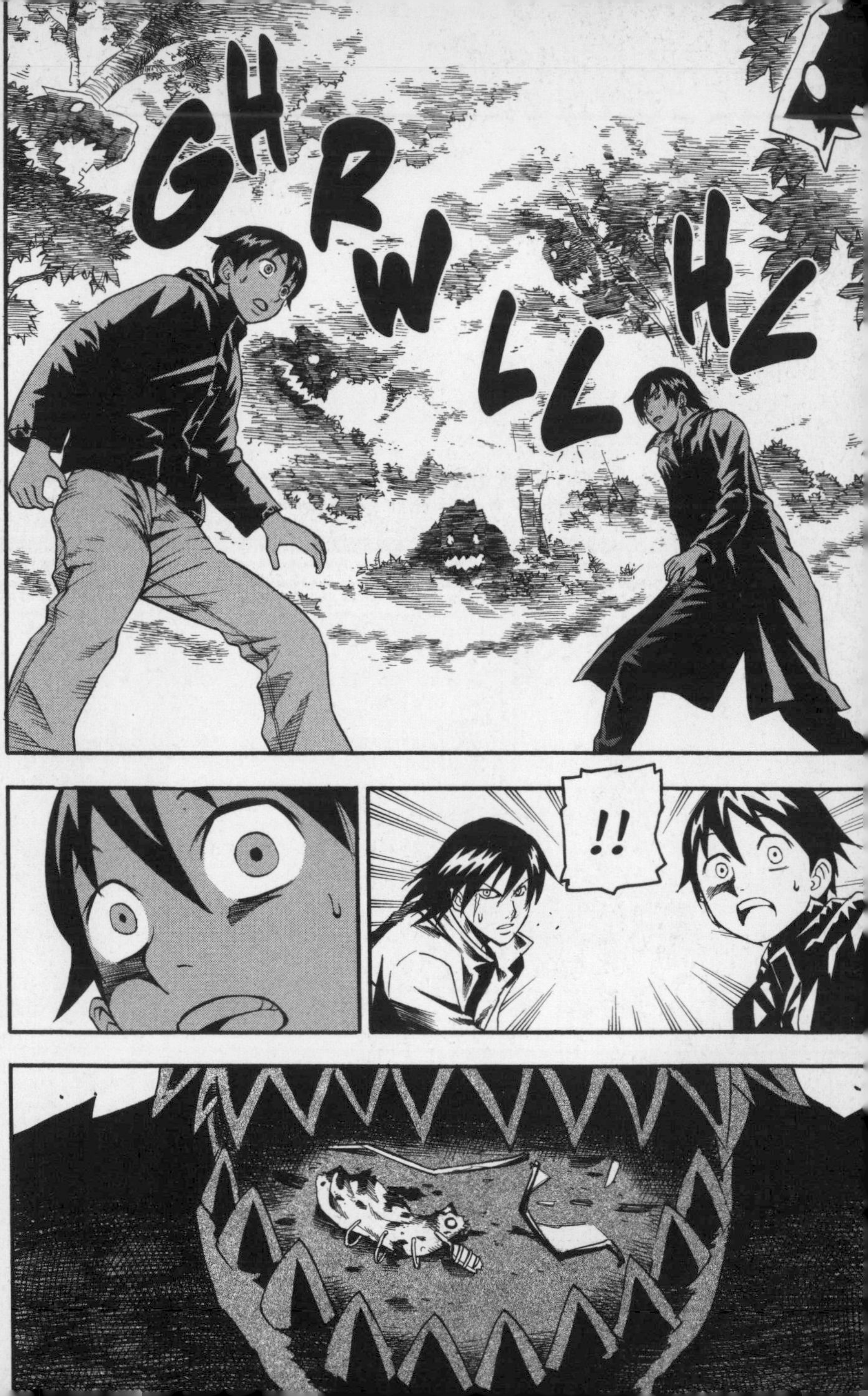
GHRWLLHL
!!

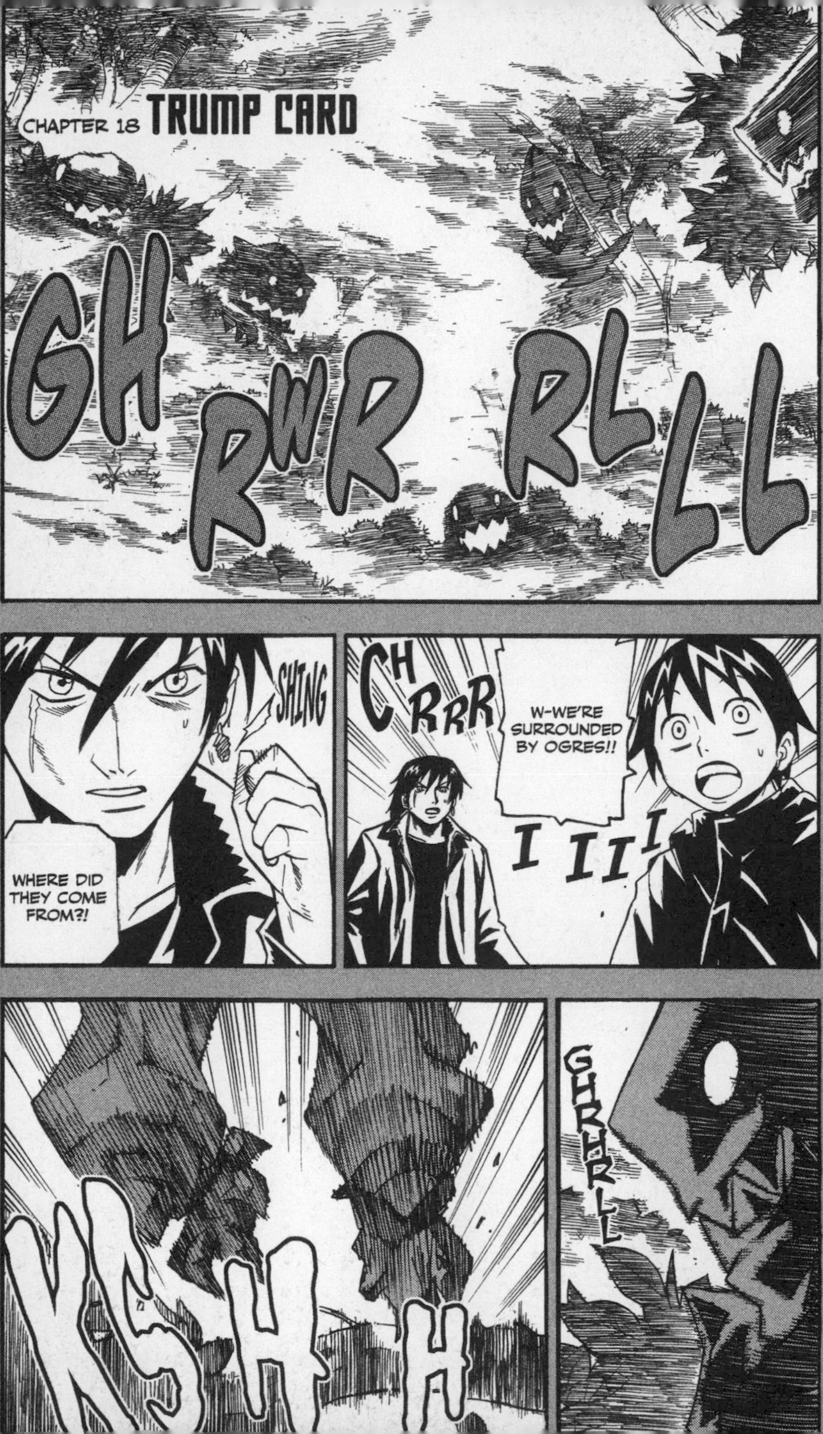
CHAPTER 18 TRUMP CARD
GHRWRRLLL
CHRRR
W-WE'RE SURROUNDED BY OGRES!!
IIII
SHING
WHERE DID THEY COME FROM?!
GHRHRLL
KSHH

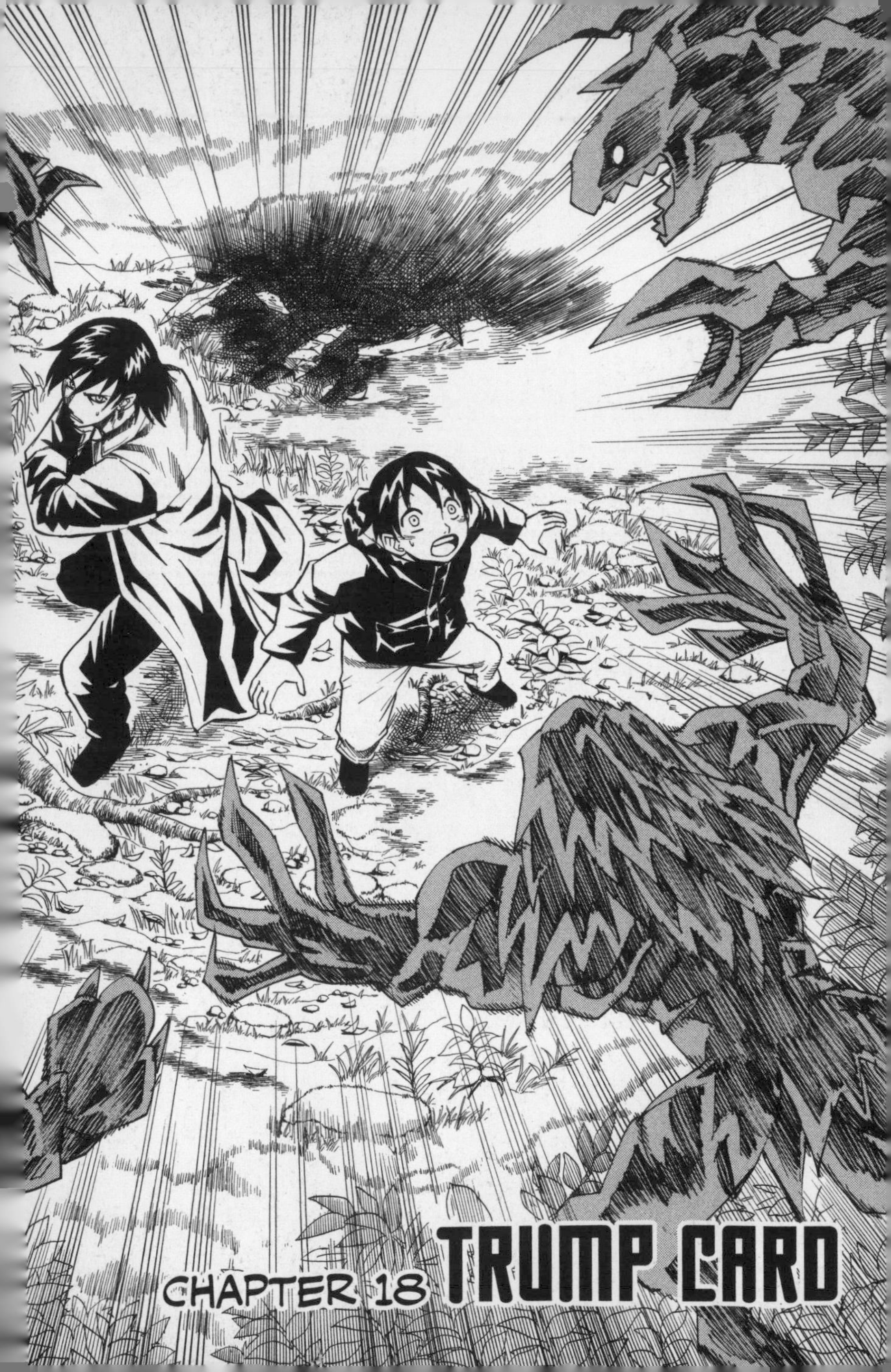
CHAPTER 18
TRUMP CARD

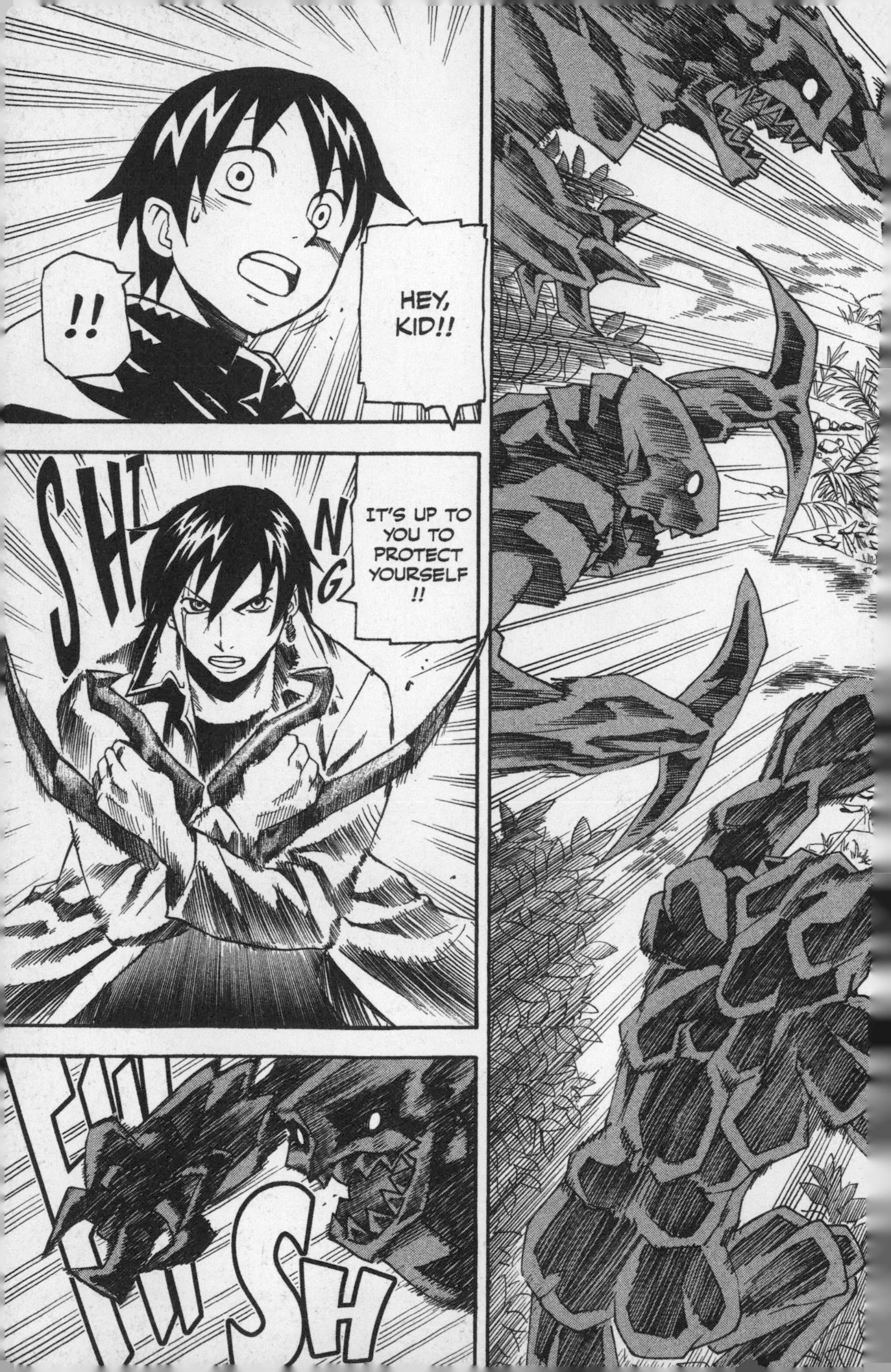
HEY, KID!!
!!
IT'S UP TO YOU TO PROTECT YOURSELF !!
SHING
SH

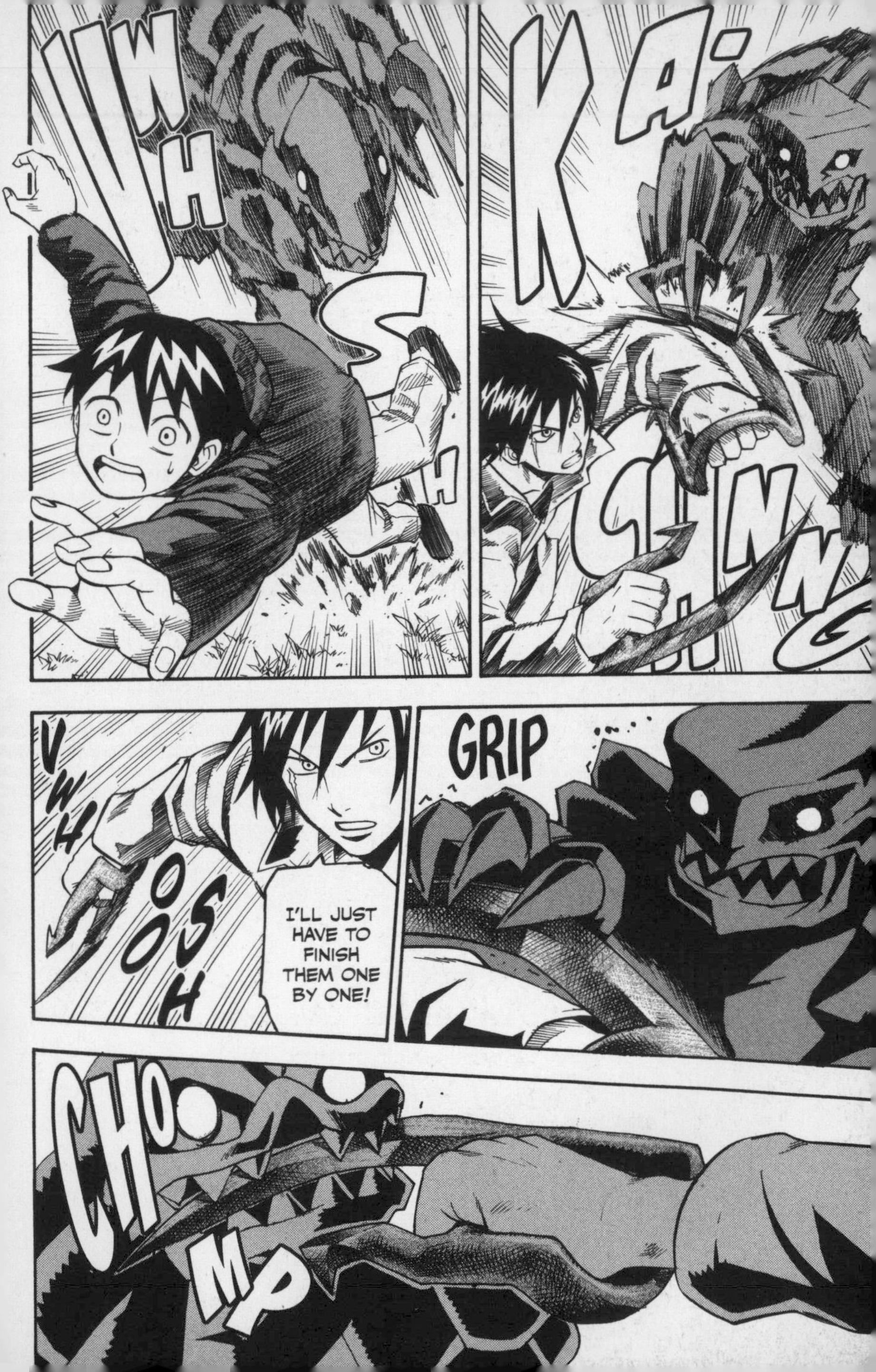
GRIP
I'LL JUST HAVE TO FINISH THEM ONE BY ONE!
CHOMP

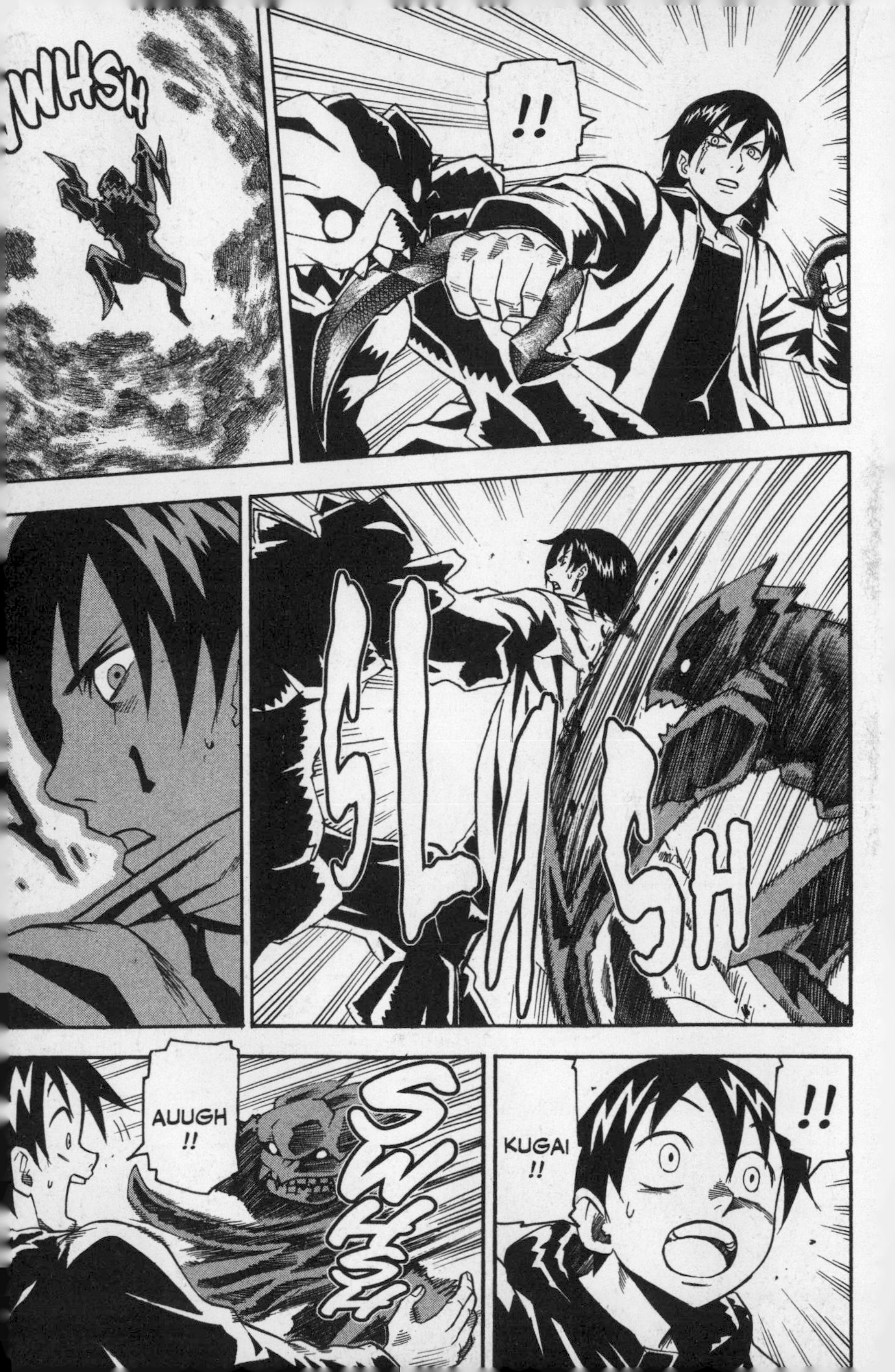

!!
WHSH
SLASH
!!
KUGAI !!
AUUGH !!

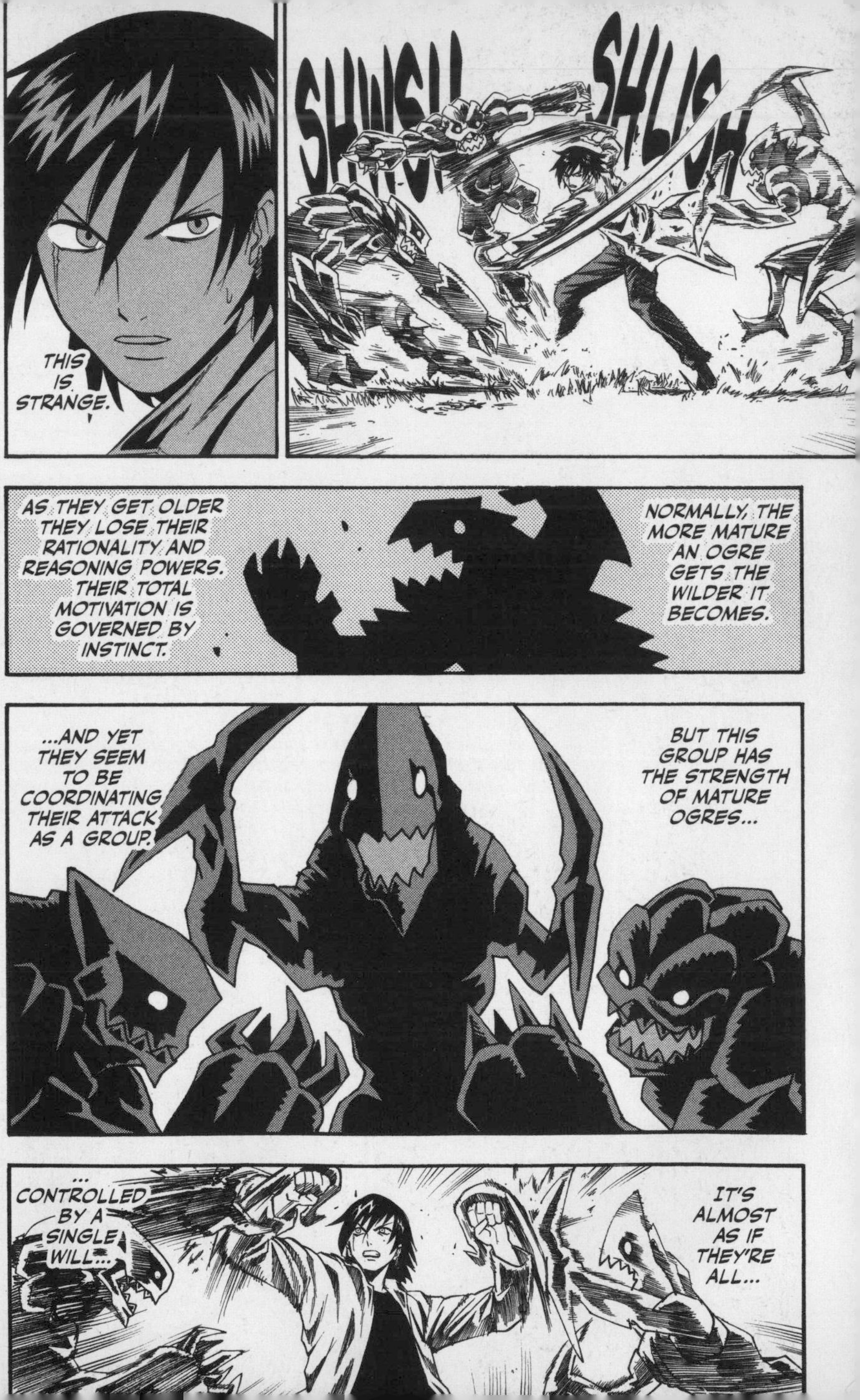
SHLISH
SHUSH
THIS IS STRANGE.
NORMALLY, THE MORE MATURE AN OGRE GETS THE WILDER IT BECOMES.
AS THEY GET OLDER THEY LOSE THEIR RATIONALITY AND REASONING POWERS. THEIR TOTAL MOTIVATION IS GOVERNED BY INSTINCT.
BUT THIS GROUP HAS THE STRENGTH OF MATURE OGRES...
...AND YET THEY SEEM TO BE COORDINATING THEIR ATTACK AS A GROUP.
IT'S ALMOST AS IF THEY'RE ALL...
...CONTROLLED BY A SINGLE WILL...

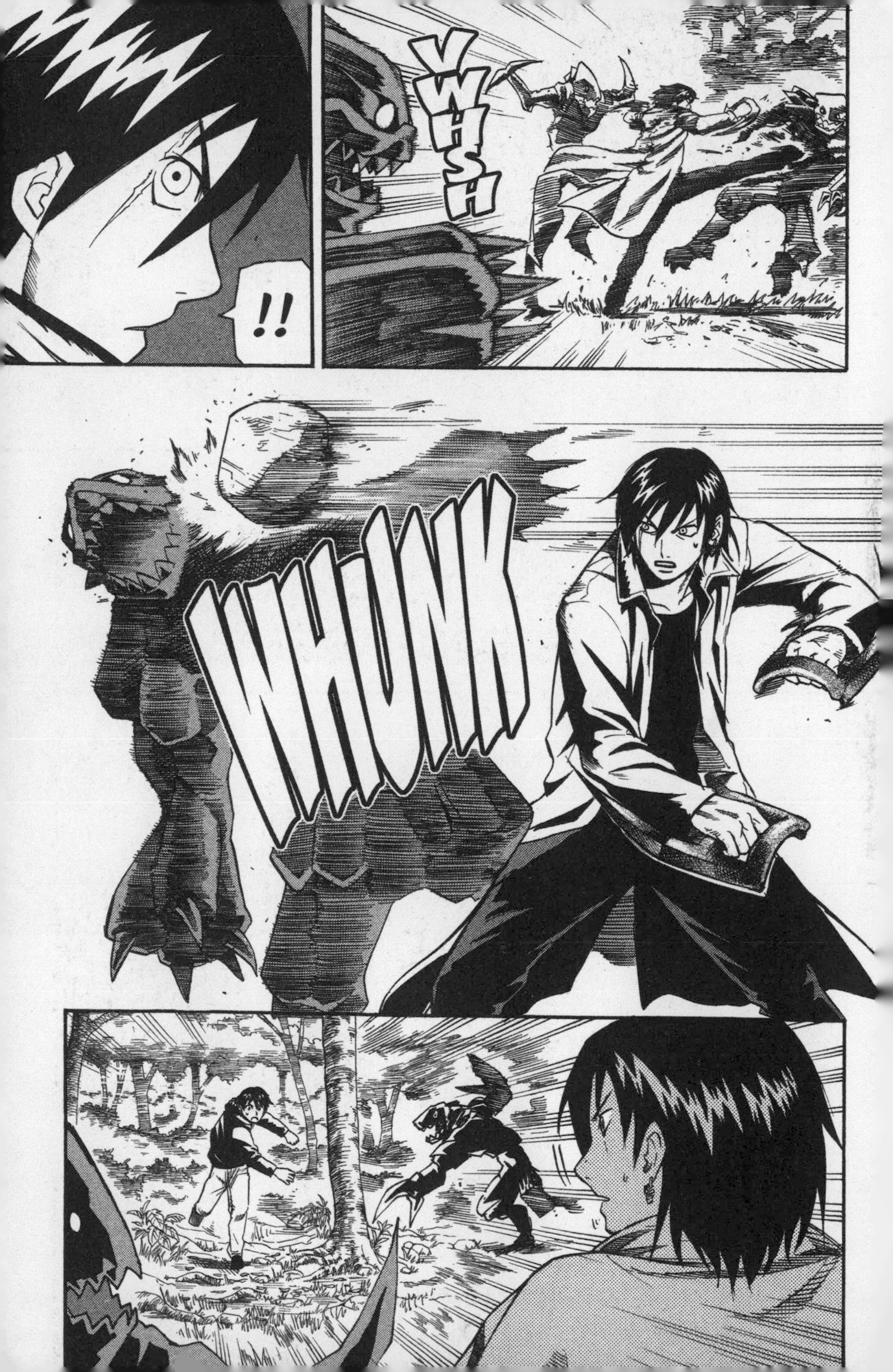
VWHSH
!!
WHUNK

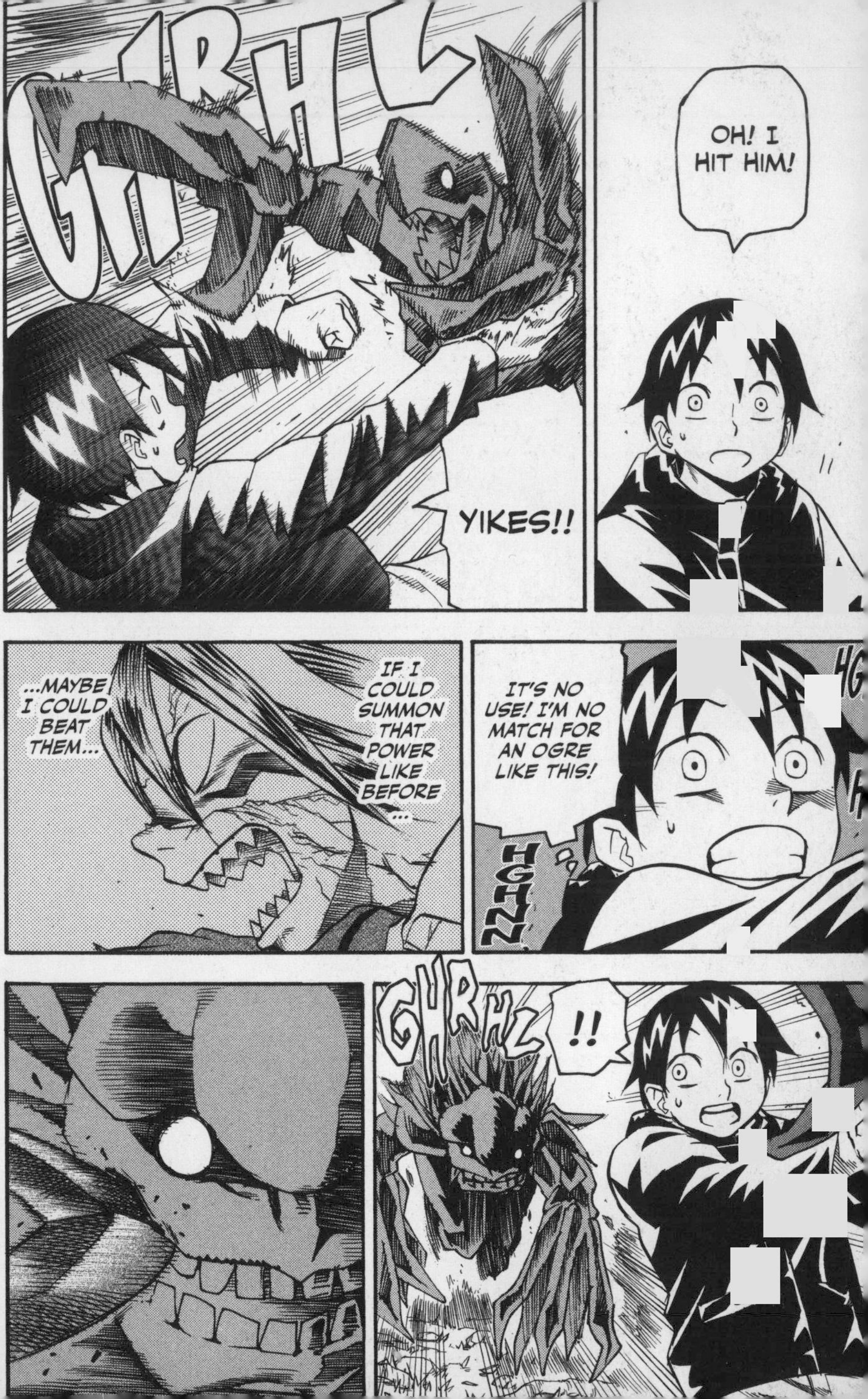
OH! I HIT HIM!
GHRHL
YIKES!!
IT'S NO USE! I'M NO MATCH FOR AN OGRE LIKE THIS!
HGHNN
IF I COULD SUMMON THAT POWER LIKE BEFORE ...
...MAYBE I COULD BEAT THEM...
GHRHL
!!

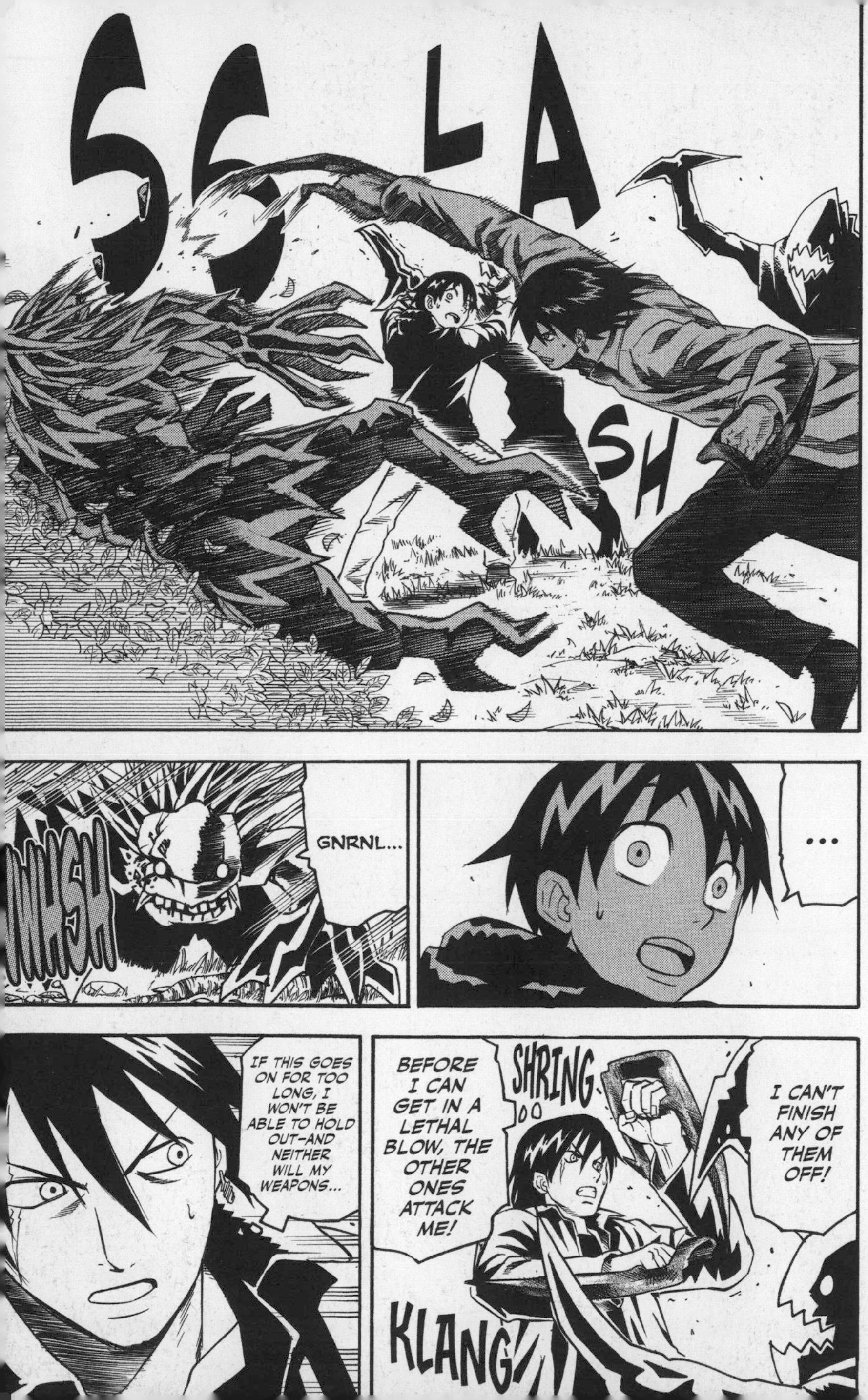
SCLASH
...
WHISH
GNRNL...
I CAN'T FINISH ANY OF THEM OFF!
SHRING
BEFORE I CAN GET IN A LETHAL BLOW, THE OTHER ONES ATTACK ME!
KLANG
IF THIS GOES ON FOR TOO LONG, I WON'T BE ABLE TO HOLD OUT—AND NEITHER WILL MY WEAPONS...

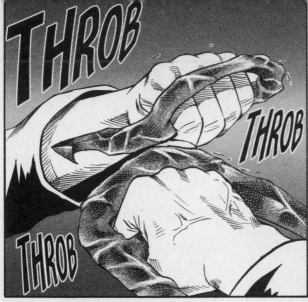

THROB

THROB

THROB

KH HR H

STAY BACK NOW!!

HEY, KID!!

KUGAI?

BWSH

IT'S DANGEROUS, BUT I HAVE TO DO IT.

?!

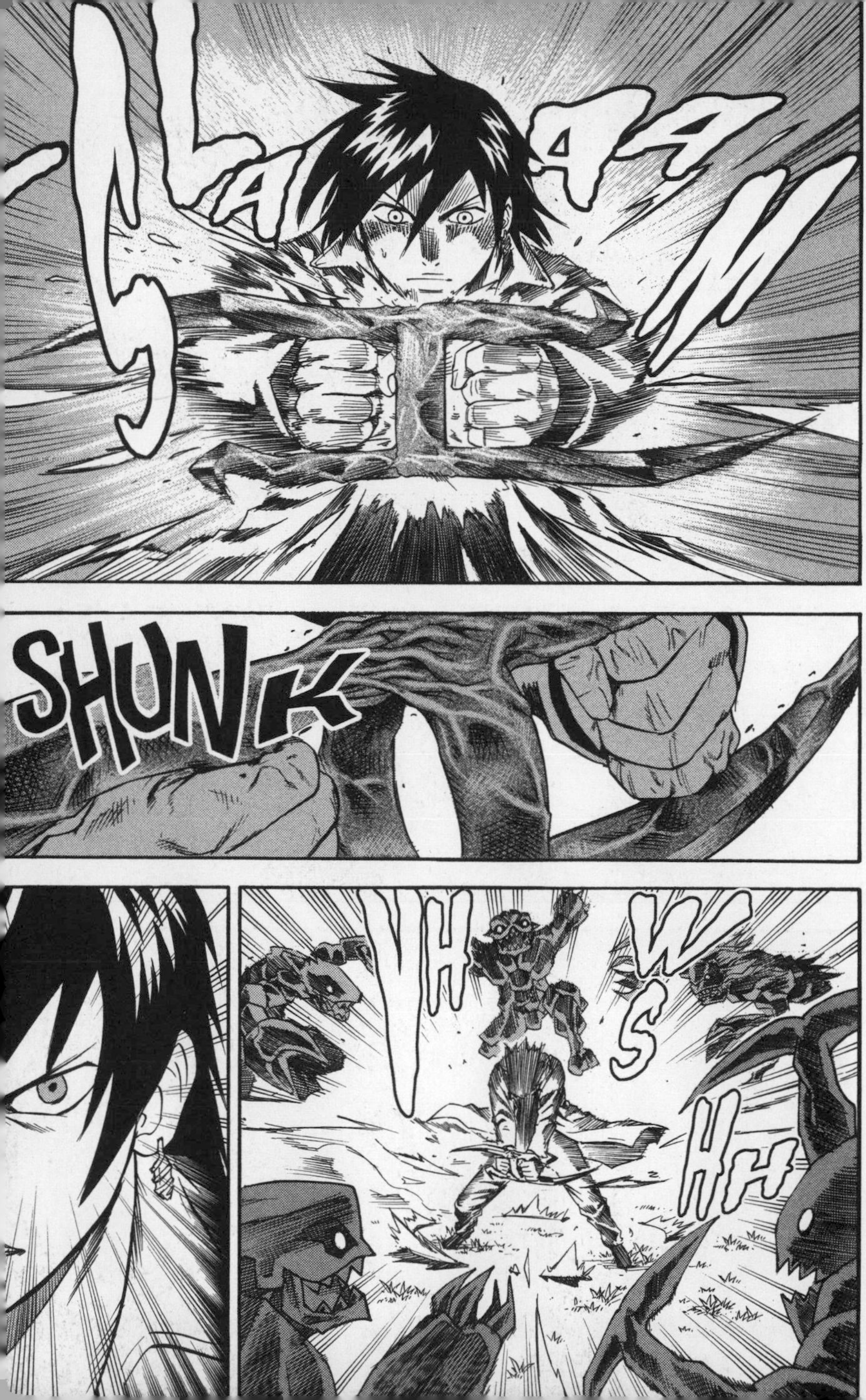
SLAAAM
SHUNK
VH
WSHH

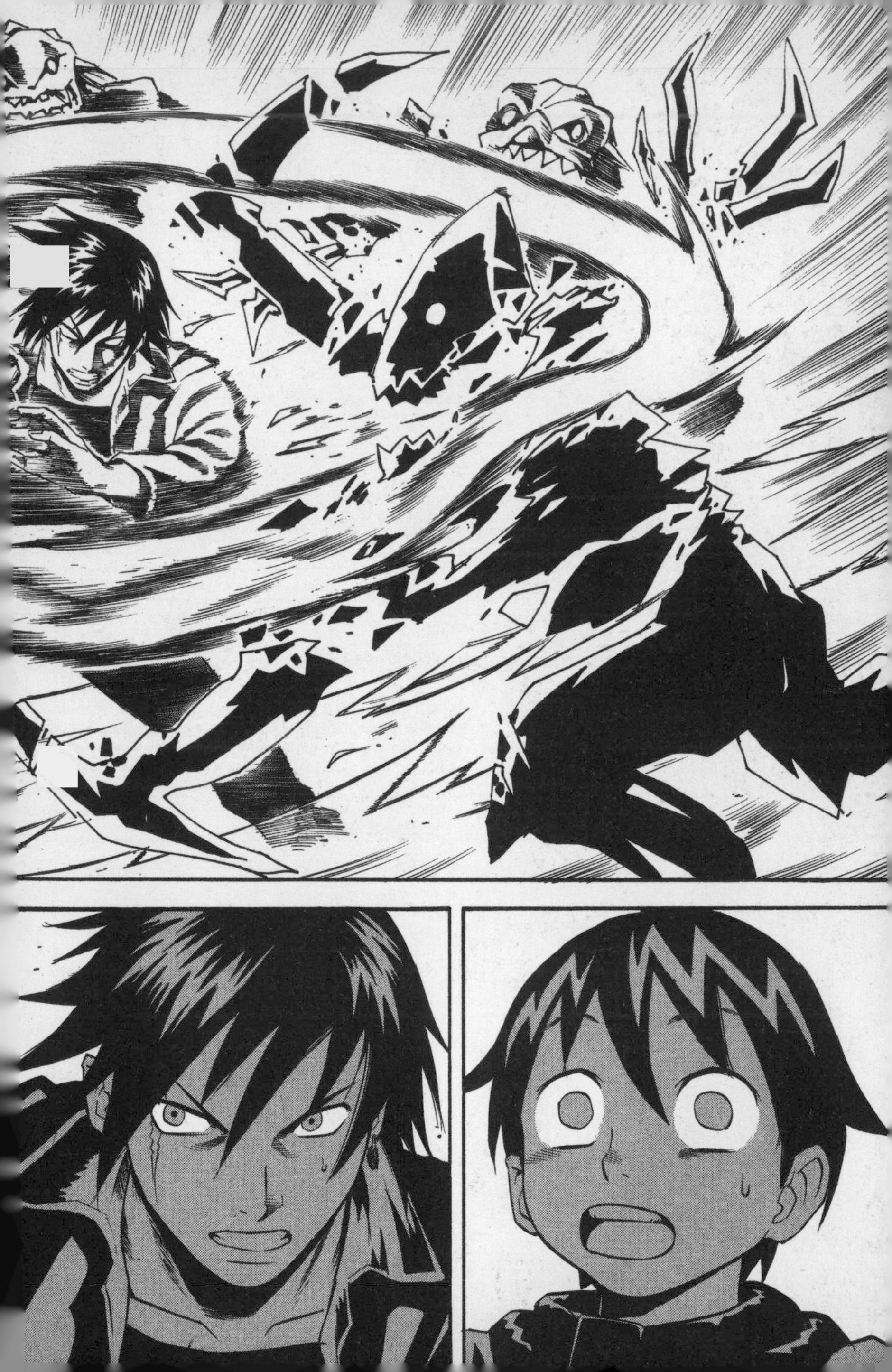

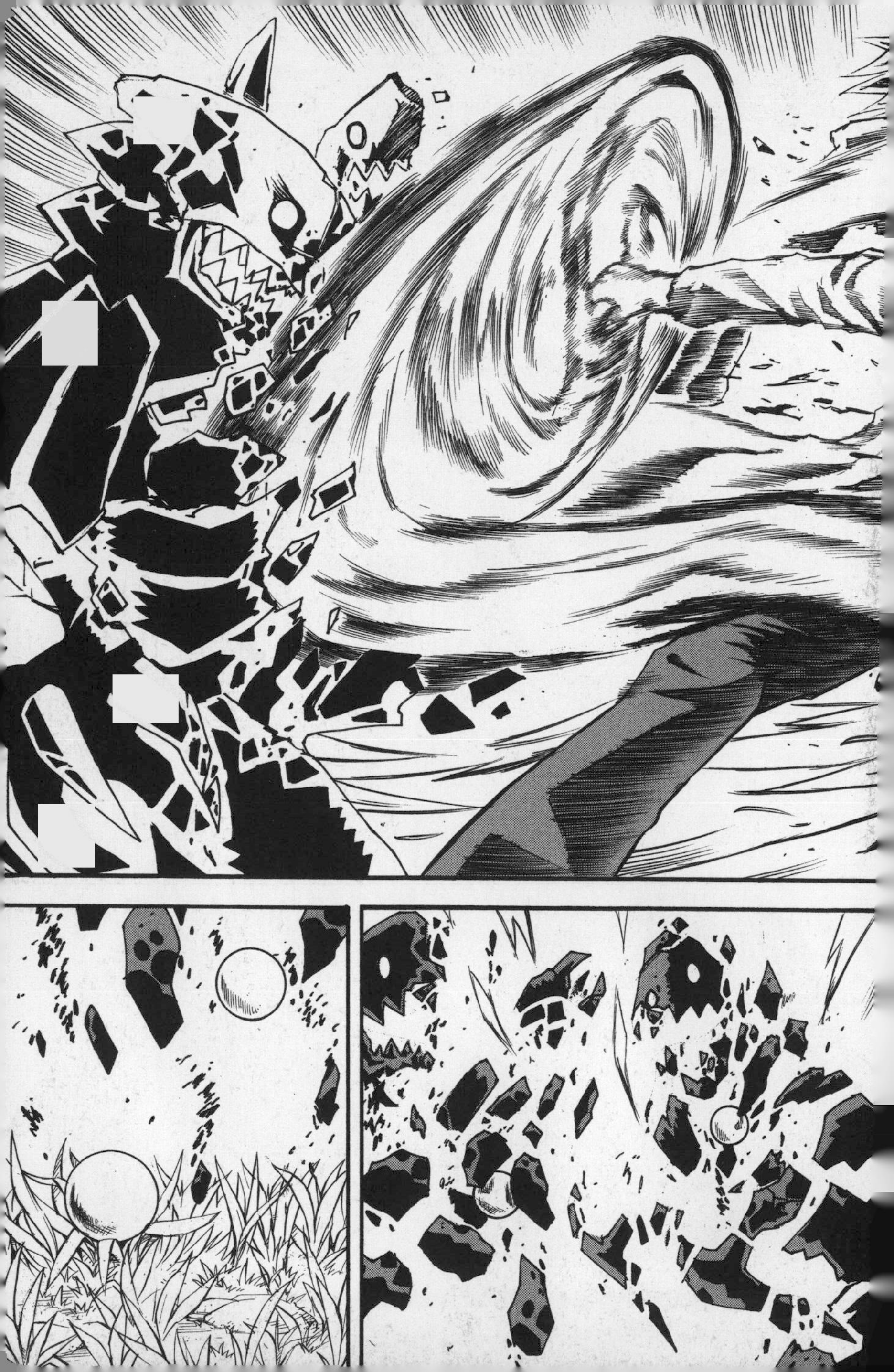

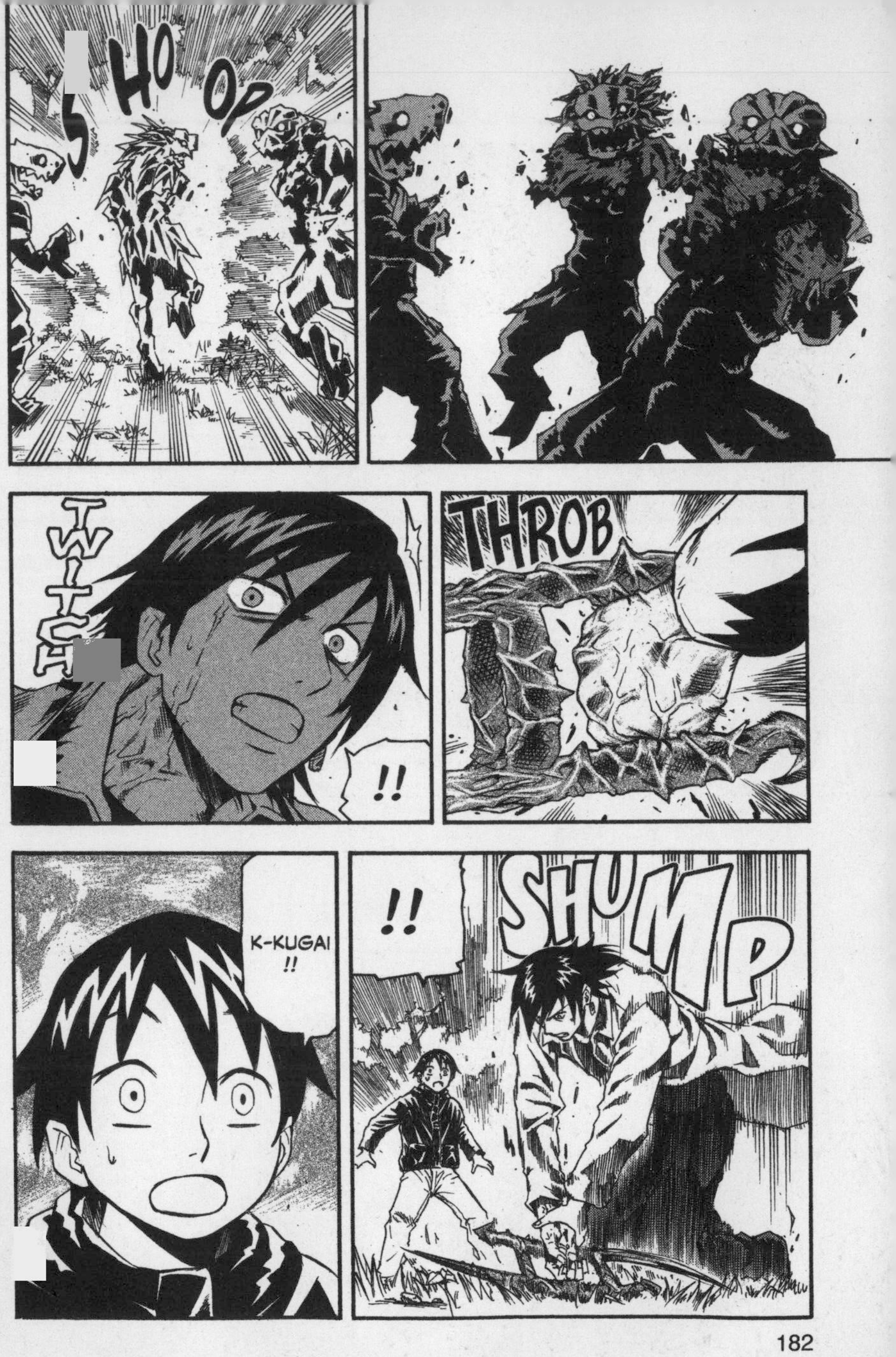
SHOOP
THROB
TWITCH
!!
!!
SHUMP
K-KUGAI !!

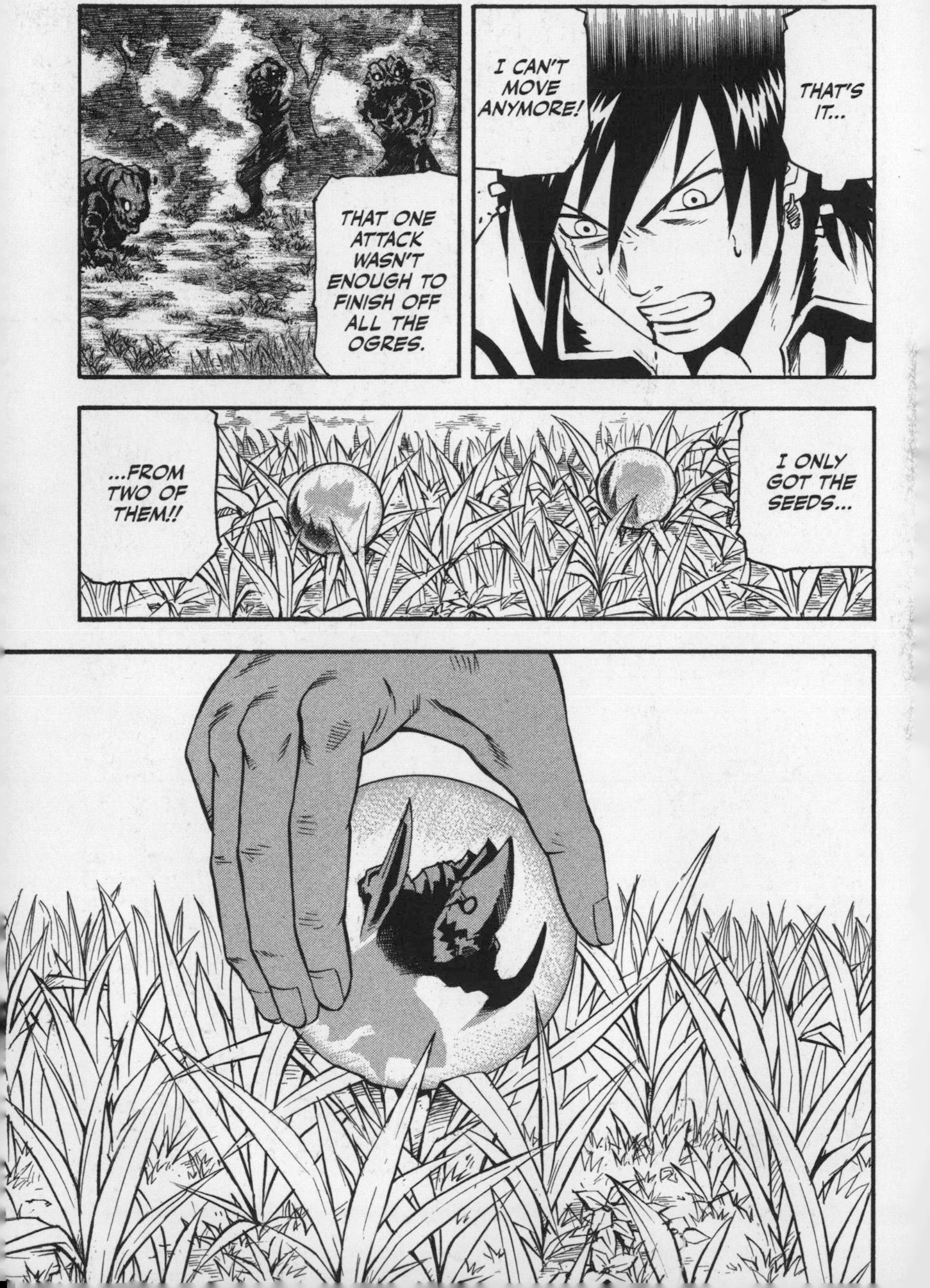
THAT'S IT...
I CAN'T MOVE ANYMORE!
THAT ONE ATTACK WASN'T ENOUGH TO FINISH OFF ALL THE OGRES.
I ONLY GOT THE SEEDS...
...FROM TWO OF THEM!!

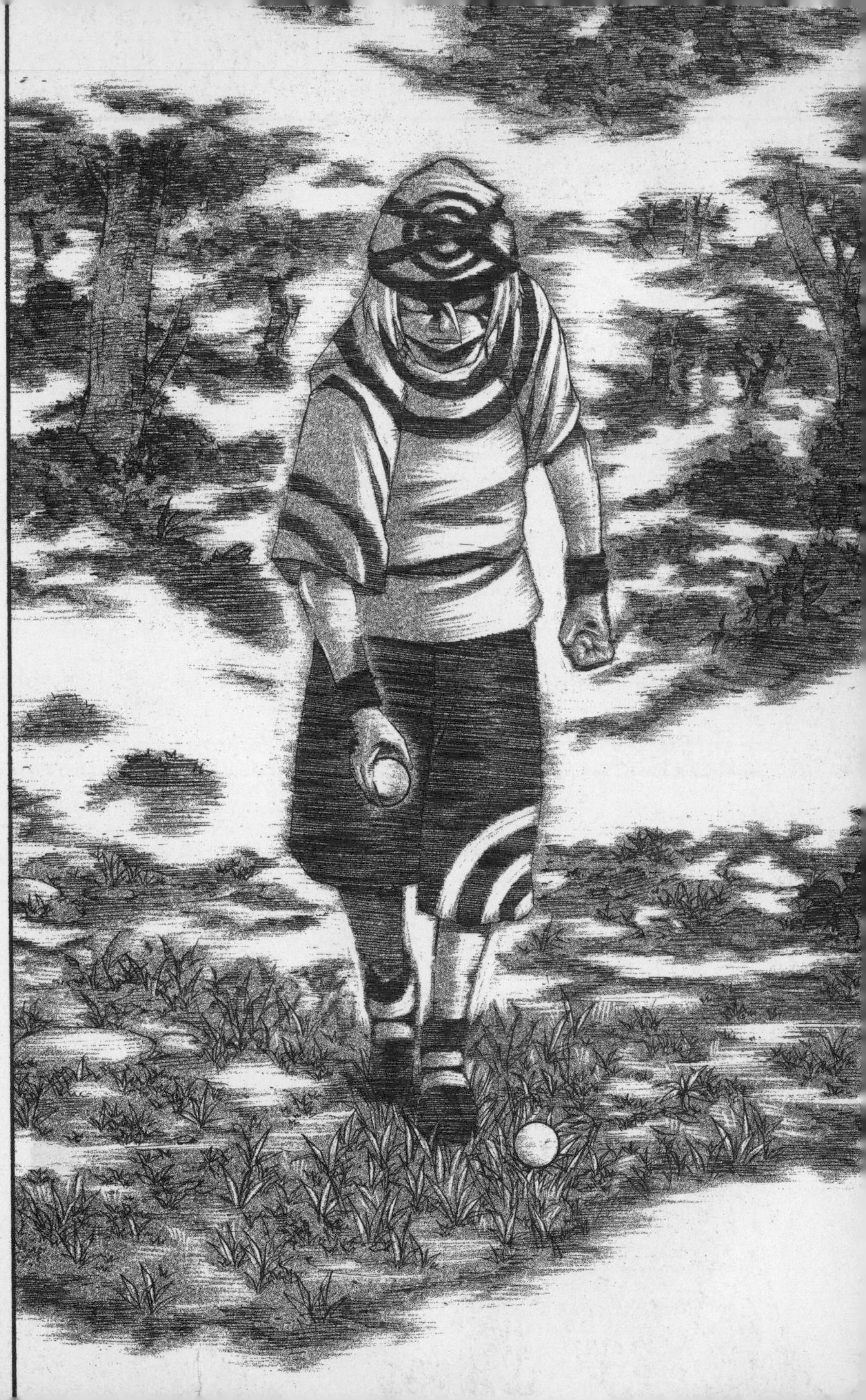

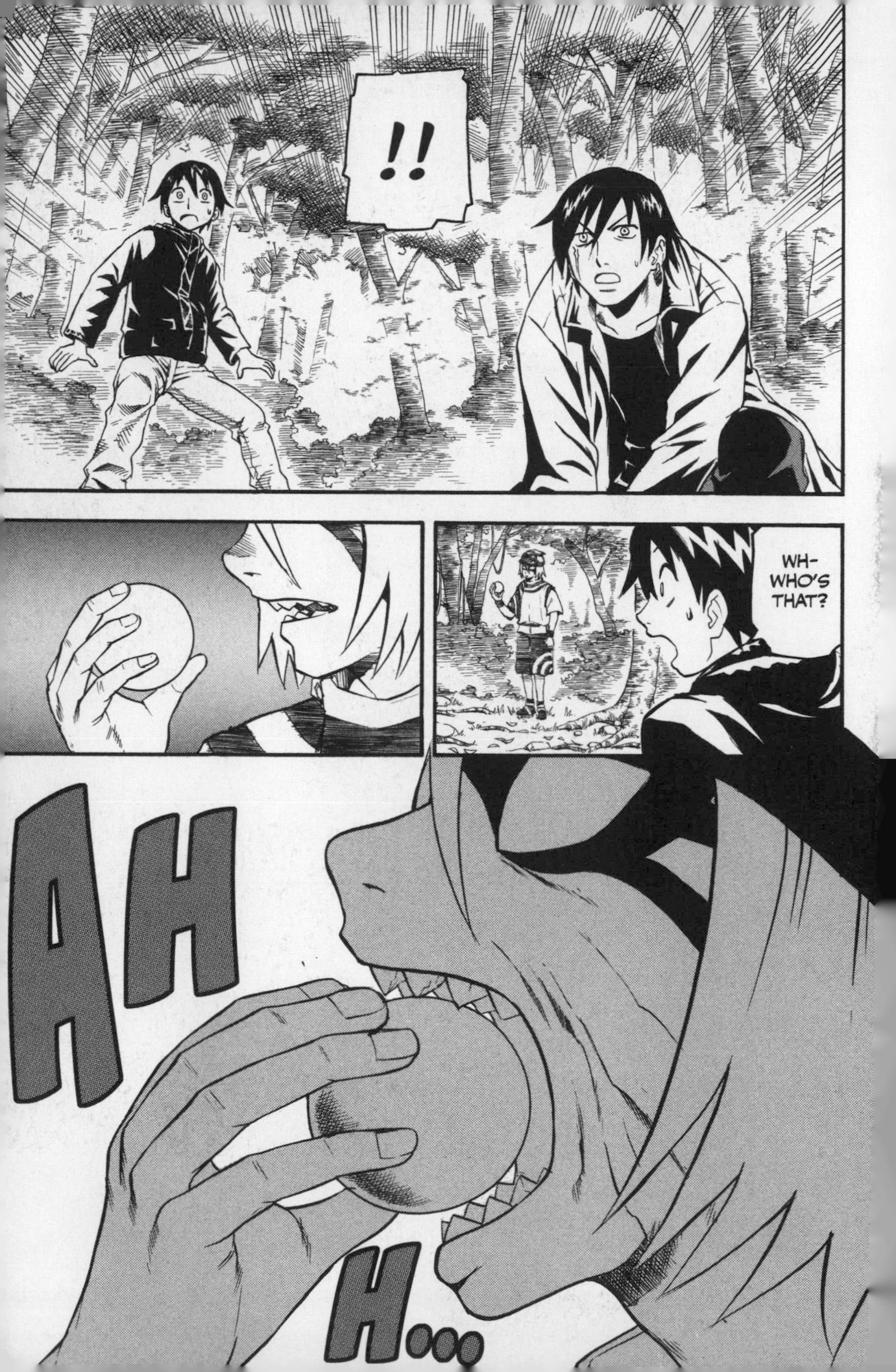
!!
WH-WHO'S THAT?
AH
H...

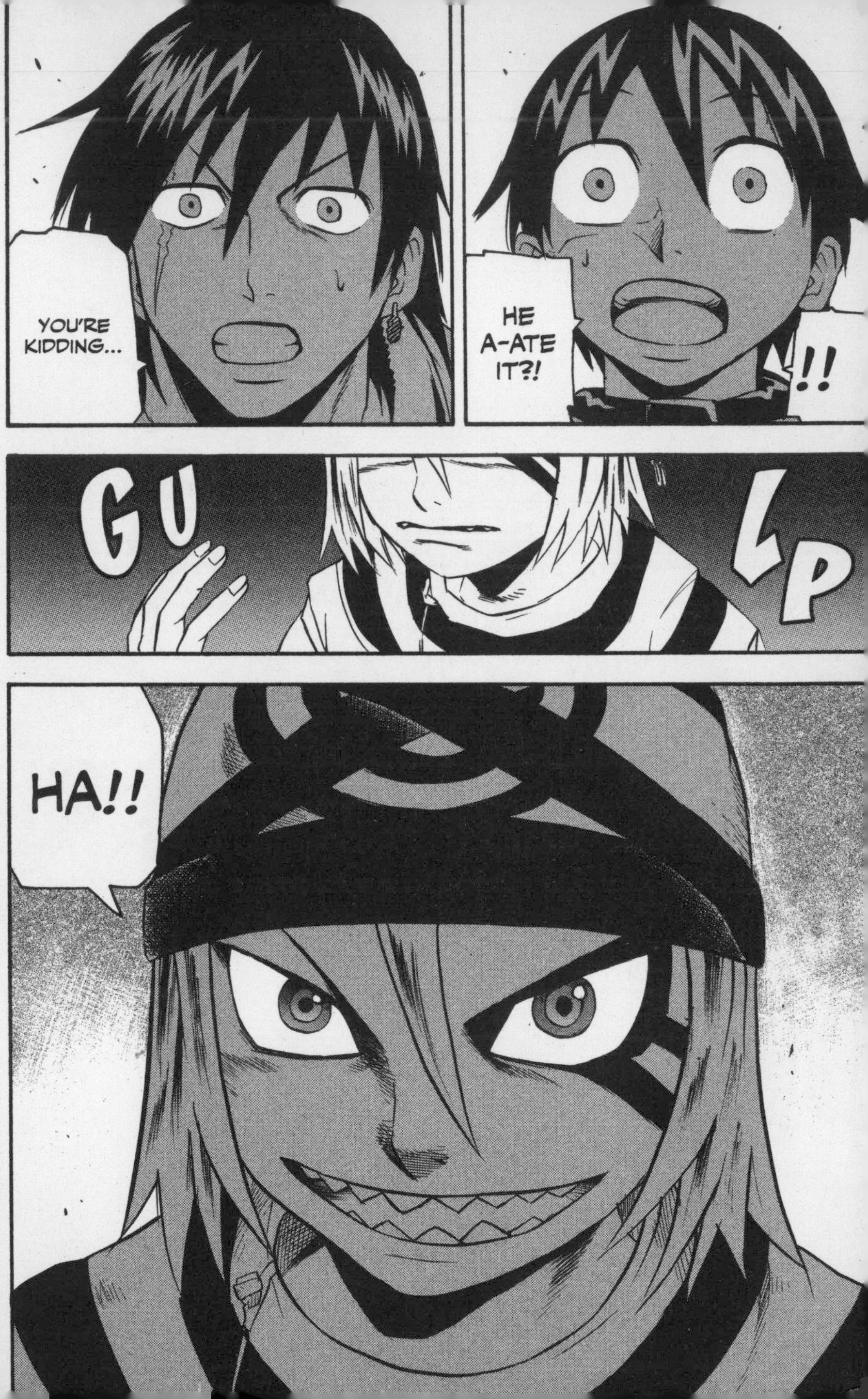
HE A-ATE IT?!
!!
YOU'RE KIDDING...
GULP
HA!!

KURO
ZAKURO

THE OGRES' KEEPERS

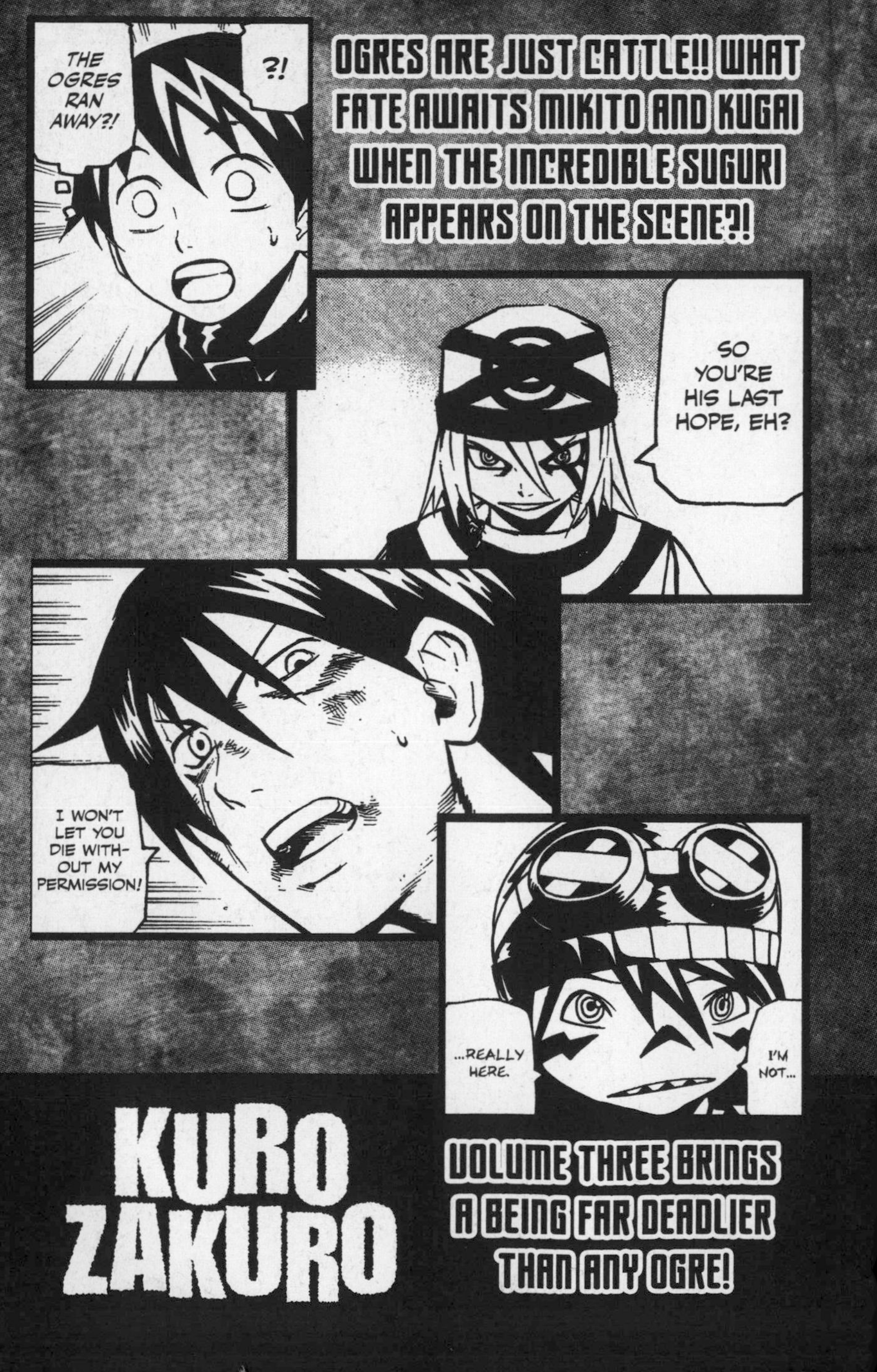
OGRES ARE JUST CATTLE!! WHAT FATE AWAITS MIKITO AND KUGAI WHEN THE INCREDIBLE SUGURI APPEARS ON THE SCENE?!
?!
THE OGRES RAN AWAY?!
SO YOU'RE HIS LAST HOPE, EH?
I WON'T LET YOU DIE WITH-OUT MY PERMISSION!
I'M NOT...
...REALLY HERE.
KURO ZAKURO
VOLUME THREE BRINGS A BEING FAR DEADLIER THAN ANY OGRE!

SPECIAL BONUS PAGE

URAZAKURO

HI, THIS IS NATSUME. THANKS SO MUCH FOR READING KUROZAKURO. I APPRECIATE IT. THERE WERE NO EXTRA PAGES IN VOLUME 1, SO THERE WAS NO BONUS MATERIAL. (IN THE END, THERE WAS A BIT OF ROOM, SO I DREW UP SOME ADS AND STUFF.) THIS TIME, I'D LIKE TO SHARE WITH YOU A LOST SEQUENCE OF STORYBOARDS THAT FOR VARIOUS REASONS NEVER SAW THE LIGHT OF DAY. IF YOU LOOK AT THE UPPER RIGHT PAGE (LABELED 10), YOU'LL PROBABLY RECOGNIZE IT IF YOU'VE ALREADY READ VOLUME 2. BUT IF YOU KEEP GOING, YOU'LL NOTICE THAT THE STORY IS COMPLETELY DIFFERENT. IT'S NOT UNUSUAL FOR A SERIOUS PART OF THE STORY TO HAVE BEEN A LIGHTHEARTED GAG IN ITS FIRST INCARNATION. I DON'T WRITE THESE MANGA JUST ANY OLD WAY I PLEASE. I PLAY WITH VARIOUS IDEAS, SELECTING THE ONES THAT SEEM LIKE THEY'LL BE THE MOST COMPELLING TO THE READERS, AND I PLEDGE TO CONTINUE WORKING HARD TO DO SO!

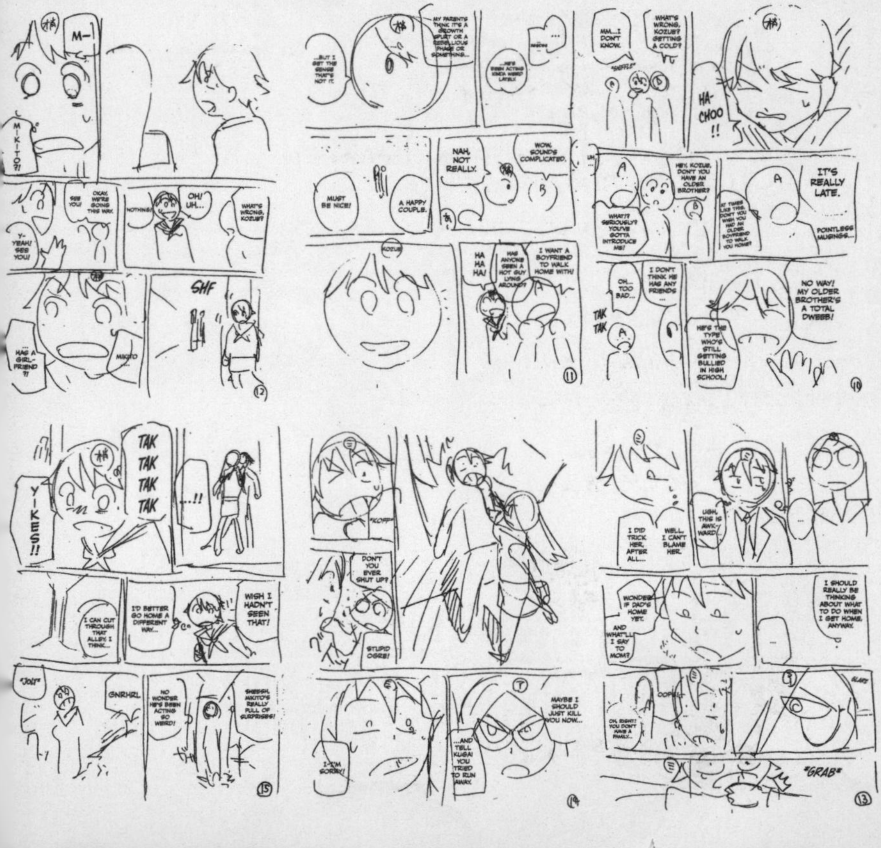
HA-CHOO!!
WHAT'S WRONG, KOZUE? GETTING A COLD?
MM...I DON'T KNOW.
SNIFFLE
IT'S REALLY LATE.
AT TIMES LIKE THIS, DON'T YOU WISH YOU HAD AN OLDER BOYFRIEND TO WALK YOU HOME?
POINTLESS MUSINGS...
HEY, KOZUE, DON'T YOU HAVE AN OLDER BROTHER?
WHAT!? SERIOUSLY? YOU'VE GOTTA INTRODUCE ME!
UH, ...
NO WAY! MY OLDER BROTHER'S A TOTAL DWEEB!
HE'S THE TYPE WHO'S STILL GETTING BULLIED IN HIGH SCHOOL!
I DON'T THINK HE HAS ANY FRIENDS ...
OH... TOO BAD...
TAK TAK
10
...
...HE'S BEEN ACTING KINDA WEIRD LATELY.
MY PARENTS THINK IT'S A GROWTH SPURT OR A REBELLIOUS PHASE OR SOMETHING...
...BUT I GET THE SENSE THAT'S NOT IT.
WOW, SOUNDS COMPLICATED.
NAH, NOT REALLY.
A HAPPY COUPLE.
MUST BE NICE!
I WANT A BOYFRIEND TO WALK HOME WITH!
HAS ANYONE SEEN A HOT GUY LYING AROUND?
HA HA HA!
KOZUE
11
M—
MIKITO?!
WHAT'S WRONG, KOZUE?
OH! UH...
NOTHING!
OKAY, WE'RE GOING THIS WAY.
SEE YOU!
Y-YEAH! SEE YOU!
SHF
MIKITO ...
...HAS A GIRLFRIEND?!
12
...
UGH, THIS IS AWKWARD...
WELL, I CAN'T BLAME HER.
I DID TRICK HER, AFTER ALL...
I SHOULD REALLY BE THINKING ABOUT WHAT TO DO WHEN I GET HOME, ANYWAY.
...
WONDER IF DAD'S HOME YET.
AND WHAT'LL I SAY TO MOM?
GLARE
OOPS!
OH, RIGHT! YOU DON'T HAVE A FAMILY...
GRAB
13
KOFF
DON'T YOU EVER SHUT UP?
STUPID OGRE!
MAYBE I SHOULD JUST KILL YOU NOW...
...AND TELL KUGAI YOU TRIED TO RUN AWAY.
I-I'M SORRY!
14
...!!
TAK TAK TAK TAK
YIKES!!
WISH I HADN'T SEEN THAT!
I'D BETTER GO HOME A DIFFERENT WAY...
I CAN CUT THROUGH THAT ALLEY, I THINK...
SHEESH, MIKITO'S REALLY FULL OF SURPRISES!
NO WONDER HE'S BEEN ACTING SO WEIRD!
GNRHRL
JOLT
15

KURO ZAKURO

Volume 2
Shonen Sunday Edition

Story and Art by
YOSHINORI NATSUME

Original Japanese edition "KUROZAKURO"
published by SHOGAKUKAN Inc.

Original Japanese cover design by Yoshiyuki Seki + Volare inc.

Translation/Camellia Nieh
Touch-up Art & Lettering/John Hunt
Cover Design/Yukiko Whitley
Interior Design/Jodie Yoshioka
Editor/Chris Mackenzie

Printed in the U.S.A.

Published by VIZ Media, LLC
P.O. Box 77010
San Francisco, CA 94107

10 9 8 7 6 5 4 3 2 1
First printing, January 2011

www.viz.com   WWW.SHONENSUNDAY.COM

PARENTAL ADVISORY
KUROZAKURO is rated T+ for Older Teen and is recommended for ages 16 and up.
FOR OLDER TEEN
ratings.viz.com

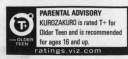

baac

With so many modern conveniences nowadays, there isn't much adventure left in life. The heroes in this story have adventures in a world very similar to the one we live in... but it's just a little different.
—Yoshinori Natsume